Bradshaw Crowdell

Ambassadors in Arms

The Story of Hawaii's 100th Battalion

Hawaii, mid-December, 1941. A machine-gun barrel points across a barbed wire-entangled beach, across the nervous white-fingered surf, beyond the purple depths, toward Japan. The helmeted heads and khaki-covered shoulders of two American soldiers are visible above the edge of the gun pit. One of them has dark brown skin, wide features, and round eyes. He is of Hawaiian ancestry. His companion's skin is of lighter brown, his face narrower, his eyes almond-shaped. He is of Japanese ancestry.

For long wordless minutes they gaze out to the place where sky and water meet. From time to time one or the other turns his head to scan the beach on his side of the emplacement, but always his eyes come back to the sea.

The Hawaiian finally speaks:

"If dey come, who you shoot? Dem or me?"

"Who you t'ink, stupid? Me as good American as you!"

A man of Japanese ancestry a good American? In the tense days after Japanese planes bombed Pearl Harbor, very few other Americans believed this could be so. To prove it, deeds would be necessary, not words. This book tells why deeds were necessary, how they were made possible, what they were—and their results.

PROLOGUE

AMBASSADORS IN ARMS

Thomas D. Murphy

SKETCHES
Yoshio Takamoto

MAPS
Tadashi K. Ohta

UNIVERSITY OF HAWAII PRESS
Honolulu, Hawaii, 1955

First Printing
**100th BATTALION
SPECIAL EDITION**
July, 1954

Second Printing
August, 1954

Third Printing
April, 1955

Copyright 1954 by
UNIVERSITY OF HAWAII PRESS

Library of Congress
Card Catalog No. 54-7835

Manufactured by
ADVERTISER PUBLISHING
COMPANY, LIMITED
Honolulu, Hawaii

Preface

Soon after I started work on this volume, a veteran of the 100th Battalion called at my home. "I hope you won't write a book making us glorious heroes that nobody will believe," he said. "But I hope, too, that being a professor, you won't write a text book on sociology that nobody will read." Before he left, however, he had added another plea, "Please try to tell it just like it happened."

I have tried to keep each of my visitor's requests in mind.

The story of the first U. S. Army unit composed of Americans of Japanese ancestry includes the special conditions under which it was organized, the problems it faced, and the way in which these were met. It is not only a record of distinguished military performance, but a record also of the extent to which the American dream has become a reality in multiracial Hawaii. In these pages, therefore, there are both glory and what my visitor would probably call sociology. It had to be that way.

The glory, it should be added, belongs primarily to the unit as a whole and to the ideals for which its members fought. The reader should know—as the veterans themselves will—that for every soldier mentioned in this book there were scores, not mentioned, who served with equal devotion and valor.

THOMAS D. MURPHY

Honolulu, Hawaii
July 1, 1954

Acknowledg-
ments

I AM GREATLY indebted to James W. Lovell, chairman of the historical committee of Club 100, who provided me with documentary material, answered questions, arranged interviews with members of his committee and other veterans of the 100th, then read and criticized the manuscript and arranged for others to read chapters covering material with which they were familiar.

I am also indebted to Dr. Kent Roberts Greenfield, Chief Historian, Office of the Chief of Military History, Department of the Army, and to Dr. Stetson Conn of his staff, for access to records on the history of the 100th and of the 442d Regimental Combat Team.

Colonel George W. Bicknell and Colonel Kendall J. Fielder, both of Honolulu, and my colleagues, Professors Robert W. Clopton, Andrew W. Lind, and Shunzo Sakamaki, read and commented on those chapters which described events or developments concerning which they had specialized knowledge. Errors of fact or interpretation, however, are mine alone.

Special thanks are due veterans Tadashi K. Ohta, who drew the maps, and Yoshio Takamoto, whose sketches—most of them made while on active service—illustrate the volume. Also to William S. Ellis, Jr., who designed the book, and to Mary Laune Aitken for her painstaking work on layout.

My research was made easier by the work of Mrs. Kathryn H. Stidham, who acquired for the Hawaii War Records Depository many of the documents used, and by the exhaustive scouting of the Depository's resources by Miss Gwenfread Allen during her research for her own book, *Hawaii's War Years, 1941–1945*.

University of Hawaii staff members who have been of great assistance include those in the Social Research Laboratory, and in the Library, especially the Hawaiiana Room and the Government Documents Collection. Miss Patsy Okamura of the secretarial staff typed and retyped the manuscript with unfailing good humor.

I am deeply indebted to my wise and capable editor, Mrs. Aldyth V. Morris, and to my wife, for her gentle and constant help.

Contents

Maps

ON DECEMBER 6, 1941, most Americans living in the mainland United States knew little more about Hawaii than that this island outpost was the seat of the great fortified Pacific naval base Pearl Harbor. The following day, however, as radio announcers and newspaper headlines spread the news of the Pearl Harbor attack, Americans found themselves grimly interested in the offshore Territory, especially in the activities of its residents of Japanese ancestry.

There were 158,000 persons of Japanese ancestry in Hawaii on December 7, 1941, about 37 per cent of the population. More than 37,000 of them had been born in Japan. They, like their fellow Islanders of Chinese, Filipino, Korean, and Portuguese ancestry, were in Hawaii because the sugar planters had needed cheap and sturdy labor in the fields. Between 1885 and 1900 thousands of young peasants had come from Japan to work as contract laborers on Hawaii's plantations. Most of them had expected to stay long enough to save what in the old country would be a modest competence, and then return home to Japan to enjoy it. A goal often mentioned was 3000 yen ($1500).

Only one of every six Japanese who came to Hawaii during those early years was a woman. A great many of the men who remained single did return to their homeland, but those who brought wives, or imported from Japan "picture brides" to whom they had become married by proxy, usually remained and lost themselves in their growing families.

Americans?

CHAPTER ONE

They saved less money than when they had been single, and postponed the journey home.

Most of these laborers stayed on at their jobs in the cane fields, living in plantation-owned houses, buying their necessities in plantation-owned stores, and sending their sick to plantation-owned hospitals. But the more ambitious ones, after working out their contract period, abandoned the cane fields, bought or leased a few acres of ground, and became truck gardeners or hog farmers. Some went into domestic service or set up small retail stores. Others became carpenters, plumbers, painters, masons, or commercial fishermen. As the Territory's economy expanded, the Japanese found their way into many other occupations. They met no such legal restrictions on economic opportunity as did the Japanese who had moved on to settle in California.

In time, as the result of long hours of hard work, strict attention to detail, constant thrift, and a certain amount of luck, a fair number of these former field hands prospered. Businesses which had been started to serve only other Japanese soon expanded to include patrons from other national stocks of Hawaii's already mixed population. Not every ambitious Japanese got ahead, but those who possessed the necessary talents often won a comfortable degree of financial security.

Over the course of the years, most of the Japanese immigrants came to be fairly content in—some even to love—the beautiful land in which their children were being born. But there always remained the idea of *Nihon e Kaeru* (going back to Japan). Among those who finally did return some went merely for a short visit, but many others bought one-way tickets planning to end their days in the land of their birth. For these folk the years away, no matter how pleasant or profitable, had been years of exile, years of longing to see again the cherry trees of home.

But, their feet once more on ancestral ground, hundreds discovered that their relatives in Japan looked on them as strangers, as "Americans." Their parents, if still alive, as well as relatives of their own generation, seemed to find them greatly altered. The returned natives realized that there had indeed been astounding changes within themselves. They had become accustomed to the free and easy social relationships of Hawaiian America, and the behavior proper in the homeland seemed restrained and stiff. They found, too, that even

2

the meager comforts enjoyed by a plantation hand in Hawaii were, for the people of his native hamlet, unhoped-for luxuries. Once greetings were over and reminiscences exhausted they often found little more to say. Many a returned Japanese realized for the first time how much Hawaii had given him and his children, how much his Island home had come to mean to him. In contrast, as the romantic dreams of the homeland dissolved, the mother country seemed to offer little but blood ties thinned by death and years of absence. It was the same kind of awakening that thousands of America's European immigrants had experienced on "going home."

Many of those who had intended to remain in Japan, now realizing they had stayed too long in the new world ever again to be content in the old, bought passage back to Hawaii. Their second homecoming was not, however, pure gladness. During the years in Hawaii they had continued to speak the mother tongue, had cherished the old customs, and had worshiped the ancestral gods. Despite this, had they, as some of their relatives seemed to think, unwittingly become more American in spirit than Japanese? But that could not be. Even if a person of Japanese ancestry were willing to renounce forever his allegiance to his native country, he still could not become an American citizen. The United States allowed naturalization to men of many other nations, but withheld it from the Japanese. How could any self-respecting person feel unity of spirit with people who scorned him? No, they were not, they could not be, Americans. But neither were they the kind of Japanese they once had been.[1]

Most members of the white minority which governed Hawaii were sure that the workers imported from Japan remained alien to the American way of life, no matter how long they lived in the Territory. Obviously their minds changed no more than did their faces. They observed all the traditions of their homeland, kept all the old birth, marriage, and funeral customs, celebrated all the ancient festivals. They worshiped in Buddhist or Shinto temples, kept to themselves, married their own kind. Only a few had joined Christian churches. Most of them spoke Hawaii's brand of pidgin English, which served as a speech bridge between all the national groups in the Islands, but only a few ever bothered to learn "real" English. They had established their own Japanese-language press, which carried reports from Domei, the official Japanese news agency. They listened to Japanese programs on the radio and went to Japanese movies. They banded together in social clubs and business associations and established their own chamber of commerce. Advertising signs in Japanese made their part of the Honolulu business district look like a transplanted section of Tokyo. Japanese flags, portraits of the Imperial family, and photographs of brothers or cousins in the uniforms of the Japanese army and navy decorated the walls of their homes. They continued to eat Japanese food, and the women wore Japanese dress in the streets. They sent their children to the public schools, as the law required, but they also sent them to private schools to be taught the Japanese language and to hear about the glories of Japan, past and present. No, they had not become Americanized.

This had never really bothered most of Hawaii's businessmen, for they had expected that the field hands would in time return to Japan. If they had not, what did it matter? Hawaii continued to need their labor. Assimilate them? Americanize them? Impossible, though something might be done—or tried at least—with the children.

As the nervous years of the 1930s passed and the militarist leaders of Japan, grabbing for a greater Asian empire, began to link their policies with those of Hitler and Mussolini, many Caucasians had misgivings. Resident Japanese were buying Japan's war bonds. They were also collecting lead foil for Japanese munition plants, contributing money to buy comfort kits for the Emperor's soldiers, even trucks and airplanes for his armed forces in Manchuria. Meanwhile Japanese stores proudly displayed the famous picture of the *San Yūshi*, the three Japanese soldiers hand-carrying a bangalore torpedo in a suicide assault against the Chinese foe. How far would the Japanese go in their loyalty to the Emperor?

Men who had previously paid little attention listened with greater concern to the few who had long warned that Japan was becoming too ambitious; that if she should test her strength against the United States Hawaii's security might be endangered from within. Pearl Harbor was only a few miles down the road from Honolulu, the largest center of Japanese population in the Territory. In addition to Honolulu and Pearl Harbor, practically all of Hawaii's military barracks, defense emplacements, and airfields were located on the island of Oahu. The terms "espionage," "sabotage," and "fifth-column activity" were now more frequently heard in bridge-table gossip. Employers began to wonder if Japanese workers were potential fifth columnists. It might have been a mistake to bring this particular group of laborers to work on Hawaii's plantations.

The children of Japanese immigrants, the *nisei*,* made up nearly half of Hawaii's public-school population. They had been christened with elaborate age-old Shinto ceremonies, and introduced to the ancestral deities. Their first baby words had been spoken in the language of their parents' homeland. From an early age they had been taught to observe the traditional habits of conduct, the correct positions for eating and sleeping, the necessity for cleanliness and neatness, the forms of "respect" language, and the way in which to bow to older folk. Their first religious ideas were associated with the small Buddhist and Shinto shrines within the home, before which their parents placed daily food offerings, bowed, announced family events to the ancestors, and lighted prayer lamps.

As they grew older the nisei took part in the making of special delicacies and in the round of preliminary parties which heralded the approach of New Year's, the most important Japanese holiday. In the early morning hours they awakened to the customary firecrackers, took the prescribed bath of purification, and then, after a breakfast of traditional foods, went off with their mothers to visit the temples. Returning home, they joined in the eating, entertaining, and visiting which filled the rest of the day. On Girl's Day, March 3, dolls were given to each girl child and doll collections were exhibited. On Hana Matsuri, April 8, the birthday of the Buddha, the children brought flowers to the shrines, drank flower tea, watched the image of the Enlightened One being drawn through the streets, and attended large communal gatherings of the Japanese people at which girls danced in his honor. On Boy's Day, May 5, red paper carp, symbols of virility and courage, swam above the roof tops in the trade winds. The young had a special place in the annual *Bon* celebrations held in July and August, when ceremonies in honor of the dead were performed in homes and at temples, and kimono-clad teen-agers danced in the temple yards. The birthday of the reigning Emperor was a holiday for the language schools, and was of great importance in some sections, especially the more rural plantation settlements, where the population was predominantly Japanese.

Within the home, during their most formative years, the young nisei were conditioned to act according to traditional codes of be-

---

* This Japanese word, meaning second generation, distinguishes those born in America from their Japanese immigrant parents, the *issei*, or first generation.

havior. They were taught to recognize the complete supremacy of the father, the precedence of the oldest son, and the superiority of the male. Indebtedness for parental care was so great, they were informed, that it could be repaid, and then only in part, by giving as good or better upbringing to the children they themselves would some day have. Only by repayment of all obligations to others could they maintain that self-respect which was the mark of a well-bred man or woman. For the person who had done one a kindness there should always be an equal or greater return. Right conduct meant restraint and self-discipline, and, if need be, sacrifice of personal happiness. The man worthy of respect was the one who knew the rules of life and observed them. He was strong in character. The individual who did not know what society demanded, or, knowing, broke the code, was either badly schooled or a moral weakling, and in any case an object of scorn.

Concepts such as these seemed strange to the *haoles** of Hawaii, educated in the American tradition of equality, individuality, and freedom, but it was hoped that the public schools might wean the nisei away from the more undesirable ones. But many agreed that such virtues as respect for superiors, obedience to authority, and uncomplaining acceptance of duty were well worth teaching to the nisei, destined as they were to take their fathers' places in the fields. Far better for the younger workers to hold fast to these precepts than to embrace too quickly ideals of individuality and equality which might lead to discontent and economic and social unrest.

Thus far there seemed no cause for great concern about the kind of training the *issei*** were giving their children. But before coming to Hawaii the issei had been taught a duty which transcended all others, that of complete and selfless loyalty to the Emperor, high priest and supreme symbol of the Japanese nation. Had the alien father taught his American-born children this obligation also?

Through the doors of Hawaii's schools, over the years, the young Japanese-Americans passed into a wider world than their parents had ever known. In classroom and schoolyard they studied and played with children of the other national stocks and mixtures which made up Hawaii's multi-racial population. When they entered school they

* An Island term applied (by themselves as well as by others) to white residents.
** See footnote, page 5.

6

were already fluent in pidgin English,* the one common tongue of the Islands. Though the teachers did their best to help them learn "standard" English, the efforts were not strikingly successful. Some of the Island-born teachers, themselves children of immigrants from the Orient, had spoken pidgin from childhood and had not, despite their training, acquired ease in speaking English. The biggest obstacle, however, was the fact that other pupils scoffed at those who tried outside the classroom to speak as the teacher said they should.

Mastery of the English language is not, however, necessary for the understanding and practice of democratic principles. It was to be supposed that just as the Mainland school system had molded the children of non-English speaking European immigrants into the American pattern, so also would Hawaii's schools bring these young Orientals to understanding of, love for, and allegiance to, the ideas and ideals which were the core of American life. Despite warnings of possible contrary result, the children and grandchildren of European parents had grown up to become solid and devoted citizens. Why should the process of assimilation by education not work as well in Hawaii? The public-school teachers of the Islands had faith that it would, so they not only taught the nisei children the theories of American democracy, but gave them opportunity, in classroom and extracurricular activities, to practice them.[2]

In 1937 a joint committee of United States senators and representatives conducted hearings in the Islands to investigate Hawaii's readiness for statehood. Their final report stated that the "public schools of Hawaii are the foundations of good citizenship. As a part of their curriculum they inculcate the basic principles of American democracy

---

* The following sample is based on the Hawaiian-pidgin version of "Cinderella" by Leslie Vincent and Emery Nemethy in *Paradise of the Pacific*, June, 1951, with revisions by Elsie Toyama:

"One time dere wuz one ono-looking wahine who wuz kine, an' gentle like one dove, an' dey been call her Cinderalla. She nevah get one house for herself, but she wen' live wit' a mean wahine who get two pilau daughtah, an' she been da maid for da house.

"Cinderalla wuz call dat becuz after she been all pau her work, she sit in da kitchen an' rake for cinda for save da good kine charcoal. She even wen' wash an' wipe all da dishes, an' scrub an' sweep da floor an' take real care da rooms of da two pilau step-sistah. Da beds dey been sleep inside wuz haole kine from Sears an' Roebucks—sof' an' wit' springs inside. In dere room been mirrors dat go from da floor to da roof which dey been look demselves alla time, an' tryin' for make pretty on top da faces. But 'ats wastetime.

"Da poor Cinderalla been sleep on top one pile junk kine lauhala mats nex' by da doghouse, an' only had pilau clo's for wear. Da titas an' da moddah everytime make huhu an' yell at her for notting, but alla time Cinderalla nevah been mind, an' make da sweet kine smile.

"One day, da son of da King been send out inwitations fo' one beeg pahty. . . .' "

in the young who pass through them. With so many children of alien parentage among them a definite program of Americanization is necessary. Too much praise cannot be given to the schools of Hawaii for the splendid manner in which they have met the problem, and the great measure of success that has attended their efforts. Through the schools more than by any other means the people of Hawaii are being molded together into the American pattern and philosophy of life."[3]

However, as mentioned earlier, there were the Japanese-language schools, where more than eighty per cent of the young Japanese-Americans were receiving additional education. For an hour every school day and for a longer period on Saturday mornings they attended these private schools,* many of them conducted by Buddhist and Shinto priests. The children were taught to read and write in Japanese and were instructed in the history and culture of Japan.

In founding these schools the Japanese immigrants were following a pattern already established by European immigrants on the American Mainland, and the reasons they gave were the same. Privately financed instruction of this kind, they said, served to keep open channels of communication between themselves and their American-born children who might otherwise, in speech, habit, and thought, become too quickly separated from their parents. What some people called assimilation or Americanization might proceed much too fast for family happiness. A bridge was needed to span the rapidly widening gulf between the two generations, and the issei claimed the language school was such a bridge.

Establishments of this kind had always been criticized. Native Americans charged that the teaching of another tongue made it difficult for children to master the English language, the means through which they must learn American ideas and patterns of conduct; that the subjects taught hindered the process of Americanization and tended to perpetuate loyalty to a foreign country and culture; and that the religious teaching was alien, if not hostile, to that which formed the moral outlook of most Americans. Despite criticism, however, European-language schools had been tolerated and the United States Supreme Court had upheld their right to operate.

---

* Some of these operated between about 7:00 and 8:00 A.M., prior to the opening of public schools, but afternoon classes were the rule.

Various students of the subject said that the quarrel was based on a difference of opinion as to the speed with which the second generation should be assimilated. With or without the language schools, the end result would be the same: the young people would eventually be divorced from what were, at their strongest, only secondhand cultural influences from the parents' homeland. Why be disturbed?

Many residents of Hawaii, however, could not so calmly appraise the Japanese-language schools. The pupils were of Oriental, not Caucasian, stock. Their parents' cultural inheritance was far different from that of European immigrants, which included the teachings of Christianity as an essential element. For centuries Europeans had been developing a society in which the individual was offered wider and wider liberty of action and thought, and American civilization had been built on European foundations. Under the surface skin of cultural differences, Americans and Europeans were brothers—white brothers.

Hawaii's Japanese, on the other hand, had come from a country where the Emperor was given the honors of divinity, where books were read from right to left, where the people squatted on the floor and ate their food with sticks, where even the music seemed to the Western ear a dissonance of weird minor chords. These "coolies" came from a country which had emerged only within recent times from cultural isolation and military feudalism, a nation whose false front of representative institutions could not hide the fact that the mass of the people neither understood nor exercised democratic self-government. Power-hungry militarists had recently hurled that empire into a career of conquest aimed not only at domination over Asia but at the weakening of American power and influence in the Pacific. To the *haoles*, this was the cultural background of more than one-third of the population of Hawaii, America's greatest Pacific bastion.

In view of these facts, how could Mainland experience with the children of European immigrants form an adequate yardstick by which to measure Hawaii's far greater task of making the nisei good Americans? How could one observe the Japanese-language schools without feeling deep concern?

It was true that in the 1930s the teachers no longer openly urged loyalty to the Emperor; they no longer used textbooks prepared by the Imperial department of education, but these changes had been secured only by long-continued pressure. In 1917 these schools had been attacked in the Territorial legislature; in 1920 a report by the United States Bureau of Education had recommended their abolition; and from 1920 to 1925 a series of legislative acts had sought to regulate and eventually eliminate them. After 1927, when the United States Supreme Court had declared the latest of these laws unconstitutional, a compromise had been reached: teachers were to be required to pass tests in English, American government, and history, and the schools were to be conducted under supervision of the Territorial department of public instruction.

Criticism continued, nevertheless, increased as Japan proceeded with her Chinese adventure, and swelled to new heights when Japan joined the Rome-Berlin Axis. It came not only from the type of zealot who always demands one hundred per cent Americanism of his own brand, but also from more sober citizens. Who could be sure that the priest-professors who travelled to and from Japan were not propaganda agents, insidiously attempting to maintain and strengthen their students' inherited ties of loyalty to the Emperor? In the late 1930s, residents of Hawaii who had previously given the matter little thought began to ask whether tolerance in educational matters might not go too far.

The Japanese residents defended their schools: though necessary now, they would disappear as the first generation died off. The texts in present use did not teach loyalty to Japan. Each year alien teachers made up a smaller percentage of the instructional staffs: in 1936, for instance, citizens comprised 40.9 per cent of the whole number as compared with 20.5 per cent in 1928. The schools taught ethical concepts of which all Americans approved. In their classrooms the nisei learned such virtues as filial piety, a sense of family responsibility, honesty, industry, co-operation, integrity, loyalty, kindness, and courage. These ethical values were, the issei claimed, often neglected in the public schools, which stressed "efficiency and the idea of success for its own sake." The language schools were in large part responsible for the high degree of morality and law observance for which the Japanese residents were noted. In many Japanese families both parents had to work outside the home in order to support the children, and the extra hour spent in school helped keep the young ones out of trouble. It was also economically advantageous for the nisei to know Japanese: good positions available to them were not so plentiful that they could afford to ignore opportunities with firms whose customers spoke only Japanese.[4]

The language schools continued to operate. Both those who attacked and those who defended them would have been surprised if they had polled the pupils. They would have found most of them very reluctant students. Regular public-school attendance was bad enough, but when the afternoon bell rang and the rest of their fellow sufferers rushed out to freedom, the nisei faced another hour of even stricter classroom discipline. They must try to master the woeful complexities of the Kanji,* penning these ideographs because "such training molded character," while their non-Japanese friends were whooping away at barefoot baseball, basketball, or football. They resented that lost hour of play, but they had more complex emotions too.

While the young nisei were being forced by their parents to study customs, concepts, and a language which set them farther apart from their public-school friends, the entire non-Japanese community was telling them that they were American citizens and that they should think and act like Americans. As they tried more and more to conform to the demands of the world outside the home, their parents seemed to understand them less and less. Though their parents might be different, there was no reason why they must be different. As an expression of their feelings many of the boys flouted the authority of their instructors and ridiculed as *Jappan bobora* (Japanese pumpkin heads) those who showed an interest in things Japanese. As they grew older and, in true American fashion, gradually wore down parental authority, hundreds, with the grudging consent of their parents, dropped out of the language schools.[5]

Much as these schools figured in public discussion, they were only a symbol of deeper problems. The nisei lived in two societies. The home, the language school, and the Japanese community formed one. Surrounding this smaller world was the rest of American Hawaii. Much of what the children learned in one society they were expected to forget or disregard in the other.

At the family table they ate large quantities of fish, rice, and vegetables cooked in Japanese fashion. At the homes of friends, at public-school cafeterias, and in restaurants they sampled other dishes,

* Chinese ideographs used with Japanese phonetic scripts in the school primers.

becoming as familiar with hot dogs, hamburgers, corned beef hash, and pie a la mode as any other children. At home they ate with chopsticks; outside they learned to use the knife and fork. In the home they learned the strict code of etiquette which governed their relationships with parents and other elders; outside they saw and envied the more casual relationships between children and parents of Hawaiian or European ancestry. Within the Japanese community they celebrated New Year's, the *Bon*, and other festivals; in the public schools they fashioned Easter baskets, danced around the Maypole, dressed as Pilgrims for Thanksgiving pageants, sang "Silent Night, Holy Night," and helped decorate the classroom Christmas tree.

Their parents and language-school instructors stressed respect for elders and unquestioning obedience to family. But in the public schools, in connection with the planning and interpretation of study units, or participation in student government, or arrangements for social affairs, their teachers asked them to express their own ideas and welcomed suggestions for group activities. Parents and Japanese instructors taught the concealment of emotions in public, but away from the older folk the nisei joked and giggled and laughed with other American kids and cheered themselves hoarse at high school games. The issei frowned on American social dancing, but their children learned the newest steps, and either wore down parental objections or attended such dances without permission. When they had the money for a movie they spent it to see films made not in Japan but in Hollywood.

Torn by the conflict between cultural patterns, it was little wonder that the young folk were often perplexed, sometimes dismayed, and sometimes angry. Under which banner should a person march? Should he keep one foot in each camp, or should he step once and for all into one camp or the other?

As the years passed there were, however, indications as to what the final decision would be. At American dances the boys picked their own partners, and as they grew older they began to choose their own wives. In Japan the parents had always arranged marriages; in Hawaii the children gradually came to choose their mates (though once the couple had fallen in love, formal arrangements between the families were still made by the traditional marriage brokers or "go-betweens"). Weddings were still elaborate, with costly banquets and many changes of bridal costume, but, as in the case of the "go-betweens," it was easy to yield to filial piety and ancestral custom once the right of free choice had been won. By the 1930s, the ceremonies were more simple, more "American," and though marriages to non-Japanese were still unusual and often violently opposed by the parents, such unions no longer shocked the Japanese community as they once had.[6]

The nisei were taught the religious beliefs of their ancestors, and if they learned the ethical principles involved and participated in the more important religious ceremonies their parents were content. As the boys became men, many began to think of formal religion as something for the womenfolk, the shrine ceremonies as a necessary bore put up with to please the females.

A small minority of the issei, however, had become Christians, and their children and other school friends invited nisei pals to Christian church services and social gatherings. Some liked what they heard and saw, and, despite family objections, deserted the ancestral gods. These young converts often viewed their change of religion as simply another step in the process of becoming Americans.

Some converts found that their new church affiliations helped them make friendships with Americans of other national strains and brought them out of the strictly Japanese community into the wider stream of Hawaii's social life. It helped them feel that they really had a place in American society. The number of nisei who became Christians was not great, but each year a few more made this transfer of spiritual loyalty. Another inherited allegiance was being gradually dissolved.*

Whether the nisei made their social contacts outside the Japanese community through the Christian church, the public school, the business life of the community, or through participation in civic affairs, most of their new friendships were with other non-Caucasians, who comprised almost two-thirds of the population. The *haoles*, who had been the first immigrants to the Islands after their discovery by Captain Cook in 1778, had a strong hold in Hawaii. They had financial and political power, and they set the standards of personal success toward which imported workers had learned to strive. As a rule they

---

* A father often consented to this step, not because he considered Christianity a better religion than Buddhism, but because he would rather have his child attend some church than none at all.

mixed socially only with other whites. Numerically, however, the *haoles* were in the minority, and the nisei could still feel that they "belonged," even though they might have no Caucasian friends.

In American society there had always been one fairly sure path by which the children of immigrants could gain social standing. As they graduated from unskilled to skilled labor their prestige rose with their incomes. Generally, the public school had formed the first rung of the ladder to financial and social success.

The overwhelming majority of the issei were of peasant stock and had had only elementary schooling in Japan. But they, like many of America's European immigrants, wanted their children to have a better education than they had had. So they scraped and saved to pay book-rental fees and keep their children in the public schools beyond the minimum period required by law.[7] As a result every year more nisei graduated from the Territorial high schools, the University of Hawaii, or Mainland colleges. Some entered Japanese-owned firms or started their own small enterprises, some were hired by the plantations or the big companies in Honolulu. Many became public-school teachers, others secured civil service jobs. An increasing number, financed by their parents and other relatives, studied at professional schools on the Mainland and then returned to Hawaii as doctors, lawyers, and dentists. At first most of their clients were from the Japanese community, but in time Islanders of other nationalities also sought their services.

Executive positions on plantations and in other big *haole*-controlled establishments were practically closed to nisei as well as to other Orientals. These posts usually went to the younger Island-born whites or to imported Mainland Caucasians. This caused resentment among those who saw the better jobs monopolized by men whose chief, and sometimes only, claim to such positions seemed to lie in the color of their skin. Some of the young Orientals called it racial discrimination, and contrasted the schoolbook statements that equality of opportunity was a basic part of American democracy with the practices of the "real" Americans who dominated Hawaii's economic life.

Often those who complained did not know that similar patterns of job distribution had long been practiced on the Mainland, in situations where skin color was not in question. The sons and daughters of European immigrants had experienced similar discrimination.

They, too, had seen the best jobs go to those whose fathers or grandfathers or great-grandfathers had been born in the United States. An executive of Anglo-Saxon Protestant descent had often preferred to offer a position of responsibility in his firm to a candidate who was of the same national and cultural ancestry as his own, rather than to the son of, for instance, a Russian Jew, or an Italian Catholic. He wanted a person of "his own kind," a person he could trust and mingle with socially. And the immigrants or their children usually hired "their own," too. It might not be democratic, but it was done.

In Hawaii, as on the Mainland, some doors were closed to immigrants' sons, but others were open. The census of 1940 showed that 15 per cent of the persons of Japanese ancestry in Hawaii were in preferred professional, proprietary, and managerial positions, as compared with of 13.7 per cent for the total Island population

Despite occasional grumblings about racial discrimination, most of the nisei realized how fortunate they were to have been born in Hawaii. Even if they had to study more, work harder, and be quicker to grasp at a chance than the youths with white skin, America was still the land of opportunity. Many Japanese-Americans had gotten ahead in one field or another—with brains, guts, time, and some luck, others could hope to do the same.[8]

Those nisei who visited Japan learned what chance for advancement the son of a peasant had in that land of economic castes, where the common man was harshly exploited in field and factory. They returned home thankful that their fathers had come to Hawaii. Those who travelled on the American Mainland could find like cause for thanks during any auto trip across states with large Negro populations. And though there were slums in Hawaii, on the plantations and in the towns, in any Mainland city one could find *haoles* by the thousands living in more depressing rabbit warrens. In the Islands, at least, the slum dwellers had fresh air and open windows and could get out into the sunlight the year round. As to social acceptance, Hawaii nisei could always contrast their lot with that of the Japanese in California, who lived sealed off and unaccepted by most of their fellow citizens—a ghetto-like environment which had no counterpart in Hawaii.

In the congressional report on the statehood hearings of 1937, it was observed that Hawaii's Japanese-Americans showed the same attitude toward America as had the first generation Americans of European ancestry: "an appreciation of the material benefits received; a high conception of the freedom enjoyed; and an earnest endeavor to comply with the standards of the new culture." The congressmen went on to remark that the behavior of the nisei left little to criticize and much to praise. Their record as an orderly, law-abiding group was unexcelled, and thrift, industry, and willingness to co-operate with other groups were well-marked traits. Their participation in the work of schools, churches, and civic and political organizations showed a desire to share community responsibilities with their fellow Americans in a common loyalty to American ideals and institutions. Much was made of the foreign-language schools and press, but it was pointed out that these agencies served a real purpose in the adjustment of an immigrant group to new conditions. Many European immigrants had used the same means for maintaining contact between the first and second generations. When these institutions had served their purpose they had ceased to exist, and there was no reason to doubt that Hawaii would follow the pattern already familiar on the Mainland. "The Americanization of the Japanese of Hawaii has perhaps made greater progress than it has with many immigrant groups of longer residence in America living in mainland communities." The legislators felt that time would automatically take care of many of the problems which might now seem insurmountable.[9]

In 1941 the State Department sent a special agent to the Pacific Coast states and to Hawaii. It was part of his mission to assess the possible attitudes of the residents of Japanese ancestry in the event of war with Japan. He made some shrewd observations on the position of the nisei within the Territory:

This reporter believes there is this fundamental difference between the 'Japanese Problem' on the Coast and the 'Japanese Problem' in the Hawaiian Islands. On the Coast, the Japanese are discriminated against on a racial basis. In Hawaii it is really only a social and economic basis. This is peculiarly American. In our materialistic civilization one fits in socially largely on an income basis, provided he is willing to wash his neck and give up eating with his knife. In Hawaii the Japanese fit in thus among the bulk of the inhabitants because the bulk are dark skinned of one kind or another. The whites generally are on a higher economic plane than they are on the mainland. The few Japanese who reach a position economically where they can mix with the whites are not numerous enough to make much impression even if they do resent not being asked to tea. The bulk of the whites in Hawaii would not mix anyway with stevedores or dock laborers, black or white. On the mainland there are plenty of 'Okies' to call the Japanese a 'yellow-belly' when economically and by education the Japanese may not only be their equal but their superior.

The result of this is that the Hawaiian Japanese does not suffer from the same inferiority complex or feel the same mistrust of the whites that he does on the mainland. While it is seldom on the mainland that you find even a college-educated Japanese-American citizen who talks to you wholly openly until you have gained his confidence, this is far from the case in Hawaii. Many young Japanese there are as open and frank and at ease with a white as white boys are. In a word, Hawaii is a melting pot because there are more brown skins to melt—Japanese, Hawaiian, Chinese, and Filipino.[10]

Had he had more time for investigation, this reporter might have added that though socially the nisei mixed more freely with the other dark-skinned people of Hawaii than with the whites, there were *haoles*, even in the higher social levels, who did invite Japanese-Americans to tea and to dinner and did treat them as equal fellow Americans. Not many, but enough to prove to the nisei that there were white Americans who really believed and practiced what they preached.

As the nisei grew to adult estate, got jobs, married, and had children, they became members of parent-teacher and other civic groups, joined political parties, voted, sometimes ran for office themselves, and, generally, exercised the privileges and duties of American citizens. But again they met perplexities. During the late 1930s their status as citizens became the subject of extended public discussion which once again centered around the question of loyalty.

While European immigrants had been permitted to become naturalized American citizens, Japanese immigrants had not. Until 1924 the Japanese government followed a practice almost universal among civilized nations of recognizing the children of its nationals, wherever such children were born, as citizens of Japan.* Thus, though the nisei born before 1924 were American citizens by virtue of their birth on American soil, under Japanese law they had also inherited the citizenship of their parents. They had what was known as dual citizenship. In contrast, the children of naturalized Europeans were, by both birth and inheritance, citizens of the United States alone.

---

* The United States followed the same principle, conferring its citizenship upon children born to Americans living abroad, despite the fact that some nations conferred their own citizenship on such children.

By an Imperial ordinance which became effective December 1, 1924, the government of Japan departed from usual international practice and declared that in the future it would claim no American-born child of Japanese parents as a citizen unless the parents registered the infant's name with a Japanese consulate within fourteen days of its birth. Dual citizenship would result, therefore, only when parents strongly desired that their children share their own allegiance. Procedures for formal renunciation of Japanese citizenship through registration with Imperial governmental agencies were also made somewhat less complicated. They could be used by those born before December 1, 1924, as well as by any born after that date who might, as they grew older, wish to deny the Japanese citizenship registered for them by their parents.[11]

The report of the joint congressional committee which conducted the statehood hearings of 1937 noted that the matter of dual citizenship did not arise in the case of half of the American citizens of Japanese ancestry in Hawaii, those who had been born after 1924, since only a "negligible" number of the latter had been registered by their parents as Japanese citizens. A fair number of those born before that year had also renounced their Japanese citizenship. The question of dual citizenship became a live matter only when a dual citizen, whether of Japanese or European stock, visited his parents' homeland, and so came under the jurisdiction of that country. Otherwise his rights and obligations were no different from those of other Americans. It seemed to the congressmen that the United States could set up some machinery to help all of its dual citizens rid themselves of the claims of foreign countries by application to federal officials within the framework of the American government alone. From the sentiments which committee members had heard expressed, it was obvious that the Americans of Japanese ancestry in Hawaii would give their wholehearted support to such action. In the meantime the number of dual citizens was growing less each year. The older nisei continued in increasing numbers to renounce their Japanese citizenship, and Japan had abandoned claim to the younger generation.[12]

Fellow residents who questioned the loyalty of the nisei looked at the matter much less calmly. Hawaii's concern was not with young Europeans; it was with young Japanese. Suppose, as seemed more and more likely, there should be war with Japan. All nisei of military age had been born before 1924. How many of these had renounced Japan? And what about the hundreds born in Hawaii who had been educated in Japan and had returned to the Territory to live?* These *kibei*, as they were called, were still American citizens, but after years in Japanese schools were they loyal Americans? What of their influence on the rest of the second generation?

Until their dual citizenship became the subject of much public discussion, the majority of the nisei had given the matter only passing thought. They were Americans, living in America, and Japan had no control over them. Many of those born before 1924 did not know they were dual citizens, while many born after 1924 were unaware that their parents had registered them as citizens of Japan.

Dual citizens who had decided to expatriate from Japan had found that the process of formal renunciation was by no means quick and simple, despite the procedures made available since 1924. As proof of American citizenship, it was necessary to secure a copy of one's birth certificate from either the Secretary of Hawaii or the Territorial board of health. Both offices charged fees for completing these forms. It was also necessary to get from the village master or other head of the male parent's community in Japan a copy of the census register whereon one's name appeared. If the applicant was under fifteen his parents had to make this request; if he was between fifteen and twenty they had to signify their assent; only those twenty-one or over could act alone. It usually took at least a month to obtain this second necessary document from Japan. Also the official form of renunciation had to be secured from a local Japanese newspaper office, hotel, or other establishment, and those who helped fill them out expected to be paid for their services.

Once the three forms were ready they were sent to the Japanese consulate in Honolulu, from which they were mailed to the Japanese Ministry of Home Affairs. Three or four months later the name of the person who sought expatriation was published in the Japanese government's official gazette. Then the consulate in Hawaii notified the applicant, who next wrote to the appropriate relative in Japan

---

* Children were sent to Japan to live with relatives for one or more reasons: In the homeland they would get adequate care and training at less cost or would be less of an economic handicap when both parents worked; or the parents intended some day to go back to the old country, where they would rejoin offspring who had been properly reared as good Japanese; or the father felt that schooling in Japan would be of economic advantage to the child whether he remained in that country or returned to Hawaii.

to request that his name be stricken from the local census register. This was basic procedure, but any number of complications might arise, two of which may be mentioned as typical.

In the earlier years of immigration many Japanese did not know that births were supposed to be registered with the Hawaii board of health. Plantation doctors often failed to perform this service. On the other hand, the Japanese consulate in Hawaii had numerous local agents throughout the Islands who every five years took a very careful census of the Japanese population. In the process they registered the names and birth dates of all young Japanese citizens. Applicants for expatriation therefore often learned that though their names were listed in the census registers in Japan, there was no documentary evidence in Hawaii to prove that they had been born on American soil. In such cases it was necessary for them to gather affidavits to show that they had been born in the Territory. Often both parents had died, and their friends or neighbors had moved away or were themselves dead. When the applicant found witnesses who lived on an island other than Oahu, he had the expense of bringing them to Honolulu to give testimony. In cases of this sort it was also often necessary to obtain legal advice.

Sometimes a nisei who had been born before 1924 learned that his birth had been registered with the board of health as well as with the Japanese consulate in Hawaii, but that it had never been entered in the local census list in Japan. In such a case the name would have to be recorded in that country before application could properly be made for expatriation—and then for removal of the name from the Japanese register upon which it had had to be inscribed!

To many of the dual citizens this red tape, embarrassment, and expense* was a much less formidable barrier than was parental opposition. Why, asked many of the issei, should a child be so eager to renounce forever the country of his blood? Why should he do so under pressure from people who thought his parents unworthy of American citizenship—and very probably, if the truth were told, felt the same way about himself? It was shameful, they said, like a dog, to kiss the hand that slapped one. If an expatriate should someday go to Japan to visit relatives, he would have to go through all the formalities of getting an American passport and would, in addition,

* The minimum cost was probably about $15.

have to pay for it. Suppose he should wish to get a job in Japan? No one would hire an outsider, a man who had denied his country. Expatriation would make inheritance of family properties in Japan difficult, if not impossible. Furthermore, the whole procedure was foolish and unnecessary. A nisei lost none of his rights and advantages as an American citizen by retaining Japanese citizenship—why not keep them both?

Even more important, expatriation was considered an unpardonable rejection of one's ancestors and an act of disloyalty to Japan which would bring shame and disgrace on one's family. Parents often flatly refused to co-operate in the expatriation of children who were under twenty-one; those above that age often had to defy all traditional concepts of filial piety in order to proceed.[13]

In 1938 the Hawaiian Japanese Civic Association, a nisei group, campaigned to persuade dual citizens to expatriate. During its two-week drive a thousand nisei took the first steps to make themselves legally one hundred per cent American. The same organization made similar efforts in 1939, 1940, and 1941, and each year more young Japanese-Americans renounced the land of their fathers.

In November, 1940, the leaders of the association drew up a petition for presentation to Secretary of State Cordell Hull. This document described the existing expatriation procedures as "complicated and cumbersome, entailing involved correspondence and long waiting." In many cases, it stated, "the technical difficulties are appalling, and in numerous instances more than a year elapses before the action is at long last completed." Some citizens had deferred taking the necessary steps, not only for these reasons, but also because they were unwilling to recognize a claim upon them by any other government than the United States. The whole situation brought upon the heads of Americans of Japanese ancestry much "undeserved and unwarranted" suspicion on the part of some of their fellow citizens. The petitioners realized as clearly as any the utmost importance of national unity in thought and action during a period of crisis, they regarded themselves as the equals of any other Americans in the sincerity of their allegiance to the land of their birth, and they asked that an arrangement be reached with the Japanese government which would provide a more simple procedure of expatriation.[14]

A nisei professor from the University of Hawaii delivered the key-note address at an association rally which launched a campaign for 20,000 signatures. He said, in part:

In the local situation, we Americans of Japanese ancestry happen to be the minority placed under the spotlight of suspicion. Many of our fellow Americans are not ready to accept us as fellow citizens without mental reservations, and some would even deny us the further enjoyment of American citizenship. We are subjected to many forms of discrimination. For instance, our own Navy at Pearl Harbor hesitates to employ Americans of Japanese descent on its clerical and maintenance staffs; a number of business firms seem to have an unwritten law that no Americans of Japanese ancestry shall obtain certain types of positions or rise beyond a certain rank; on some plantations, em-ployees of Japanese blood cannot sit in certain sections of the theaters. The list of specific instances of discrimination is sizable, and we have good grounds for feeling that some of our fellow Americans are not being quite fair in their treatment of us.

At the same time, we must try to be level-headed about all this. . . . we cannot expect any sudden change of feeling, for that would be too much to ask of human nature. And, too, the blame is not wholly on the other side. Either as a group, or as individuals, we ourselves may have contributed to-ward developing feeling against us, and we must now do our share toward bringing about, gradually and intelligently, a lessening to the personal and group bitternesses and tensions that are the inevitable corollary of discrimina-tory practice. . . .

Our immediate concern, at this time, is our position as loyal American citizens. Our loyalty is questioned on the ground that many citizens of Japanese ancestry have not been expatriated from the Japanese nationality, and are therefore dual citizens. . . .

The great majority of Americans of Japanese ancestry in Hawaii born prior to December 1, 1924, did not know that they were citizens of any country other than the United States of America, and many are bewildered today on finding themselves in the status of 'dual citizenship.' This bewilderment is increased by the confusion in many minds as to the proper significance of the term 'dual citizenship.' Dual citizenship is regarded as equivalent to dual allegiance by those who have not paused to consider the extremely important distinction there is between these two terms. Dual citizenship is a status automatically imposed on persons who are claimed by two governments in accordance with their respective nationality laws. Dual allegiance, on the other hand, is an attitude or position taken deliberately by individuals for reasons of their own. When this distinction between dual citizenship and dual alle-giance is more clearly realized, we shall have more intelligent understanding of the real nature of 'dual citizenship' problems. . . .

It is not difficult to see how suspicions directed against Americans of Japan-ese ancestry today might lead eventually to terrible conclusions, and, if we can, now, while it is not too late, act to clarify our positions so definitely that these suspicions will be allayed sufficiently to stabilize effectively our local situation, by all means, let us do what we can. One specific step that we can take is represented in the petition to our Secretary of State. By signing this petition, we publicly record our stand as loyal American citizens who believe in the principles of American democracy and in the magnificent idealism for which the Stars and Stripes stand.[15]

During November and December, 30,000 nisei, sixteen years and older, signed their names to the petition, and to the assertion contained therein that they had "grown up as Americans in mind and spirit, with loyal devotion to this land of our birth."

In 1938 a prominent nisei official made public some estimates as to the number of dual citizens. He stated that of the approximately 113,000 American citizens of Japanese ancestry in Hawaii, 60,000 had been born after December 1, 1924. Of the latter only 10,000 had been registered with the Japanese consulate; the remaining 50,000 were citizens of the United States alone. Of the 53,000 born before 1924, between 23,000 and 33,000 had already expatriated. If these figures were correct, between 20,000 and 30,000 nisei born before 1924, and 10,000 born after that date were still dual citizens.

These estimates were publicized by a person who was strongly urging that the nisei renounce their Japanese citizenship. In his public statements he described the many difficulties involved in the process, and gave lethargy rather than disloyalty as the main reason for the delays. Asking for sympathetic understanding from citizens of other ancestries, he told the Japanese-American to behave so as to "leave no doubt as to his loyalty and patriotism," and urged him to rise above the strictures of "a group of intolerant critics." This man would have felt no desire to overestimate the number of dual citizens, yet the lowest figure which could be derived from his calculations indicated that Japan still claimed 30,000, at least 26 per cent of the nisei, as citizens.[16]

During a period when tension between Japan and the United States was increasing month by month, how many of the dual citizens were taking steps toward expatriation?* In the spring of 1941 an official of the Japanese consulate stated that expatriation forms were

* Information secured from the records of the Japanese consulate gives the number of applications for expatriation as 391 in 1937, 1246 in 1938, 840 in 1939, 2676 in 1940, and 3598 in 1941.

being issued at the rate of 400 a month, and that the number of applications was steadily increasing. But even at this, the peak rate so far, it would take a long time to make a real dent in the ranks of the thousands of dual citizens. And though it was being stated that such birth registrations had dropped sharply since 1938, the figures released by the consulate seemed to indicate that at least one out of every ten infants of Japanese ancestry was still being listed in its files as a Japanese national.[17]

Those who made their offspring Japanese citizens were aliens and probably didn't know any better, but, said the "intolerant critics," surely there was no excuse for those Japanese-Americans who had taken no steps to indicate a clear and unmistakable allegiance to America alone!

A nisei graduate of the University of Hawaii expressed the resentment which this attitude caused among many of his fellow citizens of Japanese ancestry. In his column in one of the Honolulu newspapers he discussed a resolution endorsing expatriation which had been passed at a recent conference of young nisei, and indicated his personal approval of this action, but continued:

It is strange, however, that so much stress is laid on the dual status of Japanese-Americans when there are countless numbers of Americans of European nationalities in the United States who are in the same double category as the Japanese-Americans. The patriotism of European-Americans, for the most part, is taken for granted. To this same group of hyphenated Americans, as well as the 100 per centers, Japanese-Americans must prove their loyalty to Uncle Sam.

Expatriation will help in dissolving much of the suspicion surrounding the Japanese-Americans, but it is doubtful whether that distrust can be completely stamped out, even if it is possible for every one of the 120,000 Japanese-Americans to sever his political bonds with Japan. Nothing short of war between United States and Japan, and visible proof of patriotism by the Japanese-Americans in that war, will convince doubting Thomases of the Niseis' allegiance to the country of their birth.

His feelings thus relieved, the writer tried to be just to those of little faith, and added, "We cannot altogether blame the skeptics. They cannot see the loyalty of the heart. . . ."[18]

THE MAJOR responsibility for the internal security of the Islands rested with the Army. Naval authorities, primarily concerned with the safety of the Pacific Fleet, were intensely aware of the opportunities for espionage, sabotage, and subversive activity open to the Japanese, and seldom tried to hide their concern. Though the Army did its worrying with less publicity, military leaders in Hawaii and in Washington were fully conscious of the potential danger. It was the duty of the commanding general of the Army's Hawaiian Department not only to organize defenses against external attack but also to make preparations for possible local uprisings and sabotage. The Military Intelligence Section (G-2) at Fort Shafter had been trying for years to estimate how the Japanese in Hawaii would behave in the event of war between the Empire and the United States.[1]

The issei, with their faithful observance of Japanese holidays and their elaborate entertainments for visiting dignitaries from Japan, caused the most concern. They continued to flock to Japanese movies which extolled the invincible might of the homeland and stressed the traditional virtues of loyalty, military valor, and personal sacrifice for the Emperor. The same ideas were emphasized in the Domei news reports and also in imported Japanese phonograph records. While it was true that the films, news items, and recordings were not anti-American in tone, they certainly were pro-Japanese, and they seemed to have an enthusiastic audience

The Eyes of America

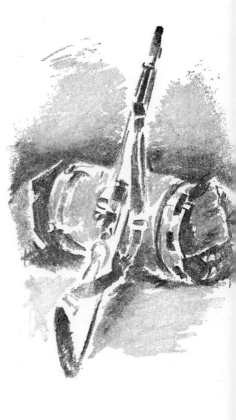

among the Japan-born. It was also apparent that the Japanese consulate in Honolulu had worked through the issei-controlled Japanese Chamber of Commerce in arranging fund-raising drives for the benefit of the Imperial war machine.

There were some nisei groups like the Hawaiian Japanese Civic Association which had campaigned for renunciation of Japanese citizenship, but it was the immigrant generation which still dominated organizational life within the Japanese community. To the Army the "loyalty" of the issei seemed dubious.

Military Intelligence also suspected the Hawaii-born youths who had been educated in Japan. There were about 600 kibei in the Islands. Many had returned to the Territory indoctrinated with the militaristic nationalism taught in Imperial schools, holding exalted views of Japan's destiny, and apparently even more devoted to that country than their parents. Some had been away so long they had practically forgotten the English language. Their ideas and manners were often ridiculed by their nisei brothers as "Japanesy." Why, wondered G-2, had a country which was rapidly conscripting for its army allowed these young men of military age to return?[2]

Military Intelligence was uncertain about the nisei. Many had visited Japan, sometimes in special tour parties sponsored by the Imperial government. They were ill at ease because of poor command of the language, and they found the ancestral village cramped and dull. Neither did they like the suspicion and reserve with which they were treated by civilians, nor the shadowing by secret police.[3] Back in Hawaii, many vowed they would never visit Japan again—once was enough. Apparently there had been no official attempt to undermine their allegiance to America, probably because the Japanese government thought they were so "Americanized" the effort would be wasted.

This did not, of course, offer any certainty as to how the Japanese-Americans would behave in case of war and possible thrusts against Hawaii. If that time came, and the nisei had to make a choice between the land of their ancestors and that of their birth, how many would prove disloyal to the United States, and who, specifically, would they be? This was the question faced by the Army's badly understaffed counterespionage group.

It was not easy to investigate nisei whose loyalty seemed doubtful. Persons of Japanese ancestry "clammed up" when questioned; they did not relish the traditionally despicable role of *inu* (dog or base informer).

It was easier to secure opinions from the non-Japanese *kamaaina* (long-resident, usually *haole*) business and professional men of the Territory, but talks with a dozen such persons uncovered as many different views. Some believed that in case of war with Japan only a few of the local Japanese would be loyal to the United States. Some were sure that their own family servants would be loyal to them as individuals and would warn them of danger, and thought the same might be true in other households. Some distrusted the issei but had full confidence in the nisei. There was no agreement, however, as to the loyalty of the Hawaii-born generation.

The business people just did not know. They were friendly, in a paternal way, with a few individuals of Japanese ancestry, usually domestics or other employees, and felt that they could vouch for them, but that was the extent of their certainty.[4]

In August, 1939, the Federal Bureau of Investigation opened a Honolulu office. Robert C. Shivers, the agent-in-charge, immediately ordered his staff "to make a thorough appraisal of all the factors which had a bearing on the internal security of the islands."

With its large and well-trained force, the FBI office took the lead in investigating the "Japanese Problem." Shivers and Colonel George W. Bicknell, head of the Army counterespionage section, worked together. From October, 1940, their staffs occupied adjacent suites in a Honolulu office building, and the two men visited back and forth, delimited spheres of effort, and pooled information. The chief of Navy Intelligence frequently conferred with them.

As Shivers' survey progressed, and the Army and FBI agents checked individual nisei, it appeared that there was no real reason to doubt the loyalty of the majority of Japanese-Americans. But it also became apparent that it would take the authorities quite some time to investigate those persons, both alien and citizen, whose attitudes were in doubt. War might not hold off much longer, and, while loyalty investigations should continue, some additional method of approach to the internal security problem should also be tried. Furthermore, unless something was done to counter what Shivers described as a popular "undercurrent of suspicion and growing fear" of the Japanese population, it would be impossible to secure united community support of defense preparations. If this psychological situation continued, and the United States went to war with Japan, the Army and Navy might be forced to divert trained personnel from battle duty to the job of keeping order within the civilian community.

A community morale campaign was planned by the FBI and Army and Navy Intelligence, with the FBI usually taking the initiative. Shivers invited some nisei, carefully selected on the advice of non-Japanese who knew them well, to help with the campaign. He told them frankly why and how they had been chosen, and asked their advice and co-operation. From their number, two advisory groups were organized in April and June, 1940. These met separately at least once a week with Shivers and one of his agents, and discussed matters relating to the Japanese population and its behavior in case of war with Japan.

In December, 1940, Hung Wai Ching, a citizen of Chinese ancestry, invited some of Oahu's civic leaders to meet and discuss plans to fight the growing public antagonism toward and distrust of local Japanese. After several sessions a steering committee was set up to carry on a quiet but vigorous campaign "to preserve Hawaii's traditional pattern of race relationships." Mr. Shivers became chairman of this group, multi-racial in composition, which called itself the Committee for Interracial Unity. Its membership included civilian business and professional leaders and the heads of the Army and Navy Intelligence services. It met every two weeks and was aided by a larger advisory committee representing every major racial group in the Territory.

The committee laid down a definite policy line: "The people of Japanese ancestry, both citizens and aliens, compose about one-third of our population. Accepted and united in purpose and action, they are an asset to the community. Rejected and treated as potential enemies, they are a burden, even a danger to our security." If a crisis came residents could and should rely on the authorities to treat the loyal with complete fairness, yet to deal sternly with the disloyal. There must be no vigilantism. What was needed was a lessening of fear, both in the minds of the non-Japanese who thought Hawaii's security might be endangered from within, and in the minds of the Japanese themselves, who feared harsh treatment in the event of war. Furthermore, a place should be found in the scheme of national defense for every loyal citizen. Loyalty could grow only if it were given a chance. It could not flourish "in an atmosphere of suspicion, discrimination, and deprival of opportunities to practice that loyalty."

Early in 1941 one of Mr. Shivers' nisei advisory groups organized the Oahu Citizens Committee for Home Defense, composed of Americans of Japanese ancestry. Its objectives were: to work with the authorities in evaluating what went on in the Japanese community, to plan for and carry out the task of bringing out more positively the inherent loyalty of the Americans of Japanese ancestry, and to prepare the people of the Japanese community psychologically for their responsibilities toward America in the event of war and the difficult position in which such an event would place them.

At a mass patriotic rally which this committee staged in June, 1941, the key speaker was the Hawaiian Department's chief of staff for Military Intelligence. He promised, as personal representative of the commanding general, that in the event of war all Island residents of Japanese ancestry would receive fair and nondiscriminatory treatment provided that their behavior indicated no disloyalty. The Army was confident that the overwhelming majority of Hawaii's Japanese were loyal to the United States, and it counted on their support in the defense effort. In return the Army would do all in its power to insure law-abiding citizens "the security of their liberties and their homes." Persons of Japanese ancestry were urged to co-operate with the authorities in countering possible espionage or sabotage by "a few mistaken individuals" whose actions might discredit their whole group.

This was the first public announcement of the Army's intended treatment of the Japanese population in case of war. Subsequent statements followed the same pattern, and in speeches before luncheon clubs, school assemblies, and other groups, Army and FBI representatives stressed the need for interracial co-operation in a united front for home defense.[5]

During the summer Navy officials urged arrest of some 234 resident Japanese consular agents who had not registered as agents of a foreign government as required by federal law. Commanding General Walter C. Short opposed such action. It would, he felt, alarm the Japanese community and sabotage the Army's civilian morale campaign. Besides, not more than 10 per cent of the issei who had failed to register knew of the law which they had violated. He wired Washington, "I believe development of loyalty among the Japanese population more important than punishment of a few individuals," and his view prevailed.[6]

Shivers had by this time become convinced that there was no reason to question the loyalty of citizens of Japanese ancestry except the small number of kibei who constituted only .345 per cent of the civilian population. He was also convinced that only a small percentage of the alien Japanese in the Islands would be actively "disloyal" to the United States in the event of a war with Japan.[7]

Cheering as these judgments were, the federal intelligence agencies saw in them no excuse for relaxation of vigilance, and during the latter months of 1941 they expanded their loyalty investigations and samplings of opinion within the Japanese community. The Army's counterespionage group within the G-2 section had grown from four regular agents in April to twelve officers and eighteen special investigators in December. The Japanese Problem almost monopolized the attention of Military Intelligence personnel.[8]

By the end of November the Army assessment of its internal security problem was roughly as follows: If war with Japan did come, and it was fought (as practically all the top planners of both armed branches thought it would be) in the western reaches of the Pacific, with no large-scale attacks against Hawaii, then the great majority of the issei could be expected to be "passively loyal" to the United States. They would probably do nothing to help Japan or to harm their hostland. Most of the nisei would act as loyal American citizens. The comparatively few fanatics classified as dangerous, issei or kibei, would be picked up by the FBI as soon as hostilities began. The rest of the residents of Japanese ancestry would be under careful surveillance.

These conclusions were based on the assumption that the actual fighting would not touch Hawaiian shores. But what if enemy troops managed to force a landing on Oahu? It could be assumed that some Japanese would remain neutral. Others would probably do everything possible to repel the enemy. There would be some who would help the invaders. Even individuals normally "loyal" to the United States might under the influence of battle hysteria throw off their newly acquired convictions and succumb to ancestral ties. But which individuals would do what? Probably many of the Japanese themselves did not know the answer to this question, nor could they know until faced with the necessity for an immediate decision.[9]

In any case, though the Army did have plans for dealing with the local Japanese in the event of an enemy invasion attempt, it was little worried about what then seemed a remote possibility.

In October, 1941, Curtis Munson compiled a report on Hawaii's "Japanese Problem" for the State Department. He noted that the FBI held the leading place in the investigation of the internal security situation and commented that this was due largely to the personality of the agent-in-charge, who had done much to gain the confidence of the Japanese and other elements in the community.* Military Intelligence agents were also working earnestly to assess the situation, under the leadership of an able reserve officer (Colonel Bicknell), who had been in the intelligence service during World War I. Naval Intelligence, a late starter, was developing an organization whose effectiveness would not reach its peak for another four or five months.

Munson further noted that the first generation Japanese in Hawaii were, like the first generation on the Pacific Coast, ideologically and culturally closest to Japan. Though many of them spoke no English, or at best pidgin, it was thought that the majority of them would prove loyal in the event of war. This was especially so because most of them lived on the land, to which they were devoted. In this connection he remarked that it seemed as if everyone in Hawaii, and especially the darker-skinned laboring classes, placed loyalty to Hawaii first and to the United States second. It was "not that they were not loyal to the nation; it was simply that they loved Hawaii." As for the nisei, the opinion of those best informed was that about 98 per cent were loyal. This would mean, however, that about 1,500 were disloyal.** The FBI reported only 400 suspects among the aliens, and its private estimate was that only fifty or sixty were "sinister."

After describing the social and economic position of Hawaii's Japanese, and contrasting their status with that of their West Coast cousins, Munson continued:

* In a subsequent report, dated December 20, Munson stated: "Your observer must note without fear or favor that 99% of the most intelligent views on the Japanese, by military, official, and civil contacts in Honolulu and the mainland, was best crystallized by two Intelligence men before the outbreak of the war. These two men are Lieutenant Commander K. D. Ringle of the 11th Naval District in Los Angeles and Mr. Shivers in Honolulu of the F.B.I." U. S. Congress, Joint Committee on the Investigation of the Pearl Harbor attack, *Pearl Harbor Attack*, Hearings, 79th Cong., 1st and 2d sess., pursuant to S. Con. Res. 27 (Washington, 1946), Part 6, p. 2688.
** The kibei were included in this figure.

In summarizing, we cannot say how loyal the Japanese in the Hawaiian group would be if there were an American Naval disaster and the Japanese fleet appeared off the Hawaiian Islands. Doubtless great numbers of them would then forget their American loyalties and shout 'Banzai' from the shore. Under those circumstances if this reporter were there he is not sure that he might not do it also to save his own skin, if not his face. Due to the fact that there are more than enough soldiers in the Islands to take care of any Japanese, even if so inclined, the Japanese will probably remain quietly at their tasks. However, in fairness to them it is only right to say that we believe the big majority anyhow would be neutral or even actively loyal.[10]

The federal agencies had done all their probing with the greatest possible secrecy and Hawaii's civilian community had no knowledge of the conclusions reached. Rumor, speculation, and misinformation continued to condition the minds of a large part of the non-Japanese population, and in 1940 and 1941, persons of Japanese ancestry, nisei as well as issei, were left in little doubt that many of their fellow residents looked on them with distrust.

Since 1927 nisei from the various islands had been holding annual "New Americans Conferences" in Honolulu. These meetings had been arranged by the Reverend Takie Okamura, a Japanese convert to Christianity who had come to Hawaii in 1894.* They were intended to help introduce the Japanese-Americans to their duties as American citizens and to correct those "mutual misunderstandings and misapprehensions" which often hindered frank and friendly relations between nisei and *haoles*, employees and employers. The delegates were carefully selected and most of them came from plantation communities. They discussed their civic responsibilities and the problems they faced in finding their places in America's social pattern. They met, talked, and lunched with various *haole* leaders (the Army and Navy each sent a representative), listened to speeches, and, generally, received much paternal advice from their mentor and the visiting elders.

Mr. Okamura had long been convinced that by continuing to operate the language schools, by registering their children as Japanese

---

* In addition to organizing and building a flourishing parish and church, this energetic and devoted clergyman had founded the first Japanese-language school in the Territory, the first Japanese library, the first Japanese magazine, and the first Japanese YMCA. He had helped many young men to secure high school and university education, and had worked unceasingly to bring about the Christianization and Americanization—he felt that each depended on the other—of Hawaii nisei.

citizens, by opposing expatriation, and by public display of Japanese customs and habits, the issei had earned much of the criticism they received from other elements in the community. Though his frequent public statements of these sentiments had made him unpopular with a great many of the Japanese, he had nevertheless continued his censure.

In the opening address of the 1940 New Americans Conference, the theme of which was "Statehood for Hawaii," Mr. Okamura claimed that the three main obstacles to statehood were: the continued existence of the Japanese-language schools, the wide prevalence of dual citizenship among the nisei, and the doubts which the American people still felt as to the assimilation and Americanization of the Japanese-Americans.

Some say in defense that the question of the loyalty of our citizens of Japanese ancestry is already clear, and that it is no longer to be doubted. They say 'dual citizenship' is not a new thing. There are a lot of dual citizens among the citizens of European descent, so why pick only on citizens of Japanese ancestry? Indeed, their reasoning sounds plausible. But there are so few Germans, French, and British in Hawaii, and they are not a serious problem. The overwhelming majority of [such] people in Hawaii are citizens of Japanese ancestry. They are holding on to American citizenship with their right, and to Japanese citizenship with their left. Which hand will they let go in the event of an emergency? That is the grave concern of Americans, and it is not unreasonable.

For years it has been customary for the older Japanese to gather at the language schools on the Emperor's birthday, or for the dedication of a Japanese school building or on other special holidays, and start their exercises with the unveiling of the Emperor's picture, profound obeisance, singing of Kimigayo, the national anthem, and reading of the Imperial Rescript.* Americans and other nationalities have seen this happen, and even the newspapers broadcast it in full detail. Being Japanese subjects, everything they do at the language schools is perfectly legitimate. No one can condemn them. But it does not seem right to the American people. These schools which ought to be the training places of future American citizens are no different from the schools for Japanese subjects and for Japan. After being educated in public schools under strong American influence, these children attend language schools in the afternoon and are brought up under Japanese influence. How can they be expected to be loyal to the American flag? Can they really be simon-pure American citizens? This again is not an unreasonable question.

---

* The "infallible" guide of educational policy in Japan, where it was publicly read with great formality on the anniversary of its issuance, October 30, 1890.

Mr. Okamura urged citizens of Japanese ancestry to act resolutely to remove the doubts which others felt as to their loyalty. "Do your duties as loyal citizens. Don't be a fence-straddler, but be strong Americans."

Other civilian speakers on the 1940 program were generally as firm, if not as blunt, in telling the delegates that they and the rest of the nisei were "facing a moment of supreme test," that they must prove their loyalty. They must "be American and nothing but American," forget their Japanese ancestry, lose themselves in the larger community, and throw off "the secretive and gregarious characteristics" which they daily displayed before people of other racial extractions. "You are not good Americans until you have cut the umbilical cord of race and have become Americans." Words would not suffice, there must be deeds.

A civilian guest, a sincere and long-time friend of the Island Japanese, who described himself as their "constant defender and supporter," discussed the language schools and the matter of dual citizenship. He knew that it took several months to secure expatriation, but the process was relatively inexpensive. In fact, to put matters bluntly, there was no excuse for those who desired to be accepted as Americans by other citizens but nevertheless failed to cut the ties which bound them to a foreign power. At least there was no excuse which would be accepted by other Americans.

The language schools, he said, also caused distrust. It was true that their legality had been upheld by the Supreme Court, but it was by no means certain that they would be upheld if again banned by law. Other Americans felt that these institutions were part of a program to keep the nisei loyal to Japan. They felt that such schools were un-American and subversive. Therefore, if Americans of Japanese ancestry wished to be accepted as citizens by other Americans, they must not only expatriate from Japan but also give up the language schools.

These *haoles* who talked so strongly were *kamaainas* who wished the nisei well and had often publicly expressed the belief that they could and would be assimilated into American life. The speakers made a distinction between themselves and the *malihinis* (newcomers from the Mainland) who often brought a ready-made mental picture of insidious, sly, inscrutable, treacherous Japanese. Yet their counsel was brusque, even stern. Nearly every speaker expressed his own belief in the loyalty of the nisei, yet listeners must have often wondered if they were regarded as possessing that single undivided allegiance so earnestly stressed. If these big men talked this way to *them*, what must they think of the rest of the Japanese-Americans?

The delegates listened respectfully to the advice with which they were, as one nisei put it, pounded.* But in subsequent discussions among themselves—in true American fashion—they argued the merit of some of the advice. True, more of the dual citizens should expatriate, but the process was by no means as easy as some of their advisers seemed to think. Though it was certainly true that the language schools did arouse suspicions which were not unreasonable, did this warrant their immediate abolition? The restraint and modesty of behavior which the nisei had been taught at home and in the language schools, and which some speakers had mentioned with approval, had probably made them backward and diffident in their social intercourse with *haoles*, and so had given some excuse for the accusations of "Japanese clannishness." Though agreed that their generation should be socially more aggressive, the delegates noted with approval a statement made by a University of Hawaii sociologist, who was present at one of the sessions, that the *haoles* "should get organized and get in with the Orientals and make them feel at home and when the Orientals feel at home with the *haoles* the function of the language schools will be almost done."

Some of the discussions dealt with the matter of economic discrimination. It was well known that the nisei had little chance to rise to executive positions in *haole* firms, and that it was the practice of such businesses to give higher pay for similar work to white workers and to import Mainlanders to fill supervisory positions. Recently citizens of Japanese ancestry had met another example of discrimination. The Army and Navy had been expanding their installations, but when Japanese-Americans applied for jobs they were turned away. "Why is it," cried one delegate "that no matter how hard we labor we have so few opportunities of rising? Is it because we are just common Japanese of the yellow race?"

Another youth who had listened to the questions asked wistfully,

* One of the guest speakers (who talked to the delegates as he would have talked to a group of young Caucasian citizens) wryly prefaced his own remarks with the observation: "It seems as though the New Americans are a peculiar target for preaching, lecturing, and scolding."

"I would like to know how we can become Americanized? What do you mean by Americanization? If we eat the way Americans do and live the way they live, will we be Americans? Unless you understand what democracy means I think it is difficult for us to become true Americans. It is not by birth but something inside. We should talk about loyalty. How loyal are we? There is reason for other people to suspect us and now is the time to take stock and inventory of ourselves and express our true opinion on how we feel and then decide definitely. People coming from Japan are loyal to Japan because they understand Japan. In my opinion the American way of life is best."

When the "New Americans" convened again in July, 1941, the advice was the same as before, though it came from a different set of notables. One speaker titled his address "The Eyes of America Are Upon You." Another civic leader, who described himself as an old and warm friend of Hawaii's Japanese, gave a talk which might appropriately have borne the same heading.

You are torn between your desire to please your grandparents and your long family line in Japan on the one hand, and the call to undivided loyalty to the land of your birth, your own nation, on the other hand. You must clearly be, and have it known to all that you are, wholly, and with undivided allegiance, Americans. . . .

Straighten out these questions of loyalty, and national unity, and fairness to your neighbours, in your own mind, so that you are personally as clear as a bell in your own thoughts. Determine that come what may, even though you be misunderstood and misconstrued, you know that your own mind is undivided and you are placing the good of your own country and your neighbors above your own selfish desires. . . .

Because he felt that his listeners had too often received similar exhortations unaccompanied by concrete suggestions as to how to act on them, this speaker told the delegates to mix into general community life, help in solving community problems, improve themselves and help others to do the same, and co-operate in programs directed toward increased national unity.

Do you know people whom you can more thoroughly convince as to the duty of undivided loyalty, allegiance, and help in the nation's emergency? Are there some who need to be brought to the attention of national officials lest they act unwisely to endanger the country? In such matters you can help. If such minds exist, you can help in solving the problems. And if you co-operate in specific ways such as have been suggested above, you will know that you are excellent Americans, and others will recognize it. Deeds count, not words alone. And if you do the things that are appropriate to the American way of life, you may enjoy inward peace, and may be confident that those in authority will approve of what you are doing and will be grateful to you for aid to our country in its emergency.

And let me close by stating that I personally know that many of you, and I have reason to believe all of you, are doing just such fine things as good citizens, American born.[11]

It was neither unnatural nor unreasonable that these businessmen should talk as they did. The public-school teachers and social and religious workers knew the nisei as students and friends but the businessmen generally knew them as employees, and felt certain of the loyalty of only the few whom they had come to know well in that relationship. The rest of the Japanese-Americans were an unknown quantity.

There were, however, some civic leaders who disliked this approach to the nisei. Such a person was Samuel Wilder King, Hawaii's delegate to Congress, part-Hawaiian and proud of it. In March he had written to a Honolulu newspaper editor:

I have felt and said repeatedly that those who believe they [the nisei] can return any loyalty towards Japan after having been born and brought up in an American environment, belittle the value of our American institutions and the great benefits our American democracy offers to the individual. I have not the slightest doubt that the overwhelming majority of our citizens of Japanese ancestry are loyal to the United States, and are making every effort to make themselves completely American. Filial devotion and other influences retard the process somewhat, but this is true of every immigrant group.

If we would quit "picking" on this group, stop continually making them the subject of suspicioning and questioning, we would help overcome these restraining influences. As it is now, we simply make it harder for these boys and girls to be good Americans because of the doubts so frequently expressed about their loyalty, and the fact that we use towards them an entirely different yardstick to measure their Americanization than we apply to any other immigrant people. I sincerely believe our newspapers and our leaders in public affairs would be rendering a great patriotic service if they would join together in a definite change of front towards these citizens, think of them as one would men of Italian, or German, or any other European ancestry, and treat them as individuals, according to merit, without continually harping on race.

King practiced what he preached. In Congress, as well as at home in Hawaii, he firmly asserted his confidence in the loyalty and Americanism of his constituents of Japanese ancestry. In March, 1941, one of them wrote him a letter of thanks:

An article appearing in the *Honolulu Advertiser*, March 23rd issue, under the caption "King Raps Misunderstanding of Japanese Situation in Isles" is highly appreciated not only by me but, I am sure, equally so by many other Americans of Japanese ancestry in Hawaii whose undivided loyalty is to the United States.

The second generation Hawaiian-born Japanese have been knocked so frequently that your views in clarifying the so-called Japanese question in Hawaii [give] us a glow of happiness and a spark of determination to live up to the faith you have bestowed upon us. Time is here or will come when you will be proud of the Americans of Japanese ancestry. We shall not fail you.[12]

In mid-November a Honolulu newspaper printed a letter from one of its subscribers. Intended as an open address to young Americans of Japanese ancestry, it was the kind of utterance which King deplored.

Now you, by fact of American birth and American citizenship on the one hand, and on the other the heritage of many generations of Japanese progenitors, are called upon to make one of the most momentous decisions that young men and women have ever faced in the history of this world.

How can a boy kill people of his own flesh and blood? And again how can a boy brought up as an American take up arms against the flag under which he has lived and flourished?

Do not hesitate. Make your decision and take your choice now. Only be sure of one thing: choose the course you believe to be right. If your heart and conscience tell you to fight for America, have no regrets. FIGHT FOR AMERICA!

If, again, your best feelings dictate the opposite policy, go to the land whence your parents came. Do not stay here and be spies or dishonest people. Have the courage of your own convictions.

Now is the time. Think and decide, and you may be sure that if you ask God to guide you, He will not let you fail![13]

When this letter appeared, some 1,500 of the young men to whom it was directed were wearing Army uniform. Inducted through the selective service system, they had been receiving military training in the Territory. Had the "best feelings" of any of these GIs suddenly urged his removal to Japan he might have met some difficulty in getting permission for the journey.

If these youths were forced to make that "momentous" decision, would each of them be ready and willing to kill Japanese soldiers? In the previous year the War Department had evidently not thought so. On August 26, 1940, during the U. S. Senate discussion of the

Burke-Wadsworth bill to establish a national selective service system for military training, Senator Robert Wagner of New York had proposed a change in the wording of the section which dealt with enlistments. His amendment, intended to assure Negroes the same rights as other citizens to enlist and to be accepted in the various branches of the armed services, would have prohibited discrimination against any volunteer on the basis of race or color.

Senator Lester Hill of Alabama opposed adoption of the proviso. He had consulted with the War Department about an amendment, previously proposed, which would have had substantially the same effect as Wagner's.

The War Department is very much opposed to this amendment. One reason is that they cite the situation with reference to Japanese-born Americans [*sic*] in Hawaii and they say: The population of Hawaii, totaling about 400,000, includes approximately 153,000 persons of Japanese racial origin. About three-fourths of these are American citizens by birth. A large number of these are, no doubt, loyal Americans, but it is well known that others are not loyal Americans. A law that would require acceptance of enlistment without regard to race of American-born Japanese who are otherwise qualified would seriously cripple the military forces of the United States in what might be a very critical area in the event of any trouble in the Pacific.

Senator Millard Tydings of Maryland elaborated the point, citing frequent mention of the large Japanese population of the Territory by members of Congress who opposed granting Hawaii statehood.

That does not infer that there are not many loyal American-Japanese in the Islands, but a great many of the Japanese in the Hawaiian Islands are of the first generation, who have even now no United States citizenship [*sic!*]. * It would be unfortunate if the garrison in the Hawaiian Islands had a large percentage of Japanese troops, the loyalty of some of whom might be questioned, particularly in the event there should be war between the United States and Japan. I think we had better leave this element out, let the Army run the Army, and not have so many generals in the United States Senate.

Other southern senators also spoke against the amendment, but it was nevertheless accepted, and the Selective Service Act, as signed by the president on September 16, provided that any person within the prescribed age limits should have the opportunity, "regardless of race or color," to enlist and be inducted into the armed forces.

* Senator Tydings had been a member of the Congressional Joint Committee on Hawaii of 1937, which had taken a great deal of testimony on the matter of dual citizenship and its relation to American and Japanese nationality laws.

It also directed that in the selection and training of men and in the interpretation and execution of the Act there should be "no discrimination against any person on account of race or color."[14]

In Hawaii the Army command knew that some potentially disloyal Japanese-Americans would be called for military service under the terms of this act. In addition to the kibei there were surely other nisei who might be a source of danger to the Territory's military security if they were taken into the Army. It had been possible to investigate the loyalty of comparatively few of the thousands of nisei who were now liable for induction.

The surest way to exclude potential traitors was mass disbarment of all citizens of Japanese ancestry or deferment of each of these whose induction number was called until his loyalty could be investigated, but the Wagner proviso made the first procedure impossible, and, though the Army did have the legal right to reject individuals on grounds of disloyalty, the second method would, in effect, constitute discrimination on the basis of race. It would contravene the spirit, if not the letter, of this federal prohibition against racial discrimination. In fact, if not in form, it would have meant mass exclusion of the nisei, and it would have bluntly notified every citizen of Japanese ancestry in the Islands that his blood made his loyalty to the United States automatically suspect. In delivering such a shattering blow to the morale of the loyal nisei it would have created a far greater threat to Hawaii's military security than the presence of a comparatively few untrustworthy soldiers within the Hawaiian garrison.

So, at least, thought Lieutenant General Charles D. Herron, commanding general of the Hawaiian Department since 1937. It was he who authorized the following direct quotation in the October 19, 1940 issue of *Collier's:* "The Army is not worried about the Japanese in Hawaii. Among them there may be a small hostile alien group, but we can handle the situation. It seems people who know least about Hawaii and live farthest away are most disturbed over this matter. People who know the Islands are not worried about possible sabotage. I say this sincerely after my years of service here. I am sold on the patriotism and Americanization of the Hawaiian people as a whole."

This statement did fit in with the current Army propaganda campaign to strengthen the allegiance of the Japanese residents, but

Herron really did have more faith than his Washington superiors in the loyalty of the nisei who would become American soldiers. He had broken with military precedent in the previous March when he had given orders that a reserve officer of Japanese ancestry be called up for extended active duty in the garrison force. There might be some recruits disloyal in spirit, but nisei inductees could be watched as they trained and those found suspect could always be retired to civilian status. Serious danger to Hawaii's defenses would arise only in case of open hostilities with Japan, in which event these soldiers could be used as unarmed service troops whose loyalty would never be tested in combat, or they could be discharged from military duty. By December, 1941, some 1,500 nisei recruits had been inducted.

They were not the first Hawaii-born men of Japanese ancestry to enter the American Army. In 1915 and 1916, when the Territory's National Guard had begun vigorous recruitment of volunteers, its officers had not encouraged enlistment of nisei. The official history of Hawaii's participation in World War I relates that while "no actual discrimination was practiced, and a few enlisted, there is evidence to show that they were not much wanted." In 1917, however, after the United States entered the war against the Central Powers, a company had been made up from the 596 nisei registered by Hawaii's selective service boards, and in August of that year it had become Company D of the Guard's 1st Regiment. Though called into federal service in June, 1918, the Guard had never left the Territory, and Company D's most notable war service was a ten-day patrol of Honolulu's water reservoirs.[15] After the war, nisei enlistment was again discouraged.

On October 15, 1940, Hawaii's National Guard once more became part of the regular Army. A few weeks before, an official report had given its strength as 110 officers and 1,741 enlisted men. Of the enlisted men, who were classified according to "racial origin," Hawaiians and part-Hawaiians numbered 732; Caucasians, 524; Chinese, 217; Puerto Ricans, 84; Filipinos, 52; Koreans, 52; Japanese, 40; colored, 2; and other, 38. Of the officers, 76 were Caucasians, 28 Hawaiians or part-Hawaiians, and 6 were Chinese.[16] (In 1940, persons of Korean ancestry composed 1.62 per cent of Hawaii's population; those of Caucasian ancestry 24.5 per cent, and those of Japanese ancestry 37.2 per cent.)

When federalized the Guard was composed of two regiments—the 298th Infantry and the 299th Infantry. The first had been recruited from Oahu volunteers and the latter from residents of other islands. There were nine nisei in the Oahu regiment: three were sergeants, old-timers in the outfit who had entered military service during World War I; one was a clerk in the Service Company; five were members of the regimental band. There were thirty-one nisei in the 299th. It was more difficult on the other islands to recruit full complements for the companies, and in these more rural areas where everyone knew everyone else, it was easier for a nisei who was well known and liked to get into the "club." On Oahu one company of the 298th was composed of Chinese-Americans, and another almost entirely of Caucasian graduates of the Reserve Officers Training Corps at Honolulu's Roosevelt High School, where most of the students were of white ancestry. These units were the exception to the rule, however, and nonsegregation was the general practice. The Hawaiian and part-Hawaiian boys, with their natural friendliness toward everyone, helped to break down racial barriers.

The 298th Infantry became part of the 21st Brigade of the Army's Hawaiian Division, and the 299th came under command of the 22d Brigade. By the end of October, 1940, both regiments were in training at Schofield Barracks on Oahu.

On December 9 the selective service boards of the Territory began to process inductees. After thirteen weeks of basic training at Schofield, most of the recruits were sent to the 298th and 299th Infantry, men from Oahu to the 298th, those from other islands to the 299th. Of the nearly 3,000 men inducted through selective service boards during the next twelve months, approximately 1,500 were nisei, a great many of whom had volunteered. About 200 were sent to Army Engineer units, but the rest went to the former National Guard regiments.

They were not segregated in separate companies, but were placed in those units where they were needed and their individual talents could be used to best advantage. They met hostility neither from their fellow inductees of other national ancestries nor from the old-timers of the Guard—the enlisted men of that organization had not been consulted on its personnel policy. To their new comrades the nisei were simply other Island boys. In the National Guard as in the general population whites had long been a minority.

Japanese-American students had been accepted in the ROTC units at Oahu high schools and at the University of Hawaii, so at least half of the nisei inductees had received military training.* Officers soon noticed the snap and efficiency they introduced into their squads and platoons. General Herron later testified that: "In the training camp they were remarkably diligent and obedient to orders. When 4 o'clock came, after a long hard day, and others turned to rest or recreation, the Japanese kept right on at drill or study. There were no malingerers among them and they were quick to learn." In a private letter he also remarked: "I will never forget how the Niseis took hold in the National Guard camp at Schofield when the first draft came in. As a class, they were the best recruits I had ever seen in 45 years."

Within a few months many of them were privates, first class, and some had become noncommissioned officers. In June, 1941, at the patriotic rally arranged by the Oahu Citizens Committee for Home Defense, General Herron's representative publicly reported: "No group of selectees is doing its work with more intelligence, enthusiasm, and efficiency than the young men of Japanese ancestry." Officers at Schofield Barracks were, he said, "unanimous in stating that these young men are solving their problems in every particular."[17]

This praise was evidently genuine. In October Munson of the State Department wrote:

Due to the preponderance of Japanese in the population of the Islands, a much greater proportion of Japanese have been called to the draft than on the mainland.** As on the mainland they are inclined to enlist before being drafted. The Army is extremely high in its praise of them as recruits. The Japanese seem to be chiefly afraid that their boys will not be given the same chance of promotion as the whites. Frankly, at first this discrimination existed. A Japanese still had to be better than a white to gain promotion. The Army is gradually eliminating even this discrimination. They have been giving them a chance at becoming officers. Recently they picked out the very best of these and put them in charge of white troops. The Army officers confessed that they held their breath. Much to their surprise and relief there was absolutely no reaction

---

* A strong argument for such training had always been that it helped Americanize the non-Caucasian youth of the Territory. It was well known, however, that the nisei who had received it were not welcome in the National Guard, and that only one or two of those who had received commissions had ever been called up for active duty.

** The preponderance was in the proportion of nisei to other young men of military age. Between 1910 and 1922, the birth rate among Japanese immigrants had been high in relation to that of other stocks, and children born during that period were now at the most acceptable military ages. Citizens of Japanese ancestry comprised 60 per cent of those inducted in Hawaii's first selective service call.

from the white troops and they liked these officers very well. Of course, these were especially good officers, but the Army is going to try more. This has been a great thing in strengthening the loyalty of the Japanese in the islands. They are beginning to feel that they are going to get a square deal and some of them are really almost pathetically exuberant.[18]

After six months training the 299th Infantry moved from Oahu, various of its elements taking stations on the islands of Maui, Molokai, Hawaii, and Kauai, the personnel assisting Army Engineers and the Works Progress Administration in construction of military installations. The 298th Infantry remained on Oahu.

On the morning of December 7, 1941, when the air arm of the Japanese Imperial Fleet attacked Pearl Harbor and military and naval airfields on Oahu, the 2d Battalion of the 298th Infantry was stationed on the windward side of the island, in positions along the shore between Bellows Field and Kualoa. The 1st Battalion was at Schofield. At the latter post ammunition for rifles and machine guns was not available to the 1st Battalion during the attack, but near Bellows Field two men of the 2d Battalion used a fleeting opportunity to fire at Zeros on their way to strafe the airstrips.

That Sunday morning a number of nisei soldiers of the 1st Battalion were on week-end pass from Schofield. Many were headed for Oahu's beaches when they heard news of the sneak attack. They hurried to the Barracks, walking or thumbing rides, bathing suits still under their arms. All reported to their units for duty. During the morning, the 1st Battalion moved by truck convoy along the North Shore, past Kahuku, to previously designated beach positions in the Kailua area.

That evening, on blacked-out Oahu, there were few persons who did not wonder whether sunrise would disclose a Japanese invasion fleet off the island's shores. Anything seemed possible. The Japanese-American soldiers at their beach posts had special reason for deep thought. That supreme test of which they had heard so much might be only a few hours away. Perhaps they hadn't much time to make up their minds as "clear as bells."

They were destined not to receive their trial by battle so soon, and decisions made that night were never put to the test. Dawn revealed no invasion armada—none ever appeared off the shores of Oahu. When the nisei did enter combat later it was because the Army was confident of their loyalty to America.

In the second week of December, 1941, however, that trust had yet to be won. When the planes with the red circles roared down on Pearl Harbor, 600 November inductees were still receiving rookie training at Schofield, 350 of whom were of Japanese ancestry. On December 7, and for the next three days, all of the 600 were put to work digging slit trenches throughout the camp area. On the evening of December 10 they were ordered to turn in their rifles and remain in their tents, and told not to leave them even for the latrine. The next morning their bivouac area was ringed by machine guns. On the 12th the machine guns had disappeared and the rifles were returned, but for the next few days ammunition was issued only for target practice. The trainees were then hurried through a shortened training program after which they were sent to the 298th and 299th Regiments and various Engineer units.

None of the men who received this special treatment ever heard or saw any official explanation of the incident. Rather incongruously, neither on December 7 nor in the days immediately following were any such special security measures taken in regard to the Japanese-Americans already in the 298th and 299th Regiments and in the Engineer battalions.

During the next six months elements of the 298th were stationed along the windward shore of Oahu, between Mokapu Point and Kualoa. They strung barbed wire, constructed and manned machine-gun emplacements, built dugouts, and patrolled the beaches. On the other islands the soldiers of the 299th had similar duties and continued to help in the building of military installations.

Staff officers of the Hawaiian Department frequently inspected the two regiments. A colonel, as he talked with the commander of the 298th Regiment, noticed a number of nisei soldiers working near that officer's tent. "You sleep here," he asked, "where these Japs can slit your throat?"

As the weeks passed, the headquarters brass had opportunity to make other and more favorable observations. The "Japs' " gun positions were well built and diligently manned; their equipment was always in good order; and they continued to work faithfully at their training exercises. Inspecting officers had to admit that, trustworthy or not, the Japanese-Americans still looked like good soldier material.

But now, even within the ranks, things were not the same for these particular trainees. Their fellows of other ancestries tried to be decent, but they couldn't forget the treacherous attack on Pearl, and neither could the men of Japanese ancestry. There wasn't quite the same easy camaraderie.[19]

When they went home on pass, the Japanese-American boys found further evidence that Hawaii's traditional garment of interracial good will was giving way at the seams.

On December 7 almost every person on Oahu must have asked himself whether the enemy had been helped by residents of Japanese ancestry. No one, military or civilian, knew, but while the enemy planes were still in the air, FBI agents were picking up aliens whose names headed the 1-A suspect lists.

At noon General Short asked the civilian governor, Joseph B. Poindexter, for a proclamation of martial law. He feared that the following morning the enemy might attempt a landing on Oahu, aided by local Japanese saboteurs. Poindexter telephoned President Roosevelt, reported the main danger was from the local Japanese, and received approval of Short's request. The governor and the general then issued previously prepared proclamations.

Army and Navy Intelligence personnel and Honolulu policemen joined the FBI in making arrests. Within three hours after the attack thirteen squads of officers had rounded up nearly every "dangerous" individual of Japanese extraction on Oahu. Next came the Caucasian enemy aliens, most of whom were taken into custody during the rest of this day and the next. By the evening of December 8, 482 persons had been interned. Of these, 370 were Japanese, most of them Buddhist or Shinto priests, language-school officials, commercial fishermen, or kibei; 98 were Germans; 14 were Italians. Several hundred persons on the 1-B list were put under close surveillance, and during the following days many of these were picked up.

Trustworthy Soldiers?

CHAPTER THREE

In his role as military governor, Short issued in quick succession a series of orders clamping rigid controls on enemy aliens. They were forbidden to change residence or occupation, or otherwise move from place to place without approval from the provost marshal. They were ordered to turn in at police stations all implements of war, fireworks, cameras, short-wave receiving sets, and other now contraband items. They were not to be at large during nightly blackouts. They could not be employed in restricted areas without official permission, nor could they buy or sell liquor. Japanese-language newspaper offices and schools were closed, and all foreign-language broadcasts were stopped.

In an order issued on December 8, Short announced, however, that so long as alien Japanese kept the peace, obeyed all laws and regulations, and avoided active hostility, they would be given the consideration due peaceful and law-abiding citizens except so far as restrictions might be necessary for their own protection and for the safety of the nation. Citizens were directed to treat them with all friendliness compatible with loyalty to the United States.[1]

Army announcements to the public were worded to indicate the assumption that both the issei and the nisei were, in the mass, "loyal," but most of the military and civilian population held no such optimistic view. Within a few hours after the blitz hundreds of people had heard and retold rumors that the local "Japs" had aided the attack. Why not? These stories were no harder to believe than that the Pacific Fleet had been bombed. On December 8, on the basis of what seemed accurate Army information, *The Honolulu Advertiser* ran a banner headline, "Saboteurs Land Here." Secretary of the Navy Frank Knox, on his return from a hurried visit to Pearl Harbor, told a newsman that Hawaii had been the scene of "the most effective fifth-column work that has come out of this war except in Norway."* And some of the tales—that Japanese maids had failed to report for work on December 7 because they had had

---

* In his report of December 20, Munson commented: "In Honolulu your observer noted that the seagoing Navy was inclined to consider everybody with slant eyes bad. . . . Your observer suspects that Secretary Knox's comparison to the Fifth Column in Norway stems from either of two things: First, a very busy man being caught by the coattails by a reporter; and second, from the *unknowing* 'eat 'em up alive' element amongst whom of necessity he was largely exposed in his hurried visit to determine responsibility." U. S. Congress, Joint Committee on the Investigation of the Pearl Harbor attack, *Pearl Harbor Attack*, Hearings, 79th Cong., 1st and 2d sess., pursuant to S. Con. Res. 27 (Washington, 1946), Part 6, p. 2688.

advance notice of the enemy attack; that a recent newspaper advertisement illustrated by a picture of bombed and sinking ships had been run as a warning to Japanese residents; that lanes cut through cane fields had guided enemy planes to Pearl Harbor; that local Japanese had deliberately blocked the Pearl Harbor road with their cars—had originated from observed, though completely misinterpreted, happenings.[2]

Checking the accuracy of such reports was necessarily slow work, and hardly had federal agents or local police run one to its source before it was replaced by another of similar nature. These stories, told on the Mainland by hysterical Army and Navy wives who had been hurriedly evacuated from the Territory, resulted in some anxious official cable queries from Washington to Army headquarters in Hawaii. Some rumors, picked up by Mainland magazines and newspapers and published as eyewitness accounts, returned to the Islands, clothed with the authority of print, and circulated as accepted fact.

One incident seemed to support the belief that there had indeed been treachery. On Saturday, December 13, four Hawaiian ranch hands from Niihau reached Kauai to report an armed Japanese aviator loose on their isolated little island. The pilot, who had crash-landed his plane on December 7, had been disarmed and kept under guard while the residents waited for the supply boat which regularly visited Niihau. Its arrival had been delayed because of the military emergency, and on December 12 the aviator had secured firearms and freedom. The four Hawaiians had rowed sixteen hours to reach Kauai with their startling news.

An Army lieutenant volunteered to lead a party to Niihau. It consisted of thirteen enlisted men, the four ranch hands, Aylmer Robinson of the family which owned Niihau, and two other civilians. Early on the 14th the lighthouse tender *Kukui* landed the expedition on the rocky east shore of Niihau. On reaching the ranch village after a seven-mile march its members learned that the enemy pilot was dead. Though wounded three times by bullets from the flier's gun, an unarmed Hawaiian had dashed the intruder's brains out against a stone wall. Investigation disclosed that the Japanese had secured his weapons through the aid of a resident nisei, Yoshio Harada, who had helped him terrorize the other inhabitants, and had then shot and killed himself after the aviator's death.

It was learned that Harada and Ishimatsu Shintani, the only Niihau residents of Japanese ancestry, had been called upon on December 7 to act as interpreters between the aviator and his captors. On the 12th the flier had sent Shintani to a ranch hand who was guarding the flier's papers, to offer a bribe for their destruction. Warned that he was likely to get into trouble for this kind of activity, Shintani replied that the pilot would kill him if he refused to do what he was told, but then went into hiding, and emerged only after the flier had been killed.* The officer in charge of the party obtained the flier's papers, which contained information relative to the plans for the bombing of Pearl Harbor, and took into protective custody Harada's widow, her young daughter, and Shintani. The wounded Hawaiian hero of the "Battle of Niihau" needed hospitalization and was also taken to Kauai. It was not generally known that the leader of the rescue party was a nisei officer, Lieutenant Jack Mizuha, of Company M, 299th Infantry, which was at this time stationed at Burns Airfield, Kauai.[3]

It was little wonder that many residents, civilian as well as military, clamored for revenge. A "Jap" in one of the bombers, or one who had come to Hawaii as an immigrant, or one born and bred in the Islands—what real difference was there? On December 7 and in the days that followed many a normally kind and reasonable person talked of shooting anyone of Japanese ancestry on sight. Others cried that mass imprisonment or mass evacuation from the Territory was the least these people deserved. These latter proposals received increasing support as newspapers began to report the drastic official measures being taken against the Japanese of the West Coast.**

While he remained in command Short relied on the advice of his G-2 staff and refused to be stampeded into overhasty and ill-considered action. The Japanese population was being carefully watched. Each day more persons on the 1-B list were taken into custody, and those who were left at large continued under constant observation.

* The evidence indicates that Shintani and Harada acted from fear for their lives rather than from loyalty to Japan. No formal charges were ever brought against Shintani or Harada's widow. See note 3.
** Ironically, the rumors of espionage and sabotage which had emanated from Hawaii had furnished invaluable ammunition for those West Coast pressure groups which demanded and secured wholesale evacuation of all residents of Japanese ancestry. Morton Grodzins; *Americans Betrayed: Politics and the Japanese Evacuation* (Chicago, 1949), pp. 84–86, 94, 109, 174, 182, 202, 205, 254; Appendix I, pp. 380 ff.; Appendix II, pp. 401–403.

Less dangerous characters were also kept under observation by special agents of Japanese ancestry, who were themselves "classified" according to degree of loyalty. Japanese families were being moved from the neighborhood of vital defense installations, and from time to time areas of predominantly Japanese population were searched for contraband articles. Violations of security regulations received prompt and severe punishment. Should the enemy attempt an invasion of Oahu, plans long prepared were ready to confine those of Japanese ancestry to their homes.[4]

Soon after December 7, representatives of the Committee for Interracial Unity called on Colonel Kendall J. Fielder, assistant chief of staff for Military Intelligence, Shivers of the FBI, and the heads of the Territorial Office of Civilian Defense, to offer whatever assistance the committee could give. A Morale Section was set up within OCD. Hung Wai Ching, a realtor of Chinese ancestry, Charles Loomis, *haole* secretary of the Honolulu branch of the Institute of Pacific Relations, and Shigeo Yoshida, nisei public-school teacher, were named co-chairmen of the new agency.

This trio, working under Colonel Fielder's personal supervision and in close contact with the FBI, served as a liaison team between the Army and the various national ancestry groups. Most of their work was in activities designed to build civilian morale and unity for the defense effort. They planned the organization of special advisory committees composed of representatives of the Japanese, Chinese, Filipino, and other communities, with special attention to the make-up and duties of the proposed Japanese group.[5]

Fear and confusion filled the Japanese community. These residents, too, had heard and believed rumors of treachery among their number. Arrests on and immediately after December 7 were not nearly so numerous as many had expected, yet no prominent member of that community could feel certain that he would not be the next to receive a visit from the police. Many kept packed suitcases ready in case they were ordered interned.

Lieutenant General Delos C. Emmons, when he relieved Short on December 17, made no immediate change in his predecessor's internal security policy. Military Intelligence reported that so far it had found no truth in any reports of espionage or sabotage by the Island Japanese, and that these residents were scrupulously observing all regulations.[6] But an enemy invasion still seemed a strong possibility, and the new commander had to prepare for every contingency.

In the latter part of January Emmons issued an order which gave some indication of his thinking.

During the previous October, a special "defense" session of the legislature had given the governor authority to organize a volunteer Territorial Guard to replace the National Guard regiments called into federal service. At the time of the "blitz" no such force had been organized, but within an hour or two thereafter the governor had ordered the adjutant general to call out the "territorial militia" and to "organize and constitute a Hawaii Territorial Guard from such of the said militia as may volunteer for service and enlist therein." He also appointed this officer commander of the ROTC in the schools, with orders to use these units as the core of the new Guard.

The University of Hawaii unit was the first ROTC contingent called up. While this was being discussed, an Army officer telephoned Short to remind him that many of the University cadets were of Japanese ancestry. Short replied that "he thought they might prove to be perfectly loyal and that we should go ahead." By 10:00 A.M. the University men reported to the Honolulu Armory for enlistment.

For the rest of that tense day and night these military auxiliaries stood armed guard at various Honolulu public buildings, utility installations, and warehouses. Next morning they were joined by a unit of Hawaiian and part-Hawaiian cadets from Kamehameha Boy's School. By December 11, when the Guard was placed under direct Army control, its complement had been recruited to a total of seventy-three officers and 1,060 enlisted men, and guardsmen were on duty at public buildings, utilities, newspaper plants, radio stations, warehouses, and reservoirs. By the end of the month 89 officers and 1,254 enlisted men patrolled 150 posts in and near Honolulu, their services making six regular garrison companies available for more important duty.[7]

On January 21, the 317 members of the unit who were of Japanese ancestry were discharged without explanation. The same day Emmons authorized formation of other civilian-military volunteer defense forces to be composed of non-Japanese persons. He also gave official recognition to the Businessmen's Military Training Corps, membership in which was restricted to Caucasians and Caucasian-Hawaiians. Its primary mission was the immobilization of enemy aliens in Honolulu and the vicinity in case of a military emergency. Since the inauguration of the BMTC at a meeting of 23 civic leaders (January 4), 1,500 volunteers had enrolled, many of them prominent executives and professional men. The Army had assigned regular officers as instructors. At one of the first staff meetings the organizer and commander had stated: "Our main job is to watch the local Japanese." Of course this directive had not been publicized.[8]

Neither press nor radio reported the discharge of the nisei from the Territorial Guard but the news quickly spread throughout the Japanese community. Although restricted by tightening controls, aware that their every move was under constant scrutiny, and oppressed by the pall of suspicion which hung over them, the Japanese residents had so far felt that at least some of them were not suspect. But this new development tended to sabotage the Army's policy of treating them as though they could be trusted.[9]

Some of the discharged University students talked things over with older friends of all nationalities. "All right," they said, "we've been kicked out. The Army and Navy won't let us enlist. But there must be some way we can show we're loyal. How?" From the Morale Section of the OCD came the suggestion that they ask Emmons for a chance to prove their loyalty.

Shortly thereafter the dischargees petitioned the military governor: "Hawaii is our home; the United States, our country. We know but one loyalty and that is to the Stars and Stripes. We wish to do our part as loyal Americans in every way possible, and we hereby offer ourselves for whatever service you may see fit to use us."

Before the end of February, 150 nisei, almost all of them University of Hawaii graduates, went to work for the Army as members of a labor unit under the U. S. Army Corps of Engineers. Their technical status was that of civilian laborers, but they lived under Army discipline, wore Army fatigue uniform, ate Army mess, and slept in Army barracks. Under command of Army officers they dug ditches, quarried rock, built barracks and warehouses, surfaced roads, and strung barbed wire along Oahu beaches.

Any one of the self-styled Varsity Victory Volunteers could have earned much more than $90 a month in jobs made plentiful by the wartime boom. Their demonstration of loyalty at personal sacrifice, in the tradition of their ancestors, was a good example to other nisei, and it helped counteract the low morale in the Japanese community which had followed their discharge. Even more important, it marked a turning point—it demonstrated that AJAs* could be loyal. Emmons, among others, was impressed.[10]

His post was one of terrible responsibility. Any dawn might show enemy landing barges headed toward Oahu. A small number of determined saboteurs could cause disastrous damage. An invasion attempt accompanied by internal uprisings and sabotage might prove catastrophic for the nation.

It was true that intelligence agencies had uncovered no evidence of sabotage or attempted sabotage by the Island Japanese either on December 7 or thereafter. This could be explained by the prompt internment of suspects and the warning thus given to others. Or it might be assumed that the enemy, hoping to capture Oahu's installations in working order, had ordered local agents and sympathizers to wait until Imperial troops began to storm the beaches. Prewar Intelligence speculation as to the wartime behavior of Hawaii Japanese had been based on a military situation far different from that which now confronted Emmons.

Naval officers insisted that their ships, installations, and fleet movements could be adequately protected against sabotage and espionage only by mass imprisonment or evacuation of the Japanese population, and various civilian authorities had demanded such action.

Long before the war planning officers of the Hawaiian Department had examined various proposed solutions to the security problem, and prominent civilians had been called upon for their opinions. One school of thought advocated mass deportation to the Mainland; another, transfer to the small island of Lanai; a third, the concentration of Oahu Japanese in large internment camps on their home island.**

A study of each scheme revealed several disadvantages. If war came, shipping space would immediately become scarce, and the first and second plans would need the services of a great many craft. Military and naval personnel in large numbers would be needed to manage these transfers. Besides, the West Coast states wanted no more Japanese, and might refuse to accept thousands of "potential sabo-

---

* It was about this time that the nisei began to insist on being referred to as AJAs (Americans of Japanese ancestry).

** Many persons in the Japanese community had learned the nature of these suggestions.

teurs." If the Japanese were removed to Lanai or some other island, the Army would face extremely difficult problems in connection with food, health, and housing. Their forced segregation would probably turn many Japanese of divided allegiance completely against the United States. In case of war with Japan, the Army intended to concentrate on Oahu all but token defense forces, and if the enemy, in an attack on the Hawaiian group, should capture the outer island on which the Japanese were interned, the embittered Japanese would probably give their liberators valuable information and aid. Internment on Oahu would mean building camps at a time when construction materials and labor would be scarce, and such compounds would probably have to be guarded by troops needed for battle service.

Not less important, the internment of more than a third of the civilian working population would disrupt the Island economy and place an additional burden on the armed forces at a time when all available manpower would be needed to maintain essential services and bolster military strength. A high percentage of skilled laborers were Japanese—in the construction trade, for instance, where their work would be even more vital to a defense than to a civilian economy. If they were removed from the labor force, thousands of Mainland workers would have to be imported at a time when shipping space would be needed for transporting troops and munitions.

It had finally been decided that the disadvantages of these plans outweighed their possible benefits. Japan would probably launch no large-scale attack against the Islands, and internal security could be provided by arrest of some of the local Japanese, house confinement for others, and surveillance for the rest.[11]

But that was before the blitz.

Emmons, in his reports to the War Department during January and February, 1942, estimated that on Oahu alone there were 30,000 aliens and citizens of Japanese ancestry who were not to be trusted in case of an enemy landing. A large proportion of the Japanese males were of military age, and many of the aliens had had military training in the Imperial Army. The Navy was strongly urging mass evacuation, and Emmons agreed that leakage of news on fleet movements could be prevented only by evacuation of the Japanese and many other unreliable residents. But he strongly disapproved as "impractical and dangerous" the plan, then under consideration by various governmental agencies and receiving Navy support, for concentration on one of the outer islands. If it were decided that, regardless of its bad effect on the loyalty of the nisei and its disruption of the Territorial economy, there had to be a mass removal, then the Japanese should be sent to the Mainland under a carefully organized system of priorities.

On February 1 Washington asked Emmons to give his views on possible evacuation to the West Coast of all enemy aliens, all subversive individuals, and all American citizens of Japanese ancestry. He was asked, in making his reply, to consider the factors of shipping shortage, possible alienation of loyal elements in the population, the likelihood of sabotage, and related matters. He replied on February 4 that for reasons of health and supply as well as of security he favored the evacuation of as many Japanese as practicable as soon as possible. There should, however, be no large-scale evacuation until the arrival of the troop reinforcements, and absolutely no advance publicity. If an invasion should come before the evacuation could be accomplished, plans were ready to "immobilize the Japanese in place."

Four days later the War Department asked for recommendations under two plans: evacuation of as many persons of Japanese ancestry, with families, as possible, or alternatively, removal only of enemy aliens and those citizens of Japanese ancestry whom the Army considered a threat to military defense. Emmons answered in regard to the first scheme that it would mean removal of 100,000 residents; to the second, that all evident suspects were already in custody. It was his opinion, however, that few Japanese residents had as yet given any real evidence of their true feelings and intentions, and that in order to insure the ejection of all disloyal individuals it would be necessary to evacuate 100,000 persons.

Washington decided to move slowly in the matter. As things stood, the Army and the War Relocation Authority* were already having more than enough trouble in connection with the mass evacuation of the West Coast Japanese, and all shipping was needed for more critical purposes. Emmons was told to ship only his most dangerous residents, and by the end of March less than 500 suspects

---

* The federal agency created by executive order on March 18 to formulate and put into effect a program for the relocation, maintenance, and supervision of evacuees.

had been sent to the Mainland. This number included aliens, more than 100 of whom were of other than Japanese ancestry, as well as citizens, most of whom were kibei. When the latter reached the Coast, federal authorities insisted that they be sent back to Hawaii because of difficulties involved, under the Constitution, in detaining them on the Mainland where martial law was not in effect.[12]

Meanwhile Emmons' G-2 officers had been assuring him that there was no crucial need for large-scale evacuation. They were now fully convinced that the local Japanese had committed no acts of espionage or sabotage before, during, or since the blitz. The most dangerous characters had been locked up and the rest, deprived of this potentially subversive leadership, had so far strictly obeyed orders. To the extent allowed, they had been co-operating in both civilian and military defense activities. Need for their labor continued desperate. Because of the manpower shortage caused by the Army's and Navy's tremendous build-up of supplies and new installations, workers of Japanese ancestry, even aliens, were being employed on every kind of construction project. As one Army officer remarked later, "If you wanted to build even a barracks, you had to get the Japanese to do it." Military Intelligence was confident that these people could be kept under control even in case of a military crisis. The Army's "firm but fair" policy had built up their confidence; they knew how much more harshly the West Coast Japanese were being handled, and they were thankful for their own better lot. If directed to stay in their homes during air raid or invasion they probably would quietly comply. Police and other security agencies could enforce such an order and, with a minimum of assistance from regular military personnel, take care of any possible attempts at sabotage.[13]

By June it had been decided that although wholesale evacuation was perhaps the safest solution to the security problem, in view of over-all military and naval plans and requirements, it was impracticable. Therefore it was proposed that a maximum of 15,000 persons be removed, with their families, this number to include those residents most likely to prove dangerous during invasion or threat thereof. The War Relocation Authority would direct the transfer to Mainland resettlement areas. By the end of June, however, Emmons reported that the internal security situation was satisfactory and did not justify any definite commitment as to the number of persons to be displaced. He asked that facilities be prepared for a movement of 5,000 with the understanding that possibly a smaller number might be shipped.*

On February 1, 1942, during the correspondence on evacuation, the War Department proposed that all soldiers of Japanese ancestry be released from active duty, discharged, or transferred. Emmons replied that he had already discharged the nisei of the Territorial Guard but that the troop shortage made it necessary to keep the Japanese-Americans serving in the former National Guard regiments even though this was causing a problem on islands other than Oahu, where excitable Filipino plantation workers, angry at the rape of their homeland, were threatening reprisals against Hawaii Japanese. When reinforcements from the Mainland arrived, however, the soldiers of Japanese ancestry in those units might be transferred or inactivated. The thought of transferring the 298th from Oahu to duty on the other islands had been abandoned because of the Filipino situation. Emmons suggested that the nisei troops might be organized as a labor corps and used to string wire on the beaches, clear areas for defensive fire, and build trails. Plantation laborers were doing this work, but it was proving a costly interruption of sugar production. Such use of their services would still give the nisei a chance to prove their loyalty. But this plan was also given up, since

* The War Department replied that by October 1 the War Relocation Authority would be able to take 3,000 evacuees. On October 13 Emmons indicated that he was now making plans to evacuate 8,000 persons all told, 3,000 in the near future, and an additional 5,000 later, but that he did not necessarily intend to send that many. Since March only one group of evacuees, consisting of 36 adult Japanese and 96 children who were to be repatriated to Japan, had been sent to the Mainland.

Between October, 1942 and March, 1943 only 930 individuals were shipped, and most of these were dependents of men already interned on the Mainland. This number was smaller than it might have been had Emmons not insisted that evacuees from the Territory, most of whom had some knowledge of military and naval dispositions, be segregated from the West Coast Japanese and not allowed repatriation to Japan. He had, as a result, been told that those suspects for whom he felt such special treatment necessary should be interned in Hawaii. Evacuation ended in March, 1943, when Emmons accepted a War Department suggestion that he suspend transfer of all Japanese except those selected for detention who were considered safe for release on the Mainland. At this time the General asked that Secretary of the Navy, Frank Knox, who had been making public statements urging large-scale evacuation, be told the Hawaiian Department's reasons for deferring or suspending such action. The Pentagon quoted Knox as replying that, while he still thought concentration of the Japanese on one of the outer islands feasible, he did not care where they were segregated as long as they were placed where they could do no harm.

As the months passed, and the prospect of invasion became less probable, talk of evacuation died out. During the course of the war only 1,450 Hawaii Japanese were taken into custody, and not all of these were evacuated. U. S. Army Forces MIDPAC. "History of U. S. Army MIDPAC," (microfilm), Part VIII, Appendix 1, pp. 11–16, in the War Records Depository, University of Hawaii, Honolulu, Hawaii. Gwenfread Allen, *Hawaii's War Years* (Honolulu: University of Hawaii Press, 1950), p. 134.

it would be discrimination on a racial basis and would be widely resented by the Japanese community.

Only a handful of nisei had been inducted since December 7, and by the end of March, on orders from the War Department, all enlistments and inductions of Americans of Japanese ancestry were discontinued except on special order in individual cases.[14] By the end of April sizable troop reinforcements had arrived on Oahu and the the other islands of the Hawaiian group.

Even before the Japanese defeat in the Southwest Pacific in the Coral Seas actions of May 7–8, Admiral Chester W. Nimitz, commander-in-chief of the United States Pacific Fleet, had intelligence of a forthcoming powerful Japanese offensive in the Central Pacific. It was expected that Midway and the western Aleutians would be the enemy's objectives. If Nimitz' forces were unable to save Midway the next attack might be against Hawaii.

On May 12 Emmons notified the Pentagon that no more than 800 of the nisei then in uniform could be absorbed into existing noncombat Army units, and recommended that all AJA officers and men in the 298th and 299th be organized into a special battalion and transferred to the Mainland. There the battalion might be stationed at an inland Army post or its personnel be dispersed among various Army combat outfits. On May 14 Nimitz, in agreement with Emmons, declared a state of "Fleet Opposed Invasion" in the Hawaiian sea frontier. (This meant that the Navy had main responsibility for repelling invasion, but command of the Army ground forces was left in Emmons' hands.) Five days later the 298th had been pulled back from the beaches to Schofield Barracks and placed in reserve, and Mainland troops had taken over its defense positions.[15]

On the 26th, as airplanes moved out to Midway, B-17s from the Mainland landed in Hawaii, and fleet units cleared Pearl Harbor headed for battle, Emmons notified Washington that the 298th Infantry had been recalled to Schofield. He described morale in the unit as very low, and again recommended that the nisei of that regiment and the 299th be gathered into a special battalion and transferred to the Mainland.

On the 28th he received a message signed by General George C. Marshall, Army chief of staff, which ordered formation of the proposed unit, over normal strength in personnel if necessary, and its evacuation to the Mainland by the first available shipping. It was also proposed that "CG AGF [Commanding General, Army Ground Forces] reorganize and train this unit as an Infantry Combat unit. Unit's weapons and motor transportation will be retained in Hawaii. Special transportation and armament required will be furnished upon arrival. Adequate information on this subject should be made available to personnel of unit in order to prevent any feeling that the men are being disarmed and sent to the mainland for internment which is definitely not the War Department's intention."

The next day General Emmons replied that the battalion, with an approximate strength of twenty-nine officers and 1,300 enlisted men, would sail about June 5.[16]

The decision to evacuate the nisei soldiers was to a large extent based on Emmons' feeling that he could not afford to take a chance on the reliability of these troops in the event of an enemy attack, but other considerations also played a part. If some Japanese did get ashore, the newly arrived American troops might mistake the nisei garrison soldiers for enemy Japanese disguised in American uniforms. The enemy might even try such a trick. In any event, the AJA soldier might find himself in as much danger from fellow Americans as from the enemy. Furthermore, the same reasons which made it unwise to have the nisei troops in Hawaii during a period of threatened invasion would apply later on when the 24th and 25th divisions* were sent westward against Japan. If the AJAs could not be dispersed among service units on Oahu and if they could not be sent against men of their own racial background, it was best that they be gotten out of the Islands.[17]

This meant they would have no opportunity to answer the question, "Who you shoot?"

---

* The removal of the men who composed the new battalion so depleted the two National Guard regiments that the 299th was inactivated and its men transferred to the 298th. Numerous subsequent transferals of personnel from the 298th to other units so changed its composition that when the regiment left Hawaii for Espiritu Santo and Guadalcanal at the end of 1943, for duty as a port service force, it contained only 15 per cent of the original personnel.

COLONEL WILHELM A. ANDERSEN, commander of the 298th Infantry, was called to the Fort Shafter headquarters of the Hawaiian Department in the early afternoon of May 29, shown the War Department message from Washington, and told to speed formation of the provisional battalion. Back at Schofield Barracks, he told his executive officer Lt. Colonel Farrant L. Turner and his plans and training officer Captain James W. Lovell of the order. Turner asked, "Who's going to command?" When Andersen mentioned someone else, Turner said, "I think it's my job." "No," said Andersen. "I need you here." Turner was insistent, Andersen firm. After they left the Colonel's office Turner asked Lovell if he would serve as his "exec" if he received command of the unit. Lovell answered "I've been thinking the same thing."

Andersen did nominate another man, but Brigadier General J. Lawton Collins, Chief of Staff of the Hawaiian Department, picked Turner for the job.

Born in Hilo on the island of Hawaii, Turner had attended the local public schools and then Punahou Academy, a private school in Honolulu. He had graduated from Wesleyan University in Connecticut, had entered the Army in 1917 as a second lieutenant in the Coast Artillery, and had won captain's rank in France. Back in Hawaii after World War I, he had worked three years as a clerk for an Oahu sugar plantation and had then joined a large building supply house. In 1942, at the age of forty-

Activation

seven, he held an important position in this company, was married, and had a son aged sixteen.

Before 1940 his contacts with the Island Japanese had been mainly with small contractors, mostly issei, whom he had learned to respect for their honesty and dependability. He had been an officer of the National Guard since 1926, and this service had put him in touch with a large cross section of Hawaii's youth but not particularly with the nisei, whom he came to know well only after many of them joined the 298th as rookies. He found them no different from other Island boys in the regiment, no less American. He did notice that they studied not only their basic manuals, but also other books on troop leadership and tactics, seemed to want to be first-class soldiers, and as a result lifted the discipline and snap of the whole outfit. One day, during training exercises, Turner told Lovell, "Jim, these nisei kids are good!" Turner had asked Collins whether the latter considered his appointment a promotion or a demotion, and Collins had said that if the unit showed up well in Mainland training "it might go somewhere." Turner was sure that if given a chance it could and, if he had anything to do with it, it would.*

Jim Lovell, whom Turner selected as his second in command, was thirty-five years old, married, and the father of a six-year-old daughter. Born in Nebraska, he had graduated from a teachers' college there, and was a member of the National Guard from 1924 to 1930, when he moved to Honolulu. For the next three years he taught mechanical drawing and coached athletics at Washington Intermediate, a school situated in a predominantly Japanese section of the city. Between 1933 and 1939 he held a similar post at Roosevelt High School. He then became boys' adviser and member of the athletic staff of Mc-Kinley High, the largest secondary school in the city, which, because of its large enrollment of students of Japanese ancestry, some Island residents called "Mikado High." In the graduate courses Lovell took at the University of Hawaii he met more AJA students.

Lovell had joined the Hawaii National Guard shortly after his arrival in the Territory, and in October, 1940 (when the 298th was federalized), he was a captain. Many of the AJA inductees, when they entered the regiment, learned with pleasure that one of their

---

* Biographical details given in this chapter have been secured by means of personal interview and letter, but not every person supplied all the data on himself; interviewees often furnished information about each other.

top officers was an old friend. By May, 1942, it was well known in the ranks that Lovell was a *haole* officer who understood the nisei and their problems. Lovell himself felt that these AJA boys were going to have some more troubles, and he might be able to help.

Orders were that the new unit, to be known tentatively as the Hawaiian Provisional Infantry Battalion, should consist of a headquarters, a headquarters company of ten officers and 250 enlisted men, and four lettered companies with five officers and 250 enlisted men in each. A lieutenant colonel, a major, five captains, and eight lieutenants were to be selected from the 298th Infantry; two captains and twelve lieutenants from the 299th. Turner was told that no officer of Japanese ancestry was to be given command of any of the rifle companies. There were, however, plenty of capable *haole* captains available for each of these posts, and Alex E. McKenzie, Philip B. Peck, Clarence R. Johnson, Charles A. Brenamen, and John A. Johnson were appointed commanders of Headquarters, A, B, C, and D companies respectively.

Alex McKenzie, thirty-two and married, was Island-born, a Punahou graduate, and an alumnus of the universities of Hawaii and Southern California. He had joined the 298th Infantry in 1937 as an enlisted man, and had been promoted to second lieutenant in 1938, and first lieutenant in 1940, just before the Guard was federalized. In May, 1942, he was commanding officer of Company C, and was made captain shortly after he reported to Schofield with his AJA soldiers. In civilian life he had been employed in the Honolulu office of the Standard Oil Company of California.

Philip Peck, thirty-seven, also a Punahou graduate, had attended the universities of Hawaii and California. Joining the 298th in 1937 as a second lieutenant, he had been promoted to first lieutenant shortly before the Guard was ordered to active duty. In civilian life he had been chief passenger clerk for the Inter-Island Steam Navigation Company and Inter-Island Airways, Ltd. He had become a captain shortly before he left Company H of the 298th to join the provisional battalion. Peck was married and had a ten-year-old son.

Clarence Johnson had come to the Territory in 1932 as a private in the peacetime Army. In 1934, when his enlistment ended, he went to work as a machinist at the Pearl Harbor Navy Yard. During the following year he joined the National Guard as an enlisted man, and within two months was made a sergeant. In 1938, after completion of the required study courses, he received a commission as second lieutenant. Raised another grade in September, 1941, he was in command of Company E of the 298th when ordered to Schofield, where he was made a captain. Johnson was thirty-three and married.

Charles Brenamen, who had served in France during World War I, had come to Oahu in 1929 as a sergeant in the regular Army. Between 1930 and 1934 he was stationed at Hilo, Hawaii, as an instructor for the National Guard. He left that post for private employment in 1934, but maintained active status as a second lieutenant. When called to federal service in 1940 he was employed as a timekeeper on a Hawaii sugar plantation and had become captain in command of Company K of the 299th Infantry. When ordered to report to Schofield he was commander of Company A of that regiment. Brenamen was forty-two, married, and had two children.

In 1934 Jack Johnson, a Punahou graduate, was star and captain of the University of Hawaii football team. The following year, as a senior, he was student commandant of the ROTC regiment. When he joined the National Guard in 1939 he was assigned as first lieutenant to Company I of the 299th Infantry, on Kauai, where he was an overseer on one of the sugar plantations. At the time of his entry into federal service with the 299th he was employed as an assistant agriculturalist by the Hawaii Sugar Planters' Association. In 1941 he was sent to officers school at Fort Benning, Georgia, for advanced training, and after completion of the course was promoted to captain. He was commanding officer of Company M of the 299th on Kauai when called to Schofield. He was twenty-eight and had been married only two months.

These *haole* company commanders could be considered *kamaainas*, with more than average knowledge of Hawaii's peoples. The three Island-bred men had known the AJAs all their lives; the other two had known some nisei in civilian life and had learned more about them since they had entered the Guard regiments as rookies. These officers could talk to the enlisted men in pidgin, which was no small advantage. A *malihini* officer would have found the normal speech of most of his men almost as unintelligible to him as Japanese.

Four AJAs were selected as officers of the Headquarters staff. Captain Taro Suzuki became supply officer, Captain John M. Tanimura utilities officer, Captain Isaac A. Kawasaki surgeon, and First Lieutenant Katsumi Kometani morale officer.

Taro Suzuki was thirty-eight, married, and had two children. Born in Honolulu, the son of a shipwright, he attended Japanese-language and public schools, as well as the University of Hawaii, where he majored in economics. He first visited the American Mainland in 1925, as one of the group of outstanding ROTC cadets annually selected to receive summer training at Fort Lewis, Washington. He received his degree and reserve commission in 1927, and then worked as clerk and later as salesman for one of the "Big Five" companies. In July, 1929, Suzuki was called up for a short tour of active Army duty—the first reserve officer of Japanese ancestry in Hawaii to receive this distinction. After his graduation from the University he maintained his Army reserve status by taking the necessary training courses, and was promoted to first lieutenant in 1932. A member and former sergeant-at-arms of the Honolulu Reserve Officers Association, he was known and liked by many regular Army and National Guard officers. When he and a few other AJA reserve officers were ordered to extended active service with the Army in 1940 the news created a gratified stir within the Japanese community. From October of that year until September, 1941, Suzuki was assigned various jobs in the Hawaiian Quartermaster Depot at Fort Armstrong, Honolulu ("They didn't quite know what to do with me") and was then transferred, with captain's rank, to McKinley High School, where he served as assistant instructor of its ROTC unit. After the blitz he was sent back to Fort Armstrong, where he was given command of the Quartermaster Depot guard detachment, and was later given a post in the Depot's newly created supply reclamation division. On June 1 he was told that Turner had asked his assigment to the new battalion.

John M. Tanimura was thirty-eight and married. His father, foreman of a plantation irrigation gang, had worked on Hawaii, Kauai, and Oahu. Tanimura, one of five children, had earned two high school diplomas, one from McKinley, the other from a Honolulu Japanese-language school. As a child he had watched and sometimes helped his father whose job as foreman of a plantation gang had involved the use of some engineering tools and principles, and John had decided that one day he would be a civil engineer. He entered the University of Hawaii in 1921, the year the ROTC training program was begun there, majored in civil engineering, and in 1925 was one of the first group of cadets chosen for advanced summer training on the West Coast. (He made two subsequent trips to the Mainland, in 1933 and 1939.) In 1926 he expatriated from Japan, received his degree and reserve commission in the Army, and went to work at $100 a month on an Oahu sugar plantation. In 1939 he opened his own office in Honolulu. During the years on the plantation he had maintained his status as a commissioned officer and through study courses had earned a first lieutenancy. In December, 1940, he was called to active duty and assigned to the Quartermaster Corps of the 64th Coast Artillery at Fort Shafter as utility officer. In February, 1942, he was promoted to captain.

Isaac Kawasaki's father came to Hawaii in the 1890's and was the first lay Japanese Christian preacher in the Territory. In 1912, at the age of seven, Isaac visited Japan with his parents. In 1925 the elder Kawasaki secured his children's expatriation from Japan. When Isaac was twelve, in his fourth year of language school and his sixth of public school, the eight members of the Kawasaki family moved to New Haven, Connecticut. After graduation from New Haven High School he attended the University of Cincinnati undergraduate and medical schools and received his medical degree in 1934. For the next five years he was resident intern at Cincinnati General Hospital and an instructor on the University of Cincinnati medical faculty. In 1939 he married, returned to Honolulu to engage in private medical practice, and secured a commission in the Army Medical Corps. Kawasaki was called to active duty in February, 1941, and was stationed at the Army Tripler General Hospital near Pearl Harbor. On December 7, he worked all day and into the night treating the wounds of servicemen injured by Japanese bullets and bombs. He was promoted to captain in February, 1942. When Kawasaki was ordered to the new battalion his commanding officer protested the the loss of one of his best aides.

Katsumi Kometani was the eldest son of a former plantation laborer who in 1941 was employed as a cook at a church-supported Christian academy for non-Caucasian children. Mrs. Kometani was the school laundress, and the children received free tuition. After graduation from high school, Katsumi went to the Mainland, where he attended Michigan State College, the University of Denver, and the University of Southern California. An excellent competitive swimmer, he received athletic scholarships, and also helped support himself by working as a houseboy, a sports reporter, and at various odd jobs as he studied for a degree in dentistry. As was a custom among Hawaii Japanese, the younger children contributed to his support, each expecting to be helped in turn.

On his return to Honolulu, where he prospered in his profession, Kometani maintained his interest in athletics, financed an amateur baseball nine, and also managed an amateur swimming team. In 1940 he took his baseball players to Japan for the Far Eastern Olympics. During this tour Japanese secret police dogged the members of his party. One day while they were absent their rooms were ransacked. As he returned from a train trip to visit relatives, one of the players learned from a boastful policeman that he had been tailed during the whole of his journey. The team members, most of them nisei, were still angry when they returned to Honolulu.

Kometani had joined the Hawaii Territorial Guard soon after its formation on December 7, and was the only nisei not discharged from that unit in January, 1942. At that time he asked his commander for release with the rest of the men, but was persuaded that he could do his friends more good by staying. He was one of the original members of the Emergency Service Committee set up by the Morale Committee in February as an advisory group on problems within the Japanese community. On May 30, when Kometani learned that a special battalion of AJA soldiers was being assembled for transfer to the Mainland, he asked Colonel Fielder and the commanding officer of the Territorial Guard to help him secure permission to join this unit. Two days later he was offered a commission in the Dental Corps, with assignment to the new outfit. This was irregular—battalions did not normally have their own dentists—but it had been decided that Kometani would make a good morale officer for the battalion. The following day, his office closed and all appointments canceled, he was at Schofield Barracks. He was thirty-six, married, and had three children. His wife had encouraged him to volunteer.

Of the original officers of the provisional battalion, twenty-four were college graduates. Sixteen had received their degrees from the University of Hawaii and six others had studied there. Fourteen of the sixteen AJA officers were alumni of that school, and in civilian life most of these graduates had been public school teachers. There was reason for the high proportion of teachers among the nisei who had college degrees—the Territorial department of public instruction had a regular salary schedule which applied equally to all teachers of whatever national ancestry. Though teachers' salaries were low in comparison to those incomes possible in other professions or in executive posts in the business world, they were high in comparison with those of minor clerkships which were often the best jobs open to the educated nisei, and in comparison with the earnings of teacher's immigrant parents they were often very high indeed.[1]

First Lieutenant Mitsuyoshi Fukuda of Company D, for instance, was an instructor in vocational agriculture in a rural intermediate school on the island of Hawaii at the time of the blitz. First Lieutenant Jack Mizuha of Headquarters Company had been a high school teacher and principal on the island of Kauai before he was ordered to active duty in September, 1941. First Lieutenant Richard Mizuta of Company B was an instructor in vocational agriculture at Hakalau Intermediate School on Hawaii when the Japanese bombed Pearl Harbor, and First Lieutenant Sakae Takahashi was a teacher of vocational agriculture at Aiea School on Oahu.

These and other AJA officers had received commissions after four years of ROTC training at the University. All had expatriated from Japan. They differed from the enlisted men mainly in degree of formal education—and even in this respect there was no wide gulf between the two groups.

At least 95 per cent of the battalion's members were the sons of immigrants. Some 35 per cent were dual citizens, and of these about 2 per cent were kibei; 85 per cent had attended Japanese-language schools. Only a few had traveled outside Hawaii, and of these, about twice as many had been to Japan as to the American Mainland. The average of public high school attendance was about three years per man. Approximately 12 per cent had gone to college, in most cases the University of Hawaii, and 5 per cent had graduated. The battalion's average score on Army intelligence tests, 103, was only 7 points below the minimum necessary for entrance to officer candidate school.

Averaging five feet four inches, the men were below the Army norm in height, and also weighed a good deal less than most Mainland trainees. The average age was 24 years, considerably higher than normal for infantry troops. Despite their age, small stature, and light weight these trainees were good soldier material. Most were in trim physical shape when they entered military service.[2] Hawaii's climate made it easy for both plantation laborers and office workers to continue outdoor exercise long after their school years were over, and the AJA soldiers were vigorous young males from a sports-minded (sometimes called a "sports-mad") community.

Neither press nor radio carried the news that a special AJA battalion was being organized. Had the fact been publicly reported, it might have added greatly to the already high nervous tension among the Territory's residents. During the last week of May, 1942, every Islander seemed to know that the fleet and garrison forces were getting ready for something big. More than the usual number of airplanes passed overhead; the Pearl Harbor Navy Yard buzzed with activity; soldiers on guard duty were more than usually alert. On May 28 a number of patients were moved from one of the Army hospitals and the story spread that this was to make room for expected battle casualties. On June 1 the Businessmen's Training Corps was called to active duty. For the next three nights, from sundown to sunrise, its members patrolled Honolulu's streets. During the day they wore their uniforms to work. On the afternoon of June 3, because of "the possibility of imminent air action," the Army urged women and children in the Honolulu Harbor area to move to the homes of friends and relatives elsewhere in the city or outside it. Block wardens went from house to house carrying the warning. Radio announcers reiterated previous instructions that gas masks were to be carried at all times.

Then, on June 4, the Navy announced that Midway was under attack. Everyone knew what this could mean for Hawaii. Residents kept their radios turned on, listened patiently to commercials, music, and frequently repeated air-raid instructions as they anxiously waited for news broadcasts of the battle. On June 5 it was announced that fighting was still in progress. Finally, on the 6th, the Navy released the news of its smashing victory, and Islanders could again breathe deeply.[3]

The day before, under naval escort, four transports had left Honolulu Harbor. To the 1,432 men of the Hawaiian Provisional Infantry Battalion who were on one of these transports, the radio report of the Japanese defeat came as especially welcome news. Knowing about the battle when they had embarked, they had assumed that if Midway were captured the Japanese fleet would probably head next for the

Hawaiian group. In case the Japanese made a landing, how would their folk be treated by the defending troops newly arrived from the American Mainland, to whom all Orientals were suspect? And how by the Japanese soldiers? Their families might receive rough handling by both sides. Now, on learning that Hawaii was no longer in immediate danger, the evacuee soldiers relaxed. Of course, their folk and friends might yet be removed to internment camps on the Mainland, but in that case they would at least be safe from physical harm.

Though relieved for their people, the troops on the *Maui* were not particularly happy about their own situation. At a time when the Army must have needed every possible soldier to man the Island defenses, they had been herded together and shipped away. They had been told at Schofield that they were going to the States to be trained for combat duty, but though some men believed this, others were skeptical. If the Army couldn't rely on a man to fight in defense of his own home, would it have enough faith in him to put him in battle somewhere else? And why were they being shipped without their guns?

They were young, however, and their spirits were resilient. "Half filled with excitement and half with puzzlement" as a member of the group later recalled their mood, they made the best of things. The ship, crowded with Army and Navy wives and their children going back to Mainland homes, made a fifteen-degree change in course every twenty minutes, and there was regular boat drill and nightly blackout. Though this was certainly no pleasure cruise, it was, nevertheless, for most of the soldier passengers, their first real ocean voyage, exciting, even enjoyable. The weather was good and only a few men were seasick. Cards and dice appeared; ukuleles came out of barracks bags; and the hours passed quickly.

On the last day blimps came out to cover the convoy; the men stared at the Golden Gate Bridge; and the *Maui* docked at Oakland. Here battalion officers learned that the unit had acquired a new name. Movement orders called it the "100th Infantry Battalion." After a quick pierside inspection by some strange officers, the soldiers moved to three waiting troop trains. Each of these took a different route for the battalion destination. The Army wanted no wild rumors floating around about this particular troop movement. Even so, there were startled faces at various of the train stops. Chinese soldiers? Japanese prisoners?

Shortly after one of the trains had pulled out of Oakland, a transportation officer approached Turner.

"Say, these men of yours are speaking Japanese!"

"Do you understand it?"

"Of course not."

"Go back and listen some more—that's pidgin English."

The boys could make themselves understood by Mainlanders when they wanted. At a Colorado station the Red Cross coffee and doughnut girls were surprised that these "Chinese" soldiers could speak English.

During the five-day journey the card and dice games continued, and more money changed pockets—large wads of it. Each man seemed to have brought at least a hundred in cash with him. In every car, during almost any waking hour, someone was generally strumming an ukulele and singing. This constant urge for song surprised the conductors, but they got used to it, and even began to recognize some of the Island melodies.

On the last day, as one of the trains rolled through Wisconsin, word was passed through the coaches that the trip would soon end. After some minutes the cars stopped at a siding. Across and parallel to the tracks ran an iron fence topped with barbed wire and studded at intervals with watch towers. It looked like an internment camp. "For half an hour we sat silently in our seats, thinking only of the worst; many were pensive with grim and hollow faces. Then, suddenly, as if to alleviate our pained thoughts, the train backed slowly out of the yard, switched to another track, and continued on."[4]

Conversation started again. Pretty soon there was another stop, at another siding. No barbed wire here. End of the line. All out. Someone expressed the hope that this was "the real McCoy."

In Hawaii, immediately after the Midway victory, Military Intelligence received reports of quiet satisfaction among the Japanese residents, but the G-2 agents shortly learned that these people had acquired a new worry. A great many of the evacuated AJA soldiers had had no opportunity to make farewell visits to their homes and so had had no chance to tell their families what the Army had promised about combat training on the Mainland. Many of the Japanese were fearful that their sons had been shipped to internment camps. Ten days after the provisional battalion had reached Camp

McCoy, however, news of their new station and intended training was released and morale within the Japanese community curved upward once again.[5]

IT HAD BEEN decided in Washington that the Provisional Battalion, on its arrival on the Mainland, would be placed under control of the commanding general, Army Ground Forces, and promptly dispatched to a training area in the Central Defense Command. There it was to be reorganized, equipped, and trained as an infantry combat unit, to be ready for field service on ten-day notice after September 30, 1942. Its nature, origin, and destination were to be kept secret.

Three training posts were suggested for the unit from Hawaii: Guernsey in Wyoming, McCoy in Wisconsin, and Leonard Wood in Mississippi. Army Ground Forces chose McCoy. It had a tent camp, one or more military police battalions were already training there, and a cantonment then under construction would be ready if winter housing proved necessary. The commanding general, 7th Army Corps, had been directed to arrange transfer from the coast, and was to report to 2d Army Headquarters "any unusual circumstances" which might be found on inspection of the unit at the debarkation point. The commanding general, 6th Army Corps Area, and the camp commandant at McCoy were being advised by letter of the nature, origin, and equipment of the battalion.

On June 10, AGF ordered 2d Army and Central Defense Command to organize, equip, and train the group as an infantry combat battalion with additional rifle companies as necessary. The

Separate Battalion

CHAPTER FIVE

orders said, "Every effort must be made to maintain morale and esprit de corps in the unit at a high level. So far as possible, officers and men must be made to feel that their unit is an honored element of the Army and that it is being trained with a view to its ultimate employment in combat."

The 2d Army recommended that the AJA unit, on its arrival at McCoy, be designated as a "separate" battalion. AGF agreed and henceforth the Hawaiian Provisional Infantry Battalion became, officially, the 100th Infantry Battalion (Separate)—and unofficially, to its members, the "One puka puka."*

On June 13, 2d Army Headquarters sent an officer to McCoy to impress on the leader of the 100th Battalion the importance of giving his men careful training and of maintaining high morale. He was also to secure information about the battalion, such as previous training of the personnel and background of the officers, particularly those of Japanese ancestry.

On June 21, 2d Army Headquarters sent a telegram to Washington: "Provided other arms and equipment furnished without delay, recent inspection 100th Inf. Bn. indicates said Command can be placed in highly efficient state combat training at early date."[1]

McCoy, used before the war as a maneuvering ground for the 6th Army Corps and also as an artillery range for the Wisconsin National Guard, was a sprawling 14,000 acres of fields and woods interspersed with creeks, gulleys, and some low hills. It was admirable terrain for drill, target practice, and mock battle, and had an adequate road net. Though the camp would later be occupied by thousands of troops, when the 100th arrived its only inhabitants were the trainees of an MP battalion, a quartermaster detachment, and some construction workers. At one corner was the internment center at which the boys had stared with dread from the train windows. Until April this compound had contained Japanese aliens and Mainland nisei as well as German and Italian aliens, and was to be used later as a prisoner-of-war camp.

Barracks were not available for some time, and mid-June nights and early mornings seemed frigid to men used to Hawaii's average seventy-five-degree temperature. During the daytime, however, no one stood still long enough to get cold. Training started immediately,

---

* *Puka* is the Hawaiian word for "hole," and has come to be used humorously for "zero," as in telephone numbers.

with rehearsal of all the military fundamentals which had been learned in Hawaii. One of the trainees later wrote, with more earnestness than style: "It was the unsatiable desire of every man in the command to achieve success in every phase of training, in hopes that the 100th Battalion of which he was a vital part would be comprised of the finest soldiers in the United States Army. . . . The feeling was ever present that he must do better than the average soldier because the eyes of all America were on him. . . . This want of confidence by some must be proved by fact."

In terms of normal military organization, the "separate" unit was an orphan. An infantry battalion is usually formed and trained with the two others which make up a regiment. It functions as part of the larger command, operates under supervision of regimental head-quarters, and trains in co-operation with elements normally provided by the mother organization: an antitank platoon, for instance, from the regiment's antitank company, a transportation platoon from the service company, a section from the medical group, and so on. Turner and his staff had to select, organize, get equipment for, and independently train personnel to perform such services.

Lovell prepared special tables showing the changes in organization made necessary by the 100th's separate status and after the usual red tape they were approved. When the authorization was finally received in mid-July the battalion command had already put most of its own suggestions into effect. By August 1 the 100th consisted of one infantry battalion, two additional rifle companies, one battalion medical section, one battalion service section, one transportation platoon, and one service company. Authority had been given to carry personnel in excess of the numbers authorized in the new tables of organization as overstrength.

More officers were needed so Turner requested twelve additional lieutenants, former residents of Hawaii if possible. Eight of those who showed up were former regular Army noncoms who had been stationed in the Islands before their transfer to Mainland officer candidate schools. As each new officer arrived, Turner gave him a full report on the kind of unit to which he had been assigned. One, learning that he had been sent to an all-AJA unit, gasped: "My God, I didn't know I was getting into this!"

"Your name is Schemel, isn't it?"

"Yes, sir."

"I see that your first name is Kurt. Born in Germany?"

"Yes, sir, in Berlin. . . . I see what you're getting at, sir. . . . If you'll have me, I'll be glad to join this outfit."

Whatever they may have felt, none of the other OCS graduates showed any chagrin at their assignment. For a time, however, it looked as though the Colonel's request for officers who had lived in Hawaii might have been a mistake. Like most soldiers of the Oahu garrison, the eight men who had been noncoms in the Territory had normally associated with civilians only when buying goods or amusement, and some of them had a tendency to look on the residents of Oriental ancestry as "gooks," Oahu as "the Rock," and the Mainland as God's only country. These particular officers showed a tendency to forget Turner's briefing on how to command American soldiers of Japanese ancestry, and an inclination to treat them as a lesser breed. The AJAs had not liked this as civilians and were no more inclined to like it as soldiers. Nevertheless, the "old horseblankets" had something to teach about drill and administration. As the enlisted men recognized this fact, and the former top sergeants began to realize that slant eyes did not prevent a man from a being a good soldier or a good Joe, the original antagonism gave way to mutual respect, and sometimes to affection.

After two months with his new outfit one of the former noncoms, a veteran of twenty-two years Army service, reported, "I'd rather have a hundred of these men behind me than a hundred of any others I've ever been with." It took another regular Army man some time to get over his surprise when he learned that some of his subordinates had spent $8.00 of their own money for the two volumes of *Tactics and Techniques of Infantry.* Apparently these were not the kind of enlisted men he was used to!

Under the Army's classification system a combat officer, after a certain length of service, is supposed to reach a certain rank by a certain age or be transferred to noncombat duty. Six of the newly commissioned veterans, all of them over thirty, were therefore made captains. This caused resentment among the AJA lieutenants who found themselves, despite seniority of battalion service, under the command of these officers. They soon realized, however, that the new captains were better qualified than themselves, and took their disappointment with good grace. Turner had not told them about the order which would in any case have kept them from such posts—

that no AJA might lead a rifle company. He intended to wait, and when a nisei was best qualified for a command, give it to him and settle with the Army afterward.

As the days passed constant drill brought additional snap and precision of movement; hikes and obstacle courses brought blisters and bruises but also more toughness. Every soldier became master of two or more weapons. Men learned to hit the ground, wriggle along earth folds or behind bushes, move from cover to cover, put machine guns and mortars quickly into firing position, dig various kinds of emplacements, work as a team in squad problems, and find their way about on night marches when one soldier could spot the man ahead only by the white paper pinned on his back.

If a squad or platoon could not advance frontally, it must dig in and deliver covering fire while a companion group moved to hit the enemy flank. "Always look for the enemy's weak spot and hit him there." Officers and men learned how to relay messages; lieutenants learned to control their platoons in advance or withdrawal; and each GI had it pounded into him that there would be neither success nor survival unless every man in every unit knew and did his job as part of the team.

The boys worked hard. One, five feet tall with boots on, came up to a seven-and-a-half-foot obstacle course barrier. He tried at least a dozen times to kick and claw his way over. Finally the captain yelled, "Don't kill yourself, Shorty. Try again later. It'll still be there," and moved away. Before the drill was over a corporal approached the captain and reported solemnly, "He finally made it, sir."

The boy who wrote that the eyes of all America were on the 100th may have been guilty of some exaggeration, but there were plenty of gimlet-eyed visitors from General Lear's headquarters, from other camps, and from Washington who dropped into the classroom unexpectedly. Visitors, wary at first, became more cordial after they had looked things over. Soon Turner began to hear favorable comments about his scholars. It began to look as if the experimental unit might be accepted as part of the regular school system.

Turner held frequent staff meetings. Often a *haole* officer, realizing that the AJA officers knew the men better than he did, asked for advice on matters of morale or discipline. Noncoms were called in to meet with commissioned officers, and went back to their men able to give them the latest news, tell them what training lay ahead and what was expected of them. Frequently the CO himself discussed beforehand in these sessions points he was planning to make in talks to the assembled battalion.

In frequent news and pep sessions attended by all personnel, Turner sometimes praised his men in mellow tones, sometimes scolded them in an angry roar. The subject might be anything from a report on recent battle problems to a warning against funny stuff with the local girls. "There's a wide-open town farther away that you can go to," he would tell them, or that Wisconsin made beer, and that it was quite impossible to drink it all up while on pass. There were to be no more attempts by those who had overstayed leave to bribe the guards at the camp gates with drinks or sandwiches. And there was always the reminder that the kind of treatment they received, inside or outside the camp, as individuals or as a unit, depended, in the final analysis, on the behavior of each soldier.

Those who found themselves on the carpet before the "Old Man" learned that he could bite as well as bark, but usually they nursed their wounds without great resentment. All but the most hardened characters emerged from such sessions a bit ashamed, for the Colonel lost no opportunity to remind them that their sins hurt not only themselves but the whole AJA outfit. More than one soldier compared the CO to the kind of father who spanks his child and then gives him a quarter to go to the movies.

Turner could be tough with his boys but he could also be tough on their behalf. When a regular army division moved from San Antonio to McCoy there were some brawls between the AJAs and the Texans. This was to be expected, but when the "Old Man" discovered that in some of these battles his runts had been the victims of a five-to-one preponderance of enemy manpower, the division's commander found an angry visitor in his office. The Texans shortly received orders to stay away from the 100th. There were some minor encounters after this (in which GIs of Mexican and Indian ancestry sometimes fought on the side of the AJAs) but there were no more near-riots.

Turner was temperamentally equipped to protect his brood. Lack of self-assurance was not one of his weaknesses, and he had been accustomed in civilian life to hold his own with other executives. In connection with National Guard matters or on a social basis he had associated with high-ranking officers on tour of duty in Hawaii.

He was not in awe of the regular Army brass, especially when he felt his men were in danger of getting an unfair deal. This national guardsman could be stubbornly insistent that his boys were not going to be treated as either second-class citizens or second-class soldiers —at least while he could make his voice heard.

On such occasions Turner spoke not only for himself but for the rest of the *kamaaina* officers from Hawaii. Occasionally an officer might silently curse one of his runty rice-eaters, ancestors included, but no outsider, no Mainlander, could make a derogatory remark about the ancestry of his soldiers and get away with it. A man doesn't allow strangers to criticize his family. Before long every AJA in the command knew that he was part of a united team.

In October some officers from Washington came to McCoy to talk with Turner and Lovell. Soon afterwards Lovell went to the capital. On his return he selected two officers and twenty-five enlisted man for a secret War Department project. On November 3, after another G-2 check, they left with Lovell for their new assignment. Ten days later Lovell returned to McCoy alone. No mention was made of where the group had gone or why.

Battalion units were now maneuvering in larger formations, in night as well as day attacks and withdrawals. The same lessons were repeated constantly. Advance as far as possible. Take up defensive positions when stopped. Call on the heavy weapons for special support fire. Let the reserve platoons through for the next punch in front or flank. Withdraw, if necessary, under covering fire. Dig in, consolidate, concentrate fire power on threatened sections, guard against enemy infiltration. After the enemy's counterattack has been stopped, push ahead again. Communications men laid wire as far as they could; medics snaked forward under fire to give aid to the wounded; and antitank men careened their guns to sectors where enemy armor threatened a breakthrough.

Among themselves officers expressed pleasure at the way the boys were learning. One of the regular army men boasted about his heavy weapons company. According to the manual, sixteen seconds was satisfactory time for setting up a heavy machine gun, and at Fort Benning they thought eleven seconds fast, but some of his boys were ready to fire in five!

In December sixty-seven more soldiers left the battalion, but there was no secrecy about their destination. Selected because of their comparative fluency in the Japanese tongue, they were to be trained as interpreters at the Military Intelligence Language Training School, Camp Savage, Minnesota.* Some Mainland AJAs were already being trained at Savage, but the men from the 100th were the first Hawaii AJAs to attend.

Not long after their arrival the commandant of the school wrote to Colonel Turner that they were better soldiers and presented a better appearance than any other single group of men in his outfit, including the Caucasian housekeeping detachment. "We are delighted with them and the excellent example they are setting our various detachments."[2]

Six months later, after intensive drill, they graduated with a working knowledge of spoken and written Japanese military terminology. Two men stayed at Savage as instructors and five went to Hawaii to recruit volunteers for their alma mater, but the rest soon left for the Pacific, where they were distributed in small teams among various combat units in widely scattered areas of operation. Here, at one time or another, many of them came under Japanese fire. Some had opportunity, gun in hand, to answer the question, "Who you shoot?" and none betrayed his trust.[3]

*Despite the fact that most of the boys had attended language school, the battalion average of proficiency in Japanese was a sore disappointment to Army linguistic experts.

SHORTLY AFTER he reached McCoy one of the AJAs wrote home: "The attitude here is not at all what I had contemplated. On the contrary the folks are nice to us."[1]

As soon as possible after their arrival soldiers on pass headed down the three-mile road into Sparta, county seat and farming center, population nearly 6,000. They bought soda or beer, hamburgers or hot dogs, ambled the streets, went to the movies, answered the townspeople's queries about themselves, and on return to camp reported the town small—only two movies—but the people friendly. With grins they told about some of the questions they had been asked, such as where in the Philippines was Hawaii, and did they have autos and electricity and movies there, and didn't the straw houses leak when it rained, and "Where did you learn English?"

Asked their nationality, some of the first scouts tried to avoid unpleasantness by saying they were Hawaiians. Not long afterward Turner, during one of his pep talks, reported having heard that he was leading "a bunch of Hawaiians." In the future there was to be no more nonsense. They were Americans of Japanese ancestry, and those who did not so describe themselves would get their ears pinned back. Turner and Lovell accepted invitations to speak before civilian luncheon groups and welcomed reporters from the local newspapers. During these sessions they emphasized the fact that their men, though of Japanese ancestry, were also

The Heart of America

American citizens and soldiers, and expressed complete confidence that they would be fairly treated by the civilians of the area. These statements were heard with cordial interest; the newsmen wrote friendly stories; and civic leaders offered all possible co-operation in establishing good relations between town and camp. The Junior Chamber of Commerce and Knights of Columbus opened their club rooms to battalion personnel, and officers and men soon received invitations to various gatherings at the town Community building.

While their leaders had been acting as advance engineers, some of the enlisted men had been moving ahead on their own. Those who had been churchgoers at home attended Sparta's churches, and almost immediately began to receive invitations from fellow worshipers to "come out to the house for a good home-cooked dinner." Before long nearly every GI had friends among the townspeople or the farmers from the surrounding country, and standing invitations to visit them when on pass. These hospitable civilians soon discovered an AJA trait which was to become known wherever the boys from Hawaii went: they never took a kindness for granted. Not only did they bring the womenfolk candy, or *leis* they had made themselves, but they also brought a cigar for the host, or, better still, offered to pitch in and help with the chores. Quick-humored and fond of fun but well-behaved and notably polite to their elders, they were usually invited to come again. Soon their new friends began to receive presents through the mail, bowls made from Hawaiian woods, *lauhala* place mats, guava jelly and poha jam, and other exciting gifts from grateful parents in Hawaii. Somewhat later, after the 100th had left McCoy, the Japanese on the island of Oahu gave a free *luau* to which every Wisconsin soldier on the island was invited.[2] Pit-roasted pig, *poi*, cocoanut pudding, hula dancers—nothing was too good for their guests.

Sparta girls were curious about these boys from the romantic Pacific islands, and found them quite different from the Hollywood portrayals of the buck-toothed, shaven-headed, heavily eye-glassed "Jap." More than one AJA was told that he was "not a bit like the movies." After a while some of the girls went to dances or the movies with the soldiers from McCoy, and eventually there were a few marriages. To only one such marriage did there seem to be loud parental objection—the bride's mother had the union immediately annulled. Another marriage ended when the groom, whose new and easy-going spouse had spent $2000 of his savings, decided to invest a remaining $500 in a divorce.

Other AJAs spent their money on themselves in Sparta's theatres, bowling alleys, skating rinks, restaurants, taverns, and lunch counters. Most had brought sizable amounts to McCoy, some of it saved from money gifts given the departing warrior in accordance with Japanese custom. They spent their savings and their pay checks in an open-handed manner more Hawaiian than Japanese. They attended church suppers, fraternal group parties, and dances. The USO became their second home and its director, Miss Alice Kenny, a friend to everyone in the outfit.

A battalion elimination tournament produced a crack baseball team. Coached by Lovell and Doc Kometani, the group first played civilian nines in the Sparta neighborhood and then branched out to tackle opposition over a much wider area. It was accompanied on these trips by a musical group selected from the best of the many singers and ukulele- and guitar-players in the outfit. These "Hawaiian Serenaders" (two Hawaiian brothers who had claimed Japanese ancestry in order to join the provisional battalion were part of the ensemble) sang and played Island songs before the games, and some of the musicians, attired in *leis* and grass skirts, performed both comic and serious hulas.

Pregame publicity by one home-town team billed the AJA players as "Native Hawaiian Soldiers," and the musicians as "Original Hawaiian Serenaders," and promised every paying customer a "Beautiful Hawaiian Lei" (these were of paper and made in Brooklyn) as a souvenir. Wearing jackets lettered with the word *Aloha*, the team played snappy ball. It won eight of fourteen games, and the Serenaders were a popular success. Both groups served the battalion as effective ambassadors of good will.

Battalion headquarters received frequent invitations to send parade detachments to patriotic celebrations and bond rallies. One of the first such groups marched into Madison's Capitol Square behind a sound-equipped police car which blared, "These soldiers fought in the Battle of Pearl Harbor; they are guests of the American Legion." Another group, singers from the battalion, entertained children at Madison's Orthopedic Hospital. On another occasion municipal officials asked that a drill unit be sent to take part in a monster Victory Rally at the University of Wisconsin fieldhouse. Men from the battalion had already visited the University campus, where students from the Islands and their Mainland friends had done everything possible to make them feel at home. During the football season busloads of AJA soldiers had come down from McCoy to cheer the Wisconsin team and afterwards add to the gaiety by singing Island songs or performing comic hulas. After their drill exhibition at the Victory Rally, members of the platoon danced with co-eds, some of them girls from Hawaii.

Shortly after the drill exhibition in the fieldhouse, a Madison judge wrote to Turner that his boys had "caught the attention of the entire assemblage by reason of their clean-cut appearance and the precision with which they executed all commands." A similar letter from another citizen described the "spontaneous and prolonged" applause which the drill team had received, and praised their "soldierly appearance and general conduct." The Mayor also wrote to commend their gentlemanly and proper conduct, and asssured the Colonel that these or any other soldiers of the 100th would receive a warm welcome in Madison on future visits.[3]

Turner had a sizable file of such reports, for his men had brought into Army life the lessons in behavior taught them by their parents and language-school teachers, and in addition they were more mature than the average GI. But the battalion had its share of drunks, women-chasers, and hell-raisers. However, these had to contend not only with military and civilian police but with members of their own group. With the whole battalion on trial, the other AJAs were not going to let a few "crazy buggas" ruin its reputation, so they policed the ranks vigorously. If doghouse discipline failed, sterner measures were used. Eventually the few who couldn't be good tried to be careful, and if one nevertheless did get himself in trouble his buddies tried to haul him away before an alarm could be sounded.

Chicago was only four hours away by train, and this city became another headquarters for those on leave. The mayor's wife, Mrs. Edward J. Kelley, active in providing recreational activity for GIs training in the area, helped arrange mass visits by battalion personnel. On the first of these excursions, two hundred soldiers from McCoy were met at the train by buses and taken to a baseball game as guests of the Cubs, then to dinner at the servicemen's center, and to a reception and dance at the University of Chicago's International House. The next day, Sunday, started with a sight-seeing tour, followed in the afternoon by a double-header at the ball park, after which buses took the group back to the train. Total expense per person was about five dollars. As the boys gradually made contact with fellow Islanders working or studying in Chicago, they seldom found themselves alone on the town during visits.

One week end in Chicago a few AJA camera fans took pictures of various points of interest. A civilian, alarmed at this approximation to his mental image of the slant-eyed, picture-taking Oriental spy, reported them to the FBI. Agents swept down, took their cameras, quizzed them thoroughly, and then set them free. Soon afterwards Turner received a sharp query from Military Intelligence. In his letter of reply Turner enclosed some newsstand picture postcards of Chicago scenes. No more was heard of the incident.

Before leaving home most of the AJAs had never traveled outside Hawaii, but now their speed and the extent of their journeyings to "see America first" amazed their officers. Every sizable city within striking distance received its share of tourists from McCoy, who got as far west as military regulations would permit persons of Japanese ancestry, as far south as New Orleans, and as far east as the Staten Island ferry view of the Statue of Liberty. This and the monuments of the nation's capital were musts for every man in the outfit, but the explorers also gazed at many intervening scenes of interest from points of vantage such as the Empire State Building's observation tower or the bleachers at Yankee Stadium. Back at camp one group proudly showed a photograph of Joe Di Maggio towering high above a group of smiling AJAs.

It is usually a happy occasion when someone from Hawaii meets a fellow resident on the Mainland. They may never have seen each other before, but their mutual affection for the Islands automatically makes them friends. One night, on Broadway, a woman stopped beside a small group of AJAs from McCoy. "You boys from Hawaii?" "Yes, ma'am," and, eagerly, "You from the Islands too?" "I left after the blitz." A little chat, a handshake all around. "Have fun. Aloha," and she was off. One of the soldiers opened his hand on a twenty-dollar bill.

The first group of soldier-tourists to reach Washington went to the Traveler's Aid desk at Union Station to ask help in getting rooms. After a series of telephone calls the woman in charge found beds for six in a small hotel. Soon afterwards the boys piled into the lobby and up to the room desk. The clerk did a double-take and called the manager; he took one look and retired to his office to make a phone call. He returned shortly to ask for identification cards; then, after further conversation with the Army officer at the other end of the line, came back reassured and cordial.

In Washington, as elsewhere, American soldiers with Japanese faces were news, and the next day the tourists were answering reporters' questions about themselves, their unit, and life in Hawaii. As always, they insisted upon the American-ness of their environment and schooling. They talked of Island baseball, basketball, and football, as well as of surfboard riding, net casting, and spearfishing. They had, they said, eaten hot dogs, hamburgers, and apple pie a la mode ever since they could walk. They also assured newsmen that radio stations and chromium-plated drugstores were as well known in the Islands, if not as common, as ukulele-playing vocalists, surfboards, and palm trees.

The AJAs were well prepared for the newsmen's questions. Soon after their arrival at McCoy, reporters and photographers had turned up at the camp. After talking with Turner and his staff the reporters had gone out to buttonhole individual GIs, cameramen trailing along taking pictures. Some of the larger papers ran special features on the AJA soldiers; many of the smaller ones carried picture stories supplied by a syndicated Sunday magazine supplement; and the big press associations sent accounts to their papers throughout the nation.[4] Paramount and Universal made newsreels in which the soldiers from Hawaii marched across movie screens to the accompaniment of martial music and running commentaries.

Reporters naturally commented on ways in which the AJAs from Hawaii were unique: their small stature; their ukuleles, guitars, and Hawaiian songs; the flat straw sandals they wore when off duty; their preference for rice rather than potatoes; the way they played practically every sport barefoot, even football; and their amazement at the girls who wore ankle socks in Wisconsin's winter climate. Newspapers ran photographs of them, grim-faced during battle practice or grinning and yelling at play.

It was also noted that they sang songs like "Don't Sit Under the Apple Tree," and called each other "Porky," "Gabby," and "Moose." They knew a lot about American history, civics, and geography, and spoke "surprisingly good English." (Former teachers would have been amazed at the effort they put into speaking correctly. They reserved pidgin for their buddies.)

When the reporters interviewed the residents of Sparta, they found them impressed by the AJAs' "good manners and high level of education," and the comparatively large proportion of lawyers, accountants, engineers, teachers, and other professionally trained individuals among enlisted men as well as officers. One journalist asked a private if he had ever been to the Mainland before. "I'm a graduate of the University of Missouri," was the reply.

Newsstand vendors said that most of the men from this battalion bought reading material other than comic books, even "serious" magazines. The local librarian reported that they took out library cards and used them, and bookstores reported greatly increased sales. An editor of one of the local newspapers wrote: "We have no riff-raff here. Our new residents are fine, clean people." Officers of the 6th Service Command said that the 100th was one of the best drilled and trained outfits encamped in the Mid-West.

When reporters asked individual AJAs the jack-pot question, "Would you fight the Japs?" the unhesitating reply was "Yes." They said the attack on Pearl Harbor was shameful; Americans didn't play that kind of dirty ball. They pointed out that most of the civilians killed during the attack were of Japanese ancestry—they had relatives and friends to avenge. The war lords of Japan obviously had not cared what happened to the Japanese living in Hawaii. The AJAs knew themselves to be American in mind and heart, but until they were given a chance to prove it in battle against Japan's troops other Americans would not. In any case they wanted combat duty, whether against the Japs or the Germans. "I want action," one AJA said. "I want to fight so my wife and four-year-old daughter in Hawaii can live in honor as loyal Americans."

As the weeks passed, enlisted men began to boast that their squad was the best squad in the best platoon in the best company of the whole outfit. The officers grinned—this was *esprit de corps*, and no combat outfit was any good without it. Perhaps, with luck, the same soldiers might have a chance later on to assert that theirs was the best battalion in the best regiment, etc., etc.

The overstrength in personnel—five companies instead of the usual three—which had at first been such a headache because Army quartermasters never quite believed that one battalion needed all the supplies requested, proved to be an asset for training purposes. In working out combat problems any two companies might substitute for an enemy battalion, with the result that the 100th was able to practice some exercises which otherwise it would have practiced only as part of a regiment. In many ways it was indeed a pint-sized regiment. When Turner received a letter from the office of the adjutant general in Washington addressed to the "Commanding General, 100th Infantry Division, Camp McCoy, Wisconsin," he proudly showed it to his men, then wrote on the envelope, "no stars, no Packard," and pasted it in his scrapbook.

The barracks, finished in September, gave some protection at night, but Wisconsin's winter wonderland was at first no source of delight to these guests from the subtropics. Men who had previously known ice only as cubes in a drink now cried, "*Auwe*, da cold!" and longed for Hawaiian sunshine. Eventually, however, they found cold weather could be a source of pleasure. They built wooden balks in the open spaces between the barracks, flooded the enclosed areas, bought skates, and began to skid around on their new ice rinks. Men who had never seen snow before ate it, rolled in it, and made snowballs. Snapshots mailed home at Christmas time showed AJAs posed with snowmen garlanded with *leis* of coal, and *Mele Kalikimaka* ("Merry Christmas" in Hawaiian) scratched in large letters in the snow at their feet.

One December night, as the wind whistled about the barracks, a large group of officers came to McCoy from Chicago. Early next morning, in weather sixteen degrees below zero, and under close observation, battalion units went through their routines. During the course of the inspection the heavy weapons company thawed out, set up, and fired its water-cooled machine guns in a performance which one of the visiting generals said was the best exhibition of practice fire he had ever seen.

On the last day of the year notice came from 2d Army headquarters that the battalion was to move to Camp Shelby, Mississippi. Most of the men agreed that if they had to leave friendly Wisconsin for the South, the orders couldn't have come at a better time. They had already gone through two stages of a three-months course of outdoor sleeping. In November it had been one night a month, in December one night a week, in January it was to have been seven consecutive nights. Not that they couldn't take it—but no one was going to be sorry to miss the final session in the open. "Mebbe mo' betta we go sout'," they agreed.

Before the departure date, set for January 6, the battalion members gave a big farewell *luau* for civilian friends in the Sparta area. They served more than a hundred pounds of steak soaked in shoyu sauce, rice in quantities never before served at any Midwestern feast, and all the other Hawaiian dishes they could get ingredients for, and the Serenaders put on the show of their lives. As the strains of "Aloha Oe" lamented evening's end and the longer parting soon to come, there were regretful handclasps all around.

This *luau* had served as at least a token of gratitude for what one AJA officer, a public-school principal in civilian life, described in a message to his former colleagues in Hawaii as "the wonderful cordiality and hospitality" of the people of Wisconsin. It could, he wrote, "really put to shame some of our much glorified and over-exaggerated Hawaiian hospitality." He told how quickly the men of the 100th had realized that in terms of attitudes toward American institutions and ideals they and their new friends were, despite differences in ancestry and environmental influence, basically one in spirit. "I am confident," he wrote, "that when this unit, the only large one representing this territory in distant lands, goes forth into whatever service it is called upon to perform, it will be outstanding and a real credit to the spirit of Hawaii Nei. It should make all of you teachers who had a part in their training proud of the fact that the sacrifices the boys may have to make, will be made for the preservation of American liberties, which they have always known and enjoyed and expect others to continue to enjoy in the Paradise of the Pacific."*

At about the same time another American, son of immigrant parents, Carl Sandburg, had written in his column in the Chicago Sunday *Times:*

One morning in March, 1934, I gave a talk, readings, and songs for the student body of 2,200 in McKinley High School in Honolulu. The Japanese boys and girls were ten to one of the Filipinos, the Portuguese and the Negroes. And they were solemn or sober, wildly amused or rollicking with laughter at the same places in the program as were the American audiences on what is called the mainland. Their language, as they spoke, was Americanese, slangy

* From a letter written by Captain Jack Mizuha, the officer who on December 15, 1941, volunteered to lead the party which went to Niihau where the Japanese aviator had crash-landed and had attempted to terrorize the inhabitants.

with point and meaning, like that of the Army men at Schofield Barracks or the Navy men at Pearl Harbor. They seemed to be thirsty to learn of American traditions.

Then the biographer of Abraham Lincoln went on to assure his readers: "Anyone who bets on the future service of the 100th Infantry Battalion of the 2d Army, in training at Camp McCoy, will not go far wrong."[5]

AT SHELBY, Mississippi, the 100th was assigned quarters at one end of the camp, in an area reserved for special units. Immediately after arrival Turner reported to headquarters of the 85th Division, to which the battalion was to be attached for training.

An officer asked Turner: "Well, did you get your Japs here all right?"

"Sir, my men are not 'Japs.' That is a term of opprobrium we use for the enemy. My troops are Americans of Japanese ancestry serving in the American Army."

The officer bristled a bit: "Well, General Haislip has called them that."

"If he wants to use that term in the office, OK, but we'd like to have it understood that we don't want it used before our men."

From that time on it was not.

Attached to the 85th, but not to any of its regiments, the battalion received orders directly from the division's G-3, which assigned officers to supervise its training. On a rainy chilly dawn, two weeks after it had reached Shelby, the 100th performed before Major General Wade H. Haislip, commander of the 85th, and his staff. Jumping from the line of departure, a live artillery barrage whistling overhead, the AJAs sprinted from cover to cover or slid forward on their wet bellies. Conscious that this was another exam that had to be passed, they threw themselves into action as though it were a case of advance or die. A few days later, at a staff critique, Haislip told his officers, "I watched the 100th

Shelby and the South

Battalion the other morning, and they're better than some of our units that have been training a lot longer. It was rotten weather, too, but they played the game."

In March, 1943, eleven recent graduates of officer candidate schools joined the team: Alexander, Anastasio, Froning, Gleicher, Grandstaff, Handley, Jakuszewski, Krivi, Lakner, Mitchell, and Rothmeller.

The same month the battalion hiked some twenty-five miles into the enormous pine-dotted plain in the midst of which Shelby sat, to take part in D-Series maneuvers with the division. During the dozen battle problems which followed, the outfit was attached to various regiments, a few days with one, then transferred to another.

During these sham engagements, fought in the chill of almost constant rain, battalion headquarters learned to work under regimental command, side by side with other battalions. The 100th advanced, took defensive positions, or withdrew, learned how to maintain contact to right, left, and rear, to co-ordinate its fire with that of companion units, and to go to their support or ask their aid as needed. As "casualties" mounted officers and men realized as never before how necessary it was for every man to be able to fill the job next above his own. It was during this period that five men of Company C earned Soldiers' Medals for saving a buddy who had gone under while trying to swim a swollen creek.

The men mentioned earlier who left McCoy on a secret mission returned to the battalion at Shelby. Since November they had been part of Army Ground Forces' special project for the experimental training of "attack" and "scout" dogs for use in jungle warfare. Because of its dense semitropical vegetation, Cat Island, about ten miles south of Gulfport, Mississippi, had been selected as the training site. To test the assumption that Japanese persons exuded a scent which dogs could be taught to recognize, the AJA soldiers had been borrowed from the 100th Battalion to act as "enemy" troops. Wearing face guards and heavily padded clothing, they concealed themselves in thickets and when discovered by the attack dogs threatened them with their weapons. The animals, who were accompanied by Caucasian trainers, were supposed to bite the "Japs." When scout dogs were being used the AJAs concentrated on evasion tactics, and the dogs were supposed to point when they smelled the foe.

The dogs—apparently unable to distinguish between Caucasian and Japanese odors—reacted in the same way whenever they detected any humans ahead. In the spring of 1943, Army Ground Forces turned Cat Island over to the Quartermaster Corps, which inaugurated another dog training program at that site, and the AJAs were released for return to the 100th.* A report submitted to the commanding general, Army Ground Forces, by the commanding officer of the training center had expressed a high degree of satisfaction with the work of the "trainers, Hawaiian, Japanese ancestry" and had stated that they "mingle perfectly with the other enlisted men."[1]

At first these secret operatives had wondered whether they did, indeed, secrete a peculiar odor, and had had nightmares in which they fought an endless succession of mastiffs from their throats, but after the first few days they had enjoyed their mission. The weather had been balmy and the swimming and fishing good. Back again with the battalion, they found adjustment to the dreary sogginess of the maneuver area difficult.

When the D-Series maneuvers ended, late in March, everyone welcomed the return to Shelby bunks, the easier routine of camp drill, off-duty gab, cards, horseplay, and sports.

At Shelby the barracks were more completely home than they had been at McCoy. In the trains on the way south the AJAs had talked about the kind of treatment they might expect from southerners and what they should do about it. It had been decided that each man, "for the sake of his friends and the good name of the battalion," should do his best to avoid racial troubles, but "should not sell himself short and be humbled into a lower rank."

At the new camp there were GIs who made cracks about "Japs" and "yellow-bellies." Some of the AJAs made it plain that those who wanted to call names must also trade punches, but generally the boys stuck to the resolve to avoid trouble, and found that the best way to do this was to stay close to their own barracks area. Here Doc Kometani worked hard to keep the men busy and cheerful. The battalion produced a basketball five which won the 85th Division trophy and a boxing team which won the post championship. These triumphs, coupled with the general report that theirs was a soldierly outfit, earned the battalion's members a certain amount of respect.

---

* The Army never employed attack dogs in overseas areas, but in 1944 and 1945 used scout dogs in the Pacific theater. Though these animals could not distinguish between Japanese and Caucasian troops, there was value, in certain situations, in their ability to warn that humans were ahead.

Passes were purposely kept at a minimum, but this was no great hardship, for the men were less eager to go to town than they had been at McCoy. There had been talk on the journey down of winning the good will of civilians in Mississippi as they had done in Wisconsin, but that idea died quickly. The 21,000 residents of Hattiesburg, a cattle, farming, and lumbering center nine miles from Shelby, had already had their quiet streets made noisy by GIs from all parts of the Union, and had experienced all the annoyances which come to a community near a military reservation. Though the merchants prospered, most of the residents would have been happier if there had been no Army installations nearby. They were already looking askance at doughboys when the first brown-skinned visitors from Shelby began to drift into town—and this was Mississippi, home state of Congressman Rankin who felt that, Japs being Japs, soldiers of that ancestry should be used, like Negroes, only for labor.

Some Hattiesburg civilians made nasty remarks; others were rude; but most were, the men agreed, just cold. This reception, contrasting as it did with Sparta's friendliness, made the boys of the 100th button up their mental overcoats. "We never warmed up to Hattiesburg," they said.

The AJAs had heard about the South's color line, but they were shocked to see it in practice—separate toilets for whites and colored; special seats in buses; restaurants and theatres for whites only; countless assertions that the Negro was inferior. Though they themselves were usually allowed in toilets, restaurants, and bus and train seats reserved for whites, they could not but feel sympathy and anger when other "colored" men were thus humbled. A Negro in Army uniform thrown out of a barber shop or beaten unconscious because he would not take one of the rear seats in a bus—why didn't more of them fight back? "Thank God I was born in Hawaii!"

At first some AJAs struck up the acquaintance of Negro soldiers or civilians and spent part of their time on leave with these new friends, but after a discussion among battalion officers and subsequent talks with the men this practice stopped. Though the whole racial situation in the South might be wrong, the 100th certainly could not change it, and association with Negroes could bring the battalion members the same treatment. The men saw the point, but were resolved that what fighting they did would be for the America represented by Wisconsin and not by Mississippi.

At Shelby, as at McCoy, each man's behavior was the concern of all. One night a group of soldiers sat singing around a campfire, cans of beer in hand. A former fisherman from a remote Island village began to sing a Japanese ballad. This was against the rules, and he was told to shut up—when the battalion had first reached the Mainland Turner had issued an order that no one in the outfit was to speak Japanese, and the men, realizing that the restriction was for their protection, had obeyed it. But the fisherman, a little drunk, continued his song. Not long, however. Doc Kometani heard no more than a few words of the forbidden tongue before he charged to the campfire and demanded that the culprit identify himself. Later, commenting on what Doc had to say, one of the boys remarked, "I nevah see da Doc move so fas' or talk so *huhu*."

Another incident showed this same concern for the good name of the 100th. Some men in Company A had come down with the measles and Captain Kawasaki, the surgeon, had ordered their unit isolated. While new cases were still being reported, the battalion received orders to get ready to move out for a battle problem. Doc Kawasaki told Turner that if A marched with the rest of the battalion the whole outfit would soon have the measles. Turner notified the commander of the regiment to which the 100th was then attached, but was told that orders were orders; those soldiers who were in bed could stay there, but the rest would march. Torn between his knowledge that if the battalion did not move it might look like malingering, and his fear that if it did, the men of A Company would infect the rest, Kawasaki offered a compromise. That company should move with the rest, but in as strict isolation as field conditions would allow. Turner reported to his superior that the 100th would be ready to go, but was then informed that the regimental surgeon, who had meanwhile been consulted, had flatly stated that the infected company should remain in its barracks. As it turned out, measles spread throughout the whole battalion despite Kawasaki's precautions.

Early in April, still attached to the 85th Division, the 100th moved by motor and rail to the immense Louisiana Maneuver Area where a number of divisions were to take part in war games. Before departure Turner "addressed the battalion in the usual informal manner but added a little solemnness. . . . He asked them to do their best job and if they demonstrated the same display of the past then this would be the end of their training and the battalion would be ready to move on to the higher stage which the whole world watched."

The next two months were rough. It was steaming hot most of the time; chiggers and ticks made life one long itch; and the poisonous coral snakes and water moccasins of the region filled the soldiers from snakeless Hawaii with dread. In imitation of real battle conditions the drinking ration was at times whittled down to a quart a day. It was often "wash when able," and then in stagnant stinking ground water. Hiking seemed endless, especially on the day the unit marched 25 miles to hit an "enemy" force from the rear. Each unit nevertheless had some experiences which were later remembered with pleasure, such as Company F's wild splash, bayonets fixed, across the Sabine River, to rout an opposing force from "vital ground."

Their unit but a tiny element in the mammoth shiftings of men and machines in this area, the men marched and countermarched but knew next to nothing of the part they played in the total picture. On his own level, however, each soldier learned more about his own job, and how much he contributed to the battalion's effectiveness.

About this time Sparta, Wisconsin, was damaged by a spring flood. The boys took up a collection and mailed the town officers a check for $343.00. One of the Sparta newspapers commented that this gift was "not only a tribute to the people of Sparta for their friendliness to these men, but it is a tribute to the men who sent it, a tribute to their loyalty to their friends."[2]

Late in May General Leslie J. McNair, Chief of Army Ground Forces and director of the war games, drove out to the 100th headquarters near the Sabine River. After answering Turner's query as to his health (he had been wounded while in North Africa on an inspection tour), he came to the point: "How are they shaping up? Do they really want to fight?" He explained that transportation had been scarce, but that the situation was getting better. "If they're as ready as you say, we'll find a place for them within the next two or three months."

On June 13 the battalion moved to Camp Claiborne, Louisiana, for two days of intensive firing practice with all weapons. When the men returned to their barracks at Shelby on the 16th they learned that 2686 AJA volunteers from Hawaii had been quartered next door. Important decisions had been made in the Islands and in Washington during the previous sixteen months.

IN HAWAII, following the Pearl Harbor attack, the Morale Committee of the Office of the Military Governor had appointed racial subcommittees. The AJA members of the Japanese subcommittee had been carefully selected to provide the Japanese community with new, able leaders of unquestioned loyalty. Shortly after their first meeting, held February 8, 1942, at which they decided to call themselves the Emergency Service Committee, they issued a statement of their aims. They would work with leaders and organizations of other racial elements in the Islands "for the preservation of Hawaii's traditional harmony among all races and promotion of a united home front" and would strive for "application of the fundamental values of American democracy in the treatment of all Americans, regardless of racial ancestry, fully realizing that military and other requirements sometimes make impossible the full application of this principle."

The Committee would attempt by education to strengthen the loyalty of citizens and aliens, would assist them in showing their loyalty by active participation in the war effort, and would help them face "realistically and cooperatively" the difficult situation in which the war had placed all persons of Japanese ancestry. In co-operation with other agencies, the Committee would also try to meet certain morale and personal needs of AJAs already in military service, and of their families, and would make plans for postwar rehabilitation,

By Our Professed Ideals

CHAPTER EIGHT

re-employment, and readjustment of both soldiers and civilians.[1]

At numerous meetings with Japanese residents, ESC speakers stressed the fair and sympathetic treatment which they had already received from the Army but warned them that its continuation must be earned. No half-way allegiance to the United States was possible. The disloyal must be exposed, and "not a single case of sabotage or subversive activity" must ever be committed. Old-country institutions, traditions, and mannerisms must be abandoned. There must be no further use of Japanese dress or tongue in public, and all commercial signs in that enemy language must be destroyed. The Japanese must, of course, obey all security restrictions to the letter, but they must do more—work harder at their jobs, join whatever war-effort organizations were open to them, buy bonds to capacity, donate to the blood bank regularly, and aid the defense effort in every other way possible.

The committee gave advice and assistance in the disposal of assets and dissolution of various Japanese organizations, including the language schools. (ESC spokesmen said the schools should not be reopened after the war.) Money thus realized was sometimes donated to Army or Navy Relief, sometimes invested in war bonds, sometimes given to the newly established Hawaii Veterans Memorial Fund of Oahu. Real estate and furnishings were given to the USO, the YMCA, and the City and County of Honolulu. A "Speak American" campaign was organized and hundreds of aliens were persuaded to attend classes in elementary English. When shoppers claimed that Japanese sales persons were discourteous or showed favoritism to customers of their own ancestry, the Committee investigated. It advised persons of Japanese ancestry to bear slighting remarks without retaliation. When outraged *haole* housewives wailed that their Japanese servants had basely deserted them (they had generally left domestic service for better-paying jobs), the ESC tactfully explained that domestics in general were taking advantage of the laws of supply and demand. When ESC members suggested to certain AJA candidates for public office that their election could have unfortunate effects, these citizens withdrew from the running. The Committee co-operated in the formation of AJA morale groups for the other islands, and made the results of its own experience available to them.

Members, taking time for this unpaid service from their regular business duties, met frequently, sometimes two or three evenings a week. Often they worked well into the night on a plan, then spent much of the following day putting it into operation. Occasionally their "high-pressure" methods were criticized, but in general the Japanese followed the new leaders willingly, grateful for the Army's generous treatment and anxious to prove they deserved it.[2]

The ESC worked within the framework of the Army's internal security policy. This G-2 program was neither soft nor sentimental—too much was at stake for that—and essential restrictions were rigidly enforced, but the Army avoided use of measures any more oppressive or discriminatory than military considerations demanded.

Within the dominant Caucasian element of Hawaii's population there was a strong difference of opinion as to the wisdom of this course of action. Some approved, or came to approve; others disapproved violently. Until the late 1930s most *haoles* had discounted as "scare talk" the warnings of potential military danger from the Island Japanese. Calamity howlers had cried for years that the Territory was in danger of being overrun and controlled by the spawning Japanese immigrants and their children. Nothing of the sort had happened, nor did it seem likely to, at least not for a long time to come. The Japanese residents were probably not as loyal as the *haoles* (how could they be expected to be?) but in the event of a war with Japan they would probably remain quiet and well-behaved while the U. S. fleet mopped up the enemy's navy in the waters far west of Hawaii. A few fanatics might attempt espionage or sabotage, but they could be taken care of. In the meantime why stir up trouble?

By December, 1941, deep suspicion had replaced this attitude in many minds, and after the Pearl Harbor attack antagonism toward the Island Japanese was open and widespread.[3] After official assurances repeated over a period of years that Oahu, the Gibraltar of the Pacific, was impregnable, the blitz came as a tremendous shock. Fear followed in its wake and widespread reports of local treachery seemed to indicate that warnings of fifth-column activity had been right.

Persons who had lost relatives or friends in the December 7 disaster were ready to agree with those who cried that the Army should stop coddling actual or potential traitors. Other residents joined the chorus, as did some of the newly arrived defense workers, to whom, quite simply, a Jap was a Jap.

The volume of criticism was directly related to the news from the Pacific war front. After release of news stories such as the fall of

Singapore, or accounts of Japanese atrocities, or information concerning fifth-column activities in Burma or India, General Emmons and his staff could expect an increased number of telephone calls or visits from residents demanding more adequate protection for their property, their lives, and their country. One G-2 officer later wrote that the demands of these persons "reached such proportions that officials charged with maintaining internal security often felt that the war was being waged against the Japanese elements of the population of Hawaii rather than against the military forces of Imperial Japan." The most exasperating of these critics were those who, readily agreeing that the local Japanese had as yet done no harm, nevertheless insisted that this was only because the time for such action was not yet ripe. The same officer wrote:

When the proper moment came, they would all rise up to wipe out the local garrison and population. How and with what this momentous stroke was to be accomplished was never explained. These rabidly anti-Japanese zealots were completely immune to either logic or reason. They brought forth all kinds of nebulous ideas and imaginary dangers but never made a single constructive suggestion as to a practical means for prevention of such possible situations. It was of no use to try to point out a common-sense approach to these problems, as such action was interpreted as an indication that the official was a "Jap-lover" or a "gullible fool." They went on their way spreading seeds of discontent, apprehension, and worry by proclaiming that no action was being taken to protect the islands from the horrible machinations of the Japanese.[4]

The most common demand was for wholesale evacuation of the Japanese population. A pamphlet published early in 1943 entitled *Shall the Japanese be Allowed to Dominate Hawaii?* revealed some of the motives underlying this agitation. The author, John R. Balch, chairman of the board of directors of a public utility company, feared that if the Japanese were allowed to continue in their present numbers as the largest racial group in Hawaii the position of all other racial groups would be jeopardized, "and as these people gain even greater political and economic control we shall be forced out of our jobs and our homes." His pamphlet contained other similar statements of belief and copies of letters in which he had suggested methods of averting the threat.

In one such letter dated August 6, 1942, to Admiral Chester W. Nimitz, Commander-in-Chief of the Pacific Fleet, and another dated November 7 to Benjamin Thoron, Director of the Division of Territories and Island Possessions of the Department of the Interior, he had urged mass evacuation of Hawaii's Japanese. He was convinced, he wrote, that the Japanese, retaining their own customs and culture, rarely allowing their blood stream to be mixed with that of other races, breeding children faster than other stocks, would, if left in their present security, "absolutely dominate" the Territory within another decade or so. On the basis of careful study during his thirty-five years in Hawaii, Balch believed that probably very few of these residents could be trusted, particularly if pressure were put on their relatives in Japan, or if American or allied armed forces should suffer further serious military reverses.

As soon as conditions warranted, therefore, at least 100,000 of these people should be moved to inland farming states, "this exodus to be of a permanent character." During the rest of the war California Filipinos could be brought in to take the vacated jobs, and afterwards Puerto Ricans and loyal Filipinos could be imported. The proposed evacuation would not only remove the danger to Hawaii's internal security but would also prevent the Territory's domination by the Japanese. Shortage of shipping space was an obstacle; the sugar and pineapple interests, in opposing the plan, had cited the economic disruption which it would entail; the Chamber of Commerce had objected, as would Quakers and other religious groups. Nevertheless Balch was convinced that his program should be adopted at once.

In a letter dated November 27, to H. J. McClatchy, executive secretary of the California Joint Immigration Committee, Balch had proposed a somewhat different method of averting Japanese control of the Territory. He had decided after deliberation that the best way to handle the proposed "migration" would be to allow the 35,000 resident alien Japanese to remain in Hawaii, but to remove American-Japanese families, totaling not less than 100,000 persons, to small resettlement colonies throughout Mainland United States. These evacuees "should never be allowed to return to the Territory" but after the war their relatives and friends might join them in their permanent exile.*

---

* McClatchy, whose racist organization had (in the name of national military security) so successfully pressured General J. L. De Witt into ordering mass evacuation of persons of Japanese ancestry from the West Coast, indicated to Balch that he was "unalterably opposed" to the removal of any of Hawaii's Japanese to any part of the Mainland! Carey McWilliams, *Prejudice. Japanese Americans: Symbol of Racial Intolerance* (Boston, 1944), pp. 143–144.

In the weeks following the Pearl Harbor attack Hawaii's Japanese, sick at heart, ashamed, and fearful, had retired into solitude and reserve. Afraid of doing or saying the wrong thing, many had done nothing. Critics had immediately cried that such sullen and treacherous demeanor was proof of their basically untrustworthy nature. Then and later, when persons of Japanese ancestry carried their gas masks more faithfully than other residents, their obedience to official instructions was interpreted as evidence that they had been warned of Japanese attacks to come. Their heavy purchases of war bonds were called "investments in a good thing," and donations to war relief funds a design to buy favor from those in power and to befool the gullible. When they abstained from violent denunciation of all "Japs" and things Japanese they were called unconverted Emperor worshipers. They were criticized for taking jobs vacated by patriotic Americans who had entered the armed forces, for earning unheard-of wages, for making huge profits in business, and for buying at bargain prices the choice residential real estate being sold by non-Orientals who were leaving the Territory.

The Island Japanese were not, however, without civilian friends. Opposed to the "get tough" faction was a smaller minority composed of social workers, clergymen, church members, teachers, and other *kamaaina* business and professional people. Some of these also irritated intelligence officials. The G-2 officer wrote of them: "In many instances they were equally as biased and unreasonable in their attitude of believing all Japanese residents to be loyal, friendly, and incapable of actions hostile to the interests of the United States. This group protested violently some of the necessary measures of protection, argued against the necessity for internment, and used every channel of approach towards bringing about a relaxation of many policies adopted by the authorities. It was necessary in some instances to adopt as severe an attitude in dealing with these zealots as was required to combat the unreasonable activities of the anti-Japanese group."[5]

There were, however, some individuals of idealistic conviction and courage whose knowledge and good sense carried weight with the military governors. One of these was Charles R. Hemenway, former school teacher, later attorney general of the Territory, and at the time of the attack, chairman of the board of a large trust company and a director of several corporations. Long active in civic as well as business affairs, Mr. Hemenway had been a member of the board of regents of the University of Hawaii for thirty years, and in this post he had come to know hundreds of students, many of whom were of Japanese ancestry. He was convinced that these nisei and the generation they represented were solidly loyal to the United States. Robert Shivers of the FBI had relied on his judgment, as had General Herron and General Short. Before December 7 Hemenway had been instrumental in getting University graduates to participate in preparations for internal security, and after that date in getting them to serve on the Emergency Service Committee. One University alumnus, who had been a member of one of Shivers' original advisory groups and had later served on the Oahu Citizens Committee for Home Defense and the Emergency Service Committee, told how he came to join the first of these.

"Mr. Hemenway called me up one day from his office. He asked me whether he could talk with me at my home. I was nobody and he was one of the most important men in the Territory so I suggested that I could save him trouble by coming to see him. He said, 'No. I'm going to ask you to do something so I'll come to see you.' He did, and I joined Shivers' committee. I would have done what he suggested if he had asked me to come to his office or his home, but he didn't. He came to see me. He was a big man, as well as a big wheel."

Hemenway was outspoken in his opposition to any rash or unnecessarily harsh discrimination against the Japanese residents. At the time of his death in 1947, the editor of a Japanese-language newspaper wrote:

In the dark and tragic days at the beginning of the war, at a time when the West Coast was succumbing to racial hysteria and engaging in the sad experiment of "relocation," there was a distinct danger that Hawaii, too, might succumb to the same disease. Many community leaders were openly—and we suppose, honestly—doubtful of the loyalty of residents of Japanese extraction. A larger group, who had worked harmoniously with their Oriental friends before the war, were hesitant about "sticking their necks out" and maintained a wait-and-see policy. For a while things hung in delicate balance.

But Charlie Hemenway wasn't afraid to "stick his neck out." He knew, out of his long, extensive, and intimate acquaintance with "his boys" at the University, that these boys were as loyal Americans as could be found anywhere in the nation. And he did not hesitate to say so. His influential position in the community, his wide and varied contacts, his unquestioned integrity, his logical reasoning, and his cool-headed conviction carried weight in critical quarters. His unflagging zeal and clear-headed advice helped immeasurably in setting up the Morale Committees which were so helpful in bringing adjustment and understanding to a community torn by doubts and apprehensions. . . .

Hawaii might have gone down the sorry road of undemocratic discrimination, as California did. We were at the cross-roads in that terrible December and it was largely due to Mr. Hemenway's courage and influence that Hawaii took the right turn instead of the wrong one. . . . The entire community, and the nation, owe him a debt of gratitude for his part in persuading us that we were justified in trying out the democratic ideals we had professed.[6]

Though citizens like Mr. Hemenway were comparatively few, their cause was nevertheless successful.

On September 14, 1942, a board of officers of the Organization and Training Division (G-3) of the War Department General Staff had recommended (a) that, in general, the military potential of the United States citizens of Japanese ancestry be considered as negative because of the universal distrust in which they were held, and (b) that certain individual United States citizens of Japanese ancestry be used for intelligence or specialized purposes.

In arriving at these recommendations, admittedly "with little factual data on the subject" the board "had been forced to rely instead on the opinions of various individuals." General John L. De Witt, the commanding general of the Western Defense Command and Fourth Army, who had urged upon his military superiors and had then supervised the mass evacuation of all persons of Japanese ancestry from the Pacific Coast, had been of the opinion that AJA soldiers should be used only in inland service commands and had recommended against their use in combat units. The commanding general of the Services of Supply, Brigadier General Raymond G. Moses, had felt that these citizens could be used with profit in either service or combat units not larger than a battalion in size, in either the European or African theaters. Lieutenant General Lesley J. McNair, commanding general of the Army Ground Forces, had recommended against their use. His attitude was based largely on the belief that their military employment might aggravate the existing public distrust of all persons of Japanese ancestry. Colonel Moses W. Pettigrew, chief, Far Eastern Group, G-2, WDGS, and Colonel Rufus S. Bratton, executive officer of the Intelligence Branch, G-2, WDGS, had expressed the opinion that the Army was passing up a considerable quantity of good manpower by its restrictive policy, and had recommended that the AJAs be used in combat units and combat theaters other than those where they would be required to fight Japanese. Pettigrew and Bratton thought that the great majority of second-generation Japanese citizens were loyal to the United States. A statement from the War Relocation Authority supported this judgment. Both Admiral Nimitz and General Emmons had believed that the AJAs should be used as combat troops. The G-2 Division of the War Department General Staff had strongly urged this policy. However, despite the preponderance of advisory opinion in favor of using the AJAs as combat troops, the G-3 board had adopted the views of De Witt and McNair.[7]

Between February, 1942 (when he had thought that 100,000 Hawaii Japanese should be evacuated to insure the removal of all disloyal individuals), and September of the same year, Emmons had obviously changed his mind. His intelligence chief, Col. Kendall J. Fielder, who had served in the same capacity under Short, had been convinced before the war that the overwhelming mass of Hawaii nisei were loyal. Their behavior during and since the Pearl Harbor bombing had strengthened his belief. They had taken over leadership of the Japanese community and had co-operated with the military in every possible way. He had heard many of them plead with tears in their eyes for a chance as soldiers to prove their loyalty. He had advised Emmons to accept the services of the Varsity Victory Volunteers and he knew how they had since behaved. He knew the record which the 100th Battalion was making at Camp McCoy. He thought that use of Hawaii AJAs in combat service would greatly strengthen the morale of the Japanese community, and was positive that as soldiers these men would perform in outstanding fashion to prove themselves and their folk loyal. By September, Fielder and Emmons were sure that it would be sound policy to allow their enlistment for combat duty in a special unit to fight in the European theater, and Fielder had supported such action in discussions with officers in the G-2 Division of the War Department General Staff.[8]

On October 2, Elmer Davis, director of the Office of War Information, wrote to President Roosevelt:

For both Mr. Eisenhower* and myself, I want to recommend that you take two actions designed to improve the morale of the American-citizen Japanese

* Milton S. Eisenhower, who had been the first director of the War Relocation Authority and was now associate director of the Office of War Information.

who were evacuated from the Pacific Coast. (1) Two bills in Congress—one aimed at depriving the nisei of citizenship and the other proposing to "intern" them for the duration of the war—have heightened the feeling that this may after all be a racial war and that, therefore, the evacuees should be looked upon as enemies. A brief public statement from you, in behalf of the loyal American citizens, would be helpful. I think WRA and the Justice Department would concur in this recommendation. (2) Loyal American citizens of Japanese descent should be permitted, after individual test, to enlist in the Army and Navy. It would hardly be fair to evacuate people and then impose normal draft procedures, but voluntary enlistment would help a lot.

This matter is of great interest to OWI. Japanese propaganda to the Philippines, Burma, and elsewhere insists that this is a racial war. We can combat this effectively with counter propaganda only if our deeds permit us to tell the truth. Moreover, as citizens ourselves who believe deeply in the things for which we fight, we cannot help but be disturbed by the insistent public misunderstanding of the Nisei; competent authorities, including Naval Intelligence people, say that fully 85 percent of the Nisei are loyal to this country and that it *is* possible to distinguish the sheep from the goats.

On October 13 Eisenhower wrote to John J. McCloy, assistant secretary of war. He described Davis' letter, and reported that the President had replied to Davis that he would be willing to allow citizens of Japanese descent to enlist in the Army for restricted duty. "I believe the President's thought was that at first the men would be assigned to functions not normally handled by soldiers and if everything went well they could later be assigned to more normal tasks." Eisenhower was, he wrote, giving McCloy this information for his own personal and confidential information "because, of course, if the President wishes to follow through in the matter he will speak directly to Secretary Stimson or yourself."

Two days later McCloy had Davis' letter on his desk. The President had sent it to Secretary of War Henry L. Stimson who had passed it on to McCloy with a request for comment. McCloy's answering memorandum, dated October 15, ran as follows:

I agree that a public statement on behalf of loyal Americans of Japanese descent from the President would be helpful.[9] I am firmly convinced that large numbers of them are loyal, and they are suffering because they are classed indiscriminately with the "goats."

I also believe that loyal American citizens of Japanese descent should be permitted, after individual test, to enlist in special units of the Army and the Navy. I believe the propaganda value of such a step would be great and I believe they would make good troops. We need not use them against members of their own race, but we could use them for many useful purposes. There is a current report by a board of officers which is adverse to these views. I have asked General McNarney* to hold it up pending an opportunity for me to express my views before final action is taken.

In short, I agree with both of Mr. Davis' suggestions as contained in his letter to the President.

After receiving McCloy's opinion, Secretary of War Stimson sent an informal note to General George C. Marshall, chief of the War Department General Staff: "I am inclined strongly to agree with the view of McCloy and Davis. I don't think you can permanently proscribe a lot of American citizens because of their racial origin. We have gone to the full limit in evacuating them—that's enough."

On November 4 Emmons received word that McCloy was personally interested in the formation of the largest possible AJA organization for combat duty in Europe and wanted recommendations on the matter from the Hawaiian Department. He replied the next day, "I hope project will receive approval as it will mean so much to this Territory. Am confident these men will give an excellent account of themselves in the European theater." On November 7 he was asked to provide data on the number of AJAs, by specified age groups, between the ages of eighteen and forty-five, the number registered with selective service, the number already examined and selected, the number now in military service within Hawaii, and the number currently furloughed to reserve status who might again be called up. He was also to estimate the total number of such soldiers obtainable by resumption of selective service and the number who might volunteer if enlistments were accepted. The project was confidential.

On November 11 Emmons received a query as to the number of selective service registrants married and in deferred status, also the number of AJA reserve officers then on active duty in his department. He replied that of the latter group three were on active duty, thirty-two remained uncalled. He also reported that all responsible agencies in the Hawaiian Department "joined in urging the desirability of the project, seeing in it, in addition to other values, the soundest possible move toward internal security." He believed that every possible effort should be made to fill whatever quota might be set, by a call for volunteers.[10]

* Lieutenant General Joseph T. McNarney, deputy chief of the War Department General Staff.

Six days later, in a memorandum which had been prepared at McCloy's request, Pettigrew presented these estimates and his own recommendations. Under the heading "General Advisability or Necessity for Such Unit" he wrote:

It is axiomatic that special units should be avoided wherever possible, since they admittedly raise special problems in organization and replacement. The Nisei, however, represent a special case. They have been indiscriminately lumped with their alien parents in the West Coast evacuation and have additionally been the subject of much discriminatory treatment within the United States Army. Their induction and enlistment was stopped March 31, 1942, and, with the exception of a small proportion having a special knowledge of the Japanese language and being used as interrogators and translators, even those already inducted, numbering 4,600, are not being used to their full military value. Our present treatment, therefore, represents almost a total waste of a very considerable and potentially valuable manpower. It further denies the whole Japanese population in America an opportunity to lay the groundwork for reacceptance into our American population after the war.

There were, Pettigrew thought, two ways to clear the situation. The Army could remove all present discriminatory measures and assign the nisei to units in the same manner as other Americans, or it could form them into a special combat unit.

The first alternative had a number of serious disadvantages. While these men were "perfectly willing to fight against the Japanese in the Pacific theater," their employment in that area would make it very simple for the enemy to infiltrate behind our lines in disguise. Another drawback lay in the existence of the West Coast evacuation zone from which the Japanese had been removed. Any military unit ordered into that area or beyond into the Pacific theater would have to have its nisei members pulled out at the last minute, with consequent detriment to the organization. Furthermore, their removal from the Pacific Coast had been accepted with good grace by the majority of the American-Japanese, and there was no point in reopening that question.

The second alternative eliminated these disadvantages, for a special unit could be trained outside the West Coast zone and earmarked for use in the European theater. Outweighing all other benefits, however, was the tremendous psychological advantage to be gained by the formation of such a unit.

This psychological value would obtain not only throughout the world, but upon our American population, and would unquestionably very greatly improve the post-war conditions of the entire Japanese-American population. From the morale standpoint, I am convinced that the unit itself would make such an effort to vindicate its people that at the end of its training it would have no superior in our entire Army as a combat unit. In substantiation of this opinion, General Emmons stated in reply to my initial request for population and conscription data that he hoped the project would receive approval, since it would mean so much to this Territory and that he was confident that these men would give an excellent account of themselves in the European theater.

Pettigrew cited figures which indicated that resumption of conscription would provide 16,800 nisei troops in addition to approximately 4,000 then in service. Emmons had estimated that Hawaii could provide 10,000 men, of whom probably 4,000 would volunteer. This pool of available manpower would be sufficient to provide and sustain an Army division, and would also take care of all future military interpreter needs. For morale purposes, voluntary enlistment should be permitted. Therefore, all existing restrictions against the conscription or voluntary enlistment of the nisei should be dropped, and Japanese aliens between the ages of eighteen and forty-five should also be allowed to volunteer. Fullest possible use should be made of the nisei reserve officers already in service, both those in the 100th Battalion and on the inactive list. Quotas should be filled by voluntary enlistment, in Hawaii for six weeks, on the Mainland for eight weeks, followed by resumption of conscription. Hawaii's tentative quota should be 7,500 men over and above those already in the Army.

On December 16, after having reviewed its September recommendations, the G-3 Division of the General Staff sent a memorandum to Chief of Staff General George C. Marshall:

From a military point of view the organization of special units composed of Nationals of another country or of American citizens who trace their ancestry to that country is undesirable. Nevertheless, in several cases other considerations have out-weighed purely military ones and such organizations have been formed, examples being the Austrian and Norwegian battalions and the two Filipino regiments. The considerations leading to the authorization of these units are present in no less degree in the case of citizens of Japanese ancestry. Actually, acceptance of these citizens into our Army might have a profound propaganda effect on certain other peoples who, at present, are more or less unfriendly to the cause of the United Nations, due to the Japanese allegation that this is a racial war. Considering the fighting qualities which enemy Japanese have demonstrated there is no reason to believe that combat units of a high degree of effectiveness could not be developed from loyal personnel of this class. In furtherance of this belief it is reasonable to assume that a particularly high degree of esprit and combativeness could be developed in such an organization due to the desire of the individuals therein to demonstrate their loyalty to the United States and to repudiate the ideologies of Japan.

This belief was based, however, on the assumption that the men who would compose such a unit or units would be completely loyal to the United States. "Since this is a matter which can best be determined by actual experience, the G-3 Division does not favor the organization initially of a unit as large as a division. Instead, it is believed that a combat team only should now be organized, this combat team being authorized a 15 per cent overstrength to provide loss replacements. Depending on experience gained with this unit later decision can be made as to organization of additional units."

The proposed team should consist of one regiment of infantry, one battalion of field artillery, and one company of engineers. It should be employed, as soon as its state of training warranted, in a theater where it would not be fighting Japanese troops. "This combat team shall be built around the 100th Infantry Battalion, Separate—now active—and shall be composed of American citizens of Japanese ancestry whose loyalty is unquestioned."

It was directed that notice of the decision be transmitted to the OWI so that it could be used for propaganda purposes.

The assistant chiefs of staff of G-1, G-2, and G-4 signed their approval of the G-3 recommendations, but the assistant chief of staff of the Operations Division gave consent only on condition that there should be "no interference or delay in the present project for use of the 100th Bn. in the Torch Theater [North Africa]." Because the G-3 Review Board had not known that the 100th was to be used in the Torch campaign then under way, and because the time required to organize and train the proposed combat team was uncertain, G-3 withdrew those recommendations which concerned the 100th so as not to interfere with existing plans. With this revision, and a proviso that the OWI postpone its propaganda until the combat team had reached an active front, the recommendations were approved by General Marshall on January 1, 1943.

Emmons received word of the decision on January 22. The new regiment was to be trained at Camp Shelby, Mississippi. Hawaii would provide 1,500 men, all in the general service classification, all able to speak English. Regimental, battalion, and company commanders would be Caucasians, but other officers, in so far as possible, would be of Japanese ancestry. Emmons asked that 635 AJA soldiers still on duty in Hawaii as service troops be allowed to enlist, but Washington replied that only lieutenants might be transferred to the combat team.

On January 28, Emmons publicly announced the War Department project and called for volunteers.

Once in a great while an opportunity presents itself to recognize an entire section of this community for their performance of duty. All of the people of the Hawaiian Islands have contributed generously to our war effort.

Among these have been the Americans of Japanese descent. Their role had not been an easy one.

Open to distrust because of their racial origin, and discriminated against in certain fields of the defense effort, they nevertheless have borne their burdens without complaint and have added materially to the strength of the Hawaiian area.

They have behaved themselves admirably under the most trying conditions, have bought great quantities of war bonds, and by the labor of their hands have added to the common defense.

Their representatives in the 100th infantry battalion, a combat unit now in training on the mainland; the Varsity Victory Volunteers, and other men of Japanese extraction in our armed forces have also established a fine record.

In view of these facts, and by War Department authority, I have been designated to offer the Americans of Japanese ancestry an additional opportunity to serve their country.

This opportunity is in the form of voluntary combat service in the armed forces.

I have been directed to induct 1,500 of them as volunteers into the Army of the United States. . . .

I am glad to make this statement to the Americans of Japanese extraction in the Hawaiian Islands. This call for volunteers affords an excellent opportunity to demonstrate the faith that the Army has in their loyalty and fighting qualities.

I believe that the response to this call will be sincere and generous and that it will have the hearty support of the parents concerned and of the community as a whole.

The manner of response and the record these men establish as fighting soldiers will be one of the best answers to those who question the loyalty of American citizens of Japanese ancestry in Hawaii.[11]

Within a week of this announcement 4,000 men signed certificates of intention to enlist. During the next few weeks 9,950 volunteered.

Emmons asked Washington for an increase in the Territory's quota and (for reasons to be explained later) was allowed to accept an additional 1,000 volunteers. He also received permission for 20 per cent of the Territory's quota to be made up of men currently on duty in the Islands in noncombat outfits. The Varsity Victory Volunteers were allowed to disband that they might enlist, and at the ceremonies which marked their inactivation, Army officers gave them warm praise for their patriotism and record of service. Emmons had been given permission to waive restrictions on the calling of AJA infantry reserve officers to active duty, and commissions were now given to fifteen of the VVVs who had completed ROTC training at the University of Hawaii and to five other AJAs. Of the *haole* officers who asked for service with the new unit two majors and three captains were accepted.

The volunteers were rigorously screened, and twenty-five officers and 2,855 enlisted men sailed for the Mainland on April 4. It had been ordered that the "mistakes" made at the time the Hawaiian Provisional Infantry Battalion sailed eleven months earlier were to be avoided at all costs, and in no case was the impression to be given that the men were under guard, even though they were traveling without arms.[12]

They arrived at Camp Shelby on April 13.

FOR A FEW DAYS after the 100th's return from the Louisiana maneuvers there was an old-home-week air about the section of Shelby where the AJA troops were quartered. Battalion "veterans" and the new arrivals from Hawaii fell on each other's backs with yelps of joy and then, more calmly, swapped tips on Army life for news from home.

Since February, when they had learned that an AJA regiment was to be formed, the soldiers of the 100th had been eagerly awaiting the arrival of the Hawaii volunteers. They had also been speculating that their own unit might serve as the trained core around which the 442d Infantry would be built. This hope was soon dashed. The Army put Mainland *haoles* into the more responsible posts in the new combat team, and most of the AJAs selected as noncommissioned officers were West Coast nisei who had been inducted before the war and had since been used as service troops at various inland camps. This development irritated the men of the 100th, especially those who had been dreaming of transfer to the 442d and promotion. It also angered the newly arrived volunteers from Hawaii, who willingly accepted the idea that Mainlanders were to be their top officers (this was probably inevitable), but strongly disliked taking orders from Coast AJAs.

There were a number of reasons for this attitude. For one thing, the Mainland AJAs usually spoke English more fluently than did the Islanders. Suddenly

Kotonks, Buddhaheads, Red Bulls

CHAPTER NINE

Hawaiian pidgin sounded crude. Also, the Coast AJAs' manners were more polished, and they were more knowledgeable about various aspects of Mainland life. These contrasts made the Hawaii AJAs seem, even to themselves, provincial, and they resented this feeling. They asked each other, if these guys were so damned Americanized, how was it there were at least two AJAs from Hawaii in the new regiment for every man from the Mainland.* Wasn't it because so few of the West Coast AJAs had volunteered that the Army had raised Hawaii's quota in order to fill up the new outfit?[1] And weren't the Mainland AJAs, who had practically all the noncom jobs, always "brown-nosing" the *haole* officers in hopes of promotion? They seemed to have a whipped-dog complex in relation to Caucasians, but at the same time seemed to nurse a deep and sullen resentment within. They didn't mix well; they kept to themselves; they were, one of the Hawaii men wrote, "never open, confident, or friendly, but hesitant, taciturn, quick to complain, critical behind backs, very ambitious for personal promotion. To their frustrated souls, military rank was a great healer of wounded pride." In contrast, the Islanders were "open, happy-go-lucky, frank, friendly" individuals, who "never tried to get ahead at another's expense."[2]

This analysis derived from lack of knowledge. Creatures of a more happy environment, the men from Hawaii had not spent their lives in an atmosphere of sweeping anti-Oriental prejudice. In the Territory, with its darker-skinned majority, color had not made them outcasts. The pidgin they spoke—and which the "coasters" ridiculed —was an amalgam of several tongues used by all Island people, not only the Japanese. Hawaii Japanese had not been brusquely pushed into what were in effect concentration camps, and her AJAs had entered military service from their homes, not, like most of the Mainland volunteers, from relocation centers. They had not been discharged from the Army and shoved into guarded camps, only to be told later that they could enlist in that same Army in order to fight democracy's battle. The Hawaii men had not had to steal away at night to enlist, as some of the Mainland volunteers had, in order to avoid retaliation from embittered fellow inmates of relocation camps. They had grown up in a land where a man of any race could

* The War Department had hoped to recruit at least 3,500 volunteers from among the AJAs in the various War Relocation Authority camps. The number recruited was approximately 1,200. For an explanation, see note 1.

walk like a man, in a more really "American" environment than the Coast AJAs had known.

This more fortunate experience showed in their general attitude toward life. Somewhat later two soldiers from the 100th visited an Idaho War Relocation center, and the editor of the camp's weekly news sheet wrote: "Their humor and happiness were contagious and all those who were fortunate enough to come in contact with these two young men were instantly infected with their joking and easygoing manner. . . . That special quality that all Hawaiian born Japanese seem to possess is enviable. They seem to take everything that comes their way with a smile. Nothing ever seems to bother them— as it does the mainlanders."[3]

Undoubtedly the Island men were less given to introversion, happier, more whole men than the West Coast AJAs, and they quickly sensed the fact. What they did not realize was that this was because fate had been kinder to them. They coined a name for the Coast nisei—"kotonk." Some claimed that it was in imitation of the noise made by the coal which these "yardbirds" had had to shovel as members of housekeeping detachments at Army posts; others said it was the sound made by their heads when Island boys knocked them together. The kotonks retaliated by calling the Hawaii men "buddhaheads." The Japanese word "*buta*" means pig, and "buddhahead" may be a corruption of "*buta* head," but it was generally thought that the term had been imported from Hawaii where it was applied to Japanese Buddhist priests who shaved their heads, and, by extension, to the Japanese residents generally. The antagonism and name-calling lasted some time.

Six months later a Hawaii volunteer wrote home that some of the Islanders in the 442d were disgusted with the way things were going. Kotonks "were still drifting in, slowing up everything," and there were still too many West Coast nisei noncoms in the regiment. But, he continued, it was not just the kotonks, nor the heat and chiggers and hard training that made the Hawaii boys lose fight. What they wanted and needed was "someone from Hawaii on top because they feel that otherwise they haven't got a damn soul to back them up— to understand their peculiar problems arising from a different social and cultural background." Some of his 442d friends had written him that they had been detailed to guard prisoners of war in Alabama where "the people treat them very well, which isn't like Mississippi."

As for himself, he wrote, "What I like about my change is the North*—the scenery, its people, its atmosphere so entirely different from the South—so much more intelligent, open, friendly and broad-minded. I still can't figure why they sent the gang [the 100th] down South when they had a nice place like McCoy."

There continued to be little incidents with the *haole* outfits at Shelby. "Funny how the McCoy gang kept out of trouble when they were down there. I guess those boys are older and know how to handle themselves better; also, having an old 'kamaaina' at their head, they must feel a greater loyalty and responsibility to their unit as a 100% Hawaii one and their conduct shows it."

Though he doubted that the 442d would ever have the 100th's kind of unity, he pictured the Island AJAs of his former outfit as "sweating it out," despite all the gripes, "from a sense of duty and loyalty to the cause for which they had volunteered," and as trying to pile up the highest training score in the Third Army. As far as training went, he doubted that any other unit could touch them, and he also thought that there was no question the 442d would show up well in combat.[4]

Discord between buddhaheads and kotonks gradually died out. Mainland and Island AJAs, living and working together, came to know each other as individuals, which led to better understanding and paved the way for respect and affection. Too, Hawaii soldiers who showed leadership qualities began to get their share of stripes. The name-calling which had begun in anger continued, but the spirit was one of friendly abuse. In fact the term "buddhahead" had been quickly adopted by both members of the 100th and other Islanders in the 442d as a means of self-identification. Its implication, they maintained, depended entirely on whether or not it was said with a smile.

It seemed to the 100th's officers that the Army could have avoided a great deal of morale trouble and delay in the 442d's training if some of the 100th's well-trained personnel had been used as part of the cadre of the new regiment. The older outfit could have supplied a number of good officers, for instance. At McCoy two men had been trained for every command post, and the jobs which would have been vacated by transfer to the regiment could have been filled im-

* He had recently been transferred from Shelby to the Camp Savage (Minnesota) Interpreters School.

mediately without much loss of battalion efficiency. Later some of the 100th's experts acted as advisers when the 442d started firing practice with automatic rifles and machine guns, and some platoons of the 100th demonstrated battle techniques, but there was no transfer of personnel.

At a review held on July 20 the 100th finally received its colors. While at McCoy the unit had decided that its motto should be "Remember Pearl Harbor," and that its shield should bear replicas of the *ape* leaf* and of the yellow feather helmet once worn by Hawaiian chieftains. These recommendations had been forwarded through proper channels, but some weeks later Turner had received official notice that the battalion motto was "Be of Good Cheer" and its emblem a red dagger. Turner, at one of his pep talks, said emphatically that no other unit had a better right to the Pearl Harbor slogan, that he saw no reason why the outfit couldn't have the insignia it wanted, and that as far as he was concerned the matter was not ended. When the colors were presented at Shelby they bore the design his men had requested.

During the latter part of July, three officers from the inspector general's staff visited the battalion, poked into every corner, and departed. They must have been satisfied—soon the camp was alive with preparations for overseas movement. During the next three weeks every soldier received a ten-day furlough. In groups of three and four, men headed for Madison, Chicago, New York, and other places north of the Mason-Dixon Line.

The directive that no AJA might command a rifle company was by this time no longer in effect, and Captains Taro Suzuki and Jack Mizuha commanded Companies B and D. Sixteen of the 100th's sixty commissioned officers were AJAs, and ten of these were first lieutenants. One day in August a sergeant received word that he was to go to officer candidate school—the first AJA from the 100th thus honored. That night the happy man and some his of buddies got gloriously drunk. However, the 100th received its departure orders the following day and the potential officer and gentleman was told that he would be needed with the battalion. As he nursed his hangover sympathetic friends assured him that he could still earn his commission—the hard way.

* Hawaiians often planted the *ape* by a gate or door or around the house to ward off evil spirits.

Volunteers from the 442d replaced six men rejected by the doctors. On learning that a dozen men had not yet signed up for Army insurance, Turner called them to headquarters. He discovered in each case that the soldier's parents were in Japan and that the son was not sure the United States would pay them his insurance money if he were killed. The Old Man talked to them on the theme "O ye of little faith," and the boys all signed the application forms.

During the last month at Shelby Turner was told that some of the higher brass were thinking of giving his men a distinctive kind of identification tag. He protested the idea and its implications, and his AJAs continued to wear the same kind as other American soldiers. Asked whether he would bank on the loyalty of all his men or would prefer to leave behind those few (mostly kibei) about whom G-2 still had some doubt, Turner said he would take them all.

"All right, we'll drop the cases. They're your responsibility now."

"Does that mean you'll destroy the dossiers you've prepared against these men?"

No assurance was given on that score, but there were no further loyalty investigations.

The battalion left Shelby on August 11 and reached Camp Kilmer, New Jersey, two days later. Embarkation orders came through at midnight August 20. An hour afterward the men filed into two trains which proceeded, shades drawn, to Brooklyn. At 5:00 A.M. they were ferried to Staten Island, where they entered the *James Parker*, a former banana and tourist boat now serving as troop ship. The convoy of which the *Parker* was part did not sail until dusk, and during the day AJAs lined the rail, gazing at Manhattan's skyline.

On this, their second ocean voyage, the enlisted men carried their primary weapons, packs, and two barracks bags, and the officers were allowed bedding rolls. The transport was packed with GIs of many units; its tiered bunks were kept warm by rotating shifts of sleepers and the troops ate only twice a day; but the sea was smooth. To fill the time there were card games, dice, singing, bull sessions, and movies for those willing to wait long enough in line. During the twelve-day voyage twelve battalion members received baptism as Christians.

Among the *Parker's* passengers were a general of the Field Artillery, his staff, and a battalion of his brigade. As the convoy neared the North African coast the general, whose artillerymen were unarmed, sent one of his officers to ask Turner if he could borrow the 100th's firearms in case the *Parker* came under air attack. "Under no circumstances," Turner replied. "If there's any shooting to be done we'll do it ourselves." The general, a German-born West Pointer, sent for Turner and when he appeared, ready for battle, told him, "I approve your stand." No enemy planes appeared, and on September 2 the convoy docked peacefully at Oran.

Debarkation took an hour, and then a motor convoy carried the battalion to a staging area on a rocky, arid mound near Fleurus, a few miles outside Oran. Previous GI occupants of this camp had dubbed it Goat Hill. Here, during the day, hot winds blew dust into tents, food, and rifles, and at night sand fleas feasted on foreign blood. The water supply from big collapsible Engineer Corps tanks was heavily chlorinated, unpleasant of taste, and so alkaline that even Army soap failed to produce suds. Soldiers who received passes for Oran switched from water to wine as soon as they left camp and even the nondrinkers found it more to their taste than the water at Goat Hill.

Much of the countryside between Fleurus and Oran was covered with wheat fields, citrus groves, and vineyards. The AJAs bought wine and watched it being made. They saw little native burros trudging along dusty roads under staggering loads; Arab masters and animals sharing the same gutters and odors as they took their siestas together; "shieks" wearing robes made of Army mattress covers, and trousers made of GI barracks bags with two holes where the legs went through. The villages were dirty and some sections of Oran filthy beyond description. "Chee, da smells!" There were, however, lots of pretty French girls with good complexions, and parts of Oran had beautiful modern buildings and were comparatively clean.

On the morning after they reached Goat Hill, Turner and Lovell jeeped into Oran to Mediterranean Base Section Headquarters. A colonel who had been with the 25th Division on Oahu before the war greeted them jovially. He didn't know what their orders were but he knew of a job they could have. Supply trains coming from Casablanca to Oran were being raided along the way by Arabs, and Uncle Sam was losing a lot of material. The 100th could patrol the route and do battle with these pilfering sons of the desert. "You don't want the job?" he asked. "But somebody's got to do it! It's good fun. Nobody gets hurt but the Arabs, and if you shoot one of them his wife gets fifty bucks and everybody's happy." As they were leaving headquarters, however, a limousine drew up and a three-star general stepped out. He told them that the 100th was slated for combat duty with the Fifth Army, and that they would receive further word at their camp.

Next day a messenger came out to Goat Hill with orders that the 100th's commander report to Fifth Army Headquarters at Mastaganuna, fifty miles away. There Turner learned that his battalion was to join the 34th Division.

This was good news. The 34th was a real fighting team. A National Guard outfit, built from Iowa, Minnesota, Nebraska, and North and South Dakota elements, it had been the first American division sent to Europe after the war started. After training in Northern Ireland the Red Bulls (so named because of their shoulder patch) had taken part in the invasion of North Africa, and had taken a mauling at Kasserine Pass where the 168th Regiment had been nearly destroyed, but had later stormed Hill 609, a crucial and strongly defended bastion in the German defenses before Tunis. After that city had surrendered, the 34th had been sent 900 miles west to the vicinity of Oran, where it was now going through intensive combat training. In the fighting so far the division's total casualties, killed, wounded, and missing, were 4,254, more than one-third of its original strength.

Back at Goat Hill word of the new attachment was passed down to the men and no one doubted any longer that the battalion would see battle. Next morning Turner, Lovell, and plans and training officer Captain Jack Johnson drove to the headquarters of the 34th, encamped in a sprawling cork forest a few miles outside Oran. Its commander asked Turner, "Do you think you can trust them to fight?"

"Absolutely."

"Good. That's all I want to know."

Major General Charles W. Ryder, the officer who asked the question, was a West Pointer, and a veteran of the first World War. After the early reverses his men had suffered he had given them the motto, "Attack, attack, attack." At this time he was driving them through practice in the lessons learned from previous mistakes, the running of obstacle courses designed by British commandos, and preparation for amphibious landings. He told Turner that the 100th would take the place of the 133d Regiment's 2d Battalion, which was acting as special military guard at General Eisenhower's headquarters in Algiers.

Two days later trucks moved the 100th into the 34th's hundred-acre bivouac. In a memorandum sent to commanders of all his units General Ryder prepared them for the battalion's coming, and on the eve of its arrival the commander of the 133d Infantry, Colonel Ray C. Fountain, called his officers together to tell them about the AJA soldiers. "They are not Japanese, but Americans born in Hawaii. They aren't asking for any special consideration and we won't give them anything that isn't given all the other units. They'll be in there taking their turn with all the rest. And tell your men not to call them Japs, or there'll be trouble."

The staff sergeant then serving as battalion historian wrote of the welcome his outfit received: "Colonel Fountain, offering another amiable gesture, turned out the band to greet the travel-worn men, delivering afterwards a cheery welcome, and at last the 100th felt it was coming to its terminal in wanderings. By nightfall fraternal soldiers from the regiment drifted over into the 100th's area and took up the singing of Hawaiian songs with the men and were soon sharing the same bottles of wine. Here was the beginning of a sacred friendship."

A few days later General Ryder asked that the battalion officers be called together; he wanted to talk to them. He told his audience, sixty commissioned and forty noncommissioned officers, what able and tricky fighters the Germans were, what counter-tactics his men had learned, and how he expected his listeners to lead their men. "You'll see your buddies hurt and killed, and maybe you'll get it next, but you'll keep on fighting. No matter what happens—your battalion may be blasted to company size, and your company to a platoon—you'll fill the place of the man that's hit, and you'll keep on fighting." Their unit would get fair play and the same kind of assignments as the others, no more, no less, and he would back it up to the best of his ability. Of course, no new combat outfit ever amounted to much until after its first victory, and he would try to see that they had a fair chance to win an initial success—"and if you do, and that's up to you, you should have no trouble from then on."

This session was good for morale. Ryder seemed to be talking as he would to any new unit; he hadn't preached; and it had sounded as though he thought the 100th would perform well.

Nine new second lieutenants now joined the battalion. Selective service men, just out of officer candidate schools, they came from one of the replacement centers near Oran. Turner had gone over the roster of available officers and had narrowed the list of those whom he would take to twelve. These he had interviewed, telling them just what they'd be getting into, and that he didn't want them unless they really wanted to join his outfit. Three said they would rather lead white troops; the others said they'd be glad to be part of the 100th. Most of them turned out to be, according to Turner, "damned good officers." The 100th became *their* outfit, and they grew fond of their buddhaheads.

Veterans of the Tunisian campaign now conducted schools for each company of the 100th, explained Jerry's bag of tricks, and passed on the lessons gained from hard experience.

When the coach of the 133d's baseball team learned that the 100th had some good players, he borrowed a pitcher, a catcher, a first baseman, and an outfielder, and with their aid his squad beat the 168th Infantry's nine, from which it had recently taken a shellacking. But his glory was short-lived. A battalion team, made up of the same loaned stars and other graduates of Hawaiian baseball diamonds, soon afterward smothered the 133d's team, 26–0.

There was little time for games, however. General Ryder had intimated that the 100th would soon see action, and on September 19 the regiment moved to Oran for shipment to Italy.

SIXTEEN DAYS before the 133d moved to Oran the British Eighth Army had invaded the Italian peninsula, and on 9 September, 1943, the Allied Fifth Army (composed of the British 10 Corps and the American VI Corps) had made an amphibious assault on the beaches of the Gulf of Salerno, south of Naples. (See campaign map, p. 124.) The Fifth Army landing was intended to secure the Salerno plain as a jumping-off place for a swing northwest to seize Naples, whose fine harbor and airfields would make it a good base for further offensive operations. Allied troops moving east from Salerno might also be able to cut off German units being pushed north by the Eighth Army.

For a time it had looked as though the Fifth Army forces might be thrown back into the sea, but their line had held, and on 15 September the Germans had gone on the defensive, making only minor jabs at the beachhead, where Fifth Army was rapidly consolidating its positions and receiving reinforcements of men and supplies.

The German strategy now planned stubborn resistance before the 10 Corps, on the Allied left, nearest Naples, to allow time to wreck the city's port installations and protect a withdrawal to the north. Delaying action before any eastward drive by the VI Corps would keep open an avenue of escape for German troops being pushed north by the Eighth Army. An orderly general withdrawal would end with the Wehrmacht's forces in position along the line of the

Mud and Blood

CHAPTER TEN

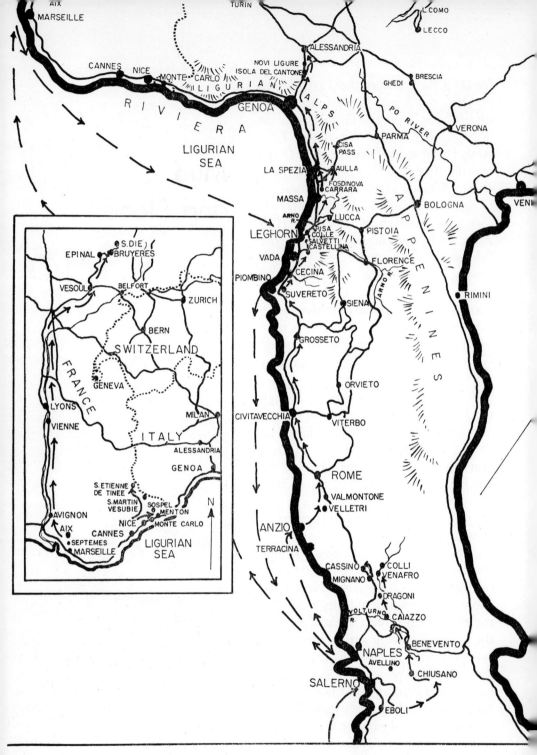

ROUTE OF CAMPAIGN, ITALY AND FRANCE

Volturno River, western section of a barrier of strong defenses which stretched across the whole of the Italian peninsula.[1]

It had been planned originally that the 34th Division would join the Fifth Army at Naples twenty-one days after the initial landings at Salerno. Fierce German resistance had changed the Allied time table, however, and the division left Oran for the beachhead on 19 September. The 100th traveled in the S. S. *Frederick Funston*, one of four ships assigned to the 133d Regiment and its equipment.

Friendly planes covered the last part of the journey and were over-head at 8:00 A.M. on 22 September as the transports reached their stations off the beachhead. Two hours later men began going down rope ladders into landing barges. Once on shore they climbed along tape-marked paths to higher ground. Looking back they could see barges and ducks shuttling between ships and shore, countless jeeps, trucks, and antitank guns and howitzers emerging from the yawning bows of the landing craft, all to the tune of roaring motors, shouted commands, and explosions, as demolition crews blew up wrecked equipment. No enemy shells fell in the landing area. That night one AJA wrote, "I never saw such efficiency in my life. Power of American Army at work. Wish I had a camera—a sight I'll never forget. This convinced me that a nation like ours can't be beaten in the war."[2]

The battalion's "extra" companies, E and F, were assigned guard duty in the beach area, E at an ammunition dump, F at a temporary airstrip which had been leveled off for use by P-40s. The other com-panies marched off the dunes via more taped paths onto hot dusty roads. A six-mile hike brought them to a bivouac area.

The big Allied push out of the Salerno plain began the next day, the 23rd. Two days later the 34th Division entered the chase after the Germans, now in retreat, and the 133d Infantry received orders to truck twenty-five miles east to the vicinity of Montecorvino-Rovella. (See map, p. 126.) As the regiment moved into action this message was being sent to officers of all Fifth Army units: "There has recently arrived in this theater a battalion of American soldiers of Japanese ancestry. These troops take particular pride in their American origin. Your command should be so informed in order that during the stress and confusion of combat, cases of mistaken identity may be avoided."

At Montecorvino the 133d received orders to move to the vicinity of Oliveto Citra in the 45th Division sector on the right flank of the Fifth Army line. It would operate as a combat team under personal

SALERNO TO S. ANGELO D'ALIFE

direction of General Ryder, commander of the 34th Division, and would proceed north and west to cut the main road leading from Avellino to Benevento, key road center on the route of enemy retreat to the Volturno River line. The 3d Division would simultaneously drive northeast against Avellino. On the 133d's right the 45th Division would guard the Fifth Army's flank and maintain contact with the British Eighth Army.

The 133d would first secure the road west from Montemarano to Avellino and would be prepared, if necessary, to assist in the capture of the latter town. It would then proceed northwest to cut the Avellino-Benevento road, along which the Germans would be attempting retreat.

On the night of 26 September the 100th moved 106 miles by truck on the narrow mountainous Contursi-Teora-Lioni-S. Angelo road to a point about ten miles past Lioni. Here it left the main highway for a secondary route which curved first southwest, then northwest, to meet the S. Angelo-Montemarano road. The autumn rains had begun, and that night, for the first time, the men slept surrounded by Italian mud.

Next morning, on the S. Angelo-Montemarano road, the 100th waded the Calore River at a place where a bridge had been blown. The men pushed ahead on foot; their transport would come up when a temporary bridge had been built. Occasional shells fell along the road but they met no Germans. As pioneers moved ahead to spot and clear mines they found some already marked by Italian civilians. In bivouac that night on the eastern outskirts of Montemarano most of the men slept in pup tents, the luckier soldiers in farmhouses and stables. It was still raining.

Next morning an Italian civilian reported that a German soldier who had been hiding in a nearby farmhouse wished to surrender. A squad from Company B brought him in, the battalion's first prisoner. He could speak a little English, and said that his mother was Irish, and his father had lived for a time in London. He asked if his captors were Chinese. Informed that they were Japanese, he registered some confusion. Had Japan, like Italy, betrayed the Fuehrer?

The battalion remained in Montemarano all day. Here a squad leader became the unit's first casualty—a passing jeep exploded a land mine and one of the fragments gave him a slight face wound.

During the afternoon the trucks again appeared. There was a terrific downpour during the night and it was still raining at 6:00 o'clock next morning as the vehicles churned forward through the mud. Bolstered by a regimental antitank platoon, the 100th was now to act as advance guard for the Combat Team.

Company B led off, out of Montemarano, off the Avellino road, and along a secondary route north through the village of Castelvetere toward high ground around Chiusano. At about 10:00 A.M., as the 3d Platoon turned a bend in the road, three German machine guns opened up, and mortar and artillery shells began to fall around the "zeroed in" road curve. Sergeant Shigeo (Joe) Takata said, "It's the first time, so I'm going first." Spotting one of the Jerry nests, he walked toward it, firing his automatic rifle. A piece of shrapnel caught him in the head. Dying, he managed to tell one of his men, who had crawled close, where the German gunners were. Before the enemy pocket was silenced another soldier had died and seven more had been wounded. The 100th had its first hero and its first claim for Purple Heart awards.

Around noon there was another check at another demolished bridge. As usual, enemy artillery had the crossing place and its neighborhood zeroed in, but despite the occasional shells thrown into the area there were no casualties. Again the trucks had to wait and again the riflemen got out and walked.

These two halts within two hours gave the men a taste of the Germans' withdrawal tactics. As their main forces moved north in good order they left behind small groups of motorized infantry supported by roving self-propelled cannon. These rear-guard fighters concentrated sudden resistance at points where they could hold the Americans back with least danger to themselves, dealt as many casualties as possible, and then ran back to their troop carriers to be driven to other favorable defensive sites. Enemy artillery kept a bead on the mined roads and destroyed bridges which the retreating army left in its wake. All the way to the Volturno American advance elements could hear the roar of German demolition charges. Mines were sown wherever the pursuing troops might attempt to build bypasses and, where the terrain made it impossible to do anything else, American engineers had to push Bailey bridges across the old abutments.

In midafternoon, after passing a junction with a road which led northeast from Chiusano, the 100th received orders to move quickly cross-country toward that town, now only about two miles away. A small mechanized enemy force retreating before the 3d Division would probably try to use a road leading north from a junction on Chiusano's western outskirts. Hurrying to get across the road first, the battalion experienced the heaviest artillery fire so far. There were a number of casualties, and the medical aid men had a chance to show their mettle. By 7:00 P.M., despite the shells, elements of the battalion were on high ground covering the junction.

Most of the enemy fire had been coming from the direction of Montefalcione, about three miles north of Chiusano. Company A was left to guard the Chiusano junction, and the other units moved up the road which ran northeast from the town. After traveling a half mile the column left the road and climbed down into a valley. At its broader end to the northwest, on a road which the Germans might use in retreat, lay Montefalcione. It was pitch dark as the men moved silently up the valley, walking over vegetable patches and groping through grapevine trellises. Dogs challenged their coming, but no mines went off and there was no enemy fire. By midnight the battalion entered the outskirts of the village without opposition, and found that the enemy had cleared out. At dawn a private on outpost duty spotted three hostile armored reconnaissance cars moving up the road from the south. Using a rifle grenade, he damaged the lead vehicle with his first shot, and all three cars turned and fled the way they had come.

In the morning, as the 100th rested in the little stone hamlet, the 1st Battalion moved through on its way to establish a roadblock at Pratola. The 3d followed, heading for Highway No. 7, which it would cut about three miles northwest of Montemiletto. Though held up for a while before Pratola by fire from enemy half-tracks, the 1st managed to push through and to set up its roadblock, helped by pressure on the north from the 3d, which moved quickly through Montemiletto and then up the La Serra-Montefusco road toward Benevento.

At about 1:00 P.M. the next day, 1 October, the 100th moved from Montefalcione to follow the 3d Battalion, and reached Montemiletto that evening. Patrols were unable to establish contact with the 3d. It rained all night and was still pouring when the 100th pushed off again the next afternoon. After crossing Highway 7 above Montemiletto and moving northwest along minor roads, the battalion entered Highway No. 7 again at S. Giorgio. Orders were to move ahead on that road on the right flank of the regiment's advance towards Benevento.

The rest of the twenty-mile march was made in darkness, through mud and cold windy rain. Bridges were down; the road was pocked with mine and shell holes; and the machine-gun and mortar men had to hand-carry their weapons and ammunition. A platoon of the 45th Reconnaissance Troop had entered Benevento during the day and had reported the city empty of Germans, who had moved north across the Calore River, but enemy artillery in the hills north of that stream still pounded at road junctions and stream crossings, and the gunners seemed to know every bend on the approach roads. Shells fell on and to the sides of Highway 7 but no one in the 100th was hit.

Things were not going so well for the 3d Battalion, on the left. Shortly before midnight, just outside Benevento, Company K reported a good many of its men wounded. A little later, as one of K's platoons reached a street corner on the outskirts, a shell exploded in the midst of a group of soldiers huddled under an awning and almost simultaneously another fell only a few yards away. The two bursts killed eleven and wounded twenty-two.

Exhausted from hours of slogging through and diving into mud, the men of the 100th passed through rubble-filled Benevento at about 1:00 A.M. Lovell led the column in single file, through alleyways across the city's southwest edge and out again. Crossing tobacco fields and small creeks, then the Montesarchio road, then a railroad farther west, the battalion finally halted and took up positions on two 200-foot hills which lay in the angle between the railroad and the Calore River. From this position the unit could protect the regiment's left flank and provide supporting fire for the 3d Battalion, which had orders to cross the Calore north of the city and establish a bridgehead on the north bank. The 1st Battalion was to take position southeast of Benevento, on the right flank.

Turner did not reach the hills until daybreak. He had been with transportation, which was supposed to reach the objective first, but had been delayed by a blown bridge. After meeting casualties of the 3d Battalion outside Benevento, he had been worried about his own boys, but had been reassured after talking with Lovell by radio.

Too badly disorganized to make the intended dawn crossing, the 3d Battalion did not reach the Calore's north bank until afternoon.

Engineers began setting up a Bailey bridge to replace the old arch, destroyed by the enemy. Shellfire held up their work but the next day, 4 October, troops of the 45th Division moved in from the right flank of the Fifth Army, crossed the new span, and took over.

The 34th Division now went into assembly areas, and the 133d Regiment camped about ten miles southwest of Benevento near S. Martino. Since Salerno the 100th had lost three men killed, twenty-three wounded. Thirteen had been injured in accidents—five when a medical section jeep turned over on the way to Benevento. Though the weather was clear at S. Martino it began to rain again on 7 October as the battalion trucked north to bivouac at Montesarchio.

After eight days here ("Filthy town. Human *kukai* all over the street. One has to weave around.") the unit moved through Airola and S. Agata into Bagnoli. As the column went through Airola children threw apples to the men in the trucks and adults happily shrieked, "Chinee? Chinee?" At Bagnoli, where Companies E and F rejoined the outfit, a hundred copies of the 34th's news bulletin were distributed. The bulletin contained a report from General Mark W. Clark, Fifth Army commander, to General Dwight Eisenhower, commander of all American forces in Europe, in which the 100th was given a pat on the back for its behavior in the advance from Montemarano to Montefalcione.* This was good for morale. "Though glum

---

* On 26 October, Washington headquarters of the Army Ground Forces sent a letter to the commanding generals of the 2d, 3d, and 4th Armies, and the 4th, 13th, and 18th Corps, all in the United States. This message quoted a War Department memorandum on the 100th's behavior in its first battle test, and asked that the content thereof be made known to all military personnel in units or installations to which AJA soldiers were assigned. The following quotation is from this letter: "A strong desire to be with their unit as it entered combat reduced absences due to sickness and hospitalization almost to zero. While the Japanese-American battalion was acting as the advance guard for a regimental combat team, the battalion advanced approximately fifteen miles in twenty-four hours, operating day and night in the face of strong enemy resistance and over difficult terrain. Although suffering casualties their advance continued on schedule. All of its weapons were used with complete assurance. A Japanese-American Sergeant who lost his life in this action has been recommended for the Distinguished Service Cross." A copy also came to 100th Battalion Headquarters.

In connection with the Volturno fighting, General Clark later wrote: "I should mention that a bright spot in this period was the performance of the 100th Battalion, which had recently been assigned to the 34th Division. . . .

"On the march to the Volturno, which was their first time in combat, they acted as an advance guard for a regimental combat team and covered a distance of almost twenty miles in twenty-four hours, despite the extreme difficulties of the mountain road. I sent a cable to Eisenhower on October 8, stating that they had seized their objective and that they were quick to react whenever the enemy offered opposition." *Calculated Risk* (New York, 1950), p. 220.

of the weather and with the fresh and bitter taste of battle within them the men's spirits were alleviated by the note of appreciation," wrote the battalion historian. During this period General Ryder gave his AJA troops another token of acceptance and esteem—the Red Bull shoulder patch.

On 15 October, the 133d remained in reserve while the 135th and 168th pushed across the Volturno River at Limatola, south of Caiazzo. As the 34th Division moved northwest it would again have to cross this stream where it looped back across the path of advance. The 133d was assigned the middle sector of the second crossing, in which the 168th would attack against Dragoni on the south side of the river, the 135th, on the right, would cross the Volturno to take Alife on the north side, and the 133d would attack north and northwest to secure a bridgehead on the Dragoni-Alife road. (See map, p. 133.)

By midafternoon, 18 October, the 133d Regiment had made its first crossing of the Volturno south of Caiazzo and was advancing under intermittent artillery fire to take part in the division's second crossing. When the regiment reached the Volturno its 1st Battalion would make a fording on the right and then move west along the north bank; the 100th would follow to the left rear of the 1st and take position on the south bank; and the 3d would move last and farther west, maintaining contact below the river with the 168th Regiment.

The 1st Battalion missed the road and waded the Volturno about two miles downstream of the intended crossing under smoke cover from its own mortars. It pushed rapidly northwest along the north bank toward the bridge on the Dragoni-Alife road. Division Headquarters sent a message that the 1st must capture the span before the Germans could destroy it, but when the battalion was only a mile away the bridge was blown.

After passing Alvignano late in the afternoon the 100th left the main road and moved directly north toward the Volturno, sometimes on secondary roads, sometimes cross-country through vineyards and orchards and over creeks. It was well after dark when the column reached the river and began to move west along its south bank. The Jerries were sending over sporadic mortar and small-arms fire. At dawn the battalion was dug in along the Dragoni-Alife road, south of the ruined bridge. The 3d Battalion met heavier resistance near Dragoni, but by dawn had taken positions along a railroad track a mile east of the town. During the 19th all units remained in place. Some "friendly" mortar shells fell in the 100th's area and, though no one was hurt, there was plenty of cursing.

Shortly after midnight, the 100th waded the chill, waist-deep river. The 3d Battalion also crossed during the night, bringing all regimental elements to the north bank. The next day was used in making ready for a night attack against S. Angelo D'Alife, seven miles northwest on one of the foothills of the Matese range. Patrols reported that the valley through which the regiment would have to advance was heavily mined and laced with machine-gun positions manned by troops of the tough 29th Panzer Grenadier Regiment. These Jerries made reconnaissance so difficult that some patrols, pinned down by fire, had to call for mortar fire and smoke shells to cover their withdrawal.

Colonel Ray Fountain, the 133d's commander, told his officers to expect heavy resistance. German artillery had

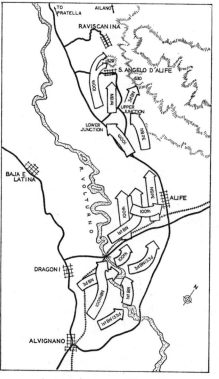

ALVIGNANO TO HILL 529

excellent observation overlooking the valley, and battalion leaders must get their troops out of the flats and to the less exposed slopes of the foothills before daylight. If a battalion were stopped it should move to the right, away from the river, toward this higher ground. The attack would be in column of battalions, the 100th leading, the 1st coming abreast later, and the 3d in reserve. The 100th would seize the upper road junction 1,000 yards east of S. Angelo; the 1st would take the lower. The 135th Infantry would be attacking on the right through Alife. There would be no rolling barrage, but the artillery would fire concentrations on request.

Company A led off in the dark at about 7:00 P.M. As the men advanced through grape trellises and vegetable gardens, or following the walls of irrigation canals, only occasional enemy shells fell in the area of attack. At about 10:30, as scouts approached one of several farmhouses along the valley floor, a door opened, and light shone forth. Moments later German machine guns opened up a constant rattle. Within a few minutes ten men of Company A were dead and about twenty had been wounded. The flats were covered with a horizontal rain of bullets, the tracers showing how neatly the enemy had interlocked his fields of fire. To continue to advance would be suicide. The greatest safety lay behind or in some kind of hummock or hollow, though these gave little protection against the mortar and artillery shells which plastered the area.

Turner ordered his men to find what cover they could, directed his mortars to try to silence the Jerry gun nests, and sent runners back to ask for support. Some men of Company A managed to get within a few yards of German machine guns before being hit, but most of that night's notable deeds occurred as men tried to fight their way back to safety. Using an automatic rifle to cover his squad's withdrawal, Pfc Thomas Yamanaga silenced an enemy gun, died firing, and so won the battalion's second Distinguished Service Cross. Lieutenant James Vaughn crawled around to encourage his men, then wriggled to the rear to ask for fire support. Ordered to return and move his platoon back, though wounded himself, he covered their withdrawal with his carbine. Private Tad Shikiya, who left his own hole to drag a moaning buddy to safety, died in the attempt. Moving around on his stomach, Private Satoshi Kadota, a medic, treated twelve casualties. Corporal Donald Hayashi took over a squad when his sergeant was wounded, gave first aid, and, for nearly two hours, covered his men's retreat single-handed. These and similar actions earned Silver Star awards.

When Turner reached the regimental command post and reported his battalion's situation, Colonel Fountain told him to pull his men back; the 1st Battalion would take over the attack. Turner protested; he had sent a platoon off to the left to envelope the German fire; if this lifted the pressure his men would advance again. No, said Fountain, he was to get his men out. Turner went back to see to it. The 1st Battalion now moved forward, angling to the right of the 100th, a bit nearer the hills. It, too, got pasted, and had to dig for cover. Meanwhile those elements of the 100th which could move back did so and angled to the right, behind the 1st Battalion, toward Alife.

By dawn Companies A and B had passed through the western outskirts of Alife, which the 135th Regiment had occupied, and were in bivouac around a cemetery near the road leading northwest from that town toward S. Angelo. They were now behind the 3d Battalion, which was farther north on the road, where German resistance had not been so strong.

When the early morning mists lifted, the 1st Battalion was still out in the most exposed part of the valley. Under enemy counter-attack it was now forced back toward the vicinity of the Dragoni-Alife bridge. During the afternoon Company C of the 100th moved up the road past Alife to rejoin A and B. The rest of the day was spent in reorganization and preparation for an attack to be made the next morning.

In the early hours of 22 October, the 3d and 100th Battalions pushed off again, the 3d heading for the upper road junction, the 100th for the lower. By nightfall neither unit had reached its objective, and the men of both were scattered along the valley slopes. This was the day soldiers of the 100th first heard the marrow-freezing moan of shells from the six-barreled electrically fired German rocket guns, the Nebelwerfers or "screaming-meemies." Eleven enemy tanks roamed directly ahead and on the left flank along the river bank. A bazooka shot, fired by a member of the 100th, destroyed one of these Mark II's, and a Piper Cub, circling the area during the afternoon, helped division artillery smash another tank and cripple four more, but the rest were still making trouble when night came. After dark the 3d and the 100th moved onto higher ground, and by early morning had secured both road junctions. Major Lovell was hit by a Nebelwerfer fragment as he led a patrol, and was sent to the rear for hospitalization.

The next day the 3d Battalion moved up the terraced sides of Hill 630, behind and northeast of S. Angelo, and the 100th pushed westward in front of the town, intending to flank it by an attack on Hill 529 to its northwest. By night the 3d was in possession of Hill 630, but the 100th had not yet reached 529.

At dawn, 24 October, the 1st Battalion, reorganized and rested, moved without resistance through the narrow streets of S. Angelo, from which the Germans had pulled back into ridges directly to the north. At the same time Companies A and C of the 100th attacked frontally against Hill 529, on whose bare cone-shaped tip stood the ruins of an old castle. A low mist made enemy artillery ineffective, but there were stubborn knots of Jerries on the forward slopes. Little progress was made during the day. When darkness came Turner sent Companies E and F to relieve A and C. In the morning the new units moved northwest, avoiding further frontal attack, to get around behind "Castle Hill," and the 1st Battalion moved from S. Angelo to flank it from the northeast. In midmorning the Jerries made their last sally, but this was repulsed with the aid of 200 rounds from the 100th's 81-mm. mortars. By noon the Germans, in danger of being pocketed, began moving down Hill 529 and into the ridges northwest of Raviscanina. The 135th Infantry now prepared to push through the 133d to take up the pursuit.

S. Angelo and its commanding heights had been secured, but it had taken five days to move seven miles north of the Dragoni-Alife bridge. Along the valley and its surrounding ridges the enemy's machine guns had fired from strongly built, cleverly concealed pillboxes. Stone walls and stone farmhouses had given the Jerry riflemen protection, and German observers had directed accurate artillery and tank fire from the hills above. Troop carriers, some of them big enough for thirty men, had shuttled back and forth, placing soldiers where needed. Some areas had been sown with mines, and booby traps had lurked in grape arbors, farmhouses, and abandoned gun positions. The 133d counted 59 men killed and 148 wounded as a result of this action. Twenty-one members of the 100th were dead, sixty-seven had been wounded, and four second lieutenants and a major had been hospitalized.

As he prepared to pursue the Germans, the commander of the 135th Regiment asked Turner for a reconnaissance report on enemy dispositions along the Alife-Pratella road. Turner sent out a patrol, and the lieutenant in command returned with a report that there were no enemy troops along the highway, but when the 3d Battalion of the 135th moved up the road that night, it ran into enemy fire and lost four men. A patrol from Company C of the 100th, detailed to guide the 135th's 2d Battalion to its line of departure for an attack toward Ailano, lost its way in the darkness, and when dawn came on 26 October, the 2d found itself several hundred yards north of its intended jumping-off-place. When the early morning fog lifted, that unit was immediately pinned down by enemy rifle and machine-gun fire. These incidents were reported to division headquarters, and also a complaint that the 100th's vehicles had been so scattered along the highway that they had delayed the 135th's night advance.

From 25 to 31 October, the 133d was in divisional reserve, and the 100th remained near S. Angelo. The field kitchen came up and there were hot meals; some supplies which had been left behind in North Africa arrived; and the men could now bathe and scrub off a two-week accumulation of mud. When a stray enemy shell whistled low over his head, an English war correspondent managed to get into a hole faster than the battalion officers he had been interviewing. A wounded German prisoner who was being treated by Doc Kawasaki was much puzzled when the battalion surgeon denied Chinese ancestry. The man's eyes bulged. "Tokyo?" he gasped.

On this, as on other similar occasions, the AJAs sometimes took grim pleasure in letting captured representatives of the "master race" guess their nationality—at times they jokingly assured their befuddled prisoners that Japan had joined Germany's enemies. It was, indeed, often easier to convince them of this than of the truth—that these soldiers with Japanese faces were American citizens. When that fact finally did dawn on some of the Jerries, they shook their heads in perplexity. "Ach, diese Amerikaner!"

During this period Turner was ordered to a hospital for rest. His superiors probably felt that an infantry battalion needed a younger, tougher officer who might be more ready to see his men shot up. The Old Man going? It was hard for the men to believe. Had they let him down during this last action? And Lovell, the officer who after Turner they would most willingly have followed, was in a hospital wounded. Turner called his boys together for a last talk. He was lucky, he told them, headed for a nice soft bed and then probably for the States. He knew they would give his successor the same loyal support they had given him. "God bless you," he said, and there were tears in many eyes.

After he had gone his successor, Major James J. Gillespie, called the officers together. Gillespie had been transferred to the 100th from the regiment's 3d Battalion where he had been executive officer. He knew how the men felt about Turner, and could guess what they were thinking. "Look," he said, "I was happy with my own outfit and I didn't ask for this job. I'm sorry you guys have lost your Pop, but believe me, before you're through you're going to lose more than one commander. Let's work together and make the best of it."

A graduate from the ranks, Gillespie was a good officer as well as a straight talker, a cool, quick-thinking tactician in battle, and a leader who deserved respect and confidence. He was also a good prophet—one month after he joined the battalion he, too, went to the hospital.

THE LAST DAY of October, 1943, the 1st and 3d battalions climbed over steep brush-covered ridges to attack and occupy Ciorlano and the high ground north and northwest of that village. (See map, p. 140.) The 100th followed in reserve. Shortly after dawn of the next day six hedge-hopping Messerschmidts strafed Companies A and C as they toiled across the hills, and twelve men were hit. Also hurt was a soldier who had been reading a comic book in what he thought was a safe hole—he received a foot wound from a fragment of an American antiaircraft shell. During the approach march, enemy shrapnel killed six men and wounded nine.

By noon, 1 November, the 1st and 3d battalions had occupied Ciorlano and the nearby heights overlooking the Volturno, and were moving down into its valley. During the day the 168th Regiment moved into Capriati. The 34th Division faced another river crossing.

In this area the Volturno was no great obstacle. It flowed through willow-clumped little islands at a depth seldom over two feet, and its waters spread no more than 800 feet at the widest point. The valley, covered with grain fields, vineyards, olive groves, and orchards, was less then two miles in width at Roccaravindola, on the right of the division's sector, and broadened to only five miles before Venafro, on the left. Once the Americans had crossed this level terrain, however, they would have to advance into bald and rugged mountains along whose crests the enemy had

Into the Hills

CHAPTER ELEVEN

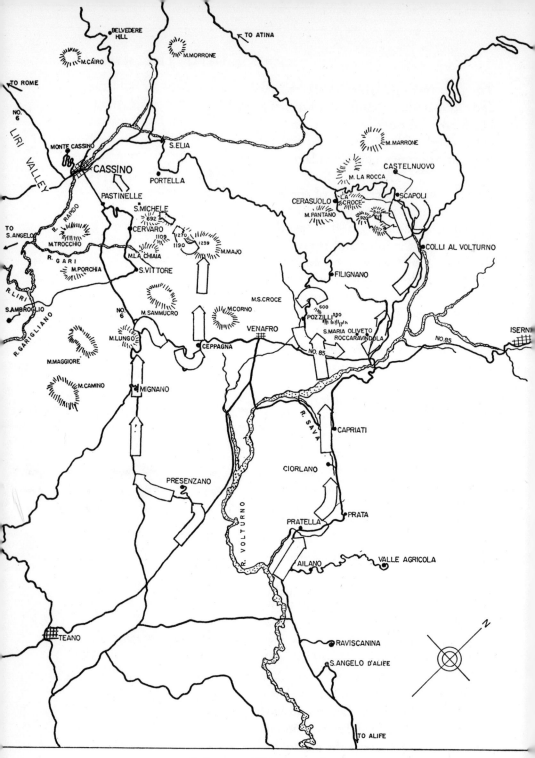

S. Angelo D'Alife to Cassino

set up a strong defensive line. The Germans intended to hold the attacking forces here until they could complete an even more formidable barrier farther to the northwest. Steep cliffs and deep canyons would make advance difficult, and only narrow unpaved roads or mule tracks crossed the hills. Troops would have to attack up mountain sides, and climb trails which jeeps could not negotiate. Supplies would have to be carried by mule train and, where the beasts couldn't make it, on the backs of riflemen.

It was planned that on the night of 3 November, the 34th Division would move across the Volturno against Roccaravindola and Santa Maria Olivetto, preliminary objectives in a push towards Colli al Volturno, farther north. The 168th Regiment would attack toward the first village, and on its left the 133d would move against Santa Maria and the hills southwest of that town. Both units would cross Route 85, which ran from Venafro to Isernia, and prevent its possible use as a path of German escape. The 179th Regiment of the 45th Division would move across the Volturno at the same time as the 34th and take Venafro. (See map, p. 143.)

Colonel Carley L. Marshall, former executive officer of the 133d, was now its commander. On the afternoon of 3 November he explained his plan of attack. The 3d Battalion would cross the Volturno first, driving on Santa Maria; the 1st would follow, but after wading the river would move left to seize Hill 550 northwest of Santa Maria. The 100th would ford farther downstream, taking ground to the rear and left of the 1st Battalion, and protecting the division's left flank and rear. German tanks and self-propelled guns were operating in this part of the valley, using olive groves for concealment, and armored enemy counterattack was to be expected. Reconnaissance showed that the flats west of the Volturno were heavily mined and booby-trapped. Between 11:30 and 12:00 P.M. an artillery concentration would pound the valley floor and the heights on the other side.

At midnight, jump-off time, the 100th had moved down from the heights about Ciorlano into the muddy delta formed by the junction of the little Sava River and the Volturno. Companies E and B led off into the chill water. On reaching the middle of the waist-deep stream they were held up for twenty minutes while "shorts" from American artillery dropped in the water ahead of them and on the west bank. Finally the fire lifted, and the men went ahead. On leaving the river the lead companies hit a thick field of S and Teller mines. Trip wires went to grapevines, fruit trees, and haystacks, and varicolored flares swished up to floodlight the valley. In an area of about a hundred square yards thirty men were hit and from then on the medics were busy. In their posts on the heights to the east, American artillery observers could check the progress of the 100th and its brother battalions by the sound of the mine explosions which punctuated the roar of mortar and artillery fire.

Lieutenant Kurt E. Schemel of C Company, the young man who had doubted whether he should join the battalion, was killed shortly after he climbed the river's west bank. He was the 100th's first commissioned officer to die in battle.

Captain Taro Suzuki and Lieutenant Young Ok Kim, scouting ahead of Company B, moved north along the side of a dirt road running northwest to Highway 85. As they approached a junction with another track leading west to 85, enemy bullets whistled in from the right. Kim yelped and fell off the road on the right; Suzuki jumped for a ditch on the left. Their men, strung out behind them along a low stone wall on Suzuki's side of the road, wheeled their weapons toward the sound of the enemy fire and let fly. The attached machine-gun section propped its guns on the walls and opened up. Staff Sergeant Robert Ozaki came up to Suzuki, who said he thought Kim had been wounded or captured. As Ozaki ordered his platoon to fix bayonets for attack the word spread down the line, and when Ozaki's men charged screaming across wall and road a good part of the rest of the company went along. The sally bagged two panicky Germans; the rest had fled after the counterblast which followed their original fire. Kim was found safe, alone, and still a bit dazed from his fall. He had probably been in more danger from his rescuers than from the Jerries. Someone later claimed that this was the first American bayonet attack in Italy.

Meanwhile a wire team of six men and a mule wandered off the projected route of advance, and the sergeant in charge decided to follow a road which he thought would bring his group back in contact with the rear of the column. It was not a good idea: the Germans had machine guns trained on all the roads, and two of them opened up on the wire party, killing three men. As the mule dashed into an olive grove, his reel making a great racket, a cascade of enemy bullets cut him to ribbons. When Company E finally spotted and silenced the German gunners the rest of the communication team crawled to safety along a ditch.

By 2:30 A.M. Companies E and B had crossed Route 85 about two hundred yards west of the Volturno and were dug in along a railroad track which ran through a depression in the valley floor. Other elements of the battalion were in olive groves between track and river. At about 5:30 A.M. the Germans threw a heavy mortar barrage against the railroad cut. It lasted half an hour, and preceded a less concentrated but steady shelling which continued throughout the day. At times enemy half-tracks rolled within a few hundred yards of the 100th's positions to deliver machine-gun and cannon fire.

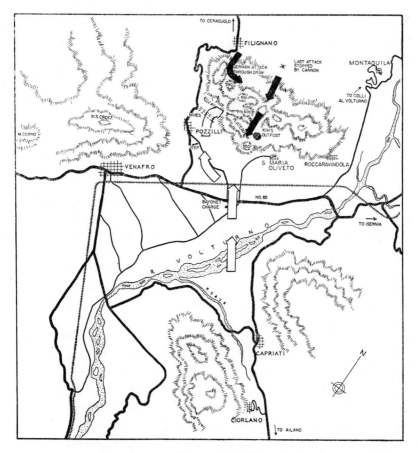

CIORLANO TO HILLS 590, 600, AND 610

Twice Jerry planes skimmed over, dropping antipersonnel bombs. During the rest of the day the battalion remained where it was, while A and C companies, in reserve, sent out patrols to maintain contact with the 179th Infantry on the left. By midnight eight men had been killed and forty-two wounded.

At daybreak next morning, 5 November, a German bayonet charge pushed the 1st Battalion off Hill 550. Three hours later Colonel Marshall ordered Gillespie to take the 100th across the valley floor and seize Hills 590, 600, and 610, on the left of the 1st Battalion. This would take some pressure off that outfit, which would try to regain Hill 550.

Gillespie knew that to advance boldly in line of skirmishers across the open terrain, with enemy guns blasting down from the heights ahead, would be sheer carnage. The only cover for a direct frontal attack was a narrow ditch, about three feet deep, which ran obliquely from the railroad toward the hills. This would not do, however, since a long, thin line of men like that, if discovered, could be cut into segments and pounded to bits at leisure. Shells fell in the olive grove where the major and his officers studied an aerial photo of the sector. Finally Gillespie decided to try an end run of about a mile to the left through the less open terrain in the direction of the village of Pozzilli, in the 45th Division sector, and then swing back to the right, toward the hills.

Gillespie and Captain Alex McKenzie, commander of E Company, led the way. There was no time for careful reconnaissance, so they scouted ahead about a hundred yards at a time, signalling back to the men to follow. In column of twos, crouching low, crawling part of the time, E and F companies crossed a dirt road leading from Route 85 to Pozzilli, and then turned right and north. As Gillespie and McKenzie clambered up a dry creek bed, they spotted an American soldier ambling toward them from the direction of Pozzilli. He said his name was Thompson; he was a paratrooper AWOL from his outfit in Naples, "looking for some excitement." He had been through Pozzilli, which he reported deserted but full of mines and booby traps, and volunteered to guide the column along a covered route to the hills northeast of the village. His offer was accepted.

When the point of the battalion was still about half a mile from the base of the cliffs, an American Armored Forces major appeared, off to the left, driving a jeep madly up the road to Pozzilli. Clouds of dust rose behind him. Two German planes circled down to investigate, spotted the vehicle, and made strafing runs, but the jeep continued to career up the road, toward which enemy artillery now began to send shells. Some of these fell near a part of the battalion column which was close to the road, and twenty men were hit. Curses as well as enemy shells followed the jeep driver as he roared out of view around a far bend.

Still unobserved (the enemy had seen only the jeep and its dust) the column came to the lower slopes of the hills at about 4:00 P.M. Here mines and booby traps barred advance. Lieutenant Lewis Key and Pfc Kenso Suga of Company E led a squad which cut trip wires, neutralized mines, and marked the path thus cleared with strips of toilet paper.* Part of the column passed through safely, but then, as some soldiers wandered from the lane, several mines exploded. Captain John A. Johnson, Jr., battalion exec, and Captain Taro Suzuki were among those wounded.

Radio was being used to control the mile-long column. Two machine-gun sections from D, the heavy weapons company, were with E and F, the lead units, but the rest of the machine guns and the mortars were in the rear. The D Company men at the end of the column misunderstood a radio message and halted to await further orders. Only when the head of the column was almost three quarters of the way up the hills did word come forward that the heavy weapons men were no longer at its tail. This could be bad. Though it was dark now, and D Company had not yet crossed the mined area, it had to push through. As soon as the Germans discovered the battalion there would be an attack, and the heavier guns would be needed.

Thompson, the volunteer guide, joined the two riflemen who were sent back to lead Company D through the mines. About forty-five minutes later explosions were heard. Soon afterwards a report came forward that the heavy weapons men were again following the column but that a few soldiers had been hit. When the two riflemen who had acted as guides returned they reported that in trying to lead some of the Company D men to safety Thompson had tripped a mine and had been blown to bits. No dog tag, letters, or other identifying marks could be found.

* Key and Suga were later awarded Silver Stars.

145

Four hours later, after a steep climb, Companies E and F reached the crest of the first hill. At the top a soldier turned on his flashlight. Someone hissed to him to douse it. He did, but the boys had seen that he was a Jerry. As he screamed and started to run he received a bullet in his back. For the next ten minutes there was heavy fire. When it ended, hand grenades had wiped out three German outposts. This had not been too difficult; the Germans had had strong dugouts on the side of the hill looking down toward the railroad and Highway 85, but had not expected an attack from the rear. The prisoners said they had thought that the Americans were still in the olive groves in the flats below. Perhaps easy living had made them negligent. Their dugouts contained eatables taken from nearby villages, as well as tinned rations and blankets, radios and binoculars, and half a butchered goat hung from a tree near one cave.

Company E spread over the first hill and, in anticipation of enemy counterattack, began digging slit trenches. No one knew whether this crest was 590, 600, or 610—there were plenty of other hills around—but it should be one of the objectives. Soldiers who had no picks used helmets and pocket knives. Company F moved along the ridge line to the northwest, to another knob (later called 590), and also began to burrow. Lieutenant Kim led a patrol to make contact with the 1st Battalion on Hill 550, estimated to be about half a mile to the southeast, and on the way surprised a German supply party. In the firing that followed seven prisoners were taken. By dawn another hill to the north (later identified as 610) had been occupied.

Surprisingly, no enemy mortar or artillery fire fell on the captured positions during the night. Dawn brought a heavy concentration of shells, but only a few men were hit. There was frost on the ground and the men could see snow-capped peaks towering in the distance. At about 10:00 A.M., a column of Germans began moving up a draw parallel to the Company F front. They met a storm of small-arms and machine-gun fire backed by 60-mm. shells. Lieutenant Neill Ray and Corporals Bert Higashi and Katsushi Tanouye, observers from Company D, crouched on the lip of a mound forward of Company F's riflemen. Enemy shells exploded all around them, but they continued calmly to direct fire down upon the Jerries. Twice driven back, the Germans twice re-formed for attack. Each time the observers directed as many as forty rounds at them. Sticking to their vantage point until the sun was directly overhead, the three finally died together in the hail of wood and metal splinters which followed a tree burst. They were posthumously awarded Silver Stars. Soon afterwards the Germans withdrew, carrying their wounded, and leaving their dead strewn along the draw.

Despite occasional rain or snow flurries it was not too cold during the day but the temperature went down sharply after dark. During their second night on the hills some men wore the clothes of dead Jerries over their own summer uniforms.

A day and a half after the hills had been captured, Company C struggled up the cliff sides carrying rations and ammunition. The food and water supplies on the hills had been exhausted, and the goat as well as other eatables found in the German dugouts had disappeared. But the main worry had been lack of shells for the mortars. Now they would be ready when the Jerries attacked again.

It had been a job to get the supplies up the mountainside. Battalion Supply had assembled a number of Italian drivers and their mules outside Pozzilli, but as the animals were being loaded a couple of enemy shells fell among them, and all that was left was some minced mule meat and some dead civilians. After that, the men of the reserve companies had to scramble up the trails carrying the goods on their own backs.

Heavy fighting was in progress in the hills around and beyond Santa Maria Olivetto, in and north of Pozzilli, and on the slopes of Mounts Santa Croce and Corno behind Venafro. Between patrol duty and preparation for another enemy attack the men of the 100th could observe the show from their own heights, see the puffs of shells, count the seconds before the sound reached them, and watch American, and, less frequently, German, planes dropping bombs or strafing.

In the afternoon of the day after the first supplies arrived there was a heavy concentration of enemy artillery against Hills 610 and 600, and German smoke shells reduced visibility to about thirty yards. Men waited tensely for an attack, but the minutes went slowly by and no Germans appeared. As the smoke began to lift a radio operator phoned the battalion command post on Hill 600. A party of about seventy Germans, carrying machine guns and mortars, was doubling across a small plateau about five hundred yards south of 600. For some moments there was shock in the command post.

Lieutenant Kim had stationed his platoon in a well-hidden spot in the draw between 600 and 550, occupied by soldiers of the 1st Battalion. The Jerries would have had to pass it, yet there had been no fire. What had Kim been doing—sleeping?

Suddenly rifle and BAR fire were heard. The platoon had evidently discovered the enemy, but had it done so soon enough? Gillespie ordered a section of heavy machine guns down from 600 to bolster the platoon's fire, and sent a squad to flank the enemy from the rear. He also telephoned the regimental command post to relay warning of the enemy's approach to the 1st Battalion. That unit soon opened up on the Jerries, who were now between two fires. After milling around for a bit, they threw down their guns and marched, hands in the air, toward the 1st Battalion positions. Kim later reported that he had intended to cut the Germans off from all possibility of retreat and had ordered his men to let them pass before opening fire. The 1st Battalion took thirty prisoners.

Enemy shelling continued during the rest of the day. At about 5:00 P.M. an observer from the regimental cannon company reported a German column moving down a draw from the north at a range of about eight hundred yards. Shells from the rear soon began whistling over the battalion's positions toward the German assault group. Their trajectory was low and some shorts caused casualties among the men on the hilltops, but most of the shells landed where they were supposed to. The battalion's 81-mm. mortars also lobbed shells among the Germans and, when they started to withdraw, plastered the path of their retreat. This proved to be the last enemy attack.[1]

For the next two days each successive battalion patrol moved farther ahead before it spotted Germans. Companies A and C, acting as a provisional battalion, were patrolling the area between the 100th and the 179th Infantry in Pozzilli. On 11 November elements of the 179th established contact with the 135th Infantry north of Filignano, and the 133d was pinched out.

Ever since the crossing of the Volturno five nights before, the 100th's medical section had been busy bringing in and patching up the wounded. Four aid men were killed and seven wounded when three litter squads received shellfire as they went to the rescue of some Company B casualties, and Doc Kawasaki had been hit as he climbed toward the hills. Men hit by shellfire on the ridges had to be carried all the way down to the aid station outside Pozzilli. Wounded men sometimes lay for hours on the cold ground before they were found and taken to the head of the trail. There they waited until other bearers came to carry them down. Sometimes it was as much as thirty hours before an injured man received medical attention. Shock and exposure caused as much damage as wounds, and more than one soldier died as he was being carried slowly down the steep track. Even in the comparative safety of the lower ground outside Pozzilli, shells sometimes fell around the surgeon's tent.

The battalion came down from the heights on 11 November. Next day the first overseas pay check came through but, with the Germans still shelling the Pozzilli area, the men waited in their slit trenches until the money came around. On 13 November enlisted men from Companies E and F were transferred to the other companies to fill the gaps made during the recent fighting, but despite these replacements A, B, C, and D still had only 150 "actives" each instead of the usual complement of 187. Since the 100th had first gone into action three officers and seventy-five enlisted men had been killed or had died of wounds, and 239 members had been wounded or injured.

On 15 November, VI Corps ordered a halt to the twelve-day-old attack into the hills. Faced by strong and stubbornly held positions in terrain ideally suited for defensive operations, and by almost insuperable problems in moving supplies across swollen streams and mucky roads, the 34th and 45th divisions had made scant progress since crossing the Volturno.

It was raining steadily and the days were growing colder. On 16 November, the 100th moved into Santa Maria Olivetto, "a nice town on a hillside," and remained there eight days. The rest was welcome, as was the opportunity to bathe and change into warm woolen underwear which had at last arrived.

Colonel Marshall inspected the battalion at Santa Maria. The new commander of the 133d, with his carefully groomed mustache with waxed spikelike points which he constantly twirled, had been awarded the Distinguished Service Cross for gallantry in Tunisia, and liked to talk about the engagement at Fondouk in which he had won it— among themselves his men called him "Von Duke." Marshall's favorite military hero was Jeb Stuart, and once the colonel got that rebel cavalryman's name into a discussion, he could be relied on to gallop down the conversational field alone. Though his officers grinned, and the enlisted men delighted in ribald cracks about the mustache, everyone respected his qualities as commander, for he really cared about the well-being of his soldiers, and gave them tough, careful training so that as many of them as possible might emerge from battle alive—thus winning himself another title, "Hard-labor Hank."

Memorial services for the boys who had died were held by bat-talion chaplain Israel Yost, a Pennsylvania-Dutch Lutheran minister who had joined the outfit at Benevento. The lanky, mild-looking, sandy-haired, bespectacled minister told how a burial detail carrying one of the 100th's dead had met a 45th Division soldier near Pozzilli, and how he had taken off his helmet and stepped off the trail as the AJA bearers went by. Yost himself had been slightly wounded helping evacuate casualties during the river crossing, but had soon been back at work in the aid station binding the wounds of his brothers—mostly Buddhist—in God.

In Hawaii, on the day memorial services were held for her son who had died on Hill 600, Yukio Asai's mother received his last letter. Written in the simplest Japanese, it was the result of much effort. Yuki had forgotten most of what he had learned in language school and had asked his buddies to help.

Dear Mother:

Old Man Winter is here in Italy and it is 2 years since I have left you and I am dreadfully homesick for you. But I am a soldier of Uncle Sam and till I fulfill my duty I must stick on my job. I am praying to God every night that you may be well till the day of my return.

I wish you were here to see me! I have begun to see and understand the world. Looking over my school days I can imagine what a problem I must have been to you. Don't laugh, Mother, but I have learned to do my own washing. One has to be in the Army before he learns to do his laundry.

Evening is fast approaching and I must say goodbye. Please take good care of yourself till I come back.

Yukio.[2]

To CAPTURE ROME, Fifth Army had to break through the enemy's newly completed Winter Line defenses which blocked entrance into the Liri Valley, gateway to that city. According to the plan issued on 24 November, 1943, the British 10 Corps and the American II Corps would move against the Camino Hill mass and Mt. Sammucro, shoulders of the Mignano Gap, in preparation for a push through the Gap and into the valley. (See map, p. 140.) From the mountains at the head of the Volturno Valley, on the Fifth Army's right flank, VI Corps would simultaneously drive west on the Colli-Atina and Filignano-S. Elia roads to seize high ground north and northwest of Cassino. If VI Corps and II Corps could then envelop the defenses of Cassino, German strongpoint on Highway 6 which led to Rome, an armored breakthrough might be made up the Liri Valley.

Scrub-covered hills and rocky ravines made up the area through which the 34th and 45th divisions of VI Corps would have to fight, and steep peaks on the right and left would confine movement to the terrain between the Colli-Atina and Filignano-S. Elia roads. The 34th Division had orders to capture the heights north and south of Cerasuolo which commanded a junction of these roads. The 133d Regiment would advance through the hills between Cerasuolo and Castelnuovo, the 1st Battalion attacking Castelnuovo, the 3d in the center moving against Mt. La Rocca, and the 100th on the left taking La Croce

I Didn't Hear a Man Complain

Hill north of Cerasuolo. (See map, p. 153.) Farther to the left, the 168th Infantry would try to capture 1600-foot Mt. Pantano, which overlooked Cerasuolo from the south. Still farther south, the 45th Division would open up a section of the Filignano-S. Elia road and assist the 168th on its right in the attack against Mt. Pantano.[1]

By 25 November, Thanksgiving Day, the 133d had moved from Scapoli to relieve the 504th Parachute Infantry in the hills about Colli at the extreme right flank of the Fifth Army line. After two weeks of steady rain the sky had cleared, and the ground was dry again. The days were not very cold, but water sometimes froze in the canteens at night, and the men of the 100th were still wearing summer uniforms over their winter underwear. Morale received a boost when Colonel Marshall reported that General Ryder and General Lucas, VI Corps commander, were pleased with the 100th's performance in its most recent engagement.

On the day after Thanksgiving the 100th received cold turkey and bread which mules had packed up the mountain trails. Part of the meat had become green on the journey, but some of the men scraped and ate it anyway, and got diarrhea.

Company C missed out on the sandwiches. On Thanksgiving Day it climbed Hill 1017, a few miles southwest of Colli. After lugging food, water, and ammunition up the 3000-foot mountain, the men encountered mortar and artillery fire at the top, but dug in without casualties. That night an officer led the 3d and weapons platoon forward to Hill 920, on the left front, which was thought to be only lightly held by the Germans. Scrambling down the sides of 1017, skirting the sides of Hill 905, a knob on its forward slope, and then crossing a wide gulch, the advance party reached the lower eastern slopes of Hill 920 in the early morning. Scouts climbed to the top of a "pimple" on the side toward Hill 1017 and returned with news of Jerries dug in on its reverse slope. Word was sent to 1017 by field telephone that one company should be able to take the hill, and this report was relayed back to battalion headquarters near Colli.

Colonel Gillespie now planned that Company C should occupy Hill 920. Meanwhile Companies A and B would move westward on the northern slopes of Hill 841, between the crest of that ridge, which would mask their approach from enemy guns on La Croce Hill, and the Rio S. Pietro. After mopping up enemy resistance, the three companies would reunite and attack La Croce Hill, from which they could deliver flanking fire on the enemy forces defending Mount Pantano, objective of the 168th Infantry. It was a nice plan.

On 29 November a column made up of Companies A and B moved to the right of Hill 1017, reached the northeast slope of Hill 841, and turned westward through the high scrub. Company B met the first resistance, from Germans in front and to the left, near the top of the ridge line. Company A was sent up the slopes to the left to

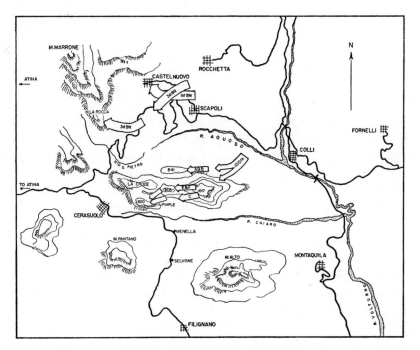

COLLI TO HILLS 841 AND 920

flank the enemy. In the ascent it found mines through which a path had to be cleared, and near the top, German wire. Enemy rifle, machine-gun, and mortar fire was heavy, and casualties mounted. It proved impossible to push the Jerries off the crest or to move west along the slopes. After several unsuccessful assaults both companies dug in.

Artillery support could not be expected; the area was evidently at extreme gun range; and the soldiers of the two companies were generally so near the enemy that shells from the rear would probably damage friend as much as foe. German shellfire knocked out three howitzers of the regimental Cannon Company, and disrupted the 4.2-inch chemical mortars. A and B had to depend on their own mortars, and it was impossible to find good observation posts from which to direct their fire.

For the next two weeks the companies tried unsuccessfully to push west. In the attacks and counterattacks of these days four men won Distinguished Service Crosses. During a flank attack by an A Company platoon, Private Shizuya Hayashi, a BAR man, charged at an enemy machine-gun nest through grenade and mortar fire, gun blasting from his hip, and killed nine Germans in the pit and two more as they fled. Shortly afterwards an enemy antiaircraft gun fired almost point blank at his assault party, but Hayashi, counterfiring, knocked out nine more and took four prisoners.

In a defensive action Corporal Masaru Suehiro of Company A stayed at his mortar observation post, though severely wounded, and called for fire which destroyed an enemy gun nest and demoralized a strong enemy party which was forming for an assault.

A squad in the Company B sector was attacked in flank by a platoon carrying rifles, grenades, automatic pistols, and machine guns. When the fight ended, twenty-seven Germans were dead, one was wounded, and another had been lucky enough to be taken prisoner. A little later the remnant of the enemy party, about four-teen men, moved in again. This time four were killed and three wounded, and the remainder withdrew. Two men, Lt. Allan Ohata and Private Mikio Hasemoto, had done all the damage. Neither had been hurt, but Hasemoto died the next day of a mortar wound as he and Ohata fought off another attack.

Despite these and other deeds of gallantry the Germans continued to control the ridge.

On the battalion's left front things had gone no better. The two platoons of Company C which had reached Hill 920 on 26 November had been ordered to establish themselves on its slopes until the rest of that company could come up from Hill 1017, but the troops on 1017 could not advance until they received more supplies from the rear. Battalion supply was short of personnel, and a detail of about twenty men had to go back from 1017 to the supply dump each night to pick up the forty-five-pound boxes of C and K rations and the five-gallon water cans which had been packed into the hills by mule train. German artillery posted on the ridges to the west made daylight movement too dangerous, and the trip to the rear area meant half a night on the steep and dangerous trails.

When the men from Hill 1017 finally joined those on Hill 920 in the early morning of 30 November, they found their comrades in pretty bad state. After knocking out several machine guns on the way, at a heavy cost in men, the two platoons had managed to climb onto the "pimple," a patch of low scrub-covered ground about twelve feet square, the highest point on the eastern slope of 920. But Germans, dug in on the pimple's reverse slope, had covered its crest with mortar fire and had forced them back down again. Behind these Jerries was a saddle, and behind this and rising from it was another knob on the western side of 920. From this point machine guns, antiaircraft guns, mortars and Nebelwerfers fired against the eastern pimple, and lobbed shells over its crest onto the eastern slopes of 920, where the two C platoons had finally dug in, about 300 yards down, at the lower edge of a belt of dense scrub timber.

During their second night on 920 a detail from Hill 1017 had gone forward to bring them food and water. Stumbling and slipping in the dark on dew-covered roots and rocks, the heavily laden men had reached 920 with only half the water left in their three five-gallon containers—about enough for one glass of water for each soldier on the slopes. The food was to have been turkey and bread, separately packed, but the boxes had gotten mixed and only the bread reached the famished men. Thirsty, hungry, miserably cold, under intermittent mortar fire and in constant expectation of counterattack, they ate their Thanksgiving dinner.

The reinforcements who finally arrived on the 30th had been able to carry little in the way of supplies. One newcomer offered his canteen, three-quarters full, to some of the parched men. "Several accepted my water with thanks, but though any one of them could have finished it in one swig they took only a mouthful and returned the rest. Others politely refused, saying, 'Keep it, you're going to need it yourself.' I thanked God I was fighting with men like these."

About 10 A.M. plans were made for another attack. Two patrols went out to reconnoiter, and returned about two hours later. One had met no Germans; the other had left two of its men dead on the side of the pimple. At noon Company C broke out of the woods and started for the top. The few who reached it died there and the line wavered and receded down the hill. Reorganizing in the woods, the company made another assault, and failed again. Against machine-gun, grenade, and mortar fire, and without artillery support, the position could not be taken. The company's mortars had no observation and were firing practically blind. Retiring through the woods, the men dug in, under a rain of enemy shells which continued all that day and night.

Next morning the men shook trees and shrubs, trying to catch dew from the leaves on their parched tongues, or chipped lumps of soil from the frozen ground and sucked at the moist dirt. Everyone was thirsty, hungry, cold, and generally miserable—but "I didn't hear a man complain, and we shared what little food and water we had."

The officer in charge of the original group on the hill had gone to the rear, a victim of shell shock. Company C's commander went back to report to battalion headquarters, taking a messenger with him, and a first sergeant was left in command of the force on 920.

Company E reached the hill about 9:00 A.M. the following day. With F, the other extra company, it had at first been held in reserve near Colli. Both these units had been so depleted by transfer of personnel to other companies that each consisted of only two skeleton rifle platoons and a machine gun squad. They had at first been ordered to Hill 1017, and had started to dig in there, but then had been told to occupy Hill 905. While organizing on that position, Company E had been ordered to leave 905 (which F would hold alone) and to move to the aid of Company C, on Hill 920. The men of E had spent the night on the trail across the gulch between 905 and 920, but were comparatively fresh, and preparations were made for another attack.

While scouting to find observation posts one artillery officer was killed and another officer and two radio men were wounded. Visibility was low, and fire directed at the German positions from the tops of neighboring hills proved of little help. It was finally decided to ask for artillery fire by map, but after several shells burst in the company area this idea was abandoned. From a nearby hill the heavy weapons company battery fired some 81-mm. mortars but without much apparent effect. At about 11:00 A.M. Company E led another attack against the hilltop, and this also failed.

By this time each unit of the combined force had suffered heavy losses. In Company C's 3d Platoon, for instance, a private first class led the eight men still able to fight. Battalion headquarters sent word to remain in position and await further orders. "This we were glad to do. We dug our slit trenches deeper and got ready for a counter-attack and a long stay." In the afternoon it became colder, and snow fell. This soon changed to rain, which lasted until evening and was caught in raincoats, shelter halves, helmets, and anything else that would hold water. Thirst was thus temporarily relieved, but clothes and shoes were wet and the ground muddy, and slit trenches filled up almost as soon as they were bailed out. Enemy mortar shells were still crunching in from the top of the hill.

Early next morning the messenger who had gone with the company commander returned. On his way back to the hill he had found a spring only about a quarter of a mile behind the outpost line, and he promised that food and water would be brought forward that night. Despite the danger of daylight travel, a detail went immediately to the spring. When night came a mule team from battalion supply dumped food and water about a half mile from the hill. For the next nine nights parties of fifteen men went back to this supply dump for rations and ammunition.

Rain began again, shortly after the food arrived, and continued for two days and two nights. There were not enough shelter halves—many of them had been used to make stretchers—but raincoats and helmets kept the men's upper parts reasonably dry. Legs and feet got soaked, however, and rather than spend the nights in their water-filled trenches men slept sitting or standing. From now on the ground was muck; trench foot became common; and at night soldiers released for treatment hobbled down the hill and across the trail to the battalion aid station three miles to the rear. To save their red, swollen, continuously aching feet they crawled over the bad places.

On the day the rain stopped, Company F arrived and its commander took control. Capable and cool, his cheerful manner lifted morale. He also brought some luck. During the rain the Jerries had continued to send over mortar fire, but now they paid less attention to the hill's forward slopes.

Though the ground remained soggy and the nights were cold and wet with heavy dew, the sun came out bright and warm. From another hill Company D's mortars began giving the Germans some of their own medicine, and communication with battalion head-quarters by radio and field telephone was better than it had been, though the communications men were still out every night splicing the wires, and the radio continued balky.

The hillside position was so near the enemy that it was necessary to speak softly, but the scrub cover acted as a screen against enemy mortar observation and made it possible to have small fires and to smoke. Soldiers who had no Coleman stoves tore their wax-covered K ration boxes into little strips, piled these carefully, and lighted them to get a smokeless fire which would heat enough water for a cup of coffee.

Evidently content where they were, the Jerries did not attack down the slopes, and there were no further assaults against the pimple. There couldn't be; despite the arrival of Companies E and F, there were less healthy men available for combat than when the two Company C platoons had first arrived at the hill.

A squad of French Senegalese troops appeared during the morning of 12 December. They were part of the 2d Moroccan Division which was being sent to relieve the 34th Division. Their white lieutenant asked a few questions, stated that he intended to scout the Jerry positions, and asked for a couple of guides. Told that a daylight patrol would be suicide, he insisted on going ahead. Orders had been received that the Frenchmen were to be given "every possible co-operation," so a request was made, reluctantly, for volunteer guides. Two sergeants offered their hides for sacrifice.

Four men went out, the French lieutenant, one of his men, and the two sergeants. Five minutes later small-arms fire was heard. Soon the Frenchman and Senegalese came dashing back through the scrub. A minute or two later the firing suddenly stopped. For a time it was very quiet. No one looked at the Frenchman. Then the two sergeants emerged quietly from the woods, grim-faced but unhurt. They reported having left a dead German near the top of the hill.

Three nights later a company of French Moroccans arrived. A big moon lighting their way, they had made little noise in the approach. By 10:00 P.M. they had taken over all positions. As the remnant of C, E, and F companies quietly left Hill 920 they carried little ammunition. Most of it had been left for the French, who were using American guns; besides, the journey back would be easier without it. Company C had started out with a hundred and seventy-five men on

Thanksgiving Day. About fifty of these now walked down the trail; the rest were in hospitals or were dead. Companies E and F had been inactivated, and the few men left in each had become part of C Company.

Elsewhere on the battalion front things had gone little better. In various aid stations, during the previous two weeks, Staff Sergeant Masaichi Goto, a battalion medic, had been making occasional hurried scribbles in his diary: "What a battle! . . . Capt. Jack Mizuha hit. Evacuated him about 2 miles on litter. . . . Major battle going on—now we hit the German Winter Line. Evacuated about 50— wish this was all over. . . . Troops on several hill tops. My men in three aid stations. It's a job to keep tab on them. . . . No progress made. . . . We are facing mortar shells, artillery, and German planes." His last notation summed up the engagement: "Evacuated about 250 in ten days."

Beyond the aid station, three miles back, trucks were waiting to carry the men to the kitchen area. Arriving there at about 2:00 A.M., they threw shelter halves on the cold wet earth and immediately dropped to sleep.

In the morning the kitchen crew put on a real feed: ham and eggs, hot cakes, bread, mush, and coffee with cream. As the boys wrapped themselves around the kind of meal they had seen in uneasy dreams on Hill 920, they began to talk, between great bites and gulps, even to joke and laugh about things that hadn't seemed so funny a short time ago, like the French "looie" scuttling back from his personal reconnaissance. Their stomachs stuffed with food for the first time in a month, many soon had diarrhea—but who cared?[2]

The Moroccans had relieved Companies A and B two nights before, and during the morning there was inquiry for friends, and exchange of bad news. In the afternoon the battalion motored to the rear to join the rest of the regiment in a bivouac near Alife. There it was learned that the 1st Battalion had not been able to pass Castelnuovo, that the 3d, in the center, had reached Mt. La Rocca and had taken a hill on the south slopes of Mt. Marrone, and that the Germans were still on Mt. Pantano, where they had been giving the 168th Infantry a rough time. Much farther south, Fifth Army troops were still trying to capture Mounts Lungo and Sammucro.

In Hawaii, about this time, Joe Takata's wife received his post-humously awarded DSC. With the approval of his parents and her own, she decided to forget the Japanese custom of distributing tea among the relatives and friends of the deceased. Instead both families donated $400 to the Red Cross, Army and Navy Relief Funds, and the Community Chest.[3]

FOR NINETEEN DAYS, as the regiment rested near Alife, men bathed, cleaned equipment, and followed a training program which combined physical hardening with scouting and patrolling. Red Cross girls provided coffee and doughnuts; there were movies every night; and the USO put on some shows. Warm showers and hot meals cheered everyone, as did the winter uniforms, overshoes, and extra blankets which were distributed. During this period the first battlefield promotion raised a master sergeant to warrant officer, junior grade, and Major Caspar Clough, a Silver Star man, came from the 1st Infantry Division to replace Major Gillespie, whose stomach ulcers had finally forced him into a hospital.

A "white Christmas" reminded the boys that, though it might seem longer, it had been only a year since they had taken photographs of snowmen at McCoy. They cut an evergreen on a nearby hill, placed it in an open area of the camp, and decorated it with pieces of tin from C ration cans and red berries from native shrubs. Chaplain Yost held a "solemn and beautiful service" before the tree and afterwards there was singing of carols.

At the end of December, 1943, as the VI Corps left the front to prepare for an amphibious assault behind the Winter Line, the French Expeditionary Force took over its sector, and the 34th Division was transferred to II Corps control. The Red Bulls moved up to relieve the 36th Division, and the 133d

More Hills

marched to an assembly area during a New Year's Eve blizzard. At Presenzano, where the regiment rested for five days, three staff sergeants of the 100th received commissions as second lieutenants.

The Germans had finally been pushed off Mounts Lungo and Sammucro. The Fifth Army prepared for the next phase of the Winter Line campaign, in which II Corps would move up into the Liri Valley, and the French would push west into the high ground north of Cassino. (See map, p. 140.) On the left of the II Corps sector, Task Force "A" (the 6th Armored Infantry reinforced by the 1st Armored Division) would capture Mt. Porchia, and the 135th Infantry of the 34th Division would take S. Vittore and Mt. la Chiaia. The 168th, on the right of the 135th, would push into the hills north of S. Vittore, break the enemy line anchored on the mountains, and outflank la Chiaia to the northeast. On the right of the 168th, the 1st Special Service Force, reinforced, would attack high in the mountains northeast of la Chiaia and Cervaro, and would then move west, flanking Cervaro from the north. After la Chiaia was taken, the 168th and 135th would converge on Cervaro. If these attacks were successful the Germans on Mt. Trocchio, last obstacle to American advance out of the Mignano Gap, would find their northern flank uncovered, and would face an all-out assault from northeast, south, and southwest.

On 5 January, the day scheduled for the beginning of these attacks, the 1st Battalion of the 133d was detached to act as reserve for Task Force "A," and moved from Presenzano to Mt. Lungo. The next day the rest of the regiment trucked to Ceppagna and then marched to an assembly area nearby. Here it came under command of the 1st Special Service Force, which, with the artillery of the 36th Division added, now formed Task Force "B." Its third regiment captured the peak of Mt. Majo (Hill 1259) on the night of 6 January and for the next three days fought off desperate German attempts to recapture that height. On 7 January the SSF's first regiment attacked toward Vischiatoro Ridge (Hill 1109), west of Mt. Majo and directly overlooking Cervaro.

The 100th and 3d battalions of the 133d had followed the third regiment of the SSF onto Mt. Majo. On the night of 7 January the 100th moved forward to take Hill 1190, a spur to the west, but lost its way in the foggy darkness, and after a three-hour march was called back to the line of departure. The next night the battalion moved forward again, and against only minor resistance climbed and took the high knobby plateau which was Hill 1190. The next two days patrols were sent to the northwest, toward Hill 1270. During this period news arrived that four staff sergeants had received commissions as second lieutenants.

At about 6:00 A.M. on 11 January the battalion moved through the fog-covered saddle between 1190 and 1270. When the haze lifted at about 10:00 A.M., the Jerries laid down heavy mortar fire and stopped Company A, the lead unit. Companies B and C swung to the right to ease the pressure, but came under mortar and small-arms fire from a flanking ridge and were unable to advance. By nightfall there had been numerous casualties, and Company C's commander had been wounded. In this action Sergeant Masaharu Takeba, whose platoon was pinned down by machine-gun fire, moved away from his men and deliberately exposed himself in order to draw the enemy fire. He died, and his family later received a Bronze Star. At dawn the 3d Battalion of the 133d was sent against the ridge on the right, and Companies A, B, and C moved frontally against Hill 1270. Fire from the 81-mm. mortars gave strong support, and by evening the battalion was mopping up the last enemy resistance on the reverse slopes of the objective.

Snow and mud had hindered the men in climbing the hill's lower slopes, and the final assault had been made above the timberline, across barren windswept rounded rock covered only by scattered patches of snow. In their solidly built dugouts, with plenty of food and ammunition, the Germans had evidently been prepared for a long stay. That night Major Clough told the officers of his new command that the day's action had been the best job of two-battalion co-ordination against a strongly emplaced enemy that he had yet seen. The enemy made no counterattacks, and both battalions rested the next day.

On 13 January, Task Force "B" was broken up, and the SSF moved out, leaving the two battalions of the 133d to maintain the advance to the west. These now moved down the lower slopes of the Mt. Majo hill mass toward the Rapido Valley, mopping up scattered enemy pockets north of the Cervaro-Cassino road. On 14 January, the 3d Battalion struck northwest from Hill 1270 and captured Hill 692, and on the 15th, the 100th dropped down into lower ground to occupy the little hamlet of S. Michele, recently evacuated by the Jerries. The next day the 100th was ordered to Cervaro but in mid-journey was told to march back to S. Michele, where it rested, sending patrols along the valley floor toward the Rapido River.

During this last week of climbing and fighting, terrain and supply difficulties had been even greater obstacles than in the fight for Hills 841 and 920. The weather was worse; the mountain trails, often above the timberline, were covered with snow, or ice, or mud on ice; and soldiers had continued to be disabled by trench foot. Mules brought K rations and ammunition as far as they could climb, and then riflemen, pack boards strapped to their backs, carried the supplies farther into the hills.

Later a wounded veteran of the battalion told a reporter of being in his foxhole, "my feet and my fingers numb from cold, and the icy rain stinging my face. . . . I would be homesick for Molokai, and the murmur of the surf on the warm sand, and it would seem far away."[1]

It sometimes took hours to move litter cases back to the battalion aid station. From that point the injured were carried down to the nearest ambulance by six-man teams, stationed at twelve relay points, each about an hour's haul from the next. The first two stages in a wounded man's journey to the hospital often took twelve to fifteen hours. Three stations along the route supplied blood plasma or other aid, and provided hot drinks and a rest place for the walking wounded.

One badly damaged boy, who had been carried into an aid tent, unstrapped his wrist watch. "Here, Sergeant, take it; I won't need it any more." He fumbled, got out his wallet, whispered, "Soldier, take my money; I won't need it," and died within a few minutes.

Another seriously wounded soldier was carried into the station where Doc Kometani was giving aid. After six hours on a litter, this man's first words were: "Doc, your assistant is dead back there. I'm sorry."

In eight days the battalion had moved only a few miles west, but two officers and eleven enlisted men had been killed, two officers and forty-four enlisted men had been wounded, and one officer and four enlisted men were "missing in action."

On 7 January, the 135th Infantry had taken S. Vittore and Mt. la Chiaia. (See map, p. 140.) On 13 January, after having captured Cervaro two days before, the 168th Infantry was on the slopes overlooking Le Pastinelle and the Rapido River plain, and only a mile from Mt. Trocchio, from which the Germans now withdrew without a fight. By 16 January the French on the north flank of the Fifth Army were in S. Elia.

The Winter Line had been broken, but now the Allies faced the more formidable Gustav Line, built by Hitler's famous Todt organization. This barrier began in the hills above S. Elia, ran along the Rapido, crossed the mountains behind Cassino, followed the Rapido and Gari rivers through the Liri Valley, and then extended through the mountains north of the Garigliano to the sea. Its immensely strong fortifications had to be cracked before there could be a breakthrough up the Liri Valley toward Rome, some ninety miles away.

Fifth Army was at this time planning an amphibious assault at Anzio, thirty-one miles south of the Italian capital. (See campaign map, p. 124.) Just prior to this intended landing the 10 and II Corps would smash at the Gustav Line. To the extent that their attack was successful it would presumably engage German reserves which might otherwise be available for use against the invasion force at Anzio. If it pierced the German defenses, Allied troops would rush up the Liri Valley to join with the beach-

Cassino

head units for a drive on Rome. Conversely, success at Anzio could perhaps be counted on to weaken the defenses of the Gustav Line by depletion of its reserves, which might be pulled north for use against the Anzio invasion.

D Day for the amphibious assault was set for 22 January. On 17 January, 10 Corps would attack across the Garigliano River on a line extending along that stream from the sea to S. Ambroglio. Three days later the 36th Division would push across the Rapido River and establish a bridgehead in the S. Angelo area. On the right of the 36th, the 34th Division would make a demonstration to keep German reserves in the Cassino area, and would hold itself ready to move across the S. Angelo bridgehead against Cassino or to pass through the 36th and up the Liri Valley to the northwest. These plans contemplated a breakthrough south of Cassino's defenses.

Though 10 Corps had established a bridgehead across the Garigliano by the end of January, it breached only the outer works of the Gustav Line, and the 36th Division's attack in the S. Angelo sector (20–22 January) had been a costly failure. As a result it was now planned that the 34th Division should cross the Rapido River in an attempt to break through the German defenses north and west of Cassino. In this area the Rapido cut across the eastern edge of the Liri Valley, flowed southwest from S. Elia and just east of Cassino, and joined the Gari River four miles below that city. West of the Rapido, the Gustav Line ran roughly southwest from Mt. Marrone to Belvedere Hill (720 metres) and then south to Monastery Hill (516 metres) on the summit of which sat the ancient and famous Abbey of Montecassino, a great rectangle of buildings dominating the Liri Valley and Highway 6, the road to Rome. (See map, p. 167.) Fifteen hundred feet below and east of the monastery lay the gray stone city of Cassino, straggling awkwardly along the steep sides of a lower hill which sloped east to the Rapido. Cassino's peacetime population was about 20,000, but the Germans had converted the place into a fortress and the inhabitants had fled.

As it crossed the Rapido above Cassino, the 34th Division would send a column down the road which entered the city west of the river. Other elements would push into the mountains about Mt. Castellone to the northwest, take high ground dominating Cassino, and debouch southwest to Piedmonte, cutting Highway 6 and pocketing German forces in the area thus enveloped.

While the high brass plotted battles yet unwon, the dogfaces of the 100th rested near S. Michele, making only reconnaissance and combat patrols during the period 16–22 January. The first patrol established contact with the French at Portella on the north, and with the 2d Battalion of the 135th on the south near Cervaro. Later missions scouted enemy defenses on the east bank of the Rapido River, looked for a likely crossing place, and engaged enemy outposts.

They reported that the Germans had dammed the river, which, diverted from its normal course, flooded the plain directly west of the battalion's positions to knee-depth. Its dried-out channel was about seventy-five feet in width and about fourteen feet deep; its

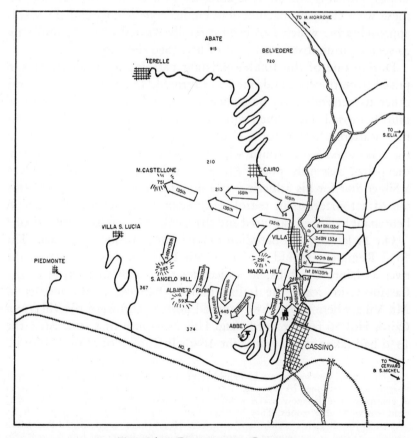

THE 34TH DIVISION AT CASSINO

east bank was of cement topped by a retaining wall which rose above the ground level to heights varying from seven to twelve feet; its west bank was of dirt and very steep. To reach the Cairo-Cassino highway the battalion would have to cross in succession a submerged road, flooded farm land, two irrigation ditches about three feet wide and four feet deep, a more shallow ditch about two feet wide and one foot deep, a muddy cornfield sown with circular, picket-type mines, and another irrigation ditch five feet wide and six feet deep. After crossing these obstacles the men would have to scale the retaining wall on the east side of the river bed, cross the channel, clamber up the dirt bank on the other side, and force their way onto the road through a double apron of mined barbed wire. Steep, barren slopes, probably mined, rose abruptly west of the highway, and on these were German machine-gun emplacements covering the whole approach area, which had been carefully cleared of brush and trees to secure an unobstructed field of fire. (See sketch p. 169.)

During one of the 100th's daylight patrols two scouts were surprised from the rear, and one was captured. The Jerries yelled to the other to surrender. As he hesitated, a hand grenade came toward him. It missed. He replied with two fragmentation grenades. As his foes scattered he ran for a nearby irrigation ditch, dived in, swam three hundred yards south with the swift current, and returned to the patrol assembly point. Pfc Sueyoshi Yamakawa later received a Silver Star for his athletic versatility. The next day, however, only ten of a fourteen-man patrol returned from a German ambush. A lieutenant had been captured and three enlisted men had been killed.*

On 24 January the battalion moved into position for attack. The 133d Regiment would lead the 34th Division's assault across the river and into the hills, its objectives the southern portion of the Cassino-Cairo road, the Italian military barracks at the hamlet of Mt. Villa where the highway turned northwest toward the village of Cairo, Hill 56 farther north, and Hill 213 south of Cairo. After the 133d had taken these points the 168th Infantry would pass through

---

* The officer, who had won a battlefield commission for gallantry in the fighting near Pozzilli, was questioned by Japanese and German military officers while he was prisoner in Germany. The Japanese asked whether the American Army gave the AJAs equal treatment with other troops. They had heard about the 100th's battle record, were interested in the allegiance which these men from Hawaii bore to the United States, and seemed surprised at the number of years of schooling the lieutenant had received. *The Honolulu Star-Bulletin*, July 2, 1945; *Pacific Citizen*, July 28, 1945.

to seize Mt. Castellone, S. Angelo Hill, and Albaneta Farm, all northwest of Cassino. On the 168th's left and within this outer encircling movement the 135th Infantry would cross the Rapido and drive into the northern end of Cassino.

From 11:30 P.M. to midnight, jump-off time, five battalions of artillery sent a cascade of fire at the German positions. The three battalions of the 133d then moved ahead abreast, the 1st on the

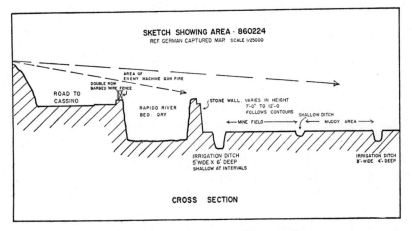

GERMAN DEFENSES AT THE RAPIDO RIVER

right, the 3d in the center, and the 100th on the left, south of the barracks. Men of the ammunition and pioneer platoon cleared paths through the mines for Companies A and C, which led the 100th's advance. Sergeant Calvin Shimogaki, his mine detector disabled by a bullet, crawled in the mud, searching with his hands for trip wires, and cleared a path five feet wide and fifty yards long.*

By 5:00 A.M. Companies A and C had reached the east bank of the river channel. Though the Germans had been shelling the approach area, casualties had been relatively light. During the morning enemy guns pummeled the river line, but there was good cover behind the retaining wall of the east bank.

On the 100th's right the 3d Battalion, under heavy fire from the direction of the Italian barracks, had placed only a few men along

* Shimogaki, who won a Silver Star for his action, was one of the forty AJAs who had been accepted into the Hawaii National Guard before October, 1940. He had been a member of the band.

the river bank, and the 1st Battalion had been stopped after 200 yards by a mine field, through which a tank battalion was now trying to clear lanes of advance.

Company B of the 100th was ordered forward to join A and C companies in preparation for an attack across the dry river channel. The men advanced across the flats under a smoke screen, some of them carrying ladders for use in scaling the embankments. When they were halfway across the wind changed, blowing away their cover, and they were stopped by a hail of machine-gun, mortar, and artillery fire from the hills across the road. Only the company commander, two other officers, and eleven enlisted men reached the east wall. Those of the company who could still move sought cover in irrigation ditches or dug into the mud.

Companies A and C were told to push across the river bed and road into the hills between the barracks and Cassino, but German fire was so intense they were unable to pass the west bank of the river channel. Major Clough was wounded in the arm, and Major Dewey, executive officer of the 133d, took temporary command of the battalion. That night Company B was pulled back from the flats. When Captain Fukuda of Company A returned from the river bank to the battalion command post he was asked what he thought of the situation. Fukuda said he thought the battalion could probably push its way into the hills, but that when it got there it would not have enough men left to hold on. Dewey had orders, however, that the battalion should attack in the morning.

Fukuda now led Dewey, Major Jack Johnson, a messenger, two wiremen, and a litter crew back toward the river wall, where a new command post was to be set up. As the group moved across the flats a German machine gun opened up from the hills ahead, spraying the area at random. Dewey and Johnson were badly wounded. Johnson, as he crawled for cover, exploded a mine and caught it full force. He died a few hours later at the aid station. Major Clough again took command of the battalion, and in the early morning hours Company C was pulled back from the river bank.

During the next day the 1st Battalion and elements of the 3d failed in an attempt to get across the highway and onto Hill 213, and at dark they were, like the 100th, in defensive positions along the river bank. During that afternoon elements of a company of the 1st Battalion, 135th Infantry, crossed the Rapido on the left of the 100th and reached the outskirts of Cassino, but flooded ditches, wire, mines, and machine-gun fire prevented further advance. That night Company A of the 100th was ordered back from the river; elements of the 1st and 3d battalions took over its position; and the 100th went into reserve at S. Michele. The 1st and 3d battalions held a line of departure for the 168th Infantry, which passed through and attacked at 7:30 the next morning, and then they too moved back across the flats, and the 133d went into divisional reserve.

Tanks preceded the 168th, and by dawn of 28 January a few soldiers had climbed part way up Hill 213 but were later forced to withdraw. Two platoons had dug in midway between Cairo and the Rapido. By dark on 29 January, the 168th had gained the lower slopes of Hills 56 and 213, and by dawn of 31 January, despite heavy casualties, it had captured these hills and had occupied Cairo. Farther north, elements of the French Expeditionary Force had taken Belvedere Hill and Abate Hill.

The night of 29 January, the 133d moved back into line to take over the defensive positions of the 135th Infantry, which now swung to the right and moved between the Italian barracks and Hill 56 for an attack against Mt. Castellone and Majola Hill. On 1 February, the 135th took these objectives and pushed south and southwest, while the 168th remained on Hills 56 and 213.

On 31 January, the 133d had finished mopping up in the barracks area, and on 1 February it sent the 3d Battalion south against Cassino along high ground west of the road as two platoons of the 756th Tank Battalion trundled down the highway and the dry river channel. Stopped on the first day by heavy enemy fire, on 2 February tanks and infantry secured a toe hold in the northern outskirts of the city, but by evening they had been pushed back up the road.

The next afternoon, 3 February, the 3d Battalion angled to the right, away from the road, and captured Hill 175, just northwest of Cassino, but heavy fire from Hill 193, directly south of 175, stopped further advance. Called "Castle Hill" because of the ruins of an old fort on its summit, Hill 193 presented an almost vertical cliff on its north face. Here and on the other heights in the sector the Germans had dug or blasted concrete and steel emplacements, some of which were large enough to contain living quarters for several troops. They were strong enough to withstand direct shell hits and were connected by trenches studded with steel-topped igloo-like machine-gun emplacements. The Todt engineers had done their work well.

The same day some tanks pushed into the northwest corner of the city, and the 1st Battalion forced its way into the northeastern out-skirts and dug in under heavy counterattack. Many of Cassino's stone houses had been made into miniature fortresses inside which the Germans had built concrete and steel antitank and machine-gun emplacements which commanded the narrow alleys. The bigger guns stopped the attacking tanks cold, and machine-gun and sniper fire mowed down attacking infantrymen.

In the hills to the northwest the 135th Infantry reached the slopes of S. Angelo Hill on 4 February, but could not push the Germans off its summit. The 1st and 2d battalions of the 135th were able to advance only a few hundred yards to the southwest against Hills 593 and 445. On 6 February two battalions of the 168th moved into action, attacking unsuccessfully against Monastery Hill (516), and on the same day the 2d Battalion of the 135th took and, with great difficulty, held Hill 593.

By 5 February all but L Company of the 3d Battalion of the 133d had moved from Hill 175 into the northwest corner of Cassino. That day the 1st Battalion relieved Company L which joined the rest of the 3d Battalion. The 1st Battalion took up the attack against Castle Hill (193) but gained little ground, and the 3d Battalion inched a little farther into Cassino's northwestern corner.

On 6 February, the 36th Division was relieved by the 2d New Zealand Division, which took over the sector south of Cassino, and the 36th swung north and to the right of the 34th Division to the Mt. Castellone area. It was intended that as the 36th jumped off for an advance southwest toward Piedmonte the 34th Division would simultaneously make another attempt against Hill 593, Monastery Hill (516), and Cassino. Possibly this time there might be a break-through to Highway 6.

The 135th Infantry of the 34th would attack in the vicinity of Hill 593, protecting the right flank of the 168th Infantry, which would make the main effort, another assault up Monastery Hill. If the 168th took the Abbey it would then drive toward Highway 6. Within these outer encircling movements the 133d Infantry would push southwest, in a tighter arc, to hem Cassino's defenders from the west. In the 133d's pivoting movement, the 3d Battalion in Cassino would serve as anchor, while the 1st Battalion farther west and the 100th on the outer rim of the arc swept south and then east against the town.

At 7:00 A.M. on 8 February, three hours after the 168th Infantry had moved against Monastery Hill, each of the 133d's battalions swung into action under smoke cover and with support by elements of the 760th Tank Battalion. Company C led the 100th down from the barracks area, climbed across ravines to a spot west of Castle Hill (193), and then turned south to climb through more gullies to Hill 165. Under smoke cover the battalion had suffered only a few casualties, but when the wind changed, lifting the smoke, machine-gun and mortar fire poured down from enemy positions on Monastery Hill to the right and from Castle Hill to the left. Several soldiers were killed; many more were wounded.

Major Lovell (whose return from the hospital on 29 January, just in time to take the 100th back into action, had been greeted with a joyous "The Major is back!") was injured and again forced out of action. Pinned down by rifle fire at the edge of a gully, he had piled up a rock shelter for his head and the upper part of his body, but had received a bullet in the chest and three in his exposed legs. Sergeant Gary Hisaoka, who had already been recommended for a Silver Star for his work in clearing mines on the Rapido's banks, started to dig a shallow ditch toward the wounded officer from his own slit trench eighteen yards away. After having burrowed eight yards he disgustedly threw down his shovel. "Hell, I'm going now." He dashed the rest of the distance, grabbed Lovell under the arms, and dragged him to safety.

A German assault gun appeared from some buildings behind the Castle, and began to pump shells down at the men on Hill 165. Rifle grenades couldn't reach it, so the same bazookaman who had ruined a German tank at Alife was called forward from a support platoon. He snaked across rocky terrain to a point within thirty yards of the gun and fired. His first shot hit one of the treads, and as bullets rattled around him he aimed again, and this time his rocket pierced the tank's armor and exploded inside. Tank-buster Masao Awakuni then crawled behind a boulder and sweated it out under sniper fire. In the dark, ten hours later, he returned to his outfit, a self-applied bandage around a wounded arm. He later received a DSC.

While the 100th had been feverishly seeking shelter on Hill 165, the 2d Battalion had had to dig in on the northwest slopes of Castle

Hill, and the 3d Battalion had been able to push only a few hundred feet into Cassino.

For the next four freezing days the men of the 100th deepened their holes and barricaded them with rocks and earth. Communication lines were constantly being cut by shellfire, and two Headquarters Company men, Pfc Akira Ishikawa and Pfc Satoshi Nakaue, later received Bronze Stars for their hours of repair work under fire. Technician Robert Oda and Sergeant Edward Saito volunteered to carry a radio from the battalion intermediate command post to the front lines about a mile forward. On the way the instrument was damaged by sniper fire and shell fragments. Dazed and bruised from being hurled among boulders by shell concussions, the men returned to the command post, secured another radio, and delivered it. They, too, received Bronze Stars.

In three days of fighting, 8–10 February, the 168th Infantry failed to take Monastery Hill, and suffered tremendous losses. On the northern slopes of Hill 593 the 135th was forced to fight furiously just to hold on.

On 11 February, II Corps mounted another attack. This time the 36th Division would try to break the German defenses along the line from Hills 593 to 374, and the 34th Division would make another try against Monastery Hill and Cassino. The 36th failed to dent the enemy defenses, and suffered heavy casualties. The 168th Infantry, so depleted in manpower that headquarters and supply personnel had to be used as reserve units, failed to gain ground on Monastery Hill, and the 135th and 133d regiments held their ground with difficulty. From now on all units held defensively while the New Zealand Corps prepared to take over from the exhausted II Corps units.

On 12 February, the 100th withdrew from its exposed position on Hill 165 and went into regimental reserve north of Hill 193 and behind the 1st Battalion. From this point Company B was sent into Cassino to aid the 3d Battalion. For four days and nights one of its squads held an ancient church which was gradually being ripped apart by enemy shells. The gray sky could be seen through a dozen holes in the roof. One shell which ripped through the floor of the loft brought down parts of skeletons which evidently had been resting comfortably for years, and bounced skulls and assorted leg and arm bones on the pavement below.

Much of the fighting inside Cassino was being done with hand grenades. A newspaper correspondent, who wanted to see the battle close up, visited Company B, remarked facetiously that he had heard that the Japanese were good baseball players, and asked about the 100th's grenade technique. He received the weary reply: "Mister, all you gotta do is trow straight and trow first. Dat's da numbah one theeng, trow first."

On 15 February, as thousands of soldiers watched with fascination and awe, 255 Allied planes dropped tons of bombs on the venerable Abbey atop Monastery Hill, and heavy guns hurled shells into its slowly disintegrating walls. During the next three days, English, Indian, and New Zealand troops tried to capture Monastery Hill and Hill 593, but failed.[1] On 22 February, when elements of the 6th New Zealand Brigade relieved the 133d Infantry, the Germans still held Cassino and the mountain defenses above it.*

In the fighting at the Rapido and around Cassino the 100th had lost four officers and forty-four enlisted men killed, twelve officers and 122 men wounded, and three officers and eight men injured. An additional seventy-five men had been hospitalized for trench foot or other ailments. When the battalion had entered Italy at Salerno it had numbered 1,300 men, and on 1 January, before its casualties in the fight through the Majo Hill mass and down to the Rapido Plain, it had had an effective strength of 832 officers and men. Before Major Lovell had led the battalion back into the fight for Cassino, the 133d's commander had told him, "I hate to have to do this, Major; they've been hit hard already, but I've got to use your fire-eaters in this attack." The 100th's effectives now totaled 521.

Back in the rest area near Alife there was again hot food and drink and a USO troupe for entertainment. Here a commissioned officer, a noncom, and a private left for the States under the Army's new system of rotation furloughs. On 10 March the unit moved to S. Giorgio near Benevento, where its first replacements, ten officers and 151 men, arrived from the 442d Regimental Combat Team at Camp Shelby. They were warmly received. At S. Giorgio, Purple Heart winners began returning from ths hospitals, sometimes as many as ten a day. With the gaps in the ranks being filled there was more

* Despite a great aerial and artillery bombardment on 15 March, followed by a tank and infantry assault which lasted eight days, the Germans held the city and Monastery Hill. Not until the third week of May were these positions finally taken.

chance of rotation for those soldiers of longest service and greatest age. Veterans began going back across the Atlantic in groups of five, some to the East Coast, some to California, and a few even to Hawaii for permanent duty. Though the 2d Battalion of the 133d Infantry arrived from North Africa and took the 100th's place within that regiment, the AJA unit continued under control of the 34th Division.

WHILE 10 CORPS and II Corps had been making unsuccessful attempts to break the Gustav Line, American and British troops of the VI Corps had made an amphibious landing at Anzio. Begun on 22 January, 1944, this operation achieved complete surprise, and enemy resistance was at first very weak. By evening of 24 January the invading force occupied a beachhead which extended fifteen miles along the coast and about seven miles inland. (See map, p. 186.) For the next five days VI Corps consolidated this position while more troops and supplies came in across the beaches.

During these days the German command rushed troops to the area, and when the Allied forces advanced again, on 30 January, they were stopped after three days by resistance which became constantly stronger as more enemy soldiers moved into line around the perimeter of the beachhead. Between 3 February and 4 March the Germans launched three major attacks, but the invaders grimly held their ground. After the third thrust failed (28 February—4 March) the enemy went on the defensive. During the eleven-week stalemate which followed, VI Corps replaced its heavy manpower losses and stock-piled thousands of tons of sea-borne supplies in preparation for a break-out smash. The Germans, meanwhile, worked constantly to strengthen their defensive line.

The invasion force occupied the central portion of a low coastal plain which extends north from Terracina through the Pontine Marshes to the Mussolini

Beach Rats

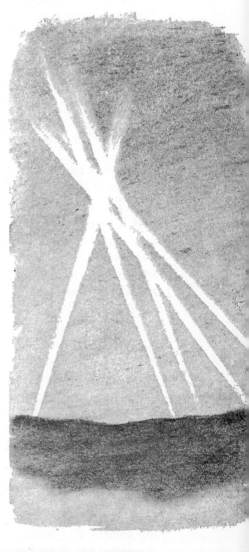

Canal southeast of Anzio and then across rolling country to the Tiber River below Rome. The twenty-six-mile perimeter of the beachhead followed the northern edge of the Mussolini Canal inland from the coast for about ten miles and then turned northeast, parallel to, but generally two or three miles south of, the Cisterna-Campoleone railroad. After it met the Anzio-Albano highway the line cut west along a ridge south of the Moletta River and back to the sea.

Northeast of Anzio, twenty miles inland, the Colli-Laziali mountain mass commanded the road net into Rome. East of these volcanic hills a three-mile-wide valley led past Velletri to Valmontone on Highway 6. On the other side of this defile rose the Lepini Mountains, stretching southeast along the inland edge of the Pontine Marshes toward Terracina on the sea. From the Lepini and Colli-Laziali heights the Germans had excellent observation over the beachhead area.[1]

The 34th Division shipped from Naples for the beachhead during the period 17–26 March. The 100th, though no longer part of the 133d Infantry, was still attached to the 34th Division, and on 24 March its members embarked in LSTs for the hundred-and-twenty-mile trip, reaching Anzio two days later. A wild crap game called Ten-Twent-Thirt, played with three dice, helped pass the time and incidentally cleaned some sailors who had joined the game. As they debarked, gazing along the villa-dotted shore line, the buddhaheads were reminded of Hawaiian beaches, but Anzio itself looked like any other war-shattered Italian town. Steel girders and shattered concrete overflowed the sidewalks; and in the shells of structures still erect, doors and windows gaped on the wreckage. Burned and twisted military vehicles, shattered trees, and skeletons of animals sprawled in and near the city.

The Red Bulls were to take over from the 3d Division west of German-held Cisterna, and the 100th moved by truck to a point south of Borgo Montello to relieve the 2d Battalion of the 30th Infantry. Compared with Anzio the countryside in this direction seemed little touched by war. Miles of flat green farm land, criss-crossed by drainage ditches, stretched off to the east. One of Mussolini's biggest public works projects had reclaimed this area from the ancient and notorious malaria-breeding Pontine Marshes, and the plain was dotted with modern two-story farmhouses, alike in design, but painted red, white, green, and yellow. Except for those male Italians who had remained as civilian laborers for the Allies, most of the peasants had been evacuated by sea, and their deserted cattle grazed in untended fields.

The new bivouac was in a patch of wooded area a few miles back from the foxholes of the front line, and here the battalion kitchen was soon serving hot meals. There was plenty of water in the irrigation ditches for bathing and laundry, and the men inherited underground dugout living quarters from their predecessors. In contrast with facilities at some previous camps these conveniences seemed very fine indeed. The Germans could, of course, reach any part of the beachhead with their shells, and the inside of a dugout was the safest place to stay, though even an underground shelter offered no sure protection from a direct hit. However, the Jerries didn't have enough guns or ammunition to pepper all parts of the beachhead all the time. In the evenings, when enemy binoculars in the hills ahead could no longer pick out objects on the plain, the boys felt sufficiently safe and cheerful to sit out in the open and talk or sing.

On 2 April Lieutenant Colonel Gordon Singles, formerly of the 69th Division, took over as battalion commander, and Major Clough, who had led the outfit since Major Lovell had been wounded, became second in command. Two days later a batch of replacements arrived, the second which had come from Camp Shelby, and this complement of eighteen officers and 261 enlisted men brought the battalion's effective strength to 1,095 officers and men, higher than at any time since the attack against Hills 841 and 920 at the end of November. Only two days of training in combat tactics could be given these latest recruits. On 6 April, the 100th was ordered to relieve the 1st Battalion of the 133d Infantry which had been in regimental reserve in the vicinity of Borgo Montello, and the relief was effected that night.

In this new position some elements of the battalion inherited dugouts and others were assigned to Mussolini's farmhouses. One company, allotted nine of the latter, divided them three to a platoon. They lay some 200 yards behind the outpost line and about 100 yards apart. Several had been either partially or completely unroofed by shellfire; most had at least one big hole in one of the walls; and of the original six rooms generally only two or three were still usable, the floors of the others being piled high with dust and rubble. In some houses the stench of dead bodies still remained. Lithographs of the "Virgin and Child" or the "Crucifixion" hung awry on the cement-powdered walls. To the surprise of the new occupants, the model farmhouses of the Fascist "New Order" had no inside toilets. Burned-out half-tracks and tanks, brown bomb and shell craters, and the remains of dead cattle spoiled the green view from the windows, and the decomposing carcasses of animals sickened the spring air.

Those soldiers assigned to dugouts found their quarters relatively safe, if not large. About three feet wide, shoulder high, and seven feet long, they had generally been built in L shape for protection even in case of a direct shell hit at the entrance. Paper or dried grass was placed on the earthen floor and then covered with blankets. Other blankets covered the walls, and to these the homesick Islanders sometimes pinned wrappers from Hawaiian pineapple cans along with the usual pin-up pictures. Five-gallon gas tins served as tables.

It was a strange kind of life. With the exception of the security guards, nearly everyone slept from dawn until midday. Except under direct orders, no one left cover during daylight. Letter-writing, checkers, cards, and napping helped fill the hours. And there was endless talk about Hawaii—"Chee, I weesh I stay relax down Waikiki makai side now. I telling you dees, no moe any kine place like da home." A cramped existence, perhaps, but restful—once one became used to the sound of intermittent shelling—and not particularly dangerous. There was always the possibility that an enemy shell might land directly on the roof of a dugout—in this area it was impossible to walk more than 100 yards in any direction without seeing a shell crater—but such accidents didn't happen very often, and even when they did, men had been known to emerge from their burrows alive. Few GIs were too lazy, however, to spend time after dark filling more sand bags to protect their shelters. Lots of jobs in the Army were "wastetime," but not this.

At sundown the beach rats emerged from their holes. Meals often owed less to the Quartermaster Corps than to skill in foraging. The Italian "paisanos" had left plenty of chickens behind; their cows seemed to offer surprisingly easy targets for German bullets; and sometimes a quick daytime shot from farmhouse or dugout bagged a rabbit which could be picked up after dark. Any plant that didn't look or taste downright poisonous was likely to find itself doing service as a vegetable. There was always some soldier who knew how to mix fresh meat, greens, and "10 in 1" rations in judicious proportions, and some of the stews that resulted were so good that men did write home about them. Broiled cow steaks were served smothered with chopped flower bulbs cooked in bouillon cube broth. Visitors from other units who stayed for a meal went away licking their chops, and the reputation of the 100th's cookery spread throughout the division. Following a practice they had adopted soon after reaching Italy, the battalion cooks continued to swap the potato ration with other outfits for rice, and the *haole* officers resignedly ate the substitute.

Red and yellow roses, dark red poppies, and pink and white carnations grew in the farmhouse gardens, and at twilight the flower-loving Islanders picked bouquets for their rooms or dugouts. May Day is known as Lei Day in Hawaii (there is an Island song to that effect) and the first day of May, 1944, also became Lei Day in Italy. That morning every man who had been able to gather enough blossoms wore a *lei* around his neck. On this same day, by happy coincidence, division supply issued the first beer rations!

At night men not assigned patrol duty filled sand bags or stood guard for others thus occupied. Jerry planes made frequent night raids, and then the sky filled with multicolored fire, as tracers climbed, ack-ack burst, and flares lighted the beachhead for miles. "It's beautiful," men said, "even if it is war."

Razor blade radios provided other entertainment for duty-free evenings. Receiving sets, made with the help of the battalion communication section, consisted of two or three double-edged safety razor blades, a few pieces of wire, and a dry battery. Small enough to fit nicely into a mess kit, they could pick up "Axis Sally," who was broadcasting nightly from Rome. The regular radio section sets had brought in her voice before the battalion had come to Anzio, but this was the first time most of the men had both leisure and facilities for frequent listening. To hear the American records Sally played (they were surprisingly up-to-date, and she occasionally played Hawaiian numbers) the men listened to her "What are you dopes fighting for?" chatter with good-humored patience. Her propaganda was as ineffectual as the German leaflets urging desertion which the boys picked up and saved as souvenirs. "The Bitch" put on a good show, her records were well chosen, and her wiles gave rise to plenty of bawdy jokes.

After Cassino, life at Anzio was more like a rest cure, but there were hours, especially those spent on patrol, when the buddhaheads wished themselves elsewhere. German motorized paratroop units were frequently sent into the American lines at night to capture prisoners and create confusion, and VI Corps ordered jeep patrols for their interception. With the windshields down for better forward visibility, and the tops folded back so that the sky could be scanned for German planes, a driver and three heavily armed companions would course the countryside within the battalion sector, eyes straining through the dark for suspicious activity.

Ordinarily a soldier assigned to this duty was in more danger from his daredevil charioteer than from the enemy, but patrol work beyond the outpost line was another matter, whether a man went out as a member of a heavily armed combat group of ten to twenty men or of a smaller reconnaissance patrol. Letters and pictures left behind, dog tags covered, canteens full to the brim so that water wouldn't slosh, men crept along the channels of drainage ditches, or through grass and shrubs, trying always to avoid paths along which mines or ambush might lurk. When an enemy flare flooded the plain with sudden light, they froze for an eternity until it finally faded out. Sometimes the burp of a German machine pistol ripped the silence, and then there would be a short confused fire-fight. On a good night even the wounded walked back, but there were evenings when some soldiers had to be carried and others remained where they had fallen.

The worst kind of duty was that spent in a foxhole on the outpost line, with the Germans only about a hundred yards ahead. It was unsafe to show any part of the body during the daytime, and, day or night, any movement had to be stealthy. The nearest buddy in the next hole was perhaps ten or twenty yards away, and no whispered conversations helped pass the endless hours. A wound received during the day had to wait for medical attention until a relief came up at dark, and then it was sometimes too late. The lonesome vigil was especially hard on the replacements newly arrived from Shelby. One went out to his post one night and was found dead the next. That was rough, and everyone who heard about it was glum for a while. Then, "Maybe he bettah off; he got no moh *pilikia* now."[2]

Of all the Anzio patrols, that led by Captain Young O. Kim and

Pfc Irving M. Akahoshi was the most daring and successful. Kim, S-2 of the battalion, was a twenty-five-year-old Los Angeles boy whose parents were born in Korea. He had joined the 100th at McCoy on graduation from an officer candidate school, had already won a Silver Star for his part in the fighting on Hills 590 and 610, and had been hospitalized for a time as a result of a wound received in that action. In almost every engagement, but especially when on patrol duty, Kim had shown an extraordinary aptitude in killing Germans. When asked to explain his success he modestly admitted that a prewar slaughterhouse job had given him specialized preparation for his present duties. Perhaps he also wanted to show his AJA comrades that Japan had not conquered his parents' homeland by reason of superior national valor. In any case Kim never seemed to get his fill of danger. Major Lovell once commented that Kim volunteered for scout duty as though it were healthy.

Patrols sent out during the first two weeks of May had captured no prisoners for interrogation, and regimental headquarters was pressing for up-to-date information on opposing forces in the sector, so, on 16 May, Kim and Akahoshi offered to go out and bag one or more Germans. Three riflemen volunteered to go along.

Leaving the Company B command post shortly before midnight, the five scouts crept along a waist-high drainage ditch through and past the enemy's forward outposts. At about 2:00 A.M. they heard some Germans digging. Kim decided to wait until dawn before going ahead. When it became light enough to see, he posted the three riflemen as cover, and he and Akahoshi moved forward again, out of the ditch now, cutting and crawling through heavy briar.

At about 9:00 A.M. they halted, and Kim peered cautiously above the scrub, looking for enemy defense posts. They left the briar and stomached their way across a field of eighteen-inch grain toward what Kim had spotted as a possible German strongpoint. Two hours and some 250 yards later they heard voices, and metallic sounds as though a gun were being cleaned. A little more wriggling, and then through the grass they could see a couple of security guards in a slit trench. At Kim's low-voiced command two Germans gazed popeyed at the barrel of a Thompson sub-machine gun and silently raised their hands. As this pair and their captors crawled stealthily away they could hear the talk and laughter of other Jerries a few yards away. By 4:00 P.M. all members of the patrol and their prisoners were back within the 100th's lines.

When General Ryder visited the battalion command post next day he called Kim in for personal commendation. Kim and Akahoshi later received DSCs. During his visit Ryder gave notice that VI Corps would soon put its breakthrough ("Buffalo") plan into operation.

On 19–20 May, Companies A and B moved from the vicinity of Borgo-Montello in the direction of Borgo Podgora to relieve two companies of the 1st Battalion, 133d Infantry. These units had suffered heavy casualties in a raid on enemy lines the day before, and regimental headquarters, anticipating a counterattack, had decided to move in fresh troops. As the relief companies came up to the 1st Battalion positions, which were under heavy mortar and artillery fire, they were given light gas masks with instructions to carry them until further notice. The rest of the 100th moved in progressively to take over, and by 22 May the whole battalion was in line, in strong defensive position. Heavy mortar fire had evidently discouraged any enemy plans for counterattack, but patrols went out frequently from both sides of no-man's-land.

On the afternoon of 22 May the command post received a message from the outpost line: a German emissary had proposed that a party be sent to pick up eight American wounded behind the enemy lines. Battalion surgeon Captain John J. Dahl and Chaplain Israel Yost drove out with two ambulances, a quarter-ton truck, and two litter squads, and proceeded to within 100 yards of the Mussolini Canal. A battalion rifleman told the party to dismount, disarm, and follow a drainage ditch out into the canal. Though the big cut measured 170 feet from bank to bank, only a low sixteen-foot-wide stream ran down its center. Within the canal Dahl and his party found, all without firearms, a lieutenant from Company A, several enlisted men, and two young German paratroopers. On the south bank a German sentinel gazed across at the group. One of the Germans could speak a little English; Chaplain Yost knew some German. It developed that the paratroopers wanted a truce so that they might bury the bodies of a dozen dead Americans still above ground within their lines. Yost replied that the battalion command had no power to make such an agreement. The Jerry spokesman and his companion saluted smartly, wheeled, and walked away.

ON THE DAY after the parley in the big ditch the 100th suddenly found itself in undisputed possession of both its banks, and sharing patrol of eight miles of the Canal Line with the 34th Reconnaissance Troop. Buffalo Plan had gone into operation at dawn; the 133d Infantry was now fighting on the right flank of a smash at Cisterna; and the Germans on the south side of the Canal were rapidly pulling back toward the threatened area.

During the previous thirteen days a combined offensive by the Fifth and Eighth Armies had broken the Gustav Line between Cassino and the sea, had outflanked the weaker Hitler line farther north, and had thrown the Germans into retreat along the southern front. By 23 May, 1944, elements of the American II Corps had reached the outskirts of Terracina, at the edge of the coastal plain below Rome, about thirty miles from Cisterna.

That same morning the seven beachhead divisions launched the first phase of their breakthrough drive, a thrust intended to cut Highway 7, most westerly of the main south-north roads to Rome. (See map, p. 186.) Once the German line had been broken in the Cisterna area, VI Corps planned a push north through the valley between the Colli Laziali and Lepini hills toward the upper end of the Liri-Sacco River valley system, at Valmontone on Highway 6. It was assumed that the threat in this area would hasten withdrawal of German units still fighting a stubborn rear-

Breakthrough to Rome

guard action against the Eighth Army in the Liri Valley, for, with Highway 7 cut, the Germans would have to rely on Highway 6 as their main path of retreat from the south.

Buffalo Plan achieved complete surprise. After elements of the 34th Division had blown gaps in the enemy mine fields before Cisterna, the 3d Division moved against the town; the 1st Armored Division (135th Infantry attached) drove to cut Highway 7 on the north, and the 1st Special Service Force (133d Infantry attached) attacked to gain the road south of Cisterna and to hold those enemy forces southeast of the Mussolini Canal which were on the right flank of the Allied advance. By evening of 25 May objectives had been attained and VI Corps held Cisterna, Cori, and Mt. Arrestino.

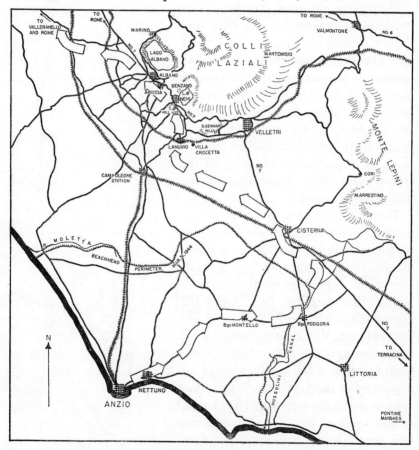

ANZIO THROUGH ALBANO

During the first day of the breakthrough many men of the 100th hardly realized that anything unusual was happening. That evening antitank men digging gun positions still worked warily, alert for the first rustle of an enemy shell—the road alongside which they were digging had frequently been plastered by enemy artillery. The next afternoon, however, American tanks and half-tracks were roaring past the antitank positions into the former enemy lines.

On 24 May a third batch of replacements arrived from Camp Shelby, and the three officers and 112 enlisted men were quickly distributed among the battalion companies. Two days later Lieutenant Kim came back from patrol with a prisoner who turned out to be a Russian who had been captured at Orel and conscripted into the Wehrmacht. He had been assigned to duty in Poland for some months, and had then been transferred to Italy by way of Czechoslovakia, Hungary, and Austria. In the few German and Italian words he knew the Russian told of having been provided with the clothes of dead Nazi soldiers—his shoes were certainly far too large—of receiving more food from the Italian military than from the Germans, and of his hope that he might be transported to the United States. He was obviously much pleased to be out of the fighting.

While the 100th had been resting the war had gone on. Along the line Velletri-Lanuvio-Campoleone Station, VI Corps had been attempting to break the southwestern anchor of the enemy defense line below Rome. The 45th Division had attacked on the west toward Campoleone; the 34th Division, in the center toward Lanuvio; and the 1st Armored Division, on the right toward Velletri. Farther east, the 3d Division had moved against Valmontone. By evening of 27 May, the 133d and 168th regiments of the 34th Division were up against strong enemy positions which ran along a line of ridges on the south slopes of Colli Laziali below the Velletri-Lanuvio-Campoleone railroad line. The 168th Regiment, on the right of the 34th Division sector, was only about two miles south of Lanuvio.

On 27 May, the 100th trucked fifteen miles northeast toward Lanuvio to replace the 135th Infantry's 2d Battalion, which had been detached for service with the 1st Armored Division. At 5:00 A.M. on 29 May, the 1st and 3d battalions of the 135th went into action at Pastroella Creek, but were stopped by intense automatic fire, and during the next two days advanced only a little more than a mile against fierce resistance. Throughout this fighting the 100th remained in regimental reserve. On the 135th's left the 45th Division and the 1st Armored Division had captured Campoleone Station but had had little success in attempting to push north toward Albano.

The night of 30–31 May, however, elements of the 36th Division captured Mt. Artemisio, northeast of Velletri, thus piercing the Velletri-Valmontone defense line, and making it possible for the 36th to drive north across the Colli Laziali mass to threaten the rear of the Velletri-Lanuvio-Albano line. On the evening of 31 May the enemy began to pull some troops out of the Lanuvio-Velletri area; the next day, 1 June, Velletri fell to the 141st Infantry of the 36th Division, and on 2 June the men of the 168th Infantry occupied Villa Crocetta and S. Gennaro Hill, strongpoints east of Lanuvio which had held them in check for six days. The Germans were, however, still fighting strongly on the left against the 135th Regiment and the 45th Division.

The 100th relieved the 1st Battalion of the 135th on 2 June at 1:25 A.M., and advanced under heavy mortar fire over hilly terrain toward the little hamlet of Pian Marano, west of Lanuvio. First direct contact with the enemy was made at 9:00 A.M., and fighting was continuous throughout the rest of the day and night. The Germans fought bitterly behind machine guns protected by mine fields, and Companies B and C had to clear lanes through the mines before they could knock out the Jerry gun nests, but by 7:20 A.M. of 3 June the battalion was in possession of Pian Marano.

For their conduct in this action six men won DSCs; one received a Silver Star; and three were awarded Bronze Stars. One of the DSC winners, Pfc Hiroshi Yasotake, of Company C, who had been ordered to cover the exposed right flank of his unit, took a post overlooking enemy positions, reported German movements, and, using his BAR and hand grenades, wounded seven Germans. In a ten-minute duel with an enemy machine gun 700 feet away, he silenced its gunners. As Company C began cleaning out enemy dugouts, this soldier also advanced. At one point in his progress he was in an abandoned gun emplacement, a German advancing through the grapevines toward him. When the enemy soldier had crawled within five yards, Yasotake riddled him. Three more Germans who tackled the gunner were wiped out at twenty yards distance.

In another part of the battalion sector Pfc Haruto Kuroda, Private Thomas Ono, and Sergeant Yukio Yokota, all of Company B, earned

DSCs by silencing five machine guns and five machine pistols and killing or capturing seventeen of the enemy within a period of three hours.

Pian Marano cost the battalion fifteen men killed, three wounded, and one missing in action. Some of the casualties resulted when the 100th was mistaken for an enemy unit and was fired upon by 45th Division artillery.

On 3 June the 168th Infantry occupied Lanuvio, and all units of the 34th Division pushed north toward Albano against rapidly weakening German resistance. The enemy was withdrawing from the Velletri-Albano line. The 36th Division, now pushing rapidly north across Colli Laziali, threatened the enemy rear, and elements of the II Corps of the Fifth Army were moving up Highway 6 north of Valmontone, circling the north side of the Colli Laziali mass on the way to Rome.

During the afternoon of 3 June Colonel Singles took command of a task force composed of the 100th, the 125th Field Artillery Battalion, the 151st Field Artillery Battalion, Company C of the 191st Tank Destroyer Battalion, Company A of the 804th Tank Destroyer Battalion, and Company C of the 84th Chemical Mortar Battalion. Supported by this firepower, Singles' foot soldiers were to mop up elements of the German 29th Panzer Group strongly emplaced on Hill 435. This knob commanded a road junction just south of Genzano which the enemy needed to keep open as an escape route for troops withdrawing up Highway 7 toward Albano and Rome.

At 8:30 P.M. Company A climbed the hill under cover of a barrage laid down by the 125th Field Artillery Battalion. When heavy machine-gun and mortar fire pinned Company A down, Company B went into action on the left, and Company C on the right. The supporting tank destroyers performed with deadly accuracy, practically all their shells landing on or within a few yards of the crest, wiping out gun emplacements and gunners, and chemical mortars simultaneously wreathed the defenders in smoke. By midnight the battalion was in undisputed possession of the mound. Company C alone had taken fifty prisoners.

During the morning of 4 June, the 133d Infantry pushed through Genzano, and all along the line the 34th Division moved north. Throughout the day "Task Force Singles" advanced so swiftly up Highway 7, through Genzano, Ariccia, and Albano, that rear and forward elements were out of communication, and the combat team itself was out of touch with the divisional command post. The Germans were in hasty retreat, and masses of Allied tanks and infantry were converging on Rome along Highways 6 and 7 and all intermediate roads.

At 3:00 P.M. the next day, ten miles beyond Valleranello, a road sign indicated that Rome was only ten kilometres ahead, but here, to the intense disgust of its members, who had hoped that theirs might be the first Allied battalion to enter the Italian capital, the 100th was ordered to halt and wait for truck transport. As the unit rested, flying columns of tanks, tank destroyers, and motorized infantry passed by, racing for the bridges across the Tiber River into Rome. By dark most of these spans were under Allied guard.

At 9:00 P.M. Colonel Single's men piled into trucks, and an hour and a half later were riding through the northwestern outskirts of the Italian capital. Only scattered cheers greeted them. Earlier in the day the first American troops had received a hysterical welcome, but the large crowds had dispersed, and now only small groups of civilians loitered on the sidewalks to discuss the events of the great day.

The original members of the 100th who rode past them also had reason to mark this date. On the 5th of June, 1942, two years ago to the day, the Hawaiian Provisional Infantry Battalion had shipped out of Honolulu Harbor on the S.S. *Maui*.

IN THE AFTERNOON of 6 June, 1944, trucks moved the battalion to an assembly area a few miles north of Rome, and here, for the first time in days, the kitchen train caught up. All the artillery units of the Singles Task Force were now released from battalion control. Next morning, on roads whose ditches were still littered with wrecked German equipment, the 100th rode to Civitavecchia, forty miles above Rome, and remained in the vicinity of that port until 10 June, when there was another move seven miles north to a quiet valley where the 34th Division had set up a rest area.

The next day, 11 June, the 3d Battalion, the 522d Field Artillery Battalion, and the 232d Engineer Company of the 442d Regimental Combat Team moved into bivouac next door to the 100th. They were followed six days later by the 2d Battalion. The AJA regiment's 1st Battalion, reduced to a skeleton force by loss of men sent to the 100th and transfer of personnel to the other battalions, had been left behind at Shelby to train replacements for the combat team. A General Order now attached the 100th Battalion to the 442d Infantry, and that regiment to the 34th Division.

Until 20 June the regiment drilled, hiked, fired rifles and heavy weapons, and practiced battle problems. The 100th's veterans did their best to prepare the new boys for combat. "My kid brother is now here with me. I hope he will be all right. Somehow his safety and welfare mean more to me than my

We Get to Wondering

own. I've given him some good GI advice, and I hope he keeps himself out of trouble."[1]

There was swimming at a newly cleared beach area and at night there were movies and band concerts. Two groups, an officer and thirty men in each, went on five-day passes to the Fifth Army Rest Center at Porto Mussolini, and each day 10 per cent of the battalion personnel got twenty-four-hour passes for Rome. At a ceremony in the divisional command post area General Ryder pinned Silver Stars on two officers and four enlisted men of the 100th, and the DSC on Masao Awakuni, who had used his bazooka so well at S. Angelo and Cassino. Two officers and fifty enlisted men went to the Vatican City and, with GIs from other outfits, had audience with the Pope.

During the periods of training, recreation, housekeeping, "hurrying up and waiting," even during battle itself, the buddhaheads had been doing a lot of thinking, and the two-week rest period gave them a chance to sort out their thoughts. They knew better than most GIs why they were risking their lives to push German soldiers off Italian mountainsides. The United States proclaimed the freedom and dignity of all men, and throughout its history had moved toward ever greater application of that principle. In the continuation of that process, which the Germans and Japanese sought to halt, the AJAs had a sizable stake, for they wanted first-class citizenship in the land of their birth. They hoped that on their return to Hawaii —for which they were often desperately homesick—they would be accorded that status. They knew that at home there were many persons who had never doubted their right to it, but they also knew that there were many others to whom a Jap would always be a Jap, who wanted wholesale evacuation of their folk, who would never have given the AJAs a chance to show their loyalty, who, after it was all over, would still deny that the deaths and wounds in Italy had proved anything.

They could not help knowing this; letters from relatives and friends told them what went on in Hawaii; and if additional proof were needed it was frequently provided in the "Letters to the Editor" columns of the Island newspapers which they received at the front. At times, therefore, some of the men were deeply troubled. A one-eyed, stump-armed veteran told a war correspondent who visited him in an Army hospital: "We get to wondering if what we did will help any in getting our people—the Japanese-Americans—from behind the eight ball. It was funny but we thought about it when we landed at Salerno. Even fighting all the time for almost a year we were conscious of a fear that people would hiss at us after the war. I was thinking about it just before the medic gave me morphine when I got it near Rome."[2]

A messenger, as he lay dying, whispered his hope "that you and the others will be fully recognized as Americans."[3]

Another member of the outfit wrote home about the "horrifying nightmare" that was battle: "You lose your buddies—fellows with whom you laughed, ate, slept, sweated. They become blood relations to you, and they die before your eyes—not a pleasant, natural death, but an unimaginable kind of mutilation mixed with groans and prayers ending in a gurgling last breath. Only five minutes ago you might have been laughing with that buddy of yours. . . ." And he reported: "Our outfit is going good. One can't help swelling up with pride to be in such a good outfit. One sees the little guys carrying the heavy weapons for miles. Guts and strength and a real appreciation of duty. . . . Nobody can love freedom and our way of life more than we do. If we return home to find that we are still Japs in the eyes of the guys who have grown fat with dough during the war, we are going to find beautiful platitudes like equality of opportunity and such blown, as we are being blown here; and then we are going to suffer as we have never before suffered, as we see that 'if we cannot win this peace, we will lose the next war' materialize into a shocking actuality. Pray God that this will never be."[4]

Members of the battalion constantly expressed regret that they could not do their fighting in the Pacific. A captain's letter gave the reason:

We have come over 12,000 miles to prove we're loyal—the proof in terms of human lives and human blood. . . . I know that the sacrifices we make here may be adequate proof, but the question of our loyalty to our country could have been settled for all time if we sacrificed our men on the battlefields of the South Pacific. Then no rabid race-hater can say, "How do we know whether these boys will fight soldiers from the land of both their parents?"

Everyone who sits in his foxhole here waiting for the day when this will be all over regrets that if he were to make sacrifices, why couldn't he have made them in the South Pacific fighting the Japs.

Well, that is fate. We'll do our best.[5]

In conversation with a war correspondent, a lieutenant voiced the same idea. "If we go home and say we've been in the war and people ask us where and we say Italy, those who doubt our loyalty will sneer and say that doesn't count because we didn't fight Japanese. All of us still hope to have an opportunity to fight in the Pacific before the war is over."[6] A newsman reported Doc Kawasaki as saying, "You know there is a cloud over all of us. So we must fight where we can to show again that we are loyal Americans. We fight for our lives as good citizens. Colonel Turner calls it a crusade. I think he's right."[7]

Occasionally a bitterly angry member of the battalion answered prejudice by word as well as deed. After reading two letters written by a Navy man who approved the way in which the West Coast had managed its "Japanese Problem," a wounded soldier retorted through one of the home newspapers.

> All the *haole* boys who were in my ward for the same simple reason as mine, who chanced to read the papers raised a helluva big rumpus. Many were from California and in "business" ever since this hell started. . . .
>
> I'm an AJA soldier from Hawaii and couldn't help notice your critical remarks about our fellow buddies; namely, the AJAs from the mainland.* I tip my hat to them, for theirs was the most trying ordeal since the outbreak of this hell. . . .
>
> Many of them will never see even the relocation centers again, for they rest in eternal sleep in some American cemetery over here. . . .
>
> Our relations (AJAs') with other American troops, especially combat troops, have been nothing but the best; also with Allied troops (British and French). We're treated as one of them and they and we have nothing but esteem and respect for each other because we understand what each goes through. . . .
>
> They also understand our plight, especially from articles such as yours.
>
> All in all, we find that the ones who actually fight this war understand us, and the ones who are in the rear area and out of this hell (like you) are our bitterest berators. . . .
>
> You talk about us not being 'assimilated' but your letter doesn't sound so 'assimilated' to me. . . .[8]

Generally, however, when a buddhahead wrote a letter in public defense of his people, his tone was more mild and conciliatory. On learning that two kibei in Hawaii had publicly renounced allegiance to the United States, a soldier wrote to his hometown paper, re-

---

* Some of the replacements from Shelby now fighting along with the 100th were volunteers from relocation camps—in which their families still remained. Their combat behavior had earned them respect.

porting the reaction among his buddies: "They know that news like that will cause a field day to those who doubted our loyalty right along. They also know that all the good work they have so nobly advanced, and will advance further, will suffer from that act in the warped minds of the public who are against us. . . . Don't judge our sympathies by the deeds of a few. Remember the many who are over here now, past, present, and future, not by persuasion, but by choice to prove to the few doubting Thomases of our great nation that there is but one country in our hearts and minds—America."[9]

Such writing became less frequent as the men learned how many champions they had in Hawaii, on the Mainland, and among the Fifth Army troops in Italy. Private citizens, newspaper editors and reporters, officials of the national government, and fellow soldiers were replying to the racists for them, and more effectively than they themselves could hope to do.

There were, they discovered, persons like the Army sergeant, stationed in Hawaii, who gave $100 to be used for the benefit of children of Japanese ancestry, and explained the gift as his personal response to the "evacuators" and others who were "systematically seeking to raise fictitious racial barriers, to foster ill feeling between different groups, to destroy the Constitution of the United States by making its provisions inapplicable to certain groups of citizens because of their ancestry, and to destroy from within everything which distinguishes us from the Axis countries and makes America really worth fighting for."[10]

There was the resident of Hawaii, drafted and stationed in the Territory, who replied to a letter writer who complained that too many AJAs were still civilians, and that too many of these young men were taking jobs vacated by soldiers of other ancestries. In his answer this particular GI remarked that he had recommended a boy of Japanese ancestry to fill the job which he himself had left.

There is no reason why I should either want or expect to take his job away from him after the war. Certainly not just because of the color of my skin, in any case.

We are supposed to be fighting for more justice and equality than now prevails over much of the world—not for the supremacy of the white or any other single race. We make a pretty poor start towards fulfilling our professed aims if we at home assert the same racial theories we find so contemptible in our enemies and set ourselves up as better than other people, entitled to all the best jobs regardless of individual merit.

195

This writer remarked that the brother of the man who now held his job had been in the Army for two years, and had done a "lot more fighting than I have or ever expect to do."[11]

There was the Texas woman who wrote to Private Mac I. Yagawa when he was in an Army hospital. Mac had been caught in a mine explosion and shrapnel had nearly torn off his right arm, had smashed his chest and punctured a lung, and had lodged in one of his feet. An article in *Collier's* about the 100th had mentioned Yagawa's wounds, and as a result he received numerous letters from well-wishers all over the country, of which this message from San Antonio was one:

The minority in this country that are preaching and practising racial intolerance are condemning the very creed for which our boys are fighting and dying. I want to be among the first to thank you, from the bottom of my heart, for what you have done for the folks back home. I have no boy to send into battle to defend our way of living and so I must depend on other mothers' sons.

I sincerely hope and pray that you will live your life out in peace, security and happiness in the country for which you fought so faithfully and hard. If it will help you on your road to recovery, I, and I am sure that thousands of other Americans who feel the same, will be stretching forth a welcoming hand to you when you are ready to take your place again in civilian life.[12]

The 100th received much favorable publicity. Very soon after the outfit entered combat, War Department press releases commended its performance. These notices were intended to stimulate morale within the battalion itself and among the AJA trainees at Shelby. They were also ammunition for the psychological warfare against Japan and Germany, as well as a means of mitigating home-front prejudice against Americans of Japanese ancestry.

On October 15, 1943, shortly after witnesses before a California legislative committee had warned of bloodshed if evacuated Japanese-Americans returned to that state, Secretary of War Stimson told newsmen about General Mark Clark's favorable report on the behavior of the AJA troops in their first experience of combat, and referred to Joe Takata's heroic death. In a speech delivered in New York on November 19, Ambassador to Japan Joseph C. Grew urged that the American people show greater tolerance for citizens of Japanese descent, and backed his plea by referring to the record of the 100th Battalion, serving "with distinction" in Italy. In March, 1944, Secretary of the Interior Harold Ickes made public mention of the "magnificent record" of the AJA unit.[13] There were other statements of similar nature, and increasingly frequent press dispatches on the progress of the unique fighting outfit from Hawaii.

This well-intentioned praise proved embarassing. The 100th had fought well, but no better than many another battalion in the Fifth Army. General Ryder, who himself never spared the unit praise which he thought deserved, said he didn't want that kind of thing. There were other units in his division which had been fighting much longer than the 100th and at least as well, and in the long run it would not help the Japanese-American outfit if other Red Bull soldiers became annoyed. Many men of the 100th laughed it off with "We not dat good." Others, more thoughtful, would have preferred to wait until the battalion had done more to earn its praise. Private Yutaka Nezu, who later died in battle, wrote to the editor of *The Honolulu Star-Bulletin:* "I'm the squad leader that was supposed to have rescued the 22 American paratroopers that was in your article about one or two months ago. I don't know who gave you the news but the rescuing statement wasn't true. We did go on that particular mission to rescue them, but when we went to that certain place there was no one to be rescued. What happened to those paratroopers I don't know. I don't mind being written up for things I did, but neither do I want to be glorified for things I didn't do."[14]

In Hawaii the publicity caused both irritation and grief.

In an editorial titled "Less Limelight Please," published on October 18, 1943, *The Honolulu Advertiser* referred to an Associated Press item about the 100th, printed two days previously by *The Honolulu Star-Bulletin*, and decried the "excessive" publicity being received by Hawaii's AJA soldiers. The *Advertiser* felt these stories not only gave Mainlanders the impression that the only fighting men from the Territory were those of Japanese blood, but also gave the local Japanese a distorted view of their own role in the national war effort.

The next day a *Star-Bulletin* editorial remarked that such complaints probably stemmed from ignorance of the fact that the War Department had "deliberately and carefully embarked on a policy of proving to the enemy—particularly to the enemy Japanese—that under the American democratic system, this country can produce and is producing young men of Japanese blood who willingly and effectively fight other men of their own race—the enemy." When the men of the 100th went into battle America was demonstrating to both Orientals and to Nazis that these soldiers were fighting, not as Japanese, but as Americans. The War Department issued news releases of the sort criticized, not only because of their interest to readers in the community from which the AJA soldiers came, but also because of their vital usefulness in the national policy. "That policy is to demonstrate that the American system works in war as in peace—supporting and nerving a united nation of many racial strains."[15]

Four months later, while the 100th was fighting through the Majo hill mass, the *Star-Bulletin* printed part of a letter written by Doc Kometani. In this message the 100th's morale officer told a member of the Emergency Service Committee of the gratitude with which the battalion members had received a substantial money gift from that group, and continued:

They are happy that you appreciate the real and actual battle they are going through for you and the people back there, and for the country which has raised us and given us a place. . . .

The 100th has received much publicity. I am writing to you in the hope that you will understand that we have no control over the front line publicity and it is not our desire. We are just some of the many American soldiers doing our share, not asking for any favor, but the chance to do our share. Then, if those beyond our control feel that we deserve such publicity, we feel cheered beyond recognition.[16]

When Turner returned home in May, 1944, he learned that the press reports had caused some unfortunate reactions among the parents of his boys. Eagerly read news items had told how well their sons were fighting, but the long casualty lists also revealed the cost. They were proud, but also fearful. There had been sudden and wide-spread mourning in Mainland home towns of other former National Guard units after a combat outfit composed of guardsmen had suffered extremely heavy casualties, and so it was now within Hawaii's Japanese community. One day a mother might receive from her son a message such as this: "It is an honor for a boy to stand for his country, and to defend the rights which he treasures dearly. I will do my utmost, so you may be assured that I shall never disgrace the name of my family, nor the fame of my country. Thoughts of you are always with me. Wherever you may be, you are my happiness." And she might learn next day, as did this mother, that her son was dead.[17]

It was good that the papers carried stories of the valor of their sons, but were they being asked to do more than their share? Was the Army giving them especially dangerous missions, either because they fought so well or because the AJA team was to be tested, as a guinea pig unit, to the utmost? The 100th's losses had actually been no higher than those of some other Fifth Army battalions, but the men's parents had no firm assurance that this was so. What they did know was that many AJAs were in Army hospitals or under Italian earth, and that the names in the newspaper lists of Hawaii's casualties were predominantly Japanese.

Shortly after his return to the Territory, Turner traveled among the Islands, and on each he talked with and to individuals and groups of persons of Japanese ancestry, an interpreter present to translate his remarks for the benefit of the older generation. He consoled the sorrowful, reassured the anxious, and chastened the spirits of the overproud. He reported that the men of the 100th had behaved themselves admirably both in training and in combat, and that the Army and other national authorities were pleased with them. In this fact the relatives and friends of the AJAs could take great and deserved pride, but though their boys were good soldiers, they were no better than many other GIs in Italy and on other fronts. And though, like other battalions, the 100th had been given some tough assignments, the Colonel firmly asserted that it had received no more than its proper share of the fighting.[18]

Turner's troops had trusted his word, and their folk did likewise. His mission was a continuation of the kind of service which had won him the Legion of Merit for the manner in which he had instilled his troops with "a high morale and *esprit de corps*" and had inspired them to "overcome the problems created by racial prejudice." The veterans for whom he had battled continued to keep in touch with him by mail from Italy, and those who returned to Hawaii dropped into his office for a chat.

"How's that contraption [a mechanical hand] working?"

"Try me out on a highball, Colonel."

As the War Department and the OWI used the 100th's story as a psychological weapon, word of the AJA battalion in Italy spread to the corners of the globe. In India, Burma, China, the Dutch East Indies, and various Pacific Islands, those former members of the battalion who were now serving as military interpreters proudly read Army newspaper reports which told of the record their former buddies were making. Not only that, but some of the Japanese prisoners whom they interrogated knew about the 100th!

Drew Pearson, Walter Winchell, and other columnists gave the battalion approving mention in their columns, and magazines of national circulation ran stories about the "GI Japyanks" of the "Purple Heart Battalion." War correspondents who wanted to see for themselves, visited the unit, talked with the men and their officers, and asked the veterans of the 34th and other divisions what they thought about their AJA fellows. The other Fifth Army GIs evidently had little but praise for the soldiers from Hawaii. The men of the battalion knew why they were receiving all the publicity, and when they talked with reporters they were modest about their deeds, but lost no opportunity to stress the aims for which they fought.

Of all the praise they received, however, neither the articles in the press nor the commendations of colonels and generals meant as much as the evidences of respect and affection shown by their comrades in arms. Within two months after they had entered combat, some buddhaheads were writing home about the Midwesterners of the 34th Division, "swell fellows as well as good fighters," with whom they were proud and happy to serve. As the months passed this feeling deepened. A former Honolulu truck gardener, a private first class, chosen by the Army to visit War Relocation Authority camps in the States, told his audiences about interracial relationships within the Fifth Army. They were, he reported, "better than OK." It was the uniform that counted, not the name or the face or whether a GI was a French-American or an Irish-American or a Japanese-American. "We are all the same. We helped each other. If we get thirsty and have no water they have canteens and gave them to us. It was the same with chocolate. Some people think there were differences. There were not. . . . We all help and are friends; like brothers, only more."[19]

In April, 1944, six Iowans of the 34th Division sent a joint letter to the Des Moines *Register* in which they stated that letters attacking the loyalty of the Japanese-Americans, published in that paper, had "made their blood boil." They had been privileged to fight beside some of these AJAs in combat, were proud of the fact, and wished to tell some people a few things:

Whenever you have been near enough to see these boys die for their country, then is the time to voice your opinion. There have been times when these Japanese, as you call them, have saved many lives, only because they have proven themselves better Americans than some that were not of Japanese descent.

When you have seen these boys blown to bits, going through shell fire that others refused to go through, sleep, when they could, in foxholes full of water, and other horrors not to be mentioned—then is the time to voice opinion. Not before. . . . If you care for any more opinions of other members of this division, ask for them.[20]

A Caucasian second lieutenant, similarly aggrieved, wrote to *Time* magazine from an Army hospital in North Carolina:

There are a lot of people in these United States who have nothing but a one-track mind. In some of the articles of your Letters to the Editors I saw some of these people in true light.

I just came from Italy where I was assigned to the Japanese 100th Infantry Battalion. I never in my life saw more of a true American than they are. To these people who don't have any military rank, probably don't even know that these little "yellow-bellies" (as one writer wrote) are saving his skin: I only wish that these people could witness these little "yellow-bellies" fight.

Ask anyone who has seen them in action against the Jerries [to] tell you about them. They'll tell you when they have them on their flanks they have security in that section. . . .

They, my friends, are not the little "yellow-bellies," you are.[21]

A wounded *haole* soldier wrote from a North Africa hospital about the way in which the white officers of the 100th, recuperating there from wounds, praised their men. "Interesting, too, are the praises they have received spontaneously from other officers here that have seen them in action or just worked with them in adjacent sectors."[22]

A lieutenant wrote to the Auburn (California) *Journal:*

The liaison officers from my battalion say that this Japanese American infantry outfit is the best damn infantry they have ever worked with. . . .

See where there is a lot of controversy about the Japanese [from the relocation camps] returning to California. Also that proper respect has not been shown to the Japanese American soldier. Things like that go against the grain with me. . . .

We had been sitting and living in foxholes at Anzio some 63 days. Then the big push out and the capture of Rome. They [the 100th Battalion] wiped out the last heavy German resistance we met some 12 miles south of Rome and then it was practically a walk into the city.

I know that all of the combat men here in Italy think the world of the Japanese-American soldiers. . . .

They have never failed to take an objective since I have been fighting with them. They have shown as much bravery as the American doughboy, and in some cases more.[23]

Major James J. Gillespie, home in Iowa in April, 1944, told the Des Moines *Tribune* about the men he had led across the Volturno and into the hills of the Winter Line.

These Hawaiian Japanese call themselves Hawaiians or just plain Americans. They've earned the right to call themselves anything they damn well please. I've never been so mad in my life as I have been since I returned to the United States and have heard cracks about Japs fighting on our side in Italy.

Anybody who calls these doughboys Japs is the most narrow-minded person I know of. These kids, so far as I'm concerned, are just as much American as I am. I'd like to hear anyone foolish enough to disparage them do it when the two Iowa battalions that fought with them and got shot at with them could hear it. . . . They're as good as any outfit I've ever been with.[24]

Gravely twisting the points of his mustache, Colonel Marshall told a war correspondent that his AJAs were "cool and aggressive under fire" and "definitely superior soldiers," and Major Clough proclaimed his enthusiasm for the "magnificent soldiers" under his command, who despite their small size carried heavy loads up and down mountain trails without a whimper. They were particularly susceptible to trench foot, which sometimes meant amputation, but bore their troubles with a good deal less complaining than the average GI. They stuck together as a unit, and did not straggle on mission. "One man never leaves another holding the bag." They got along well with men of other units. "They are fine men, and I hope America realizes it."[25]

As such expressions of good will multiplied, the buddhaheads began to feel that they could ignore or forget criticism by the "doubting Thomases." There were plenty of other kinds of Americans.

On THE MORNING of 21 June, 1944, the 442d moved north from the rest area to a bivouac southeast of Grosseto. (See campaign map, p. 124.) During a two-day stay at this place eleven men of the 100th were awarded Bronze Stars. On the 24th, after a twenty-seven-mile ride over hot, dusty secondary roads, the regiment camped near Gravasanno. From this village five more veterans left for the States. The next afternoon, 25 June, the battalion sweated out a thirteen-mile hike to an assembly area south of Suvereto. (See map, p. 205.) The 34th Division was to go into action next morning, to relieve the 36th.

Two days after the fall of Rome, some nine months after the Salerno landing, Allied troops had crossed the beaches of Normandy to establish the long-awaited Second Front. Though the war would be decided north of the Alps, much bitter fighting lay ahead in the Italian theater, and the Fifth Army's next phase line was to be the Arno River, 150 miles north of Rome. The Germans were being pursued up Highway 1 (Civitavecchia-Grosseto-Cecina-Leghorn-Pisa) and up Highway 2 (Viterbo-Orvieto-Siena-Florence). (See campaign map, p. 124.)

On 7 June, the 168th Infantry, 34th Division, occupied Civitavecchia, and three days later the 36th Division squeezed out the 34th in the coastal area. By the 11th, Viterbo had been taken by elements of the 1st Armored Division. By 20 June, Fifth Army troops in the coastal sector had estab-

We Tore Them Wide Open

CHAPTER EIGHTEEN

lished a line running east from the junction of Highways 1 and 73 above Grosseto.

At first the drive north from Rome had been rapid. The Germans had traded terrain for time, abandoning equipment and stragglers. Their resistance had been hit-and-run stuff, but during the second week of the retreat they had begun to offer stronger resistance in the rough hill country above Grosseto. Nearer the coast they also fought more persistent rear-guard actions to gain time for destruction of the port facilities of Leghorn.

In the early hours of 26 June, the 34th Division relieved the 36th. General Ryder placed the 133d Infantry on the left of his line of attack, on Highway 1, the 442d in the center, and the 168th on the right. South of the town of Suvereto the 422d relieved elements of the 517th Parachute Infantry and the 142d Infantry. Colonel Charles W. Pence, commander of the 442d, had decided to keep the 100th in reserve, and to start his advance with the 2d and 3d battalions. They made contact with enemy scouts shortly after 8:30 A.M. and pushed ahead, but by 11:00 had been halted by heavy shelling from the direction of Belvedere and the surrounding high ground which dominated the Suvereto-Sassetta road. (See map, p. 205.)

While Ryder had been making personal reconnaissance up this road, which passed west of Belvedere, scouts in a command car preceding his had been ambushed and captured, and he and his companions had had to hit the ditches and crawl back to the third command wagon.

At 6:30 A.M. the 100th had marched two miles to a new assembly area; at 9:30 it had been ordered to move forward another four miles; at 11:30, as it closed into the new location, orders came to attack at noon. With no time for adequate ground reconnaissance, Singles and his company commanders huddled over their maps and worked out a plan. They would move up between the 3d Battalion on the left and the 2d on the right, and try to flank Belvedere from the east and north. At 12:00 the outfit moved across a road which led into Suvereto and, unobserved by the enemy, began to climb up a covered trail in order to circle Belvedere from the east toward a high point slightly northwest of the village.

Company B led, followed in turn by Company A, the command group, Company C, and the 81-mm. mortar platoon. Heavy machine gun platoons accompanied the lead companies. As Company B's scouts climbed the ridge they cut telephone wires which led to an observation post on its summit but found the crest deserted. The German observers obviously had fled when they found their wires cut.

The Jerries had had a good vantage point. From this height could

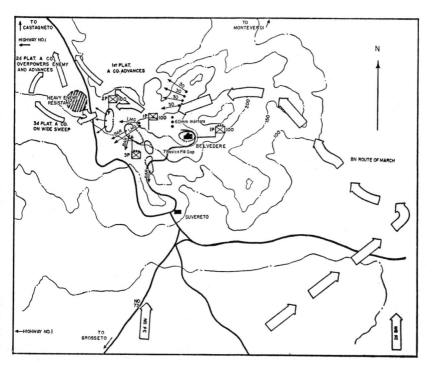

ACTION AT BELVEDERE

be seen the stone houses of Belvedere on the side of a ridge to the south. A road wound southwest out of that village to Suvereto, and above the latter town it swung north again to make a boot-shaped curve, then climbed slowly northwest toward Sassetta. Captain Sakae Takahashi, commander of Company B, spotted several German half-tracks, a few tanks, and a number of trucks and jeeps, directly across the narrow valley from the hill on which he stood. They were on both sides of the road. On the near side a three-gun battery was firing toward Suvereto. Takahashi sent a call to the regimental artillery for counter battery fire, but learned that the 522d

Field Artillery was too far back, out of range. He told Captain Paul Froning to take a section of light machine guns and a section of heavies down the slopes to shoot up the German artillery and vehicles. Lieutenant James Boodry's 2d Platoon hurried west, with another section of light machine guns, to cut the Sassetta road south of the enemy battery. Lieutenant Walter Johnston led the 3d Platoon southwest to take position on higher ground behind and to the left of Boodry's men in order to provide supporting fire and cover the entrance and exit from the road boot above Suvereto.

Sergeant Yeiki Kobashigawa took the 1st Platoon southeast in a sharp turning movement toward Belvedere. One squad he sent east of the town, another west, and the third he led into the northern end. Seven riflemen filled the gap between Johnston's and Kobashigawa's platoons. Kobashigawa and his group were well into the village when two German machine pistols opened fire from a doctor's office on the first floor of a three-story Fascist headquarters building. Loaded with grenades, and under covering fire from their comrades, the sergeant and two of his men ran for a house next to the Party building. One of the trio was hit but Kobashigawa and the other soldier made it. Four grenades went through the doctor's windows, and the machine pistols stopped. As four Germans sprinted from a side door the squad's fire killed three and wounded the other. About twenty more Jerries escaped through the back doors. Pushed from house to house, they finally tried to get away through a ravine west of the town, but were caught as they emerged by the squad which Kobashigawa had stationed on that flank. There had been no resistance at the east end, and Belvedere had been cleared of the enemy in less than an hour.

Northwest of Belvedere, Boodry's platoon, supported by 60-mm. mortars on high ground to the rear, had taken five minutes to surprise and cut down the enemy artillerymen, and the enemy howitzers were now silent.

Noticing activity around the single farmhouse east of the Sassetta road, Johnston had sent a squad against it, the rest of his platoon giving covering fire. As the assault group approached, two Germans began firing a machine gun mounted on a half-track. A well-aimed rifle grenade knocked them and their weapon apart. Grenades thrown through the windows of the house brought its occupants out with their hands up. The building had been a company command post, and material taken here included two machine-gun-armed half-tracks, a truck, and eleven jeeps, the latter still camouflaged with brush.

Followed by German infantry, a Mark IV tank now rumbled out of an olive grove west of the road toward the farmhouse and Johnston's men. When the tank was fifteen yards from him, Pfc Taneoshi Nakano put a bazooka rocket into its belly. The machine lurched forward a few yards before it blew up, and the concussion knocked Nakano unconscious. The German riflemen were picked off as they tried to withdraw. Nakano later received a Silver Star.

Farther north seventeen amphibious jeeps and a few motorcycles wheeled out of an olive grove west of the road and sped north toward Sassetta. Boodry's machine gunners waited until they couldn't miss, and then let loose. Not a jeep got by, and as each one was hit, or blocked by those ahead, the 2d Platoon's riflemen shot up the passengers as they dashed for cover. Soon afterwards four troop-loaded personnel carriers broke from another grove and lumbered up the road, trying to swing around the mess of jeeps. Two made it, but riflemen cleared the drivers' cabs of the other two, which now added to the road block. Again the riders were mowed down in the vehicles or as they poured out to run for cover. The Germans made no further attempts to use the road. A few pockets of resistance remained, but the 2d and 3d platoons had little difficulty in silencing these.

Colonel Singles now ordered Company A to head northwest and to the right of Company B against another enemy concentration farther up the Sassetta road. Boodry's platoon swung to the right in support and Johnston's also moved north, tying in with Boodry's left flank and taking defensive positions overlooking the road. A platoon of Company C, ordered from reserve and committed between the 3d Platoon and Belvedere, completed defense against possible counterattack from the west and south. Heavy machine guns from D Company came down to lower ground to back up these new dispositions. There were still Germans in the "boot" area to the south, but they found the road effectively sealed. An enemy party which tried to use it to move north from Suvereto had its ranks chopped by bullets from the heavy machine guns firing at 800-yard range.

Major Fukuda, leading the 1st Platoon of Company A north on

the east side of the Sassetta road, sent the 2d across the road to move parallel to his own party, keeping the 3d in reserve. On the east side of the road the Jerries showed little fight, and Fukuda's group moved rapidly toward Sassetta, flushing prisoners out of ditches and brush. On the west side, the 2d Platoon met heavy fire from farmhouses and had to begin cleaning these out. It was a matter of dodging through olive groves until, under covering fire, one or more men could get near enough to lob grenades through the windows. Then the Jerries either came out with raised hands or got away through doors and windows not yet under fire. The 2d Platoon leader radioed Fukuda that his men were receiving flank fire from some houses on the slopes of a ridge paralleling the road on the west, and the Major ordered his 3d Platoon across the road and up the slopes, with orders to make a wide sweep west to force the Germans out of the houses and back toward the road.

After crossing the highway the command group, which had been with the 3d Platoon, turned right to follow the 2d Platoon. Four enlisted men, messengers without previous combat experience, saw an enemy-held farmhouse and decided to capture it. As they approached, firing their rifles, some Germans went out through the rear. Nearing the house, the attacking quartet decided to make sure they were not walking into a trap, and one of them tossed a grenade through the open front door. After the explosion, a yell came from the rear of the building: "Hey, we're Americans!" Ordered to come out with hands high, three Yanks emerged. Ahead of them, their arms also lifted, came three Germans. The liberated GIs were the scouts of the 34th Division Reconnaissance Group who had been captured on the road that morning. They said they had been taken to this house, a battalion command post, and questioned. Inside was one dead German, another badly wounded, a large quantity of arms and ammunition, a couple of radios, and a large number of maps.

By about 3:00 P.M. all the farmhouses in the 2d Platoon area had been cleared. Pfc Takeo Takahashi, who later received a Silver Star for his exploit, crept seventy-five yards to surprise five guards and capture a motor pool. His booty included five quarter-ton trucks, a half-ton personnel carrier, two two-and-one-half-ton trucks, and five motorcycles.

By 3:30, three and a half hours after the battalion had marched to flank Belvedere, the enemy had been swept back up the valley, and the 1st and 2d platoons of A Company were a thousand yards northwest of Belvedere, pushing toward Sassetta, rounding up prisoners on the way. Singles now sent Company C's second platoon toward Suvereto with instructions to make contact with the regiment's 3d Battalion.

Shortly after 4:00 P.M. there was a short, fierce fire fight at Michelino, a hamlet perched above the road a couple of miles north of Belvedere, but within a half hour the Germans again ran, abandoning twelve trucks, two motorcycles with side cars, a field gun, and a tank. At 5:00 P.M. Company A took defensive positions near Pisciarello, another cluster of houses a few hundred yards farther north on high ground overlooking Sassetta. The 3d Platoon came up later, having moved up the ridge line west of the road. The other companies moved in after dark and dug in for the night.

At noon the next day, 27 June, Colonel Singles was told to move against Sassetta. The 3d Battalion, now abreast of the 100th, would attack on the left, the 2d Battalion remaining in reserve. The 522d Artillery and the mortars of both battalions delivered a preparatory barrage.

In this area a deep ravine bordered the Sassetta road on the east, and the attack would have to be made west of the road. Companies A and C started, A nearest the road, C abreast on the left along the slopes of a ridge, and B in reserve, behind A. The 3d Battalion, farther west, moved north along the ridge line. German guns north of Sassetta shelled the road behind Company A but sent no salvos into the town, where their own rear guards were holed in. The men of A moved into Sassetta against fire from machine-gun and sniper pockets. It was slow going, but not too costly. The Germans would fire for a while and then duck away.

In one building a squad found a headquarters company driver who, thinking the town had already been cleaned up, had driven his truck right into the main street. Learning his mistake when German slugs began whistling about his ears, he had rocketed from his vehicle into the nearest cellar.

Company A made another find during the afternoon, a wineshop loaded with cognac, Benedictine, and other potables. All the bottles were soon in a truck bound for the battalion kitchen area. As they searched houses, the boys looked for rice, picked up a sack here and there, and liberated, among other things, some pigs and chickens.

At dusk Company C worked down into Sassetta from the west and northwest, and by 9:00 P.M. the village was secure, with a block set up on the road leading north.

It was a pleasant change to occupy a town where the Jerries hadn't had time to evacuate all the food and wine, and that night the men ate and drank well. On any military reckoning they had earned a good meal. Since noon of the previous day the battalion had killed 178 of the enemy, wounded twenty, and rounded up seventy-three prisoners. Materiel taken or destroyed included forty-six vehicles of various types, trucks, half-tracks and motorcycles, plus five tanks, three artillery pieces, one self-propelled howitzer, and two antitank guns. And in the whole of the 100th only four men had been killed, seven wounded![1]

During the night the 3d Battalion pushed toward Castagneto on the road northwest from Sassetta to Highway 1. Some elements wandered northeast and came under fire from an enemy block at the road junction above Sassetta, but the Germans thought themselves in danger of being outflanked and pulled out in haste, leaving behind them a half-track, two 81-mm. mortars, and much other equipment.

The next morning, 28 June, the 100th moved up to the junction—many of the boys still dressing chickens as they marched, leaving a trail of feathers and gizzards behind them*—and took positions covering the roads to Castagneto on the left and Monteverdi on the right. During the day the 2d Battalion moved through the 3d, cleared Castagneto, and moved two miles past that place until halted by artillery fire.

The 135th Infantry passed through the 442d the next day, and the 100th and 2d battalions were ordered to Bibbona as divisional reserve. When this order came the 100th's cooks had just finished roasting a pig, but they hurriedly whacked the carcass into chunks, and each company got a section to work on during the journey. The 3d Battalion trucked to Monteverdi to guard the division's

---

* Usually a chicken passed from hand to hand, throughout the squad, each man plucking his share of feathers. Ryder once remarked that after the 100th's men had been foraging they were one of the most nondescript outfits ever seen on the march. As the battalion left a town, one buddhahead might be plucking a chicken, another holding a rabbit by the ears, another carrying a load of vegetables and a liberated pot in which to cook them, and still others hustling a reluctant pig toward the next bivouac.

extreme flank, and stayed there for a day and a half before rejoining the rest of the Combat Team at Bibbona.

Three weeks later Fifth Army Headquarters recommended the 100th for a Presidential Unit Citation "for outstanding performance of duty in action on 26 and 27 June in the vicinity of Belvedere and Sassetta, Italy," where "with insufficient time for proper physical reconnaissance but with a determined desire to fulfill its important mission, the battalion had quickly formulated its plan and launched the operation . . . [against] a large and determined force of German infantry and field artillery, including self-propelled guns and tanks." The citation read, in part:

The 100th Battalion was assigned the mission of neutralizing a strongly defended German center of resistance at Belvedere, Italy, which dominated a vital highway and seriously impeded an American infantry division's northward advance. . . . All three companies went into action boldly facing murderous fire from all types of weapons and tanks and at times fighting without artillery support. Doggedly the members of the 100th Infantry Battalion fought their way into the strongly defended positions. The stubborn desire of the men to close with a numerically superior enemy and the rapidity with which they fought enabled the 100th Infantry Battalion to destroy completely the right flank positions of a German Army . . . forcing the remainder of a completely disrupted battalion to surrender approximately 10 kilometers of ground. In addition large quantities of enemy weapons, vehicles and equipment were either captured or destroyed, while the American infantry division operating in the sector was able to continue its rapid advance. The fortitude and intrepidity displayed by the officers and men of the 100th Infantry Battalion reflects the finest traditions of the Army of the United States.

Another version, written by a member of the battalion, was less grandiose:

On our last push up here, we had a field day with the Jerries. We caught them from the left flank, and just tore them wide open. Those Jerries were so surprised that they couldn't even believe they were actually surrounded. Our boys killed a lot . . . and captured many more. Our mortars and machine guns did a superb job of firing. We went in so fast and so far that we even caught artillery pieces still firing. Most of the Jerries tried to escape by vehicles and cycles but were caught by machine guns and just a handful got away. The boys really enjoyed it, although now when I think of it, it's brutal and inhuman!

The boys had enjoyed it because this time the Nazis had had to stick around and take it, instead of dishing it out and running. "Dees time we really bust 'em up."

ON 1 JULY, 1944, after three days of the heaviest fighting since Rome, the 133d Infantry captured Cecina, 20 miles below Leghorn on Highway 1. (See campaign map, p. 124.) East of the city the 135th and 168th regiments had crossed the Cecina River and were north of Highway 68. Spearheading the Fifth Army drive, the 34th Division would now push straight north to the Arno River, bypassing and isolating Leghorn. Only an armored task force would move up Highway 1 where it entered mountainous terrain above Cecina. The rest of the division would attack through the inland valley north of Cecina, the 135th Infantry pinching out the 133d at that town and moving up the western side of the valley, the 442d advancing up its center, and the 168th following the eastern ridge line.

On 2 July, the 442d was in action north of the Cecina, the 100th and 2d battalions moving ahead against light rear-guard resistance. At noon, two days later, the 3d Battalion relieved the 100th, which now sent two officers and forty enlisted men to Cecina to march in a review honoring Secretary of War Stimson. During the ceremonies Ryder patted Bronze Star wearer Captain Takahashi on the back and remarked to the guest of honor, "This is my best outfit."

While the 100th was in reserve the 2d Battalion captured Hill 140 after a hard-fought battle. Though held up for a time by shelling from Rosignano, a hilltop town which the Germans were

To the Arno

stubbornly defending, the 3d Battalion, on the left, finally managed to push abreast of the 2d. In the early hours of 7 July, the 100th relieved the 2d.

Singles had orders to seize high ground northwest of Castellina, which the 168th Infantry had not been able to take. In a surprise assault, just after dawn, Company C's 2d Platoon took a position overlooking the Castellina-Rosignano road. In this attack Lieutenant Takeichi Miyashiro led a squad against a farmhouse from which machine-gun fire had been harassing his platoon's left flank. Killing one of the gunners and wounding another, the squad occupied the house and manned its windows in preparation for a Jerry counter-attack. When this came Miyashiro told his men to hold fire until the Germans were within ten yards. They did, and their delayed blast broke the attack. An hour later the enemy moved in again. Firing a BAR, the lieutenant cut down five Germans, and when his gun jammed, grabbed a carbine and kept shooting. The Jerries pulled off. After a longer pause, they tried again, this time after preliminary mortar and artillery shelling. Under four direct hits by 88's the heavy stone walls of the house began to crumble, and when 170's began falling close Miyashiro told his men to duck out. He stayed, and as the now confident Germans got close cut loose with another BAR. This time the remnant of the enemy group gave up for good. For his morning's work the lieutenant later received a DSC.

On the left the 3d Platoon had met heavy fire, but when elements of the 2d Platoon moved over in support, the Germans retired, and the high ground was secured.

In midmorning Company B moved east on the road to Castellina. Not far from the town, scouts spotted three enemy tanks approaching from that village, with a force of infantry of about company strength behind them. Pfc Richard Okazaki carried his bazooka forward and then waited for the Jerries in a shallow roadside ditch. Though a Cub plane had meanwhile sighted the tanks, and American shells had begun to fall along the road, he stayed put, and when the lead tank was a hundred yards away put a rocket into it. Astride the narrow road, burning, its ammunition exploding, the machine effectively blocked the track. Deprived of their armor, with shells slamming around them, the enemy company withdrew toward Castellina. From a house above the road Pfc Masaichi Miyashiro, a Company B sniper, bagged ten Germans at 300 yards. As the Jerry party moved farther away, he climbed to the second floor, readjusted his sights, and hit several more, one at 800 yards. Both Okazaki and Miyashiro later received Silver Stars.

By noon scouts made contact with the 168th Infantry north of Castellina, now empty of Germans. During the afternoon and evening the battalion marched across heavily wooded terrain to cut a road which led west from Pomaia, a mile and a half above Castellina, toward Rosignano. Battalion pioneers easily spotted paths through mine fields from which the Jerries, in their haste, had not removed the "Achtung, Minen" signs. On the left the 3d Battalion had crossed the Castellina-Rosignano road and was also moving north.

At dawn, after three hours sleep, the 100th pressed forward again, A on the right, B on the left, C in reserve. Company A was stopped for a time by machine guns in a wood on the right flank toward Pomaia, but a bayonet charge wiped out this opposition. The next strong resistance came at a little settlement on the Pomaia-Rosignano road, a few houses clustered around an old castle on the boundary between the two companies. Two platoons from A and one from B converged on the hamlet and cleared its houses, but three machine guns still continued to fire from within the castle. Pfc Kiichi Koda, of Company A, who had already taken part in the bayonet assault, volunteered to lead a squad against the structure, and under covering fire from his men crept around the walls, tossing grenades into each window. Then he led the way into the building, where he was killed by an enemy grenade. His squad wiped out ten Jerries and captured three more. A DSC went to his family.

As Company C marched west from Pomaia during the afternoon six men were killed and thirteen wounded when enemy self-propelled guns shelled the column. For the rest of the day the battalion rested in defensive positions near the castle. During the night the 2d Battalion took positions abreast of the 100th, relieving the 3d, which had also fought its way across the road, farther west towards Rosignano.

On 9 July, the 100th and the 2d moved ahead about a mile against scattered sniper fire. Company A overran a small rear-guard party on its right near Scopeto and captured seven prisoners, two motorcycles, a reconnaissance car, and a jeep. Soon after midnight, after a few hours sleep, both battalions pushed ahead again. When enemy artillery observers spotted them shortly after dawn they had covered only 600 yards of very rough terrain. The 100th now began to receive heavy shelling from Pastina on the east, and the 2d Battalion caught fire from a ridge due north. Maps found on a dead German showed enemy guns zeroed in on the area directly ahead, and it was decided to make an end run to the right, with the 100th swinging against Pastina.

The next morning the 100th moved through some deep draws to take positions on Pastina's southeastern outskirts. A radio call brought excellent support from the 522d Artillery, and, with help from their own 81-mm. mortars, Companies A and B cleared part of the village by nightfall. The Jerries pulled out of the hamlet under cover of darkness; the 3d Battalion moved in during the morning, and the 100th moved south to a bivouac near Castellina.

By the 15th the Combat Team had pushed through Pieve San Luce, Lorenzano, and Orciano, and that night the 100th moved out of the valley to act as reserve for the 135th Infantry, which was driving for Leghorn.

The rest of the 442d continued north, took the hilltop town of Luciano on the 16th against stiff resistance, and by the 19th was at Colle Salvetti. From this high point it was possible to see the leaning Tower of Pisa.

On the 19th, the 100th moved into Leghorn, where battalion personnel guarded key installations and acted as military police. On their first day in the city some of the boys discovered a big brewery, and liberated fifty gallons of beer. Civilians were eager to trade rice for chocolate bars and tinned rations, and that evening's meal was most satisfactory. There was good news also—two officers and seventeen enlisted men were going to get thirty-day furloughs to Hawaii!

Meanwhile, off to the northeast, the 442d was sending patrols toward the Arno. One party followed a partisan guide into Pisa to contact a resistance leader, spent a night hidden in an attic, and returned with valuable information.

On the 21st the Combat Team took positions west of Pontedera and slightly north of No. 67, the Leghorn-Florence Highway, but was relieved that night by troops of the 133d and 135th regiments and trucked southeast to Vada, a huge 34th Division rest center on the coast a few miles above Cecina. On the 25th the 100th moved down from Leghorn to rejoin the Combat Team.

Vada was the best rest camp so far. Short hours of training were followed by swimming, good dinners, movies, and USO shows. "It's a Manuela-boy life," one soldier wrote. "The seacoast along here is almost like that of Hawaii." The regiment put on some genuine Hawaiian *luaus*, with *kalua* (pit-roasted) pig, and the cooks prepared as many Island dishes as the available Italian foodstuffs would provide.[1]

From Vada the boys had frequent passes during which they added to the knowledge of Italy and Italians which they had already acquired in fighting their way through mountains and villages. In their letters they constantly dwelt upon the contrast between the striking beauty of the country and the shocking misery of most of its people. Sections of the Italian shore line made them homesick for the radiant beaches of Hawaii. In spring and summer the valleys were lovely, the hills high and green, and the sky overhead so blue and clear that everything reminded them of the Islands. A distant view of a village perched on the mountain slope was "like a fairy tale. That is when the town is enveloped in clouds. Guess you read about castles in the clouds . . . it's just like that, very beautiful."[2] On closer approach, however, even if it were undamaged by battle, the cloud-town usually turned out to be a dirty and poverty-stricken village. All too often the place and its inhabitants showed the marks of war. One man wrote, "We saw many beautiful churches and scriptures of our Lord and also statues which were very old but very beautiful, but many of the beautiful things have been bombed by airplanes or fired by big guns and it's really a pitiful sight."

Another commented that the "lot of the Italians whose homes are in the battle area (or post battle areas) is a poor one. The retreating German Army takes whatever they can, leaving the poor farmers with hardly anything for the winter. Some of their homes are in ruins—and Sunny Italy gets quite cold, misty and damp in the winter. The nights are anything but warm. . . . The people are very emotional and I have come across a few who, in telling me of their plight, actually burst into tears."

Despite the sorrow and additional destitution which the Germans had brought upon them, the Italian people always seemed friendly and kind. As the AJA troops marched through their towns they brought out bread and cheese, water, grapes, and wine, "and just yelled at us and tried to make us take it."

One day as we were going through a town we stopped for a rest. The people all came out with chairs and put them on the road and just made us sit down and brought out wine and bread with cheese. They also brought out large jars of water. Most of the boys cared for water more than anything else because it was quite hot those days and after a long hike there's nothing that can beat a good drink of water. Some of the boys stole a drink of wine while the officers weren't looking. . . .

The Italian people had not seen cigarets or candy for over a year so the children just beg for candy and they are really happy whenever we gave them. I enjoyed giving candy to the kids rather than eating them myself. . . . The men ask for cigarets and that's one thing the boys get disgusted because they don't have enough for themselves. They just beg for cigarets so some boys pity them and give them. The boys in the front have three or four packs a week and big smokers usually suffer for a smoke. . . .

Men constantly wrote about the hospitality of these war-distressed people. "It's surprising how the Italian people take you into their homes and treat you so kindly. They haven't much to offer but what they have they give without holding back and mind you the wine they serve isn't the kind they sell in the vino shops—water mixed with wine to make up for quantity."

Some observers remarked that the soldiers from Hawaii, generous with their candy and cigarets, seemed to get along better with the Italians than most GIs. Whether or not this was true, when they wrote about their new friends the AJAs certainly expressed pity. "The civilians here are very poor and have little or no food. When I go to town I carry candy in my pocket and the children sure do appreciate American candy. I feel sorry for these people who have such poor homes but they make the best of what they have."[3]

Sometimes sympathy and friendship ripened into warmer emotion. While other Joes headed for the hot spots, a few soldiers used their furloughs to revisit homes of fondly remembered signorine. Some of the romances ended in marriage and plans for a new and far-off home for the bride after the war.

Under their dirt and poverty the "paisanos" were the same sort of simple, friendly, hospitable human beings as the kind farmers of Wisconsin or the buddhaheads' own parents, who frequently invited lonely *haole* GIs stationed in Hawaii to family dinner.

Most of the men at Vada rest camp managed a visit to the Italian capital. One wrote: "There is a four-piece string orchestra on the bandstand playing 'Deep Purple' and the violin is really beautiful.

To top it all, I've got a nice glass of cognac to keep me in the right frame of mind."[4]

On 27 July General Mark Clark decorated the battalion's colors and guidons with the blue streamer of the Distinguished Unit Citation, granted for the "Battle of Belvedere." One of the boys later wrote home, "I shall never forget one part of his speech, and I can quote him verbatim. 'All you Americans of Japanese ancestry should be proud of yourselves! The 34th Division is proud of you! The 5th Army is proud of you! America is proud of you!' . . . We all felt so good. Such words mean so much to us. The general's speech will ring forever in my ears."

Another soldier wrote, "I hope that the people of Hawaii fully appreciate the significance of this citation because it is not every day that a unit as a whole gets a pat on the back from Washington."[5]

Among the individual awards presented at this time was a DSC to Lieutenant Allan Ohata for his part in the fighting near Cerasuolo eight months before, and a Silver Star for Captain Mitsuyoshi Fukuda, commander of Company A, for his leadership at Belvedere.

While at Vada the regiment furnished guards of honor for reviews before King George VI of England, the head of the U. S. Army Service Forces, and an American undersecretary of war. Companies A and B of the 100th alternated in five-day guard stints in Leghorn. During these days of rest the battalion held memorial services for its dead. "When the names of those killed were called, I tried to shut my eyes but the faces of all my buddies killed, including an awfully good kid whom I had taught in school floated one after another before me. And the tears that rained down my face were as easy to hold back as a 16-inch shell from a battleship. The names and faces appeared endless. It was very painful."[6]

It was during the Vada stay that the men learned that the "100th Battalion (Separate)" had been redesignated the "100th Battalion, 442d Regiment" and was now officially part of the Combat Team. The old-timers of the 100th disliked the change, and their loss of separate identity.

This feeling was understandable. The 100th had been the guinea-pig AJA combat outfit. Those who had been at Camp McCoy, and many of the men who had joined the unit later, felt that it was their record in training and combat which had made the formation of the 442d possible and had given the newer organization a chance at combat. Now the 100th was to be submerged in the younger and larger group. At this time men of other regiments and some war correspondents were still calling all AJA soldiers members of the "famous 100th Infantry Battalion," but the veterans of that proud unit could see that the time might soon come when the 100th would be mentioned as "a battalion of the famous 442d Infantry." Jealous of their unique record, they did not want it forgotten or appropriated. Perhaps their heads had swelled a bit, but they had done some effective fighting, and the Army public relations section and the newsmen had for some time been telling the public—and indirectly the men themselves—that they were pretty hot stuff.

Though understandable, this part of their reaction to the news was more emotional than reasonable. It was logical that the Army should make the battalion an integral part of the 442d.* But there were other factors involved. When the 442d was first being formed at Shelby, the 100th had been given no part in the Combat Team's organization, and its officers had received no commands in the larger group. As the battalion's casualty lists had mounted during eight and a half months of combat, replacement officers had come from Shelby to fill posts which might often have been given to the 100th's own experienced veterans. Many a battle-wise noncom had really led a platoon until his new lieutenant had gotten his bearings and some combat experience. The 100th hadn't had a chance to officer the new regiment, but youngsters from the 442d—often three or four years junior to the men they would command—were being sent to lead units of the 100th. It was true that the great majority of the new officers did well in their commands, established rapport with their men, identified themselves with the outfit, and shared the older veterans' pride in it, but replacement was a continuous process which frequently caused personal strain. In any outfit the battle-scarred veteran tends to be cool to the replacement until he has been tested in combat, and is even more skeptical when the new man is an untried officer. And there was always some frustration when an ambitious soldier had to revert to subordinate status after a brief taste of command.

* As has been noted previously, the G-3 Division of the War Department General Staff had intended, in December, 1942, that the Combat Team be built around the 100th, but this had not been done because of the projected use of that battalion in North Africa. What could be more sensible, in 1944, than that the Army adapt its original plan and provide the untried 442d, as it entered battle, with a core of seasoned troops?

When the 2d and 3d battalions arrived in Italy, the 100th's officers volunteered to help train these units for combat. The offer was not flatly refused, but those who made it got the impression that their aid was not considered necessary. The attitude conveyed was one of "Hands off. We won't need your help. We're as good as you are." Perhaps it wasn't intended, but the result was the same as though it had been. What was behind it? A feeling that the new men must stand on their own feet? A little envy within the new command? No matter what the cause, a number of the 100th's officers became irritated. From now on they would lay themselves open to no more rebuffs.

Resentment was not confined to the officers; it was shared by the enlisted men as well. They felt that too many of these untried GIs acted too damn cocky for kids whose insides had not yet melted in battle fright. Some of them had been heard to boast that *their* outfit was composed of volunteers, not of draftees.

On the other hand, the rank and file of the 442d had expected the 100th's veterans to act as big brothers and give them guidance, but when advice was offered they often resented (as younger brothers will) the attitude of condescension which seemed to go with it. As a result their attitude tended to be, "All right, we'll show them."

That was the way things were when the 442d first entered battle below Suvereto. In that action the new battalions didn't cover themselves with glory and, though the 100th itself was no dazzling success against its first really stiff opposition at S. Angelo, its members were not exactly unhappy that they had had to mop up the Germans at Belvedere. A replacement who had joined the 100th just six weeks before that engagement wrote home after it was over:

The 442d has been committed, and I'm afraid there will be some very unsatisfactory remarks about it going home soon. However, I hope you'll try to wise up those people by telling them that from my point of view they did as well as any new outfit could do. The men here expected too much out of them and expectations were not fulfilled. I've defended my former outfit by telling all skeptics that, give them time and we will see. I only hope that there will be a re-shuffle within the organization, especially officers. There is also present that feeling of rivalry, especially on the part of my outfit toward the 442d. Our boys have humored these new boys needlessly, and I can't see how there can be coordination as long as that feeling exists. I earnestly pray that before our next contact with the enemy, a more friendly feeling will exist between these two outfits.

On hearing the news of the 100th's change in title and status, the same soldier wrote:

> We've been officially assigned to the 442d and now are known as the 100th Battalion, 442d Infantry Regiment, and I'm afraid our A.P.O. will be changed to 464. The original boys from the 100th really detest it, and I don't blame them. All the boys are so proud of the 100th that they prefer to remain a separate battalion. So I'm theoretically back with the 442d and don't think much of it either.* Too bad we couldn't have someone like Colonel Turner, a kamaaina, to command the 442d. That, I believe, is the key reason for the difference in performance and attitude of the 100th and 442d.[7]

On 15 August, the 442d was detached from the 34th Division and attached to the 85th Division of II Corps. Two days later it was transferred to the 88th Division. The 100th Battalion, which was not included in these shifts, was assigned to the 107th AAA Group of Task Force 45, a provisional division under IV Corps control which was composed largely of antiaircraft soldiers serving as infantry troops. On the 16th the battalion moved to a point about four miles east of Pisa, where it relieved two AA units, one English and one American, and took quarters in farmhouses on the flats south of the Arno River.

Fifth Army troops now held the Arno's right bank on a thirty-five-mile front from the sea to the Elsa River, twenty miles west of Florence. Only light screening forces held the ground immediately south of the river. The bulk of the Army was resting and training in rear areas, preparing for the next big push. This would include a crossing in force, an advance across the Arno valley, and an assault on the German's Gothic Line in the Appenines fifteen miles north.

For two weeks the 100th held a thinly extended half-mile line, and sent frequent patrols toward the river's south bank. On the last day of August, IV Corps learned that the enemy was withdrawing from the river line west of Florence, and ordered a general advance. On 1 September, the 100th crossed its sector of the waist-deep Arno without opposition. That night engineers put a bridge across the river, and artillery and tanks followed.

---

* The men of the Combat Team were surprised and somewhat chagrined to learn that members of the 442d who had left Shelby only a short time before as replacements for the 100th had made a transfer of loyalty and now identified themselves completely with the 100th. Both officers and enlisted men of the 442d found it difficult to adjust to the fact that the 100th simply refused to be absorbed. For a long time, in fact, its members wore the Red Bull shoulder patch of the 34th Division in preference to that of the 442d.

The next morning, as the battalion pushed across the plain, its only opposition came from two machine guns. The next day the men dug in north of the main Pisa-Pistoia highway along the south bank of the Serchio River about five miles northeast of Pisa. The 434th Provisional Infantry Battalion took over the sector on 5 September, and the 100th moved south to Castiglioncello on Highway 1 below Leghorn. Since Sassetta, the battalion had lost three officers and thirty-three men killed, and eleven officers and 158 men wounded.

During the last two weeks of August, the 2d and 3d battalions of the 442d had been patrolling a six-mile line west of Florence. On 1 September they had established a bridgehead across the Arno, and on 6 September they had been detached from the 88th Division and moved southwest to Castiglioncello.

Here, three days later, General Mark Clark again presented battle awards, and Colonel Singles received the Legion of Merit for his leadership in the drive from Anzio to the Arno, "a material factor in perpetuating the 100th Infantry Battalion's reputation as an effective, hard-hitting, and well-disciplined combat unit." The next day the Combat Team trucked forty miles south to Piombino, where the 100th embarked on the *John Holmes*. The ship had only two latrines for its 1000 passengers, and was so crowded that many had to sleep on deck. It arrived in Naples Harbor at about midnight 11 September.

For the next eight days the regiment bivouacked outside Naples, and during this period 181 replacements arrived from Camp Shelby. Each day 10 per cent of the personnel received passes to visit the city. A man's view of people depends, of course, on the kind he meets. "I guess about 90% of the people in Napoli are either prostitutes or pimps," wrote one soldier. But another AJA left Naples with different memories.

I have become wonderful friends with an Italian family in Naples. They speak a little pidgin English, and with a smattering of Italian on my part, we manage to converse well enough. The oldest of the seven children is a boy of 15. They invited me to stay overnight. We had spaghetti for supper. I noticed I was the only one at the table who had an extra plate containing a piece of beef steak and I did not touch it. When I saw the children gulp their spaghetti clean from their plates, I pushed the meat towards the kind hearted wife and asked her to divide the meat among the children who I knew were still hungry. All at once the children and the man and wife cried out and begged and forced me to eat the meat. Can you imagine anything like it?

The husband asked me to write him every week. I promised to do so. If he didn't hear from me, I added with a laugh, it meant I was dead. Immediately the man sprang up and cried, "Don't talk like that! You are too young to die! God will take care of you!" He got out a glass and poured me his best wine, all the while begging me not to talk or think of dying because he knew God was with me.

When it was time to leave, I tried to put some money in his hand but he refused vigorously. "Write to me," he kept repeating. Then the children began to cry. I shook hands all around, the children hugging me or kissing me. Then as I stood by the door, the man and wife and children all dropped to their knees and bowing their heads prayed to God for my safety. Their kindness, their affection, their sincerity, were beginning to overwhelm me. I started to get a lump in my throat, so I turned around and left them quickly. Sometimes it gets hard to remember that American soldiers are supposed to be hard boiled![8]

During this period "Club 100" came into being. The idea had been in the men's minds since 1943, when representatives from each company at Camp McCoy had met and decided that veterans of the 100th should have a clubhouse in Hawaii after the war. A fund had been started, to which members had continued to contribute a percentage of their pay. The collections had been sent to Charles Hemenway in Honolulu for investment, and the total was now over $30,000. At Naples, delegates from each company met and approved by-laws and elected officers. Doc Kometani was the first president; Leslie F. Deacon, Hawaii Delegate to Congress Joseph R. Farrington, and Mr. Hemenway were elected honorary members.

On 21 September, the 442d moved to Staging Area No. 11 at Bagnoli, and five days later Singles' men were climbing from LSTs into the USS *Samuel Chase*, which started for Marseille on 27 September. The American Seventh Army had invaded the French Riviera on 15 August, and since that date had been moving swiftly north toward the Rhine. Already two-thirds of the Fifth Army's personnel had been transferred from Italy to the new front, and now the buddhaheads were also going to see France.

For some time they had been hearing of Allied successes north of the Alps, and on the boat they talked of being home by Christmas.

AT NOON, 29 September, 1944, after a rough trip, the *Chase* anchored off Marseille Harbor; at 1:00 P.M. the battalion began to move ashore in landing craft; at 5:00 it left the docks for a railroad station, and at 5:30 was in a cattle train of the forty-man-eight-horse type, bound for Septemes, about eight miles northwest of the port. One of the passengers later described the ride as horrible, but it lasted only four hours, and shortly after midnight the unit marched into a bivouac area a mile outside Septemes.

The next week it rained and the wind blew, as the men slogged in mud, fired and tested newly issued equipment, and heard soldiers back from the front warn of miserably cold days and nights ahead. Most of the veterans of the outfit had a working knowledge of Italian, and those who secured passes for Marseille and nearby Aix had little difficulty with language, since many of the French spoke Italian. And if a man knew neither Italian nor French he could always ask some one who did. ("Eh, Joe, how you say 'sleep' in French?") The girls were attractive, though not as buxom as the Italian *wahines*, and the civilians of the area seemed a little more "sophisticated and well-kept" than the Italians. Their brandy was excellent but, like all other French goods, was as high-priced as any in Naples or Rome.

On 9 October the Combat Team began a two-and-a-half-day, 430-mile motor journey up the Rhone Valley. Many of the trucks had no canvas, and

Come and Get Us

it was a cold and rainy trip. They passed Avignon, Lyon, Vienne, and Vesoul, and finally stopped, ten miles behind the front lines, in the Vosges Mountains near Charmois devant Bruyeres. (See campaign map, p. 124.) The regiment, now attached to the 36th Division, a Texas outfit, camped in an evergreen forest. Colonel Singles conferred with his officers about the fighting to come, and information and instructions were relayed to the men. On Sunday there was a simple church service in an open glade among the towering pines. The congregation sang "The Church in the Wildwood" and "Sweet Hour of Prayer" and recited the Twenty-Third Psalm, "Yea, though I walk through the valley of the shadow of Death, I will fear no evil. . . ." The padre gave a brief sermon on that real brotherhood of man which he hoped might follow the war, and the meeting ended with singing "America the Beautiful," "The Battle Hymn of the Republic," and "The Lord's Prayer."

Sunday chow included a new and welcome ingredient—mushrooms. Civilians had been seen gathering them near the bivouac area, and, on the theory that anything a Frenchman could eat couldn't hurt a GI stomach, the boys picked some and gave them to the cooks. No stomach pumps were needed.

That evening many wrote letters home.

I suppose tonight can be called the eve of another tough fight. You see, tomorrow night we move out and go knocking at Jerry's back door, and everybody knows that since we're engaging him finally on his own home soil, he is going to put up resistance like he never did. . . . I know you're always praying for me, and although I go in scared as hell, I know everything will be alright. . . .

It's raining and it's cold, and the rain drops splashing on my tent make me feel very lonesome. I'd like to think of this place in comparison with the area in upper Nuuanu [a Honolulu valley], but this rain and cold makes it impossible for me to picture this place as beautiful. . . .

Your letter of September 9th came yesterday, and when I think of it as the 75th Saturday edition, I realize how long I've been away from Paradise, and long for it so much the more. . . .*

About being divorced from the 442d. That was only temporary; we're again back with them, and I'm glad. It's too bad that ill feeling exists between the 100th and the 442d. After all, the boys are almost all hawaiian, and what's bad for one is bad for the other. . . .

* The recipient of this letter was a *haole* Honolulu businessman, who devoted a large part of his free time to writing to his young AJA friends ("adopted sons" he called them) who had gone into the Army.

I'm sorry ———— is having such a rough time back there. However, will you give him this from me—do not leave your home station if at all possible. Home is swell.[1]

On 14 October the regiment moved forward, its goal Bruyeres, population 4,000, situated at the junction of three roads, one of which led northeast through St. Dié to Strasbourg, the 36th Division's main objective. (See map, p. 228.) Four enemy-held hills arced from northwest to east above Bruyeres, and these would have to be cleared before that town could be secured. After an advance through high forest from the northwest the 2d Battalion would attack Hill B, a wooded mound directly north of Bruyeres, and the 100th would clear Hill A, north and slightly west of Hill B.

It was still raining as the 100th marched east along the top of a pine-covered ridge toward the first phase line, a mile west of the town. The 2d Battalion moved abreast on the right, and a battalion of the 179th Infantry, 45th Division, was on the left. In addition to its own artillery, the Combat Team had with it Company C, 636th Tank Destroyer Battalion, Company D, 83d Chemical Mortar Battalion, and the tanks of Company B, 752d Tank Battalion. Elements of the 36th Cavalry Reconnaissance Troop and the 88th Medical Collecting Company were also attached. The opposed forces were reported to consist of a depleted infantry regiment bolstered by a machine-gun battalion and a tank platoon. At dusk, which came between 4:00 and 5:00 P.M. here in the misty dripping forest, the soldiers dug slit trenches and rested in preparation for the morrow's fighting.

At 8:00 the next morning, as the regiment again moved forward, shells from the 522d's cannon whined overhead, just clearing the tree tops. A platoon of Company B led off for the 100th and covered 300 yards before it met machine-gun and sniper fire backed by enemy shelling. Captain Sakae Takahashi asked for tank fire, which helped silence this first resistance, and five Germans came forward to surrender. Moving on, Company B came to a mine field covered by tank and infantry fire. Bazooka teams were sent forward to try their luck against German tanks which were firing flat ahead at the leading platoon. Rockets hit two of them, but they withdrew under their own power. An enemy bazooka meanwhile disabled one of two American tanks which were moving along the narrow dirt road which separated Company B from Company C on its right. Braving sniper fire, men of the ammunition and pioneer platoon swept the mine field, and the battalion advance continued. Company B now bypassed a mine-protected road block of felled trees, but when an engineer platoon came up to clear this barricade four Jerry machine

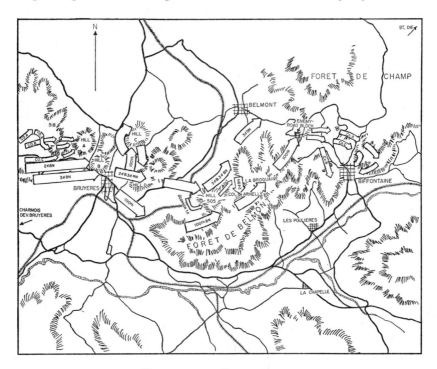

BRUYERES TO BIFFONTAINE

guns opened up, and a squad had to go back to help mop up the nest.

Swinging left behind Company B into the 45th Division sector to guard against an attack from that flank, Company A got caught in a half-hour volley of shells, and twenty men were wounded, one fatally. An attached mortar platoon from D Company also suffered twelve casualties. Three-fourths of the enemy shells were exploding as tree bursts, sending hundreds of knifelike steel and wood fragments down among the advancing troops.

Late in the afternoon the battalion dug in. The soldiers covered their dugouts with logs, primarily as protection against shell fragments, but also in the vain hope that they might help keep the rain out. In these cold wet holes men huddled together for warmth. During the night the Jerries delivered harassing mortar and artillery fire, and were answered in kind.

At 8:30 A.M. the 100th and 2d Battalions shoved off again, Company B still on the left on Hill 518, Company C on its right moving along the slopes of Hill 555, and the 2d Battalion climbing the same hill farther south. By noon Company B had descended to the lower edge of the forest, east of which stretched a hundred yards of treeless valley. On the other side of the valley rose their objective, Hill A, 1,800 feet high, thickly wooded and steep, and about a half mile northwest of Bruyeres. Enemy artillery and mortars were raking the forest fringe where Takahashi's men rested. Directly below, on the western edge of the flats, lay three red-tile-roofed stone farmhouses, within and behind which were about fifty Germans. Company B's lead platoon concentrated fire against the buildings, and a platoon of C Company gave fire support from the right. The defenders of the farmhouses replied with rifles, carbines, and machine guns, but toward dark they withdrew across the valley under protection of heavy fire from the guns on Hill A. Company A moved up from the rear into position between Companies B and C, and the three units got ready for another rainy night.

During the course of the day the 2d Battalion had reached the forest edge, had cleared some houses on the western edge of the flats, and had repulsed a Jerry advance across the valley floor from Hill B. This attack had been preceded by a barrage from mortars, self-propelled cannon, and tanks and, after an hour's close-quarter fighting, had been broken only with the aid of hundreds of rounds from Combat Team artillery and mortars.

The next morning at 7:30 the German command threw its troops into another assault across the flats. Two companies drove against the 2d Battalion and another against the 100th. By 8:30 this second attack had been broken. An hour later, just as Singles was ordering a counterattack, the Jerries again moved out into the open. As the leading elements of this new and more determined drive reached the forest edge, Singles formed his men into a semicircular defense ring, and called for all possible support from the 442d's guns. Some Germans penetrated part of the battalion line, but under a torrent of pistol, grenade, carbine, and automatic weapons fire, they were mowed down, and the Jerry wave washed back across the open ground. Companies B and C soon moved across the valley toward Hill A, but could not reach the woods, and withdrew.

In fierce fighting, during which it used six bazooka teams to hold off enemy tanks, the 2d Battalion had meanwhile repulsed another enemy attack.

During the afternoon, under cover of a low-hanging mist, a five-man patrol from Company C crossed the flats to the foot of Hill A and occupied a vacant farmhouse. Lieutenant Masamao Otake left his men in this building and went on to the next, several hundred feet away. He found it deserted but, as he prepared to leave, was discovered and surrounded. Fighting it out alone, he killed several of the enemy before he fell under a machine-gun burst. The rest of his patrol managed to get back to the battalion after dark. Otake's bravery won a posthumous DSC.

Colonel Pence, commander of the 442d, now ordered the 3d Battalion forward into position along the lower slopes of Hill 555, south of the 2d Battalion, in preparation for a morning attack in which the 3d would move against Bruyeres, the 2d against Hill B, and the 100th against Hill A.

At 9:53 A.M., 18 October, every available mortar and piece of artillery attached to the Combat Team opened up in a thirty-five-minute barrage. At 10:15, a few minutes before jump-off time, chemical mortars smoked up the town and the two hills. It was still raining. A combat patrol from Company B led off for the 100th, and the rest of that company followed, supported by two tanks and two tank destroyers. Half a platoon from Company C advanced on the right flank. The rest of C, which had two medium tanks and tank destroyers attached, fired support from the forest edge, and protected the battalion's right flank. Company A, which had moved to the battalion's left, followed Company B.

The advance patrol took two prisoners, groggy from the preliminary barrage, at the foot of Hill A. Battalion mortars and machine guns raked the lower slopes of the objective, and tanks and tank destroyers slammed shells into the higher woods as Company B's platoons, and then A's, zigzagged in waves across the flats. While some squads engaged Germans in the farmhouses at the eastern edge of the valley, the rest of the attacking force plunged into the forest, and, dodging from tree to tree, worked slowly up the stiff slopes, using grenades to root out stubborn gun nests. By 3:00 A.M. the summit of the hill had been taken and Company C was mopping up as it climbed from the valley. By 6:00 P.M. Companies A and B were dug in on the eastern slope, Company C on the northern, and the D Company mortars were in position to give protection from counterattack to the east or north. The Germans had lost thirty killed and twenty wounded, and the 100th had taken a hundred prisoners, twelve machine guns and about thirty automatic weapons.

Meanwhile the 2d Battalion had pushed across the wider flats on the right and had seized Hill B. Company I of the 3d Battalion had helped in this attack by a flank drive up the southern slopes immediately north of Bruyeres. Company L of the 3d Battalion had swung into the town from the north, and by 6:30 P.M. had made contact with elements of the 143d Infantry, which had been fighting its way into the streets from the south. A group of Jerries held out for some hours in buildings around the central square, but by midnight enemy resistance had ended.

The next morning the 100th remained on Hill A as the 2d and 3d battalions moved against Hill D (595) southeast of Bruyeres. By early afternoon they had cleaned up this mound and were heading eastward to cut the road which led northeast from Bruyeres to Belmont. By 6:00 P.M. they had crossed this road, were dug in west of the railroad track which paralleled it, and were facing a strong enemy force which lay about a hundred yards to the east, below the Belmont Forest. But now the Combat Team had advanced so far and fast that it was holding an exposed 2000-yard salient. There were still some enemy troops on Hill C (578) northeast of Bruyeres, and neither the 179th Infantry on the 442d's left flank nor the 143d on its right had pushed abreast.

During the afternoon Pence had told Singles that the 100th must capture Hill C by noon of the following day, and Singles had moved his men down into the north end of Bruyeres. The next morning, 20 October, after a preparatory barrage, Company B moved along a track which skirted Hill D, and then, under smoke cover, began to cross the open terrain between that mound and Hill C. Farther west, Company C followed a covered route across the flats. Company B's smoke was dispersed by wind, and when enemy mortars wounded some men in its attached machine-gun platoon Singles ordered B to swing to the left and follow C. The two units encountered only minor resistance on the objective and by noon had cleared its summit. Company A followed from Bruyeres, circling the base of the knoll and mopping up enemy remnants.

Meanwhile the 2d and 3d battalions were fighting off an enemy attack from across the railroad, and the units left behind to guard Hill D were battling a force of about a hundred Germans which had infiltrated their positions during the night. In midafternoon Company C and a platoon from Company A moved across from Hill C to help against these Jerries.

At about the same time an enemy armored column began to move down the Belmont-Bruyeres road. If not stopped it would split the regiment through the middle. Pence sent tanks, tank destroyers, the 3d Platoon of Company A, and some engineers to meet the threat, but before this task group could come within striking distance of the enemy armor, four cruising Thunderbolts spotted the German column, bombed and strafed it, and knocked out seven vehicles. The rest of the German force pulled back up the road toward Belmont.

By 5:00 P.M. the 2d and 3d battalions had pushed their opponents back and had crossed the railbed, but had been stopped by mine fields on the lower slopes of Hill 505, a projecting ridge of the Belmont Forest which commanded both road and railroad track.

Defense plans taken from the body of an enemy officer now formed the basis for a plan to turn the German position. During the night the reserve companies of the 2d and 3d battalions were brought together in a task force to which wire, radio, and mine-sweeping crews were attached, and Major Emmet O'Connor, executive officer of the 3d Battalion, took command of this unit. Before dawn it moved up the southern face of Hill 505 to hit the Germans in flank. Simultaneously the 2d and 3d battalions advanced up the western slopes along paths which engineers had cleared through mine fields during the night.

At 7:00 A.M. the 100th marched up the Belmont road and then climbed into the forest south of Hill 505. On the way Companies D and B, at the tail of the column, were strafed by two enemy planes which suddenly appeared from under low cloud cover. Luckily, in their single pass they roared down at right angles to the road, and there were no casualties among the soldiers who had hurled themselves into the roadside ditches. Later, in the woods, five men of D Company were wounded by shell fragments.

At about noon scouts on the left contacted the O'Connor Task

Force. Hill 505 had been taken, and O'Connor's men were advancing north along the forest slopes above the Belmont road to reunite with other elements of the 2d and 3d battalions at La Broquaine.

Within the wet forest the 100th meanwhile pushed northeast, its objective a midway point on the Belmont-Biffontaine road. Twice enemy patrols fired from the flanks, but the battalion met no frontal resistance, and in midafternoon reached the fifteen-foot dirt track and set up a roadblock. Scouts now reported Germans in front and on both flanks. If the Jerries had enough men for the purpose they could isolate the 100th, but when Singles contacted the regimental command post he was told to establish an all-around defense for the night, and to swing right against Biffontaine in the morning. Shortly after his call went through the telephone went dead, and a wire patrol found forty feet of cable gone from the line. It was an anxious night, but quiet except for the capture of a Jerry ration party headed for Belmont, and the crump of the battalion's own mortars as they covered avenues of approach to the bivouac area.

Early in the morning the Division Commander radioed instructions that the 100th should take high ground north and west of Biffontaine and should also block the roads leading south from the town. It was planned that the 3d Battalion, on the left, would attack across the Belmont-Biffontaine road while the 7th Infantry of the 3d Division, farther west, advanced north of Belmont. On the 442d's right the 143d Infantry would move up toward Biffontaine through the valley between Les Poulieres and La Chapelle.

Swinging to the right, Companies C and A occupied two wooded hills which projected from the Belmont Forest just north and northeast of Biffontaine. Company B occupied a spur southwest of Biffontaine and its attached mortar platoon took positions from which the roads leading south could be shelled. During the morning Company C, which was on the northernmost of the two hills above the town, sent a seven-man combat reconnaissance patrol toward its outskirts. Spotting a party of about twenty Jerries, the patrol attacked and took fourteen prisoners.

Singles now ordered Company C down from its hill to cross the hundred yards of open terrain which stretched toward the northern part of Biffontaine. Company A, on the height to the left of Company C, would also send one of its platoons across the flats. Company B would simultaneously make a push east from the forest edge, leaving the men of its attached mortar platoon behind as riflemen to protect its exposed right flank.

It was midafternoon when this pincer movement began. The Company C platoon and a platoon of heavy weapons from Company D moved swiftly across the open fields and occupied some houses in the northern outskirts. In one of these buildings a squad captured a German Signal Corps command post, complete with major, lieutenant, staff of enlisted aides, radios, maps, machine pistols, rifles, and quantities of bullets and grenades. The platoon from A was held up for a time by machine-gun fire but also forced its way into the town. In a three-hour battle Company B meanwhile fought its way across the valley and pushed from house to house in the western part of Biffontaine while an attached platoon of heavy machine guns from Company D shot up enemy vehicles and personnel trying to move out to the south. By 5:00 P.M. the battalion held the town, but Singles expected counterattack, and ordered every house prepared for defense.

Since 8:30 in the morning the 3d Battalion had been fighting northeast along the Biffontaine-Belmont road. At noon it was a half mile west of the 100th, meeting strong opposition, and harassed by enemy shells coming from the left, the front, and the right flanks. Some Thunderbolts came over and temporarily silenced the German artillery, but after they left the Jerry guns opened up again. The 2d Battalion had climbed into the Belmont Forest from La Broquaine to take positions southwest of Biffontaine, covering the 100th's right flank, but had met with trouble on the way. During the previous night about a hundred Germans had used bicycles to move south on the Les Poulieres road and had then climbed into the forest to occupy a high spur, the Col de L'Arnelle, which overlooked the path of the 2d Battalion's projected march. It took that unit a large part of the day to dislodge the Germans.

Pence was becoming increasingly worried about the 100th. During the afternoon he sent an armored task force down the soggy Belmont-Biffontaine road to try to push through with rations, water, and ammunition. Some soldiers of the Company A platoon rode on the tanks, which soon ran into Jerry small-arms fire. Sergeant Itsumu Sasaoka, firing a machine gun atop one of the tanks, was badly wounded but kept shooting until they had pushed past the enemy fire. Then, weakened by loss of blood, he fell to the ground. Later reported missing in action, he was awarded a DSC. The tanks struggled ahead a little farther, but were finally stopped by a roadblock defended by fifty Jerries. Some of the riflemen tried to push on through the woods, but none reached Biffontaine that day.

As darkness came the 100th still held that town, but was without flank protection and in danger of being surrounded and cut to pieces. A German counterattack from the south came at dusk. Tanks followed by infantry advanced to within fifty yards of the first houses and began pumping shells into their brick walls. As these crumbled most of the defenders ducked into the cellars, but they rushed upstairs again whenever guards at the windows yelled that the Jerry infantry were starting to move in. The attack was beaten off, but there were two more before midnight. Each was repulsed, but only after some murderous close-quarter shooting. During these assaults some of the Germans shouted, "Surrender! You are surrounded." In reply they heard yells of "Go to hell!" and "Come and get us!" and received a hail of bullets and grenades. The battalion's ammunition supply was now low, and some of their defense fire came from German weapons captured earlier that day at the Signal Corps post. After the third attack the Jerries gave up for the night.

Through his English-speaking aide the captured German major had been gleefully telling Captain Bill Pye of C Company that he had better surrender. Pye tried to bluff but the Nazi wasn't fooled; he knew the battalion was isolated. "Why be killed for nothing? Surrender now, and save your soldiers' lives." Garrulous with anticipated triumph, he boasted that one German was the equal of six "gutless Italians," gave the "decadent French" little higher rank in valor, and asserted that the Yanks and British would soon be hurled out of France and back across the Channel. He shut up, however, after the last attack failed, and gave his interpreter a rest.

North and west of Biffontaine there was confused fighting in the darkness as the A and D company platoons still on the heights fought off raids by enemy patrols. During the night enemy shells searched the hills and exploded throughout the town. A regimental supply party was struggling from Bruyeres through the Belmont Forest toward Biffontaine, its members hand-carrying rations and ammunition under protection of Company G of the 2d Battalion. Climbing for hours along slippery tracks, unable to locate the 100th's mortar men on the hill southwest of Biffontaine, the supply men finally dumped their loads and turned back. About midmorning scouts from the mortar platoon found the material about 350 yards behind their hill. The ammunition, which was badly needed, was hurried to all elements of the battalion, but there was no rush about the rations—later in the day, when elements of the 3d Battalion reached Biffontaine, they found the town's supposedly famishing defenders plentifully supplied with chickens, eggs, and even bread from the town bakery.

At dawn an enemy patrol jumped a party of litter bearers and wounded soldiers which had been struggling north from Biffontaine toward Belmont. Only two men escaped, Captain Young Kim and a medic, Private Richard Chinen, both of them walking wounded. The other eighteen spent the rest of the war in German hospitals or prison camps.

In Biffontaine, the Nazi major requested a change of quarters. The previous evening he had insisted that because of his rank he should be given a second-floor room, complete with bed and bedding, and his captors had wearily assented. His men had slept in the cellar. It now seemed that the officer had not rested well; shells had been bursting too near the house. He asked that his mattress and blankets be transferred to the cellar. Given the choice of downstairs quarters, without mattress or conversation with his fellow prisoners, or his previous accommodations, the major decided to descend to the level of his men.

At 10:30 A.M. the commander of the division radioed Singles to hold out; the rest of the 442d would push through, and the 141st and 143d Infantry would move up on the flanks. Enemy artillery shelled Biffontaine throughout the cold, rainy day. At dusk, after a half-hour barrage, the Jerries again attacked behind tanks and anti-aircraft guns. This time, however, the 100th had reinforcements. The Yank tanks had finally broken through to the town and the platoon from Company A and elements of the 3d Battalion had come in behind. Thus supported, the garrison beat off this final assault.

At noon the next day, 25 October, units of the 143d Infantry moved into Biffontaine from the south, and the 100th pulled back to Belmont with the rest of the 442d. In the three-day battle for Biffontaine the battalion had killed or wounded at least forty Germans and had taken about the same number prisoner. Captured equipment included a two-and-one-half-ton loaded ammunition carrier, a reconn car, two ambulances, three sedans, two antitank guns, six machine pistols, one hundred rifles, seven radios, three switchboards, a large assortment of maps—and a number of American Red Cross prisoner-of-war parcels. When the 100th had started for Bruyeres its effective strength had been thirty-six officers and 823 men. In the eleven days which had since passed it had lost twenty-one killed, 122 wounded, and eighteen captured.

In the fighting at Biffontaine and around Bruyeres most of the Jerry troops had been either Volksturm men—striplings and middle-aged Germans hastily taught how to fire a gun and then rushed to the defense of the Fatherland—or Czechs and Poles impressed into the battered Wehrmacht to fill gaps in the ranks of the master race. A sprinkling of Hitler's SS men had stiffened the enemy units, had driven the raw cannon fodder to attack, and had themselves fought desperately.

At Belmont there were hot showers, dry clothes, two pairs of woolen socks for each man, letters from home, and eighty-five much needed replacements. The soldier who had written about "another tough fight" wrote once again to his *haole* "Pop":

It's been almost two weeks since I last wrote you. . . . I'm afraid those two weeks of silence, with delay en route to boot, is going to cause you undue alarm and I hate to think about the days to come, when you go around wondering whether I am alright or not. All throughout the ordeals of the past ten odd days, I had thought of you, and hoped for a chance to drop you a note, but, unlike Italy, that chance never came until today. Please forgive me, Pop, and join me in thanking the Lord for sparing me again.

As I told you in my last letter, our expectations for some real tough fighting were right. From the day we contacted Jerry up until we were pulled back for rest, it was one hard series of continuous fighting. When I think of the time we went through, I get goose pimples all over me. . . .

I now have a Purple Heart and a Cluster, all collected in two short days. However, the so-called wounds were slight, and after treatment at the aid station, I was able to report back to my unit. . . .

Well, I guess I'll call it quits as far as the war is concerned. It's getting colder and colder here by the day, even if Indian Summer is supposed to be here. It's so very misty, and it rains a lot, so you can imagine how it is in our holes in the woods.

Yesterday, when we pulled back, I had 20 letters waiting for me. Your two letters dated Sept. 4th and 17th were among those, and they certainly lifted up this tired soul. Whenever I read your letters, my cares of the day are gone, and no matter how tired and sulky I am, after I'm through reading your letters, I feel really happy.

Your "Observations on Americanism" certainly hits the spot. . . . I'm having the company officers of Japanese ancestry read it, and later on I plan to pass it on to Captain Kometani. I sincerely hope that other Americans (haoles) will come to understand us as much as you and many others in Hawaii have come to know us. Here's hoping that all these things will in the near future take root and blossom into something big.[2]

EVERYONE in the battalion had expected a few days of rest at Belmont, but within thirty-six hours the 442d was pulled out of reserve, to attempt the rescue of the 1st Battalion, 141st Infantry, a Texas unit which had been surrounded in the forest two miles east of Biffontaine. At 4:00 A.M., 27 October, 1944, the 3d and 100th battalions moved east from Belmont. Medium tanks from Company B of the 753d Tank Battalion, a platoon from the regimental Cannon Company, Company D of the 83d Chemical Mortar Battalion, and a platoon of the 232d Engineers accompanied the 100th, and similar units supported the 3d. The 522d and 133d Field Artillery would fire on call.

The 100th was to swing northeast of Biffontaine, and then turn southeast through the western part of a high wooded ridge which skirted the Biffontaine-La Houssiere Valley. (See map, p. 241.) The 3d Battalion, on the left of the 100th, would make a wider arc on the same course, and the 2d Battalion would push northeast of Biffontaine, protecting the Combat Team's left flank.

Slogging through rain and mud in the predawn blackness, each soldier followed the piece of white paper pinned on the back of the man ahead. At 8:00 A.M. there was a two-hour rest, and then, after a final check on rations and ammunition, the battalion pushed forward. Company B advanced on the left, along both sides of a dirt track which followed the top of the forest ridge.

Lost Battalion

Company A marched on B's right, along the western slope, and was followed by Company C. Heavy weapons sections accompanied Companies A and B. On the right of the 100th, nearer the valley which stretched from La Houssiere to Biffontaine, the 2d and 3d battalions of the 141st Infantry were still trying to move forward to reach their comrades of the 1st Battalion, who were encircled only a little more than a mile to the south.

Soon after 8:00 A.M., the 100th met fire from well-camouflaged outposts. Two tanks moved up the soggy road to help out, but the first struck a mine and lost a tread, and the second could not pass; the track was too narrow and the trees at its edge too thick. Advance platoons silenced enemy gun nests with co-ordinated rifle, machine-gun, and grenade fire, but progress was slow throughout the day, and by nightfall the 100th had moved ahead only 900 feet. Again that night, as in the approach to Bruyeres and Biffontaine, tree bursts made it necessary to roof sleeping holes with logs. There was sporadic outpost fire into the blackness as each side waited for daylight.

In the cold, rainy dawn the 100th attacked again, with Company C now in the center of the line. As the first wave crossed an east-west ridge which intersected the path of advance and moved down into the draw behind it, enemy mortar and artillery shells suddenly blanketed this saddle, and seventeen men were hit. Jerry had pulled one of his old tricks. Those who could, ran for the reverse slope and dug furiously. For nearly an hour enemy guns pounded the draw, the ridge, and its reverse slope. Even the oldest of the 100th's veterans couldn't remember a worse barrage. Despite heavy support fire from the attached guns and from friendly artillery farther back, when night came the battalion had gained only a few hundred feet, and a German mine field lay ahead. The Volksturm boys might not know much about war—the few who were captured talked freely but knew surprisingly little about their own company dispositions— but their officers were taking every advantage of terrain. Well sheltered, the Germans had only to stay in their holes and fire their guns.

Since morning the 100th had lost five men killed and thirty-seven wounded. Among the dead was Silver Star winner Lieutenant James Boodry, battalion S-3, the tough little Massachusetts man of French Canadian ancestry who had once said that he would be willing to lead his AJA soldiers anywhere. Litter bearers were having a rough time getting casualties out of the woods to the road, and with jeeps and ambulances constantly bogging in the muck, the wounded still had a long journey to Belmont ahead of them. Rations and ammunition had to be hand-carried from the road after dark.

During the night engineers cleared paths through the mines, and early in the morning three Thunderbolts blasted the German positions. At about 9:00 A.M. the battalion pushed forward once more.

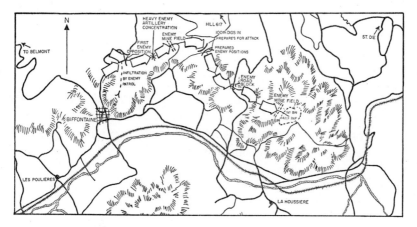

BIFFONTAINE TO THE "LOST BATTALION"

German tanks were now looping shells up into the woods from a valley to the east. At noon it was discovered that an enemy patrol had climbed from the valley floor on the right rear of the battalion, had captured a lone medic, and had cut the wire between the rear and forward command posts. Singles couldn't afford a strong patrol to guard this flank but sent a messenger back to the 141st Infantry, asking that outfit to push forward and give his men some protection.

Aided by fire from tanks and artillery, by midafternoon the battalion had gained another thousand feet of forest, but was now up against a strongly prepared enemy line which stretched along still another east-west ridge. Here the terrain offered no chance for a flanking move; only a frontal assault would do the job. After a preparatory barrage all three companies jumped off, moving up the slopes in waves of squads and platoons, firing from the hip when within range of German hand grenades. The most severe fighting took place around an enemy roadblock at a break in the ridge, but all along the line there were furious small battles. The Germans finally pulled back, leaving fifty-five dead sprawled around the road-block and in or near the entrances to their bunkers. Very few prisoners had been taken. The German command was determined, probably for morale purposes, to capture the Texas unit and had ordered a battle to the death to hold off the rescue force.

In this latest struggle the commander of Company C and both of his lieutenants had been wounded, so one of Company B's two unwounded commissioned officers took over. As darkness fell the battalion dug in and prepared for a German counterattack. None came, though it was thought that the Texans must now be only a few hundreds yards away.

Those soldiers who could still fight groaned awake before dawn and made ready for one more push. Company A had seventy-seven effectives, Company B had seventy-six, and Company C had eighty. The Combat Team threw all its firepower into a barrage against the last German hill above the encircled battalion, and the groggy remnant of the 100th stumbled slowly ahead. Ten hours and 2,000 feet later the 2d Platoon of Company B cut a path through the last Jerry mine field and made contact with an outpost of the beleaguered force. On the left, where, during four days of battle, the 3d Battalion had been constantly abreast of the 100th, a patrol from Company I broke through at about the same time.

The 100th quickly formed a protective corridor, and as the big Texans passed through to safety, they pumped the hands of their small, brown, weary but grinning rescuers. It was a haggard-looking bunch of soldiers who shambled through the lane. Isolated for seven days, ringed in an area 1,200 feet in diameter, the encircled force had fought off a series of attacks, but had been unable to push its way out. Though the enemy had been forced to divert more and more of its strength against the 442d, it had still covered the trapped unit with machine-gun and mortar fire. For several days American planes had been dropping ballast tanks filled with supplies, but most of these had fallen outside the ring, and when a load had fallen within it, rations, ammunition, and medicine had splattered widely, and had had to be hunted for at night. Drinking water had come from a small spring, guarded constantly by machine guns, and from rain caught in tent canvas. Many of the wounded had died for lack of medical attention, many men hobbled with trench foot, and, on the day of their rescue, most of the "able" remnant were physically and nervously exhausted.*

The 100th now had about 200 effectives left in the three rifle companies, and had lost eight men killed, ninety-nine wounded, and one man missing. It had killed seventy-five Germans and had taken eight prisoners. The 3d Battalion of the 442d had also been badly battered. On the first day it had met tank and half-track fire, on the second day a strongly held roadblock, on the third the same fiercely defended hill line against which the 100th had thrown itself, and on the final day the last ridge behind which the Texans had been ringed. On the 442d's left flank the 2d Battalion had ended a three-day battle to take Hill 617 northeast of Biffontaine by coupling an assault on its northern face with a feint attack up the western slopes.

For the 100th's veterans this last fight had been as bad as anything they had experienced in Italy, where there had been plenty of mountains and freezing weather, but not the constant tree bursts on all sides, day and night. In Italy a man had sometimes been at the bottom of a hill shooting up, sometimes at the top shooting down, but at least he had generally known the enemy was in front of him, and could guess how many Jerries there were, and where they were. Here in the foggy semidark of the forest the tree trunks often cut visibility to five or ten yards, and a man couldn't see ahead, or around, or behind, or guess where the next bullet might come from.

On the day after they reached the Texans, 31 October, the 100th and 3d Battalions moved south, taking positions overlooking the road from Biffontaine which circled the southern edge of the forest ridge on its way toward St. Dié. On 1 November, the 100th was in defensive position guarding a roadblock to the right rear of the 3d Battalion. More men had been evacuated for trench foot or fatigue and the combined effective strength of the rifle companies was now 175 men. For the next few days patrols scouted to the valley floor on the south and west. Heavier clothing was issued; a new type of field jacket, a woolen sweater, shoe pacs, and waterproof shoes. The 100th was in reserve on 5 November when the 2d and 3d battalions

---

* The Combat Team later received a bronze plaque inscribed as follows: "To the 442nd Infantry Regiment. With Deep Sincerity and Upmost [sic] Appreciation For The Gallant Fight To Effect Our Rescue After We Had Been Isolated For Seven Days.—1st Bn., 141st Infantry Regiment, Biffontaine, France, from 24th to 30th October 1944."

descended from the edge of the forest to seize positions along the railroad track which curved about its tip. On the 7th and 8th, as this job was being finished, the 100th moved back to Bruyeres over the first snow.

The boys' tails had probably never dragged so low as on the morning they reached the Texans, but, with that job finished pride in their unit reached new heights. Their gang had again come through when the chips were down. Shoulders were stiff, chins up, as what was left of the outfit moved into Bruyeres. But though the spirit was the same as that when the 100th had been mauled at Cassino and had pasted the Jerries at Belvedere, the flesh was not. Now, in each skeleton company, only eight or nine soldiers could say they had crossed the beach at Salerno, and half of these had carried the scars of previous battles into this last mission. The rest were men who had originally come in as replacements. When the 3d Platoon of Company A started out to rescue the trapped Texans, only two of its members were veterans of Camp McCoy, and neither of these reached the "lost battalion."

On 9 November, 1944, the 2d and 3d battalions moved back to Bruyeres. On the 13th, as these units returned into the snow-covered forest for a four-day spell of patrol duty, the 100th was ordered south to the 45th Division rest area at Bain-les-Bains, fifteen miles southwest of Epinal. West Pointer Singles had persuaded some of his fellow alumni on the 7th Army staff that his outfit had earned a rest. As far as his men were concerned, the Colonel couldn't have done them a greater service. There was general agreement that the only good thing about the Vosges Mountains had been the mushrooms.

At Bain-les-Bains, a spa where in peacetime Europe's rich came to bathe or drink the mineral waters, the 45th Division men seemed well acquainted with the 100th's reputation and most recent performance, and treated the AJA soldiers royally. After a three-day stay they moved south to Nice, the famous resort city on the French Riviera, where the 100th was attached to the 44th Anti-aircraft Brigade. (See campaign map, p. 124.) Two days later the battalion trucked forty miles north of Nice to relieve a parachute unit which had been patrolling the Franco-Italian border. The new front would be a twelve-mile stretch of the snow-covered mountain region between S. Etienne de Tinee and S. Martin de Vesubie. Now the buddhaheads were going to be Alpine troops!

Billeted in small resort hotels or in private homes—Singles had the mayor's house at S. Martin—they tramped on

Riviera Holiday

long patrols through the deep snows, uniforms covered by white parkas, but at night returned to hot meals and real beds. The two villages were peaceful and unscarred by war, and the friendly civilians were deeply appreciative when the battalion furnished an honor guard for the funeral of a native son, a former ski champion, who had died while fighting in the Free French forces.

At a couple of evening dances the boys tried to teach the sturdy farm girls American steps and to persuade the local musicians to "swing it." Some soldiers caught nice fat trout in the mountain streams and others borrowed or rented skis and spilled their way down some of the lesser slopes—though the photos they sent home generally showed them in upright stance. Thanksgiving Day was the best since McCoy, with plenty of turkey and fixings and wine by the quart, all enjoyed in an atmosphere of peace.

After eleven days in this winter wonderland the battalion returned to Nice and then moved east by truck along the scenic coastal highway to Menton, a town just about a mile from the Italian border. As they gazed at the green and purple ocean, fringed by sunny beaches, at palm trees along the roadside, bougainvillea vines on villa walls, and mountains which towered to the left above the road, the boys agreed that this was the nearest thing to Hawaiian scenery they had met so far. "No coconut trees, but date palms, and that's good enough for me."[1]

Company command posts were set up in homes or hotels either in Menton or the nearby village of Castellar. Riflemen rode north on the Menton-Sospel road, then trudged eastward across snowy slopes to take over the comfortable dugouts of a First Special Service Forces battalion. The rest of the 442d had moved into this frontier sector a few days previously, and the 100th's line of patrol stretched north from Menton to meet that of the 3d Battalion at Mt. Grammondo. The 2d Battalion patrolled north of the 3d near Peira Cava on the left flank of the regiment's eighteen-mile line.

During the next fourteen weeks troops from other commands occasionally took over in the Peira Cava area, and at such times the 2d Battalion alternated with the 3d in patrol of the Sospel sector, but throughout this period the 100th remained on the right of the line. Elements of an engineer battalion and a medical collecting company were attached to the regiment, and antitank, antiaircraft, and pack artillery backed up its guns. Almost every day one or more British destroyers moved down the coast, shelling enemy shore installations or positions on the Italian side of the border.

It was a comparatively quiet front. Soldiers on patrol sometimes stepped on mines or met sniper fire, and there was sporadic shelling from both sides of the border, but the war would not be won or lost in the Alpes Maritimes, and the German and Italian Fascist units across the frontier were not looking for trouble. The 442d sent out daily patrols, but these generally reported "all quiet." Wounded men returned from hospitals, and replacements poured in, received training in rear areas, after which they came forward to take their turns at patrol.

In mid-December "Joe" Farrington, Hawaii Delegate to Congress, visited the 100th, bringing news of home and a promise to do what he could about getting more furloughs to "Paradise."* A few days later a one-man enemy submarine came into Menton harbor by mistake, and guards at one of the 100th's antitank outposts took its operator captive. A stir of activity passed along the front at the turn of the year, when the Germans far to the north attempted a breakthrough in the Ardennes, and the Battle of the Bulge was being fought. All units of the 442d were alerted for German paratroopers who might descend behind the lines in American uniform, and the 3d Battalion established a reserve line behind the other units, but nothing happened.

In the 100th's sector the most eventful skirmish came in January, when a nine-man patrol discovered some enemy troops holed up in a hunting shack between the lines. A quick raid netted fourteen prisoners, eight of them Italian, six German. One of the attack group was killed, and two of the prisoners died of wounds.

Patrol duty was frigid work. "Whenever it gets too cold for me, I think of Waikiki Beach, and swear by all the gods that when this war is over, I'll never leave the Islands, that for six months I'm just going to loaf around down at the beaches and get back all the warmth that I have lost since I left the Islands." But the dugouts were dry and comfortable and gripers shut up when reminded of the Vosges. "If we stay here for the duration it'll be all right with me," was the general attitude.

In midmonth Singles received a full colonelcy and orders trans-

---

* Mr. Farrington was owner of *The Honolulu Star-Bulletin*, whose attitude towards the 100th, and toward AJAs generally, had been one of sympathy and support.

ferring him to command of the 397th Infantry. He had been offered a regiment before, but although he was a grey-haired thirty-nine, and old for the rugged life of a front-line battalion commander, he had refused in order to stick with what he called his "little Army." Now that things were quiet and the outfit was in trim shape again, he was ready to leave. The boys were sorry to see him go, but knew he deserved the promotion. Major Alex McKenzie filled in until Lt. Colonel James E. Conley, 2d Battalion commander, was transferred to leadership of the 100th. Conley was a former National Guardsmen who had built a reputation as a good combat officer—and he was a *kamaaina*, a Maui Island man.

At the end of January it was learned that Companies F and L of the 3d Battalion were going to receive Presidential Unit Citations for their part in the fighting around Bruyeres. Everyone in the 100th was happy, for it was generally agreed that the 2d and 3d battalions had done some really first-class fighting during the last seven months, especially during the actions in France.

Things seemed to be gradually working out as they had in the case of the early antagonism between the buddhaheads and the kotonks. The men from the relocation camps who had joined the 100th as replacements from Shelby had proved good soldiers—and good Joes, too, as those who had shared foxholes with them had come to know. The feeling between the 100th and the rest of the 442d would probably die out in the same way.

Both the Americans and their foes were sending spies across the Italian-French border, and the 100th passed various friendly agents through its lines. Menton was cluttered with Allied military intelligence agents interrogating line-crossers suspected of hostile espionage, and their own returned employees. In this area strange things were always happening. One day regimental artillery observers directing counter-battery fire against enemy guns saw some of their own short rounds explode in a field between the lines where what seemed to be Italian women were working. As they gazed through their binoculars the observers saw the "ladies" pull up their skirts, revealing Fascist uniform trousers, and sprint for cover.

Except for the cold, life in the hills was quite comfortable, but a five-day leave in Menton was something to look forward to. The battalion had taken over the Hotel Imperial, a 635-room luxury establishment on a hilltop overlooking the sea which during this period housed at least a hundred soldiers at a time. Even though its upper three floors were unused—shells had punctured the roof and walls in a few places—there was still more than enough guest room. Hot water came from the faucets; the lights clicked on and off; the beds were soft; the room radiators were warm; and the windows gave wonderful views of mountain or sea. Doc Kometani, who served as hotel manager, had a civilian staff of about sixteen laundresses, cooks, maids, and waitresses, plus ten GI aides, and his nonpaying guests didn't have to lift a hand. As one of them remarked, "It's just like sitting on the *lanai* of the Royal Hawaiian."

Men wandered around the modern lower part of Menton, climbed narrow brick-cobbled alleys into its higher ancient section, and peered into the shell-pierced seventeenth-century cathedral of S. Michele, within which broken window glass littered the pavement. The local sights were few, however, and the restees were soon ready for more stimulating recreation. Menton was officially a combat area and, of its normal civilian population of about a thousand, only a few essential civilians remained, but the girls of the licensed houses had evidently been included in this category, and were cordial to all visitors.

Twenty-four-hour passes were available for Beausoleil, population 5,000, about five miles up the coastal road and just outside Monte Carlo, which was in the officially out-of-bounds principality of Monaco. In Beausoleil all the shops, taverns, and restaurants were open, and the boys bought souvenirs, ate and drank all they could, and cultivated the civilians, who could generally understand GI Italian. Fraternization came fast. With their tinned rations to help fill the stew pot, and their cigarets and chocolate bars, the soldiers made welcome dinner guests. They in turn drank their hosts' good unwatered wine and danced gleefully with their daughters. Johnny's Bar was a favorite drinking place and hangout. Its owner was a pleasant Frenchman who spoke English fluently, and his newest crop of soldier customers became fond of him, his Swiss spouse, and his pretty daughter who helped out at the bar. One private spent practically all of his leave in a vain attempt to sell the family on his qualifications as a potential husband and son-in-law.

Doc Kometani hired the town's civic auditorium for regular Thursday night dances at which the regimental orchestra furnished music and the local girls quickly learned American dance steps—in fact, at the end of the 100th's stay, some could even do a passable imitation of the hula.

With his cigarets selling at $20 a carton and his chocolate bars at $2 each, any soldier could drink as much cognac or brandy as his stomach would take. Practically every man in the battalion had some Hennessy or Martel or Courvoisier with which to drink the New Year in, but none of the French liquor, no matter what its quality, could take the place of American whiskey. "Today we got our whiskey ration, 1 bottle of Schenley's Reserve. I'm taking it up to the hills tomorrow and we're going to have a helluva time with my boys. I've got a bottle of Hennessy too, so we ought to be able to get the boys warm, at least." Each man received a ration of a half dozen bottles of American beer a week, but it wasn't quite the thing for midwinter guzzling. "It really gives you the shakes unless you have a nice fireplace with a roaring fire."

Though it was off-limits, some GIs managed to get into the Casino at Monte Carlo. Those who did usually saved a couple of chips to stack away among their other souvenirs. Some passes allowed visits to Nice or Cannes, and a few officers secured eighteen-day furloughs for Paris. It took six days in a two-and-a-half-ton truck to reach that city, but those who made the trip said it was worth it, especially the visits to the Bal Tabarin, Chantilly Club, Casino De Paris, and Folies Bergeres. "The French certainly take pride in beautiful breasts, and they've got them; however, I prefer the American taste for beautiful legs. The Parisian women are really beautiful. I'm glad I can now say I saw them."

Early in March a boxing match with a French Army team was arranged for the 16th, at the Beausoleil civic auditorium. On the 14th, however, the Combat Team received word that it was to be relieved by French troops and on the night of the 16th the 100th left Menton by truck. As the column rode through Beausoleil Johnny, his wife, his daughter, and many others were in the streets to bid the buddhaheads not "Bon Voyage!" but "Aloha!"

AFTER A SHORT stopover in Nice the regiment entrained for Marseille. The 100th stayed four days at a bivouac near that port, from which it embarked on 23 March, 1945, in three LSTs for an unknown destination. A day and a half of guessing what this might be ended with an announcement, at Sunday morning church services, that the ships would dock at Leghorn at noon. All identifying insignia were to be removed from uniforms and helmets; the 442d's return to Italy was to be kept secret. Trucks carried the battalion from the harbor to a staging area near Pisa where, during the next three days, it received new rifles, machine guns, mortars, and vehicles to replace those left behind at Marseille.

On the night of 28 March, the 100th moved to an assembly area about eight miles north of Lucca. For six days its members practiced battle problems, trained replacements, ate dust on hikes along nearby trails, and fired and adjusted the new weapons. Engineers who demonstrated the Germans' newer and nastier mines met none of the bored disinterest common at other kinds of briefings—those on the causes and cures of venereal disease, for instance. A soldier who stepped on a mine generally had little chance thereafter to court lesser evils.

It was now announced that the 442d would be attached to the 92d, a Negro division, and would go into action on the extreme left flank of the Fifth Army line, along the Ligurian coast.

Florida to Ohio

During the previous September, while the Combat Team had been moving from the Arno River line to Marseille, the Fifth Army had crossed the Arno Valley and had broken through the center of the Germans' Gothic Line. This barrier against allied entrance into the Po Valley began on the Ligurian seacoast below Genoa and after running through the Northern Appenines crossed the peninsula to the Adriatic below Rimini. (See campaign map, p. 124.) At the end of September its only unbroken part had been the sector bordering the Ligurian Sea on the Fifth Army's extreme left flank. It had been thought at that time that the Allied forces might quickly drive through the Appenines, emerge into the plain of the Po River, and either push the Germans north through the passes of the Alps, or mop them up in the Po Valley, the last large segment of Italy still under their control. Hitler's armies elsewhere in Europe were in retreat under the hammer blows of the Americans, British, and Russians, and it seemed reasonable to believe that the depleted Nazi divisions in Italy might be finished off by the end of the year. By the end of October, however, the Fifth Army advance had slowly ground to a stop against the fourth of a series of German delaying lines in the mountains north of the Gothic Line, and for the next five months General Mark Clark had rested his weary troops and stock-piled supplies for a spring offensive.

The Germans had built strong fortifications across the narrow Ligurian coastal plain north of the Arno's mouth, and in the mountains which ran southeast above these flats and then swung east and inland above the Arno Valley. The Serchio Valley above Lucca was the only sizable river gap which broke this mountain line east of the coastal plain. During the latter part of December a German reconnaissance in force had pushed two battalions of the 92d Division southward through that valley, one of them in sad disorganization, and British Indian troops had had to be sent in to retake the lost ground. On 4 February, the 92d had begun a series of limited objective attacks north into the Serchio Valley and up the Ligurian Plain, but in seven days of fighting had made no appreciable gains.

Fifth Army planned to start its spring offensive with a diversionary attack in this coastal area a few days before its main effort, a drive into the mountains near Bologna. A push aimed at capture of Massa and exploitation north towards the naval base at La Spezia might draw some part of the enemy's small tactical reserve from the Bologna area. In any case, it should pin down the German Grenadier and Italian Fascist Bersagliere troops in the threatened sector. As a result of the disappointing showing of the 92d Division it was decided that only one of its regiments, the 370th Infantry (reconstructed from the best fighters in the division), would take part in the diversionary attack, and that this unit should be coupled with the 442d Combat Team. The 473d Infantry, an outfit composed of former antiaircraft artillerymen, would also be placed under divisional control for the push.

On 3 April General Mark Clark visited the 100th, which held a formation in his honor. He told its members, "I welcome the 100th Infantry Battalion back to Italy. I hated to see you leave the 5th Army, but it was considered necessary that you go to the support of the invading troops in southern France. I have followed closely your splendid record. . . . I remember the time when the 100th battalion received the distinguished unit badges and more than 100 other medals that I have presented at various times. I have seen you in action and know your ability. . . . You of all battalions, I pledge, will share in the great victory ahead."[1] That night the 442d moved north into the mountains to take over positions of the 371st Infantry in preparation for a jump-off at dawn on 5 April.

On the left of the area of proposed attack, a three-mile-wide coastal plain stretched from the mouth of the Arno north to the valley of the Magra River east of La Spezia. Highway 1 ran through this flat terrain, past Massa to La Spezia, but could be used only if the Germans were forced from the numerous fortified river and canal lines which ran west from the mountains to the sea, intersecting the whole length of the plain. It would be futile to attempt to flank these positions through the sharp peaks and deep gorges of the Ligurian Alps on the right, but in the lesser hills between these peaks and the sea such a strategy might be practicable. If the Germans could be pushed off this high ground they would have to pull back up the coastal flats.

It was planned that the 370th Infantry would move north through the hills nearest the sea while the 442d attacked through the higher ridges farther inland. Along these latter slopes the Germans had prepared an elaborate system of bunkers and pillboxes, blasted out of solid rock, reinforced with concrete, and sited for interlacing fire.

Mountain peaks gave excellent observation for enemy mobile artillery, and for the long range coastal guns of the Punta Bianca peninsula below La Spezia.

At the start of the Combat Team's thrust its 3d Battalion, the attack unit farthest from the sea, would advance west from the vicinity of Azzano against 2,800-foot Mt. Fragolita (Hill 912), from which the enemy had superb observation over the whole coastal area. The 100th would advance north from the vicinity of Vallechia over Mt. Caualla, which it would take over from elements of the 371st Infantry. (See map, p. 256.) It would then move against "Georgia" Hill and "Ohio" Hills 1, 2, and 3, a series of saw tooths from 1,300 to 1,800 feet in height stretching from "Florida"* Hill, a northern extension of Mt. Caualla, to 2,000-foot Mt. Cerreta (Hill 702). After the 3d Battalion had seized Mt. Fragolita and the 100th had crossed Ohio 3, the two units would make a junction on Mt. Cerreta, pinching the enemy off his high defenses. The 370th Infantry would meanwhile be pushing north through the lower hills above the plain.

On 4 April, the 100th climbed from Pietrasanta, where fruit trees bloomed in bursts of white, yellow, and pink blossoms, past Vallechia and up tortuous goat tracks and across high ridges to Mt. Caualla. On that sunny afternoon Lt. Colonel Conley brought his company commanders, platoon lieutenants, and platoon sergeants up to Florida, jumping-off-place for the next morning's attack. Directly ahead was the ridge line which had to be taken. Its right side dropped at a ninety-degree angle to one valley floor; its left sloped more gradually into another. An attempt at an enveloping attack through the valley on its right would be murder. If the battalion were to try an advance along the flats on the left and then up the long scantily covered slopes, the men would be exposed to zeroed-in artillery, mortar, and machine-gun fire long before they got near the dug-in defenders. The third alternative was a push along the top of the ridge line. Here, however, where the saw teeth were all separated by steep draws, the men would have to push down the northern slope of each individual summit before they could battle their way up the face of the next.

The officers looked through binoculars, heard reports by staff

---

* Artillerymen had given the spurs these names as target designations.

members of the 371st Infantry, and looked at a sand table reproduction of the area. Colonel Conley decided to attack along the top of the ridge line. There would, at the start at least, be only enough room to deploy one company at a time, and a sliding movement would have to be employed, company passing company on the left as each pressed ahead into action. It would probably be rough going, but there might be an element of surprise in the plan, and the battalion would depend on artillery and mortar fire and smoke concentrations to blind enemy observation.

Officers of the 371st reported that on the forward slope of Georgia, the first objective, the German emplacements were protected by a series of U-shaped trenches, sixty feet in width, forty-five feet in length. Nonmetallic Shu mines, undetectable by mine sweepers, had been planted forward of the trenches in an area between seventy-five and 150 feet in depth. Along the flanks of their defenses the Jerries had sown booby-trapped egg grenades, and the few narrow trails on the left face of the ridge line were zeroed in by machine guns and mortars. The enemy was reported to have light machine guns backed by 50-mm., 81-mm., and 120-mm. mortars, also 20-mm. antiaircraft guns and some mobile antitank, antiaircraft 75's. The veteran German troopers who held the ridge line could be expected to put up stubborn resistance.

At 4:55 A.M., 5 April, explosives began to rain on the Georgia and Ohio Hills. The shells came from the 105-mm. howitzers of the 599th Field Artillery Battalion, the 155-mm. howitzers of the 329th Field Artillery Battalion, five 57-mm. antitank guns, some 90-mm. rifles of the 894th Tank Destroyer Battalion, and nine 81-mm. mortars of Company D and Company M of the 371st Infantry. After ten minutes most of the guns ceased fire, but high explosives and smoke shells continued to land intermittently on Ohio 1 and a spur dubbed "Rocky Ridge," 200 yards north of Georgia, which ran at right angles from the third Ohio spur into the valley on the battalion's left, giving enemy artillery observers an excellent view of the 100th's line of advance. During the shelling, the 1st Platoon of Company B suffered eight casualties from 155-mm. short rounds.

Company B, holding the line of departure, had one platoon on the left side of Florida's summit and one on the right. Five minutes before the barrage lifted Company A moved through Company B and deployed its 2d Platoon to the right, its 3d to the left, and its

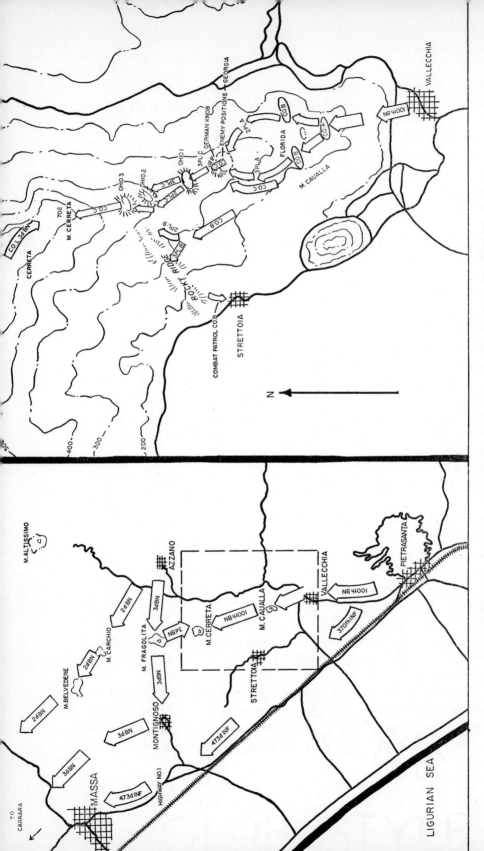

THE 442D CRACKS THE MOUNTAIN LINE. (Details of 100th's advance in blowup, right.)

1st at center rear, in support. Two of Company D's machine-gun platoons gave covering fire from high points on Florida. In the gray light A's scouts stalked 150 yards without meeting resistance—in their carefully concealed positions the Germans were holding their fire. Georgia's top was only seventy-five yards away as the 3d Platoon's first squad formed a skirmish line, and its second and third squads swung wide to come in on the left flank. At about sixty yards a scout of the 2d Platoon stepped on a mine and was blown apart, and in the next few moments seven more mines were tripped, and then all hell broke loose. On the left the 3d Platoon lost eight soldiers to machine-gun fire. As they crawled through the mine field the men of the 2d Platoon met machine-gun fire from the front and left, and enemy grenades lobbed down from directly above.

Pfc Sadao Munemori, a Los Angeles boy, a volunteer from a relocation center who had come to the battalion as a replacement, now took command of his squad from its wounded leader. Rising from a shell crater in which he and a couple of buddies had taken cover, he tossed a grenade which destroyed a machine gun twenty feet ahead. As he knelt on the crater edge, getting ready for another throw, an enemy grenade hit his helmet and bounced off into the shell hole. Munemori dived on top of it. The blast tore away half of his face and torso, and he died, but he had saved his comrades, who suffered only minor wounds. He was awarded the nation's highest military decoration, the Congressional Medal of Honor.

Using hand grenades, the 3d Platoon wiped out four emplacements and pushed into the enemy trenches. When the Germans in front of the 2d Platoon saw themselves thus flanked, they dodged up over the crest and down the reverse slope. It had taken Company A less than half an hour to reach Georgia's summit. The Jerries now sent up two red flares, a call for support shelling, and enemy guns laid down a heavy concentration on Georgia's summit and southern face. Unable to advance down the northern slope, Company A dug in.

At about 6:00 A.M., as Company C began to move forward on Florida to pass through Company B, two mortar shells fell into a squad of its 3d Platoon, killing six men and wounding seven. As the company moved down toward Georgia enemy guns filled the intervening draw with shrapnel, smoke, and dust, and two officers of an attached heavy weapons platoon were wounded, one of them mortally. Passing to the left of Company A, on Georgia, C's 1st

Platoon went over this summit and down, but was soon pinned flat by fire from a knob on its northern slope. Company A blanketed that mound and Ohio 1 with bazooka rockets and rifle grenades, and under this cover the C Platoon pulled back over Georgia's crest. Company D's 81-mm. mortars, now set up on Georgia's southern face, pounded the enemy as elements of A and C companies made repeated unsuccessful attacks in the face of enemy mines, automatic weapons, and artillery shells which came in from the Ohios, Rocky Ridge, the hills across the valley on the left, and even from the Punta Bianca coastal guns far to the north. The enemy mine fields made it impossible for either company to send more than one platoon forward at a time, and, in the fighting for caves and trenches, hand grenades were freely used by both sides. Friendly shorts occasionally fell among the attacking troops. Colonel Conley asked the regiment for engineer teams to help blast the enemy strong points, but none appeared. He also asked for flame throwers, and late in the afternoon two of these were provided, but the men who were hastily taught their use could not get near enough to the enemy positions to be effective.

Patrols which went out at dusk to see whether Jerry might be withdrawing under cover of his own heavy shelling met intense small-arms fire. At 9:00 P.M., as a lieutenant led two enlisted men to establish an outpost on Georgia's forward slope, he tripped a mine and lost his foot. During the night Captain George Grandstaff's supply company brought rations and ammunition forward by pack board and hand from Florida, to which the Captain had led a mule train. Two captured enemy scouts reported that the enemy had not known that AJA troops were in the sector until they had attacked. At the end of the day the battalion had lost fourteen killed and fifty-six wounded.

It was now planned that at dawn Company C would assault the Ohio spurs, Company B would move to the left against Rocky Ridge, and Company A would deliver supporting fire from Georgia and then follow up the attack.

At 5:30 A.M., its advance screened by mortar, artillery, and smoke concentrations, the 2d Platoon of C, one light machine-gun section attached, moved to the left to flank the knob on Georgia's northern slope. Pushing north through scrub brush and small trees, the platoon skirted a narrow trail and then, when almost to the rear of the knob, cut east and began to work up to the bunkers. Its 1st squad deployed to the left, its 2d to the right; its 3d, with the light machine guns, stayed behind on a small mound to form a base of fire. When the leading scouts were forty yards from the top of the objective, Jerry machine guns opened up and grenades, some of them strung in sixes, began to fall among the attackers. Under covering fire from their comrades three men of the 2d squad climbed within twenty feet of the first bunker and hurled grenades. Seven Germans came out with arms raised, and from a nearby emplacement another seven surrendered before they were fired upon. Four enemy dead lay about. In each of the captured dugouts there was plenty of ammunition and food.

The 3d squad had been under heavy fire from another German nest, but now, as the 2d squad provided covering fire, the men of the 3d climbed ahead, and in ten minutes had surrounded and silenced this position, killing three defenders and capturing eleven. Booty included two machine guns and a radio set. By 9:00 A.M. the enemy had been cleared from Georgia's forward slope.

Earlier in the morning the chemical mortars had been effective in blinding enemy observation, but now as the wind became stronger, the Jerries were able to lay down heavy concentrations of fire on Georgia and the approaches to the Ohios. Colonel Conley asked for close air support, and at 9:30 four Thunderbolts roared low overhead to blast the enemy strongpoints. On the first run against the Ohios and Rocky Ridge their bombs dropped much too close to the battalion's positions, and Conley, in telephone contact through the Tactical Air Command officer, called them off target. He had some smoke shells lobbed to guide their aim, and on the next three bombing and rocketing runs they were "right on." In their fourth and final pass they strafed the enemy positions. This was the first tactical air support the battalion had ever received, and a beautiful example of air-ground co-ordination.

Now two battalions of 155-mm. howitzers began a ten-minute barrage, behind which Company B headed for Rocky Ridge, and Company C for Ohio 1. The 3d Platoon of Company C stormed up Ohio 1 and rounded up forty dazed enemy soldiers. Leaving mopping-up operations for the other platoons, the 3d veered to the right flank of Ohio 2, and in a short fierce fight overran the enemy posts here, capturing eight prisoners. Meanwhile the 2d Platoon had pushed across the left slope of Ohio 2, leaving the 1st Platoon behind to consolidate Ohio 1. Now the 3d Platoon stopped to organize Ohio 2, and the 2d Platoon set out for Ohio 3 and took that hill, overwhelming three machine-gun positions and capturing fourteen prisoners. This was accomplished by 11:00 A.M. Twenty-two more Germans were captured during the next hour and a half, in mopping-up operations on the three hills.

On the battalion's left, as Company B moved through the draw between Georgia and Ohio 3 toward Rocky Ridge, enemy mines killed three men and wounded four. When the company was within 200 yards of its objective, the 2d Platoon went to the right to attack in the direction of Ohio 3, and the 3d moved to the left along the slopes toward the ridge crest itself. After using trench knives to clear a fifty-yard path through a mine field, the 2d Platoon took a large bunker in which it killed two defenders and captured seven more, and seized a mortar, an antitank gun, three rocket launchers, and a large number of mines.

Meanwhile advance elements of the 3d Platoon had walked into the middle of a mine field before the first charge exploded. Almost immediately nine others were set off. Three men were killed and seven wounded, and sixteen mines had to be neutralized before the survivors could get out of the trap. Ordering his men to swing right of the mined area, the platoon leader called for artillery support. After a ten-minute barrage by 155-mm. howitzers, scouts reported that the Jerries had evidently pulled back over the top of the ridge, but as the platoon moved ahead five Germans crawled out of holes to surrender. Near the ridge top, a scout stepped on a mine, and simultaneously a concealed pillbox opened up with a bazooka and grenades. Within a few minutes, under a blast of fire from rifles and tommy guns, its three defenders shouted surrender. By noon Company B had mopped up six more bunkers and was in secure possession of Rocky Ridge. Four Germans had been killed; two had been wounded, and twenty-four were prisoners. Company B had lost eight men killed and seventeen wounded.

At 3:00 P.M., Company C moved from Ohio 3 to join the 3d Battalion of the 442d in cleaning off Mt. Cerreta (Hill 702). Meeting only slight resistance, it took six prisoners on the way. At 9:00 P.M., the 3d Platoon made contact with Company L, which had silenced several enemy positions en route from Mt. Fragolita (Hill 912), which had been captured by the 3d Battalion on the previous day. On Mt. Cerreta captured equipment included 2,000 hand grenades, about a hundred bazooka shells, scores of rifle grenades, more than a hundred mines, a two-day supply of rations, and a surprising amount of American equipment: sleeping bags, blankets, rations, toilet articles, rifles, and ammunition.

Company A now sat on Ohios 1 and 2, and Company B remained in defensive position on Rocky Ridge. The second day of the battle had cost the battalion fourteen killed and thirty-nine wounded. At least half of these casualties had been caused by mines.

During this day, 6 April, the 2d Battalion had sent Company F to clear off Mt. Carchio (Hill 1095), and the rest of that unit had moved northwest of Mt. Fragolita toward Mt. Belvedere (Hill 897).

It had taken the Combat Team two days to break a defense line which the enemy had held for six months. On the regiment's left the 370th Infantry had been less successful. Pushed back in disorder after a two-mile advance on the morning of 5 April, an attack which it planned for the next morning was called off when the enemy intercepted the battle orders. Another plan of attack for the afternoon of the 6th had been cancelled when it was discovered that straggling had reduced the effective strength of the regiment's 2d Battalion to eighty-eight men. As a result of the 370th's inability to advance the 442d's left flank was now exposed for a depth of two and a half miles.

On the morning of 7 April Company B of the 100th sent a reinforced combat patrol two miles southwest to make contact with the 370th. Climbing down into the valley west of Rocky Ridge and taking a covered route across the flats, the party climbed to a high point above Strettoia, in which there appeared no sign of life. When the patrol entered its main street at 3:00 P.M., six dead Germans were found sprawled around a gutted American tank. An hour later a soldier spotted some men of the 370th coming into the town from the south, and after contact had been made the reconnaissance group returned to Rocky Ridge.

During the same day, after bitter fighting, the 2d Battalion had cleared a German machine-gun battalion from the slopes of Mt. Belvedere. The 100th and 3d battalions meanwhile rested, consolidated their positions, and rounded up more German prisoners. Captives reported that the three 80-man companies which had borne the brunt of the 100th's initial assault had been wiped out as fighting units, and that the other companies of the 1,000-man defending force had suffered heavy casualties. The German commander had originally ordered a fight to the death, but on the second night of the battle had directed his units to disengage and regroup in the hills farther north. It was not known how many of the enemy had been wounded, but the 100th had killed twenty-four and had captured 131. Some of the prisoners said they thought the fighting in Italy would soon be ended.

The battalion remained on its hill, in regimental reserve, for the next two days. For "outstanding accomplishments in combat" on the ridge line and in the previous engagements in the Bruyeres-Biffontaine area it was later awarded the Oak Leaf Cluster to the Presidential Unit Citation.

DURING THE next five days the Combat
Team moved rapidly ahead. Enemy
troops now fought only brief delaying
actions as they pulled back through the
hills and up the coastal plain. On 8
April, 1945, the 3d Battalion pushed
west along a ridge to Montignoso
two miles south of Massa, and established contact with the 473d Infantry,
which was driving for that town. (See
map, chap. 23, p. 256.) Company G of
the 2d Battalion simultaneously attacked
along a spur running west from Mt.
Belvedere to the eastern outskirts of
Massa, and Company E occupied the
village of Altagnana northeast of that
city. On the 9th, Company F captured
Pariana, nearer Massa, against a defense
by about 150 Germans.

On the 10th, the 3d Battalion crossed
the Frigido River unopposed and occupied high ground south of Carrara and
northeast of Massa, while Company E
of the 2d Battalion seized 3,200-foot
Mt. Brugiano which dominated Carrara
from the southeast. Elements of the
370th had taken over the hills which
the 100th had won, and that battalion
was in action again, on the Combat
Team's right flank, Company B pushing through Altagnana to occupy the
village of Antona.

On the 9th the 473d Infantry had
advanced across tank traps and mine
fields in the coastal flats to enter the
outskirts of Massa, and two tank battalions had reached the city's center
before being forced out again by heavy
shellfire. Meanwhile, however, the 442d

Mopping Up

had been outflanking Massa from the east, and, on the morning of 10 April, the 473d, which had replaced the dispirited 370th,* met little opposition as it moved into the city.

The 442d had recently been meeting armed bands of Italian partisans equipped with Office of Strategic Services credentials, and when Company L entered Carrara on the 11th, it found the enemy gone and resistance fighters in complete control. The residents shouted their welcome, threw flowers in the streets, and offered wine.

---

* In the history of the Fifth Army, *From Salerno to the Alps*, this statement appears: "The Nisei of the 100th Battalion and the 442d Regimental Combat Team knew that they were battling to redeem their friends and relatives at home from unjust prejudice, and so these men laid down their lives before the German machine guns in almost prodigal abandon. On the other hand, the Negroes of the 92d Division, insufficiently motivated to battle, did not perform as well as might be hoped." Chester G. Starr, ed., *From Salerno to the Alps: A History of the Fifth Army, 1943–1945* (1st ed., Washington, 1948), p. 422.

General Mark Clark has written that of the ten American infantry divisions in action in the Fifth Army in Italy, "the 92nd Division's accomplishments were less favorable than any of the white divisions." But he also added: "At the same time, it would be dishonest and unfair to future Negro soldiers to overlook the serious handicaps which they had to overcome. Leadership was one of the biggest problems. There were many illiterates among the Negro troops; hence it took longer to train them, and there was, in general, a reluctance to accept responsibility for the hard, routine, discipline that is essential in wartime. This failure I view not as a reflection on the Negro soldier or officer, but as a reflection on our handling of minority problems at home. The Negro had not had the opportunity to develop qualities of leadership. Most of all, perhaps, the Negro soldier needed greater incentive, a feeling that he was fighting for his home and country and that he was fighting as an equal. Only the proper environment in his own country can provide such an incentive." *Calculated Risk* (New York, 1950), p. 414.

In an article, "Report on the Negro Soldier," published in *Harpers* magazine, April, 1946, Warman Welliver, who was an officer of the 92d Division during this campaign, makes some observations on the performance and motivations of Negro and AJA soldiers: "In Italy there wasn't a GI in a thousand who would not have been proud to fight beside a Japanese-American soldier. Every story of brutality and cheap discrimination against Nisei in the states was considered a personal affront to almost every soldier there. The main reason for this was that the Nisei battalion (later regiment) fought so outstandingly well. As far as the white American GI was concerned, the Japanese-American would have been welcome in any unit on equal terms. Yet the same white GI, at least in Italy, had a high average level of prejudice against Negroes. The only way to overcome this prejudice is to prove that the American-Negro can become—and he can with proper help from his country—as good a soldier as any other American."

Welliver goes on to explain why, in his estimation, the nisei fought so much better than the Negroes. "The two groups are hardly comparable in any way except that they are both non-white minority groups. The Nisei were probably better educated than the average white soldier, the penalty for their failure was more obvious, and the degree of discrimination against them had been infinitely lower in civilian life. This latter point was particularly true in Hawaii, and the original Nisei combat unit was a Hawaiian National Guard organization with white officers who had worked with the men for years. Actually the differing backgrounds of the Negroes and the Nisei emphasize our failure to give our colored minority a decent civilian life."

One of their spokesmen was a civilian who had fought in the American Army during the first World War.

Company K, unopposed, now advanced two miles north of Carrara, taking Sorgnano and Gragnana. On the right flank, the 100th marched eight miles along a high mountain trail from Antona to Colonnata east of Carrara, its progress hindered only by joyful "paisanos" who were returning to Carrara along the same narrow track. In its advance the battalion liberated seven Russian prisoners from a small German labor camp. Swinging down from the hills to set up roadblocks around Colonnata, the 100th rested for a day, as did the rest of the regiment, while the Engineer Company worked furiously to clear the mined Massa-Carrara road. The Combat Team had outrun its supplies, and though airdrops had been tried, most of the loads had tumbled over cliffsides. The Massa-Carrara road was open by evening of the 12th, but jeeps had to bounce the 100th's supplies from Carrara to Colonnata over the ties of an old railroad track. (See campaign map, p. 124.)

At 7:30 on the morning of the 13th the 2d Battalion marched toward Mt. Pizzaculo, three miles northwest of Gragnana and commanding the Carrara-Gragnana-Castelpoggio-Fosdinova road. As the unit approached this objective enemy guns opened up from its summit on the east of the road and from Fort Bastione on the west, forcing the 2d to dig in and stay for the rest of the day. The same morning, as the 100th passed through the northern outskirts of Carrara en route to Gragnana, it narrowly missed the opening salvos of an all-day shelling of the marble city by the Punta Bianca coastal rifles. During this march, word of President Roosevelt's death passed along the line, and with it shock and grief—there was not a man in the battalion who could not recall the President's statement that "Americanism is a matter of the mind and heart; Americanism is not, and never was, a matter of race or ancestry."

At noon, in Gragnana, as the men began to eat the first kitchen-cooked food they had had for days, a barrage hit the town. Two men were killed and twelve wounded, and during the next six hours the men sweated it out, barricading themselves in the strongest houses of the town.

That night Company B was ordered northwest to Castelpoggio to protect 2d Battalion command post installations which were vulnerable to attack from Fort Bastione. At 5:00 A.M. the next morning, 14 October, under cover of a predawn mist, about eighty Germans struck at the 3d Platoon position on a hill at the east end of the village. Backed by fire from self-propelled guns, armed with bazookas, machine guns, machine pistols, and grenades, they overwhelmed the outposts in their first rush, and ten of them infiltrated the platoon area. Within thirty minutes however, the 3d had regrouped its fire; the enemy leader had been killed; and the attackers had been driven back into the draw from which they had climbed. Under machine-gun and mortar fire they pulled back over the next hill, leaving sixteen dead, twenty wounded, and ten prisoners. The defenders had lost six killed and three wounded.

In a two-hour battle which started at 8:00 A.M., Company G of the 2d Battalion stormed the crest of Mt. Pizzaculo, and by nightfall had cleared its reverse slopes, with a day's bag of twelve Germans killed and fifty-four captured. Meanwhile Company A had moved up from Gragnana, swinging left of Castelpoggio in support of the 2d Battalion's attack.

During the afternoon Company C had been ordered to move west of Gragnana in an attack on Hills 574 and 580 in the La Bandita range whence the enemy was directing heavy artillery fire at the 473d Infantry as it advanced up the coastal plain. Both of these spurs were to have been secured by troops of the Engineer Company, now serving as riflemen, but the Engineers had taken only some nearby knobs. Company C was held up overnight by enemy fire, but cleared the hills with the aid of a dawn barrage, at the cost of three killed and ten wounded. After the Engineers had moved up to garrison the captured knobs, Company C moved back to Castelpoggio.

During the same morning, 15 April, Company G had taken Fort Bastione, and Company F, with a platoon from G, had pushed northwest to seize Mt. Grugola, another hill overlooking the road to Fosdinova. Company A had remained behind on Mt. Pizzaculo.

Though the Combat Team had been advancing less rapidly during the last two days, the main purpose of the Ligurian Coast offensive had been achieved. The enemy forces in this sector had been badly hurt, and all their available reserves had been thrown into the defense. The Germans had also moved a battalion from their small tactical reserve in front of the main body of the Fifth Army, and had thrown it into the threatened sector just before the Allied Command had launched its big offensive in the Bologna area on the morning of the 14th.

On 16 April Company B relieved Company G at Fort Bastione and mopped up in that area. Marching northwest toward Fosdinova the next morning, it was checked by heavy shelling, and while Company C now moved from Castelpoggio to replace Company A on Mt. Pizzaculo, the latter unit moved north to a position abreast of Company B. At 8:00 A.M. Company B sent out two ten-men patrols, one toward Gignago a mile south of Fosdinova and the other southeast in the direction of Casale. The Gignago patrol failed to return, and the next morning, 18 April, a combat patrol from Company C went out to look for it. As the searchers followed telephone wire which led to Casale, they heard sounds of combat. Approaching cautiously, they discovered the lost patrol beleaguered in a farmhouse and battling a surrounding enemy force. The newcomers hit the Germans from two sides, and were now joined by some members of the patrol, who escaped during the shooting. The enemy then tried to wipe out their combined parties. Five of the Company B men had already been wounded, and in the shooting which continued during the night two of the rescue patrol were killed and two wounded. Covering a litter squad which had come to evacuate its casualties, the group fought its way to safety during the early hours of the next morning.

Back with their outfit, the men of the "lost" patrol told their story. They had unwittingly set up an observation post in a house only fifty yards from an enemy position and had been surrounded by Jerries. A teen-age corporal had been sent to the house to demand surrender. Making the youngster prisoner, the patrol had fired its defiance, and during the shooting which followed their captive had been hit. They had dressed his wound, had given him all the cigarets he could use, and had lighted them for him—his hands trembled so much he was unable to light them himself.

The previous day, 18 April, Company K had seized Mt. Tomaggiora northeast of Fosdinova and Company L had pushed northwest of Mt. Grugola to a position east of the town. On the 19th, Companies A and L joined forces to capture Hill 605 which commanded a road junction north of Fosdinova, and Company L then swung north against Mt. Nebbione, which commanded the Fosdinova-Tendola-San Terenzo-Aulla road.

Partisans were now reported gaining control of the highways leading north from Genoa, and if this were true then the German forces at La Spezia and other coastal points would be forced to depend for their retreat on Highway 62, which passed through Aulla toward Cisa Pass and Parma in the Po Valley. Mt. Nebbione and the hills around it were the last high defensive grounds which the enemy held south of Aulla, and he was trying to hold these ridges as long as possible to protect his escape route through that town. On the 19th and 20th, the 3d Battalion continued the attack on Mt. Nebbione from the south, and the 2d tried to encircle it from the west, but these thrusts failed. Though the coastal guns at Punta Bianca were now silent, and partisans reported that the La Spezia garrison had withdrawn, enemy troops and artillery were still being used to hold the Combat Team in check.

Colonel Vergil R. Miller now decided to regroup his forces and make his main effort in the vicinity of Mt. Tomaggiora, about two miles east of Mt. Nebbione. On the 20th and 21st, the 100th took the villages of Marciaso and Posterla, southeast and northeast of Tomaggiora, and elements of the 2d and 3d battalions flanked Mt. Nebbione to push northeast toward Tendola. On the 22nd, Company A of the 100th took a hill overlooking the hamlet of Viano, while off to the left Company K of the 3d Battalion battled to seize Tendola.

The next morning Company A occupied deserted Viano. Patrols all along the regimental front were now reporting that the enemy had withdrawn. In midafternoon Major Fukuda took command of a task force composed of his own B Company, Company F of the 2d Battalion, an antitank platoon, and wire and radio crews, and led it northwest across rocky trails to cut the road junction at Aulla, ten miles away. As his group moved north the rest of the 100th left Viano in care of the Antitank Company, and then headed back to Carrara.

On this same day, 23 April, the 3d Battalion occupied Mt. Nebbione, and, northwest of it, Mt. Carbolo. On the right the 2d Battalion met stiff resistance before routing some Italian Bersagliere troops whom the Germans had left behind at San Terenzo. These Fascists suffered forty casualties and 135 were taken prisoner.

On the 24th, as the 2d Battalion and "Task Force Fukuda" moved in from the south and southeast, the enemy withdrew from Aulla.

As Fukuda's men approached the city they were met by happy civilians offering flowers and wine.

From now on it was all coasting. Fifth Army's main attack had pulverized the German defenses on the east in the Bologna area; American columns were racing north, east, and west across the Po Valley; and from the Adriatic to the Ligurian Coast enemy troops were surrendering in droves.

When the 473d Infantry reached Genoa on 27 April the German commander had already surrendered his garrison and the city to partisan control, and when the 3d Battalion of the 442d trucked in the next day, its members rode in street cars to their posts on the outskirts.

Meanwhile the 100th had been alternately riding—sometimes on partisan trucks—and marching north on Highway 1. At stops along the way Italians had cheered, thrown flowers, offered *vino*, made speeches, and demanded similar oral effusions. Colonel Conley and the other officers had occasionally responded with minuteman speeches. On the 28th, elements of the battalion rode tanks to Isola del Cantone to close the mountain pass between Genoa and the Lombardy Plain. One squad brought in thirty-two officers and 300 enlisted men.

"This past couple of days have been really like a circus. We've routed Jerry so badly that he has quit in great masses. When 1,700 Jerries surrender to two rifle companies that's one for the book. I've seen 10 Jerries well dug in stop an entire rifle company, and to see an outfit of battalion strength surrender en masse like this is really a surprise. They're giving up by the thousands and it's good to see them come dragging their tails in with that lost defeated look so very evident on their faces."[1]

On 30 April the battalion moved back near Genoa, and spent Lei Day in more comfortable surroundings than those enjoyed at Anzio a year before. On 2 May, the day the war in Italy officially ended, the outfit travelled north to Allessandria by truck and train to take postitions at the northern edge of the city. Two days later it moved south to Novi Ligure to join the rest of the Combat Team. Here all personnel shed battle dress, bathed, shaved, and relaxed. Word of Germany's surrender arrived on 8 May. Men got out the bottles saved for this occasion and toasted each other, but there was little boisterous jubilation. The news did not excite; it dazed.

Today was supposed to be V-E day, but I don't know. I wonder if November 11, 1918, was like this too. If today is V-E day, it certainly didn't strike me the way I thought it would. . . . Officially the war ended here on May 2, but because we had been on the pursuit for almost a week before the 2nd when the final surrender notice came out we were not too surprised. But believe you me, there were times when I prayed that the war would end, times when we slunk away in our fox holes. It's good to know that we will no longer be sweating it out, and of course the probability of seeing Diamond Head again really makes me happy. Don't know how long we will be here, but I know it's not too soon that we will be sailing toward Aloha Land. . . . It's really too bad about our mutual friend [a comrade]. I hope Louise can bear the burden without having to suffer too much. What hurts is that, with the war so close to an end, he should have been so unfortunate. Hawaii has lost a good man. I hope this is the last of the heartaches.[2]

Since the start of the Ligurian Campaign on 5 April, thirty-nine members of the battalion had died and 194 had been wounded.

On 16 May the Combat Team, now relieved from attachment to the 92d Division, trucked 125 miles to Ghedi Airfield, a Fifth Army Enemy Concentration Area, in a pleasant ride across the farmlands like "one Manoa Valley after another . . . everything is so green."[3] At Ghedi the regiment passed under control of the 71st AAA Brigade and began processing prisoners. During the next eight days the 100th searched, queried, and DDT'd over 25,000 German and Italian Fascist troops, plus a weird assortment of women camp followers and former inmates of German prison camps. "It's a filthy job, frisking them, but it's filthy killing them too."[4] Major Alex McKenzie alone processed nine German generals. Most of the once proud soldiers of the mighty Wehrmacht were lousy, unkempt, and, with the exception of some of their officers, docile. One of the latter, an English-speaking captain, defiantly maintained that the war was not yet won and told his AJA interrogators that America would still have to fight *their* people and then the Russians.

It was dirty work, and baking hot around the dusty airfield, but there were compensations. The engineers rigged showers which were kept busy day and night. Many of the boys cooled themselves off by careening around in captured jeeps and motorcycles until they were ordered to turn them in. Other loot included truckloads of cognac, rum, and champagne, and while the liquor lasted each man had a bottle a week with which to wash down the dust. And, for the first time since Salerno, there was no longer need to scrounge around for rice—it was, the cooks discovered, one of the Po Valley's staple crops!

Evening jam sessions by the regimental band helped break the monotony of cards, letter-writing, and endless talk about going home—many high-point men were already on their way back to the States. There were plenty of passes for Milan or the 442d's own rest center at San Pellegrino.

On 14 June the regiment moved about sixty miles to Lecco on beautiful Lake Como. Five days later notice came that the 442d had been designated a Category II unit, available for duty in the Pacific against the Japanese. On 7 July the regiment rode to the Pisa-Florence-Leghorn area and began to guard supply and munitions dumps and prisoner-of-war camps.

During July and August a number of men from the 100th volunteered for interpreter service in the Pacific theater, and departed for Army language schools in the States. Some soldiers attended sessions at the Army Study Center in Florence, and athletes from the battalion helped the 442d's swimming team capture every blue ribbon but one in the Fifth Army championship finals.

From now on it was just a matter of waiting for orders to ship back to the States, and high-point veterans were constantly leaving. Those who remained behind continued to amuse themselves as best they could. The battalion supplied its quota for a small but fast regimental football team which placed third in the Army's "Leghorn League," and played two post-season games against the hitherto unbeaten and unscored-on "Blue Devils," champions of the 88th Division. It won the first 7 to 6 at Leghorn's "Yankee Stadium" on Christmas Day, and tied the other 13 to 13 at the 88th's home park near Trieste on New Year's Day.

In December, the 100th's own orchestra, "The Beachcombers," played in Rome, at the personal invitation of Prince Umberto, Lieutenant General of the Realm and Crown Prince of Italy. Their host heard Hawaiian music, received *leis*, watched hula dances, and seemed much pleased by the entertainment. Only a few of the musicians had been with the original "Hawaiian Serenaders" at Camp McCoy, but the spirit of this performance in Rome was the same as that of the performances at baseball games in Wisconsin, where the legend on the players' uniforms had symbolized their desire to serve as ambassadors of good will for their outfit and their folk, and had proclaimed the friendly feeling expressed in Hawaii's traditional word of greeting, "*Aloha.*"

THE ORIGINAL members of the battalion, the "men of McCoy," were largely motivated by a desire to prove their own devotion to the nation and its ideals, and that of their folk, and to justify the confidence and trust of those other Americans of Hawaii who had believed in them.

By May, 1945, they, and the replacements who later joined the outfit, had accomplished this, and more. Even before the 100th went to Italy, its record in training had become an example which could be pointed to by those who believed in the basic loyalty of America's citizens of Japanese ancestry, and urged that they be given fair play and an opportunity to volunteer for military service.

After the battalion had entered battle and its record had received publicity, the 100th had become, for AJAs throughout the land, a symbol of their loyalty. "As its participation in the Italian campaign became more widely recognized, an increasing proportion of high-school and college Nisei volunteered for the companion 442nd all-Nisei battalion [sic]."[1] Hawaii's volunteers for the 442d, training at Shelby, constantly expressed the hope that they would live up to the record set by the men of the 100th.

When the War Department announced, in January, 1944, that AJAs would henceforth be called into military service by normal selective service procedures, on a basis of equality with all other male citizens of military age, it listed, as the major factors in this

Mission Accomplished

CHAPTER TWENTY-FIVE

decision, the "excellent showing" which the 442d had made in training, and the "outstanding record" which the 100th had made in battle.[2]

During the summer of 1944, the War Relocation Authority began a campaign to counteract charges circulated about the Japanese-American people and to win acceptance for those who were resettling from the relocation centers. In working toward this end the agency attempted to focus public attention on the really essential issues of its program and "on the military record of the Nisei soldiers."

This campaign was so effective, the authority later reported, that by the early fall of 1944 "it was no longer fashionable over most areas of the country to fling irresponsible accusations at the Japanese American people and to demand further restrictions of their liberties." An editorial which appeared in the Omaha *World Herald* on October 22, 1944, was typical of a point of view which had gained increasingly wider acceptance among fair-minded journalists. This editorial mentioned a letter which the *Herald* had received from H. J. McClatchy of the California Joint Immigration Committee, in which he proposed enactment of legislation canceling the American citizenship of all who claimed its privileges, yet, under the dual citizenship theory, owed "their first allegiance to an overseas government." The *Herald* editor commented:

The Californian's proposal would . . . give the Nisei baiters on the West Coast a handy brush with which to smear all Japanese Americans—loyal and disloyal alike. It would provide a further argument with which to bar from the Pacific Coast a sizable group of American citizens who were slapped into concentration camps at the outbreak of the war. That move may have been justifiable from a military viewpoint, but continuation of the ban after the war's end would be an entirely different matter.

The best answer to the McClatchy proposal comes from Cassino, where the 100th Infantry Battalion, composed of Japanese Americans, carved a permanent niche for itself in American military annals.[3]

Typical of the effect of that unit's record on the thinking of GIs, as well as of editors, was a letter written from Italy to the Chicago *Sun*. Its soldier author mentioned "reading in American magazines and newspapers letters condemning all Japanese, regardless of birth, in the most bitter, intolerant, and un-American manner. . . . You can imagine my feelings, then, when we heard that the unit which we were relieving at Cassino was the famous 100th Infantry Battalion, consisting exclusively of Japanese Americans. You can well imagine what we thought of this bigoted group in the United States which was seeking to make life unbearable for the parents and families of these men who, we learned, protested their withdrawal from Cassino although they had been decimated by wounds and disease."[4]

The 100th's name had become a rallying cry for those who asked justice for the Mainland AJAs. Even though at Cassino and afterwards, the replacements who were Mainlanders were always a minority of the 100th's membership, in the public mind the important fact was that this fighting outfit was composed of men of Japanese ancestry.

WRA was able to capitalize on this fact in connection with its efforts to secure acceptance for the West Coast evacuees whom it was trying to relocate in the North Central and Eastern States. In the fall of 1944, at WRA request, the Army assigned Lieutenant Spark M. Matsunaga, one of the original members of the 100th, to that agency, which booked him for a series of speaking engagements before civic and professional clubs and religious groups in cities where WRA was trying to find employment, housing, and public acceptance for its wards. Matsunaga, who had been twice wounded (the second time at Cassino) and declared physically unfit for further combat, told his audiences of the fine battle record of those of his comrades of the 100th who had volunteered for military service from relocation camps, and asked that their civilian relatives, and all AJAs, be given a fair break. One auditor commented that the lieutenant's talk had inspired more tolerance in thirty minutes than other methods could in thirty years. Another remarked that in the audience of which he had been a part many persons had been unable to hold back their tears, and a clergyman reported that after Matsunaga's speech men of his congregation had come to him to express shame for their previous attitudes toward AJAs.

When the "Hawaiians" of the 100th realized that its record was being used to help the kotonks and their families, their reaction was "So much the better." Sometimes they wondered whether they themselves would have volunteered from relocation centers or would have done as well in battle had they been in these boys' shoes. Colonel Turner had once said that they were engaged in a crusade. Perhaps it was a much wider one than most of them had at first realized. Funny, though, that a man should have to kill other men in order to make it possible to build a more decent world.

Throughout the fall of 1944 and the spring of 1945, the Army's Western Defense Command allowed increasing numbers of Japanese-American evacuees to return to their home communities on the Pacific Coast, but beginning in late January and reaching a climax of effort toward the end of spring, "the anti-evacuee elements of the west coast population employed practically every weapon short of lynching and murder to keep the people of Japanese ancestry from returning to the area."[5]

On June 15, 1945, Captain George H. Grandstaff, then on furlough from the 100th, wrote to the War Department from his home in Azusa, California, to ask that he be given a chance to speak against these outrages to public audiences throughout his home state. Grandstaff had joined the 100th at Camp Shelby and had been its supply officer. (Hospitalized for two months as a result of a wound received in the Volturno River crossing, he had rejoined the battalion in time for the Cassino action. In 1945 he wore a Purple Heart with two clusters, and a Silver Star for gallantry in the fight to rescue the "lost battalion.") He explained the reason for his request:

> As one of the few white officers who have served with the Japanese American 100th Battalion for some two and a half years, my main interest is to see that the splendid work they have done in combat is called to the attention of the people of the Pacific Coast in order that Japanese Americans who desire to return here may receive fair treatment. The thought in . . . [my] mind . . . was that a white officer who had lived in California most of his life could emphasize their splendid combat record as no Japanese American could. Racial prejudice would not enter the minds of the audience where I am concerned.

The War Department approved, and Captain Grandstaff was assigned to the War Relocation Authority for a thirty-day tour of duty in the Pacific Coast area. The following excerpts are from speeches made during this assignment:

> One night in particular (at Cassino) will always remain in my mind. Some forty enlisted men and I had picked a spot at which to meet at 2000. I was delayed by a persistent mortar barrage and arrived about three quarters of an hour late. Instead of forty men there was only one. Upon questioning him, I found that the balance were up in that barrage hunting for me because they knew that I was alone. There are many fancy definitions of 'loyalty' but when those men straggled in at dawn after an all night search for me I needed no dictionary for my interpretation of the word. . . .

I came home to what I thought would be a land of the free; to a people I thought had learned from this war to respect the rights of fellow citizens; to a people who had, I thought, learned that racial discrimination and democracy don't jibe. And yet one of the first shocks that stabbed me in the stomach like a cold bayonet was to find racial prejudice and discrimination against the fathers, mothers, sisters, and kid brothers of the men in my outfit. And I find this same discrimination against even the returned veterans themselves. I asked for and received orders from the war department to speak out on this subject. I don't know of anyone who has a better right to do so.[6]

Four other officers—three from the 442d, and one who had supervised the activities of AJA interpreters in the Pacific theater of operations—were subsequently given similar assignments. These speakers were, WRA later reported, some of the most effective allies which it had in its campaign to regain status for the evacuated AJAs. "Although they certainly did not succeed in entirely eliminating anti-Nisei prejudice from the west coast region, they unquestionably dealt it one of the heaviest and most crippling blows which it has suffered since its birth in the early 1900's."[7]

Haole GIs in outfits with which the AJAs had campaigned reacted vigorously when news of the latest outbreaks of racial discrimination reached them. In August, 1945, every man in Company D, 168th Infantry, which had fought alongside the 100th from Salerno to the Arno River, signed the following statement:

From Company D, 168th Regiment, 34th Division to the 100th Battalion in appreciation of the heroic and meritorious achievements of our fellow Americans in the 100th Battalion and the 442d Infantry Regiment. We do hereby assert that our help can be counted upon to convince the folks back home that you are fully deserving of all the privileges with which we are ourselves bestowed.

It is a privilege and honor to acknowledge the members of the 100th Battalion and the 442d Regiment as fellow Americans. We are duly proud to say "Well Done" to you and yours.[8]

After the 100th had become an element of the 442d, the War Department and other interested agencies had concentrated publicity on the Combat Team as a whole, but the role which the 100th had played as guinea-pig unit and its effect on GI attitudes continued to be remembered. In a military history of the 34th Division published after the war the author wrote:

The brilliantly successful performance of the 100th Battalion, Nisei troops, had persuaded Higher Command at home that more Japanese-Americans should be committed to battle. Accordingly the 442nd Infantry Combat Team was sent over from the states to join the Division. The battle-tired 100th, still maintaining its identity, joined the 442nd. . . .

As men of the 34th observed the battle conduct of the Nisei, they grew to resent the treatment accorded the parents and relatives of these little, brown fighters. They resented the confiscation of their property and the herding of their families into concentration camps at home, while their sons were dying by the hundreds in the cause of human liberty. They determined then to raise their voices in protest and to demand justice and recompense for the wrongs inflicted upon these people.[9]

In 1947, in his book *Back Home*, Bill Mauldin summed up the kind of GI thinking which the 100th's combat performance had started, and the 442d's had so well reinforced.

But if my prejudices had just sort of disappeared, I became positively lyrical about the Japanese-Americans. I saw a great deal of them in Italy where they had been formed into a battalion that fought with the 34th Division, and into two full regiments [*sic*] that sort of free-lanced around doing heavy fighting for everybody. Some of the boys in those outfits were from the West Coast, and some from Hawaii. A great deal has been written about their prowess, and I won't go into details, except to say that, to my knowledge and the knowledge of numerous others who had the opportunity of watching a lot of different outfits overseas, no combat unit in the army could exceed them in loyalty, hard work, courage, and sacrifice. Hardly a man of them hadn't been decorated at least twice, and their casualty lists were appalling. And if a skeptic wonders whether these aren't just "Japanese characteristics," he would do well to stifle the thought if he is around an infantry veteran who had experience with the Nisei units. Except for facial characteristics, there was nothing to identify them with the soldiers who fought for the land of Hirohito.

We all heard a lot about suicide attacks and thirty-mile marches performed, with a handful of rice, by the Imperial Japanese Army. If these Nisei in Italy didn't get fed right, they raised hell just like any other American soldier. They liked to come to town on passes and make whoopee as much as anyone else, and they certainly wanted to survive the war as much as their fellow soldiers in other units. But when they were in the line, they worked harder than anybody else because they wanted to prove something. They were willing to take extra chances and do extra jobs in hopes that a grateful nation would maybe give their families, many of whom were in concentration camps formally known as "relocation centers" a few breaks that were long overdue. A lot of us in Italy used to scratch our heads and wonder how we would feel if we were wearing the uniform of a country that mistreated our families. Most of us came to the conclusion that we would be pretty damn sulky about it, and we marveled at those guys who didn't sulk but took a positive attitude about it and showed more character and guts per man than any ten of the rest of us. As far as the army in Italy was concerned, the Nisei could do no wrong. We were proud to be wearing the same uniform.[10]

In December, 1944, from "Somewhere in France," an AJA from Hawaii had written home that he and his buddies "had risked life and limb time and time again that persons of Japanese descent may walk the streets in dignity and honor after this holocaust is over."[11]

The men of the 100th could justly claim a large share of the credit for the extent to which that goal had been achieved when the war came to an end.

For most of the men of the outfit, however, the primary concern in 1945 was their return to Hawaii. What would things be like back home? By V-J day many veterans were already back in the Islands on furlough, and after that date the others returned in small batches, so that there never was any formal homecoming, with ceremonies and so on. It mattered little. It was enough, at first, to be home, and to loll in the sun, and to marvel that one still lived.

There were problems, nevertheless. From Camp McCoy to the Po Valley, various members of the battalion had been writing to members of the Emergency Service Committee encouraging them in their leadership of the Japanese community and supporting their campaigns to persuade the issei to abandon "old country" institutions, traditions, and mannerisms. These letters urged that the older folk give up the speaking of Japanese if they could speak English, talk out boldly against the Emperor, follow the leadership of the ESC faithfully, and generally leave no doubt in anyone's mind that they were heart and soul in the war, not only against Germany but also against Japan. Wounded men who returned home said the same things. Just because the AJA soldiers had made a good battle record, the issei had no right to become complacent. After Germany was finished there would still be the fight to crush Japan, and then people of Japanese ancestry would be more "on the spot" than ever before. The gains that the second generation had made toward first-class American citizenship must not be lost because some of the issei thought more of their own mental and physical comfort than they did of America.

It was with chagrin, therefore, that returned soldiers heard, during the summer and fall of 1945, that many of the younger nisei were blown up with pride because of the publicity given their soldier brothers and had become arrogantly disrespectful to persons of other racial ancestries; and that the older folk were reverting quickly to the "old country" ways laid aside during the war. It was even more shocking to learn that a small but fanatical group among the issei flatly refused to believe that "invincible" Japan had been crushed—even insisted among themselves that she had won the war—and were joining recently formed religious-nationalistic organizations within which they gave each other mutual support for their delusions. Angered AJA veterans protested unofficially to the leaders of these movements and officially to federal authorities.[12]

It was developments within the Japanese community such as these which Doc Kometani had in mind as he spoke, an interpreter at his side, to audiences throughout the Territory:

We who by God's will were permitted to return and you who are fortunate to be here have a challenge—an obligation to those who now peacefully sleep under the white crosses in Italy and France—to build a better Hawaii.

By the blood and tears of our people we have earned a place for ourselves in this community. We have made tremendous gains in recent years and we must strive to maintain and extend them.

To the older people, I wish to address a special appeal at this time. We of the second and third generations are Americans by right and choice. Our future is here in America. We ask you to use your influence to help us become better Americans. You have helped to make our position here secure by your admirable conduct and participation in the war effort. If you permit the revival of certain institutions which have placed us "on the spot," you will undo the wonderful work of the boys in uniform. We owe you a great debt of gratitude and if you will exert your influence to bring about a greater assimilation of our young people and better relations among Hawaii's people you will earn the everlasting gratitude of posterity. You will thereby be laying a solid foundation for the future of American citizens of Japanese ancestry in Hawaii.

I have been back only a few weeks but I have observed trends and events which I am afraid might endanger the traditional feeling of racial tolerance in Hawaii. The beauty and greatness of Hawaii we have long cherished to return to lie in our friendly relationships with all the races in Hawaii. That is one of the things we fought this war for. Selfishly speaking, we who are not yet fully accepted as citizens with all the rights and privileges will be the ones who stand to lose most if racial antagonisms spread throughout the territory. I plead with you to exert your utmost to maintain friendly relationships with people of all races. Let us keep the aloha spirit alive in Hawaii.

The highest aspiration of our boys in uniform is to return to a Hawaii where a citizen irrespective of ancestry will share and share equally in the rights as well as the responsibilities of citizenship. We have helped win the war on the battlefront but we have not yet won the war on the homefront. We shall have won only when we attain those things for which our country is dedicated, namely, equality of opportunity and the dignity of man.

This battle for acceptance on a free and equal basis will be a long and tedious one. The important thing is to see that progress is made. There will be times when we will become a bit impatient. It is imperative that we main- tain a broad outlook, a historical perspective, if you will. There are some things we can do to hasten our acceptance in this democratic community.

It is important that we actively participate in the life of the community, especially in those activities that involve people of all races. There are many organizations formed along interest rather than racial lines. It is important that we not only join them but assume the full responsibilities of membership.

Then too, I feel that we should do our part in bringing about a greater intermingling of the races on a genuinely social basis. I think it will be an excellent idea for us to cultivate the friendship of at least one person from each racial group in Hawaii.

All of us need to examine our own prejudices before we condemn others and before we can honestly plead for equal treatment. Our attitude toward other races, toward the haoles, toward certain people in our own race, certainly can be improved. Because of our numerical strength, we can contribute a great deal to make Hawaii a happy and prosperous land.

We in Hawaii today stand squarely at the crossroads. One road leads to democracy and racial tolerance for which many of our boys paid the supreme sacrifice on the battlefields of this war. The other leads to racial strife, intoler- ance and greed which will inevitably breed wars. We who have seen the horrors and tragedies of war hope that our children and children's children will be spared what we have just finished. The men who were laid to rest under the thousands of white crosses all over the world will not rest in peace unless we are able to fulfill their hopes and dreams of creating a better Hawaii, a better world.[13]

It was easy enough to tell those of Japanese ancestry to maintain a calm and broad outlook, but it was sometimes difficult for AJA veterans to maintain it, when they encountered criticism that they had returned home with too "cocky" an attitude. Charlie Hemenway exasperatedly commented that those who made the charge had had, before the war, a concept of the nisei as a lesser breed of second-class status who were supposed to be properly respectful, submissive, and grateful for all small favors. Now that these boys had come home from the war with a greater degree of self-assurance and a feeling that they had earned first-class citizenship, some of the Island people still persisted in treating them as inferiors. The veterans naturally refused to take it, and they were called "cocky."

In an interview with a newsman, Corporal Tad Kanda, a veteran of the 100th, patiently and tactfully explained the situation.

Some of our old friends think that we are cocky since we have returned to Hawaii. It's regrettable because we aren't. We've done only what millions of other men were doing.

The trouble is that we have seen how the other side of the world lives. It has broadened our sphere of interest and sometimes our old friends don't understand.

Most of us feel that we had too much publicity and we realize the only reason for it was that we . . . were the only unit of our kind. When occasionally some AJA starts to brag, the rest of us quiet him immediately. We have a reputation to live up to, and we are not going to have it spoiled by a few individuals.[14]

Despite such explanations the matter of publicity continued to be a cause of irritation. Many Islanders who had never been hostile to the AJAs had found themselves annoyed at the amount of print devoted to the deeds of the 100th and the 442d. Other Hawaii boys, not of Japanese ancestry, had served in the nation's armed forces, even though not in such large numbers. Why this constant barrage of articles which, by comparison, made the individual services of these other soldiers seem inconsequential? Mainlanders were probably getting the idea that the only servicemen from Hawaii had been the AJAs!

It was a natural reaction. It was easy, now that the nisei had proved themselves, to forget what things had been like for these young men from 1939 through 1943. It was also easy for some Islanders to forget—and for others perhaps difficult to realize—that the achievement of the 100th, the 442d, and the AJA interpreters, was not simply a Hawaiian story, but one which had implications for the whole of the nation. Men of good will, sitting at typewriters in the War Department and in other governmental agencies, in newspaper offices, behind magazine desks, and elsewhere, saw the story of the nisei servicemen from the Islands as an American saga. They wanted the contrast between Hawaii's spirit of *aloha* and California's intolerance—and the wartime results which had stemmed from each— to be known to as many Americans as possible. Harry Truman had succinctly expressed this viewpoint when he had reviewed 500 veterans of the 442d at the White House. "You fought not only the enemy but you fought prejudice—and you have won. Keep up that fight and we will continue to win—to make this great republic stand for just what the Constitution says it stands for—the welfare of all of the people all of the time. Bring forward the colors."[15]

At the congressional hearings on statehood held in Hawaii in 1946 and 1948 a few of the irreconcilables still publicly expressed their doubts as to the matter of loyalty, brought forth the old suspicions, and leveled the new charge of "cockiness."[16] Making reply, an AJA veteran said, in part:

We AJAs have always been accepted as Americans by our friends of other racial groups in Hawaii. It was a natural pattern that, together with the thousands of other sons of Hawaii, we did, as good Americans, our duty on the battlefronts and on the homefront. . . .

Not by our own doing, but by order of the War Department, many of our group fought as members of the 100th Infantry Battalion and of the 442nd Regimental Combat Team and, because we were a unique group, we made good newspaper copy.

This, gentlemen, was not of our asking or doing. We simply did our duty as did thousands of other sons of Hawaii, as did millions of other Americans, and we as an ethnic group do not claim credit. If any credit is due us as sons of Hawaii, that credit should go to the entire territory which educated us and had faith in us.

We fulfilled our duties . . . not so much to prove our loyalty, but more to justify the faith that our friends in Hawaii reposed in us. . . .

With the few who, in spite of the hundreds of white crosses that mark the graves of our fallen comrades in Italy, France, Germany, and the South Pacific, will still have you believe that we are not Americans, we are not too much concerned with. For when a man loves his country so well that he is willing to give his life in service to it, there is certainly nothing further one can do.[17]

There was, in fact, little need to be concerned about the "few." Testimony at both hearings showed an overwhelming feeling that the wartime services of the AJAs had buried the loyalty question for good, and dual citizenship, once such a hot issue, was hardly mentioned. As Hawaii's struggle for statehood continued, it was significant that both overt and secret opponents of that movement shifted their ground, and now concentrated attention on the matter of Communist leadership within Hawaii's union movement.

As the months passed, those fears of a rebirth of racial feeling which Captain Kometani had expressed proved groundless. The mass delusions of the fanatical issei minority died away, and though the rest of the Japanese aliens gradually sank comfortably back into more and more of the prewar ways, no one seemed to mind much as Japanese speech began to be heard again in public places, the temples were reopened, Japanese-language programs reappeared on the radio, and Japanese movies were again shown in the theatres. The AJA veterans could see that because they had worn the Army uniform and had fought for their native land, their parents had achieved a stronger feeling of "belonging," a greater sense of identification with America.* They felt, indeed, that this was one of the greatest results their military service had wrought.[18] As for the return of many of the prewar customs, the veterans gradually came to feel that perhaps the old people should be allowed a little comfort during their declining years. After all, when one came to think of it, now that all the shouting and shooting were over, what real harm had most of the old institutions done, even the language schools, which were gradually being reopened?[19] If lack of public opposition meant consent, the rest of the community seemed to agree.

Veterans had other problems, however, than those of status and community relationships. A man had to eat, and try to make some plans for the future. Most of the boys went back to their old jobs, but there were some significant changes in the vocational pattern. Some of the Big Five companies gave jobs in the executive ranks to AJA officers of the battalion. Other officers and some enlisted men decided to make the Army a career, and were assigned to occupation duty in Japan, where they served as interpreters between the land of their ancestors and that of their birth. Many men took advantage of their GI Bill rights, and either enrolled or re-enrolled at the University of Hawaii or Mainland colleges. Some who were already college graduates (notably the public-school teachers) went to Mainland universities for graduate work in law, medicine, dentistry, and other presumably more profitable professions.

There was a spate of marriages as men decided to make up for lost years and settle down, and the slow trend toward more matings with girls of other than Japanese stock again showed up in the newspaper announcements. Italian, French, and Mainland *haole* girls who had married members of the battalion came to the Islands to join their husbands in a community where interracial marriages offered more promise of happiness than in most other places on the globe. Men again took part in the activities of organizations in

---

* During the war parents of soldiers had often inquired when they could be naturalized. Even the loss of a son tended to make them feel closer to America. Very few of the issei who had sons in the Army participated in the religious-nationalistic organizations mentioned above—and those who did were invariably already estranged from their children. See note 18.

which they had been members before the war, and, with a new sense of maturity and a stronger sense of "belonging," participated more actively in the affairs of the community.

In public office, as in other spheres, the new status of the AJA became increasingly evident. In 1952 Sakae Takahashi, former captain in the 100th, once a school teacher, now a lawyer, was appointed treasurer of the Territory by the Democratic Governor, Oren E. Long. Takahashi, the first AJA in the history of the Territory to receive a post in a governor's cabinet, was shortly joined by Attorney General Michiro Watanabe, another AJA. When Samuel W. King became Republican Governor in 1953, he named Howard K. Hiroki, a veteran of the 100th, Territorial auditor, and appointed Doctor Katsumi Kometani and lawyer Jack Mizuha (another former school teacher) chairman of the Territory's Board of Commissioners of Public Instruction and member of the Board of Regents of the University of Hawaii respectively. The same pattern was apparent throughout lower echelons of public trust. In ten short years the old order of things had changed considerably.

Inactivated in August, 1946, the 442d was reactivated in August, 1947, as an organized reserve component of the Army, the first such unit ever established in Hawaii. The 100th Battalion continued to be the regiment's 1st battalion, but retained its own distinctive number. It was announced that the 442d would, at least at first, be a Class C unit, composed only of commissioned officers. Though most of those who joined the organization were AJAs, commissions were open to men of other ancestries. It was the Army's intention that if the regiment were later expanded to greater strength, it should be a completely interracial outfit.

By June of 1950, when the Korean War began, the 442d was still in class C status. The 24th and 25th Regular Army divisions, whose peacetime base was Hawaii, were on occupation duty in Japan. Early in July, elements of the 24th were the first American troops sent into Korea to fight the delaying action which saved the Pusan perimeter, and the 25th soon followed its brother unit into action. In June the 5th Regimental Combat Team, back from occupation duty in Korea, was training in Hawaii, which had furnished more than 40 per cent of its volunteers. In July this unit was rushed to the Pusan perimeter. As the selective service system stepped up its calls, thousands of Hawaii's young men went through the fourteen-week basic training course at Schofield Barracks and then went to Korea. At first the 5th Regimental Combat Team, the 24th and 25th divisions, the 1st Cavalry Division, and the 7th Infantry Division had more men from the Territory in their ranks than did most other units, but by 1953 Islanders could be found doing every sort of duty in every sort of combat outfit.

As the bloody fighting continued, and Hawaii's cost in wounded and dead mounted—at the end of 1953 its ratio in terms of population was three and a half times that of the nation as a whole-grief struck more widely than it ever had during World War II, when the casualty lists had been predominantly composed of Japanese names. Every segment of the population now had its share of sacrifice.[20] The title now applied to the 5th Regimental Combat Team, "Hawaii's Own," was more truly meaningful than it had been when used to denote the 442d, or the 298th Regiment after that unit had been gutted by removal of the men who formed the original membership of the 100th Battalion. In the newspapers now there was no mention of the racial ancestry of dead or wounded, and as veterans came home on rotation, or from hospitals, or, after the truce was signed, from prisoner-of-war camps, they returned simply as Island boys who had done their duty against the newest threat to freedom.

Though some veterans of the 100th and of the 442d were in Korea and once again engaged in hill fighting,* this was mostly the younger men's war, and most of the veterans of these units continued their civilian lives and interests. Among these were membership in veterans' organizations such as Club 100 and the 442d Club.

Under the terms of its by-laws, Club 100 was intended to serve not only as a social and mutual assistance organization for members and their families, but also as an association dedicated to promoting the unity and welfare of all the people of Hawaii. Quietly and efficiently, without any more publicity than was necessary, the Club worked toward both goals. In 1952, as it proceeded to build a bigger meeting place, its list of completed projects testified that the second of these had not been neglected. When the new building was form-

---

* Young O. Kim of Los Angeles, whose father had been born in Seoul, and whose mother had been born thirty miles south of that city, was again in the middle of the fighting, now as Major Kim, commander of the 1st Battalion of the 31st Infantry. A war correspondent quoted Kim's CO as calling him "the best battalion commander in Korea." *The Honolulu Advertiser*, February 1, 1952.

ally opened in July, its owners announced that it was intended to serve not only members of the Club 100 but the whole community. In an editorial congratulating the organization, *The Honolulu Star-Bulletin* commented: "It is in the finest tradition of service that the Club 100 operates today. It is no self-seeking 'veterans' lobby.' It has the broad community view. And, on its tenth anniversary, the 100th can take pride not only in its battle honors, but in the peacetime records many of its members have made in their community."[21]

A few weeks before, a committee of officers and members of the Club had met to select a slogan to mark the forthcoming anniversary. Many had been suggested, and one by one eliminated as either too long, or too complex, or as seeming too assertive of military performance or too remindful of the battalion's racial composition. What was wanted was a slogan safe from possible misinterpretation, yet expressive of what the 100th stood for. The slogan finally chosen was: "For Continuing Service."

This book is based mainly on manuscript sources in the Hawaii War Records Depository (HWRD) at the University of Hawaii Library, Honolulu. Full documentation for all titles listed below will be found in the bibliography.

Notes and References

CHAPTER ONE

1. For comment on the reactions of those who experienced disillusionment on their return from Hawaii to Japan, see Romanzo Adams, *Interracial Marriage in Hawaii: A Study of the Mutually Conditioned Processes of Acculturation and Amalgamation* (New York, 1937), pp. 259 f.; Andrew W. Lind, *An Island Community: Ecological Succession in Hawaii* (Chicago, 1938), pp. 265, 282; Lind, *Hawaii's Japanese: An Experiment in Democracy* (Princeton, 1946), p. 32; William Carlson Smith, *Americans in Process: A Study of Our Citizens of Oriental Ancestry* (Ann Arbor, 1937), p. 324, n. 10; U. S. Congress, House, Subcommittee of the Committee on the Territories, *Statehood for Hawaii*, Hearings, 74th Cong., 1st sess., pursuant to H. Res. 3034 (Washington, 1936), p. 229; U. S. Congress, Joint Committee on Hawaii, *Statehood for Hawaii*, Hearings, 75th Cong., 2d sess., pursuant to S. Con. Res. 18 (Washington, 1938), pp. 106, 153, 188, 427, 596; U. S. Congress, Joint Committee on the Investigation of the Pearl Harbor Attack, *Pearl Harbor Attack*, Hearings, 79th Cong., 1st and 2d sess., pursuant to S. Con. Res. 27 (Washington, 1946), Part 35, p. 263; Misako Yamamoto, "Cultural Conflicts and Accommodations of the First and Second Generation Japanese," *Social Process in Hawaii*, IV (May, 1938), 41, 48; and Yukiko Kimura, "Psychological Aspects of Japanese Immigration," *Social Process in Hawaii*, VI (July, 1940), 21.

Ruth Benedict, in *The Chrysanthemum and the Sword* (Boston, 1946), analyzes the difficulties of adjustment experienced by Japanese who returned to the homeland after living in America. It should be kept in mind, however, that only a minority of the married issei were able to return to Japan; that not all of these decided, after reaching the homeland, to return to Hawaii; and that for most of those who remained in the Territory "the growing duration of their exile . . . served commonly only to increase their sense of nostalgic longing for the homeland and their idealization of it as a symbol of social perfection." It was usually those who had the opportunity to contrast the dream with the reality who experienced change of heart. Yukiko Kimura, "A Sociological Analysis of Types of Social Readjustment of Alien Japanese in Hawaii Since the War" (Master's thesis, University of Hawaii, 1947), pp. 8–14.

2. In 1929 more than 25 per cent of Hawaii's public school teachers were of Chinese, Japanese, or Korean ancestry. By 1940 about 44 per cent were of Oriental ancestry, of which 755, or 23 per cent, were nisei. Smith, *Americans in Process*, p. 296, n. 7; U. S. Congress, House, Subcommittee of the Com-

mittee on the Territories, *Statehood for Hawaii*, Hearings, 79th Cong., 2d sess., pursuant to H. Res. 236 (Washington, 1946), p. 585.

3. U. S. Congress, Joint Committee on Hawaii, *Statehood for Hawaii*, Report, S. Doc. 151 (Washington, 1938), p. 91.

"When children reach the age of the upper grammar grades, it is very common to have them won over to the American way by our school teachers. They compare the freedom of the American school with what seems to them the unfreedom of their home life and they are sold on Americanism. They believe that their teacher knows more than their parents and they are proud of the fact that they are Americans. Frequently you will hear a boy say without thinking, 'My father is just a Chinese man.' " Testimony of Romanzo Adams in *Statehood for Hawaii*, Hearings (1936), p. 42.

"In Hawaii, where the Orientals are in the majority and the contacts with white people are limited, the teacher occupies a strategic position. The children of Oriental extraction are eager to become Americans, and the teacher is the one representative of the American community with whom they make close contacts. She becomes the pattern for their Americanism. In the main, teachers are kind and helpful, and thus the pupils idealize them, come under their moral domination, and think of following their example vocationally." Smith, *Americans in Process*, p. 83.

On the more democratic and "progressive" methods of instruction introduced into the public secondary schools during the 1920s and 1930s, see Benjamin O. Wist, *A Century of Public Education in Hawaii, October 15, 1840, to October 15, 1940* (Honolulu, 1940), pp. 158, 179, 190–192; Helen G. Pratt, *Hawaii: Off-Shore Territory* (New York, 1944), pp. 265–267; and Adams, *Interracial Marriage*, p. 308.

4. *Statehood for Hawaii*, Hearings (1936), p. 32; *Statehood for Hawaii*, Hearings (1938), pp. 470–473, 296, 316, 319, 470–473, 539; *Statehood for Hawaii*, Report (1938), pp. 44–46; *Hawaii Hochi*, July 29, August 5, 1940. For more detailed discussion of the Territory's Japanese-language schools, their purposes and effects, see Smith, *Americans in Process*, chap. XIII, "The Language Situation," and Bradford Smith, *Americans from Japan* (1st ed., Philadelphia, 1948), pp. 115 ff.

5. As to the reluctance with which the nisei attended these schools, and the slight impression which they made on some of their pupils, see testimony by a nisei, a public school teacher who had himself "gone through the mill," in *Statehood for Hawaii*, Hearings (1938), pp. 315, 320, 321. See also similar testimony, pp. 296, 471.

In an unpublished Master's thesis, "A Study of the Attitudes of the Japanese in Hawaii Toward the Japanese Language Schools" (University of Hawaii, 1943), Katsumi Onishi, another nisei, also indicates that the pupils in these schools, especially the boys, resented their enforced attendance, but reports that more than 80 per cent of the language-school alumni whom he questioned in 1937 stated that they would be willing to send their own children to such schools and only 3 per cent thought that Hawaii would be better off without these institutions. Responses indicative of approval increased in ratio to the age and length of attendance of the alumni queried, with a corresponding stress on both the ethical and economic values of such training. Of the nisei questioned in 1937, about 64 per cent felt that the people of Hawaii, in general, did not appreciate the worth of these schools, and only 3 per cent felt that the Territory would be better off without them.

In response to questions asked during preparation of a sociological study made in 1941, only 10 per cent of a sample group of nisei language-school alumni indicated that their attendance had helped them in securing employment; only 17 per cent cited ability to read and write Japanese as a result of their studies; only 6 per cent mentioned gain in moral perception as a result of their attendance; and 21 per cent stated that they saw no value at all in their language-school training. Yukiko Kimura, "A Study of Problems and Attitudes of Second Generation Boys of Oriental Ancestry in Hawaii" (University of Hawaii Social Research Laboratory, 1941), pp. 5–8.

6. In the early 1930s the ratio of outmarriages was about one in twenty; by the beginning of the 1940s it was approximately one in fifteen. *Statehood for Hawaii*, Hearings (1946), p. 67.

7. In 1937 the Hawaii Congress of Parents and Teachers issued a statement which bitterly deplored the fees which the inadequately financed public schools asked for book rental in all grades, and the additional charges demanded for study of certain elective subjects in the high schools. These, it was claimed, rested most heavily on parents of the lower economic classes, and had the additional effect of cutting down high school attendance on the part of children of such persons, who made up most of the Territory's population. "Hawaii alone of all political units collects considerable sums for essential school needs from parents by a tax on children." *Statehood for Hawaii*, Hearings (1936),

pp. 665–673. See pp. 498–499 for testimony in which the chairman of the Territory's Board of Commissioners of Public Instruction testified as to these fees.

In addition to the book rental and other levies mentioned above, in 1933 the legislature had imposed a ten-dollar tuition charge for every child attending grades nine to twelve inclusive. In 1937 this was done away with as a result of public clamor, but the other fees remained. Wist, *A Century of Public Education*, pp. 180, 181. For description of the attitude toward free public instruction which lay behind the imposition of such charges, see also pp. 162–170. In 1954 the question of school fees and their relation to free public education was still a live issue in Hawaii.

8. The existence of racial discrimination in employment practice was frequently mentioned by observers of the Hawaiian scene. Romanzo Adams remarked that if a considerable number of positions usually reserved for whites were thrown open to all comers on an equal competitive basis regardless of ancestry there would probably be "a movement of some Caucasian boys to the mainland." *The Education of the Boys of Hawaii and Their Economic Outlook* (Honolulu, 1928), p. 19. See also pp. 30, 42, 43, 46–53. Other comments on employment policies may be found in Joseph Barber, Jr., *Hawaii: Restless Rampart* (Indianapolis, 1941), pp. 63, 144, 245, 246; Sidney L. Gulick, *Mixing the Races in Hawaii: A Study of the Coming Neo-Hawaiian American Race* (Boston, 1937), pp. 195–198; Lind, *An Island Community*, p. 273; Smith, *Americans in Process*, pp. 76–78, 81, 85–87, 207, 283, n. 2; and in "Aspects of Prejudice in the Territory of Hawaii," a report on the third annual regional conference of the Territorial Conference of Social Work, September 22–24, 1944 (Honolulu, 1944), pp. 24–34.

On the other hand, Adams, Lind, and Smith, all professional sociologists, emphasized the fact that race was not by any means an insurmountable barrier to economic advancement, as indicated by the number of nisei who had managed to "get ahead." Adams, *op. cit.*, pp. 32, 39; Lind, *op. cit.*, pp. 200, 201, 245, 273, and Smith, *op. cit.*, p. 109.

9. *Statehood for Hawaii*, Report (1938), p. 41.

10. *Pearl Harbor Attack*, Hearings, Part 6, p. 2694. Previous observers had drawn similar conclusions:

"The gradual acquisition in Hawaii of a population of considerable racial and cultural diversity has made it difficult if not impossible for any one racial group to maintain rigorous discriminatory and unfriendly attitudes toward other groups. Apparently racial prejudice is most effective where there are just two racial groups." Adams, *Interracial Marriage*, p. 161.

"Because of the large proportion of resident *haoles* who have greater wealth or superior positions and because of the superior educational and social advantages enjoyed by many, it is a group that would be segregated to a certain extent even if there were no question of race." Adams, *op. cit.*, p. 125.

"That there has not been more friction is due to the fact that the problem has been dealt with otherwise than it has been on the Pacific Coast; and also, it must be stated in all fairness, because, the social psychology of the Japanese and their position in the community is free from some elements which have been sources of irritation in California and elsewhere. It must always be remembered that here in Hawaii we have no white laboring class for the Japanese to antagonize by competition and that the Japanese, moreover, never pushed themselves into Hawaii. They came by invitation—although, of course, they come no more since the 'Gentlemen's Agreement.'

"As a result of these conditions the Japanese have never felt that they have been looked upon with hostility and the effect upon their psychology is marked. They are distinctly more approachable and less inscrutable than on the mainland where their situation and consequently, their psychology sometimes has an Ishmaelitish tendency. They are also less isolated. More and more, as school children, clerks, and workingmen, they blend into the community, even though they seldom intermarry with other races." Albert W. Palmer, *The Human Side of Hawaii* (Boston, 1924), p. 104.

"The young people of Oriental parentage in Honolulu behave as if they actually belonged to the community; in California many appear timid and ill at ease. It has been noted that several from Hawaii have been able to gain a more ready entrée into the white group than those born in the states. The Hawaiian-reared are so natural in their behavior that certain white Americans recognize in them likenesses to themselves and accept them." Smith, *Americans in Process*, p. 25.

For other like comment, see Adams, *op. cit.*, p. 319; Gulick, *Mixing the Races*, p. 190; and *Statehood for Hawaii*, Hearings (1936), pp. 39, 40.

11. Kiyosue Inui, *The Unsolved Problem of the Pacific* (Tokyo, 1925), pp. 258–261, 313, 320.

Though Japan thus provided a definite process for renunciation of her citizenship for children born abroad to her citizens, she also conducted, every five years, a careful census by her consular agents of persons born in Japan but living abroad, and of the children of such persons whose Japanese citizenship had not been renounced either by direct action (in the case of those born before December 1, 1924) or by omission of registration (in the case of those born after that date). The fact that many Japanese residing in Hawaii were acting as agents of the Japanese government in making such censuses caused much criticism among the non-Japanese of the Territory during the later 1930s.

12. *Statehood for Hawaii*, Report (1938), pp. 43, 44.

13. Much of this material is derived from *Statehood for Hawaii*, Hearings (1938). See pp. 41–42, 47, 56–58, 66–70, 112–116, 146–152, 170, 173, 179, 180, 188–191, 197–200, 215, 227, 283, 288, 291–295, 303, 308, 309, 313, 314, 317, 318, 322, 323, 361–363, 365, 375, 389, 418, 419, 438–464, 473, 475–477, 481, 482, 523, 524, 532, 538–541, 586–588, 596–599. See also *Pearl Harbor Attack*, Hearings, Part 35, p. 265, and *14th New Americans Conference, July 15 to 21, 1940* (Honolulu, 1940), p. 94.

In 1937 McKinley High of Honolulu, largest secondary school in the Territory, conducted a poll on dual citizenship among its nisei students, who were more numerous in proportion to total enrollment than in any other public educational instutition in Hawaii. Of the 3415 young Japanese-Americans who filled out the questionnaires (which were to be returned unsigned) 1485 indicated that they thought themselves dual citizens, though many of these were not sure of their status. Of those who thought they had dual status, 270 indicated intention to expatriate during the next year; 464 wrote that they would probably do so within the next five years. Answers of the 176 who "doubted" that they would expatriate indicated that many of these were "doubtful" of their status, or "doubtful" that the step was necessary. According to school officials many nisei saw no point in giving up an allegiance which they did not believe they had ever owned. The survey showed 207 students who felt fairly certain that they would not expatriate, either because their parents had not registered them as Japanese citizens, or, as in the case of girls not liable for American or Japanese military conscription, because it was not felt to be necessary. (It was legally possible that a nisei who visited Japan might be conscripted into the Imperial army.)

Only sixty-nine nisei gave reasons for their intention not to expatriate. Of this number, seventeen expected to go to Japan, twenty-one faced parental objections, five had already expatriated, twelve were satisfied with their dual status, six wanted to "stay Japanese," and three mentioned American racial prejudice as justification for their attitudes. *The Honolulu Advertiser*, November 16, 1937.

The dual status of the nisei is discussed in Morton Grodzins, *Americans Betrayed: Politics and the Japanese Evacuation* (Chicago, 1949), pp. 149–155; Yamato Ichihashi, *Japanese in the United States: A Critical Study of the Problems of the Japanese Immigrants and Their Children* (Stanford, 1932), pp. 322–324; Smith, *Americans from Japan*, pp. 147–151; and Edward K. Strong, *The Second-Generation Japanese Problem* (Stanford, 1934), pp. 140–144.

14. *The Honolulu Star-Bulletin*, November 8, 1940.

In 1919 the American-Japanese Association of Hawaii had petitioned the Imperial government for a change in its nationality laws: "The present Japanese law as to declaration of citizenship works a great hardship for us. The question of dual citizenship and the criticisms which have been directed against American-born Japanese have caused us to feel that some legislation should be passed by the country of our ancestors that will free us from any obligation to it, and allow those of us, who have located within the United States with the purpose and intention of remaining and interesting ourselves in the affairs of that country, to show that we can be good and loyal citizens of the country of our adoption." The petitioners asked that a law be enacted "whereby those of Japanese descent can select their own citizenship without restriction of law, and, having once made such selection, can remain as citizens of that country without any question of dual allegiance." They also simultaneously memorialized President Wilson, asking his aid in securing revision of the Japanese law. Kiyoshi K. Kawakami, *The Real Japanese Question* (New York, 1921), p. 186.

15. Ethel J. Spaulding, ed., *We Americans in Hawaii* (Honolulu, 1941), pp. 16–18. This pamphlet contains much other interesting material on dual citizenship.

16. *The Honolulu Star-Bulletin*, February 10, 1938; September 4, 28, November 13, 25, 1940.

17. Spaulding, *We Americans in Hawaii*, p. 23; and *The Honolulu Star-Bulletin*, for dates cited in n. 16.

Mr. Melville A. Taff, Jr., formerly administrative officer and registrar of the Territory's board of health, told the author that until 1934 it was possible to check the number of births of children of Japanese ancestry registered with the Bureau against those registered at the Japanese consulate, and that the totals showed a very high coincidence. He attributed this to the fear of issei parents that if their children were not registered as Japanese nationals, relatives in Japan would be discriminated against by government authorities.

Figures secured by the author from the Japanese consulate in Honolulu and from the Territory's board of health show that during the period July 1, 1940–June 30, 1941, of the 3248 nisei babies born in the Territory 885 were registered with the consulate.

It was impossible during the prewar years to secure any accurate figures on the number of nisei who were dual citizens. The only source of authentic data was the Japanese consulate, which evidently gave out only information which suited its convenience. In January, 1942, the chief of the Honolulu branch of the FBI gave testimony to this effect before the Roberts Commission. At that time he "guessed" that the number of Island nisei who were dual citizens was "quite higher" than 60 per cent, and that in Honolulu there were no more than 15,000 nisei who had expatriated from Japan. *Pearl Harbor Attack*, Hearings, Part 23, p. 878.

The U. S. Census of 1940 reported residents of Hawaii of Japanese ancestry as numbering 157,990. Data in the files of the Overseas Japanese Section of the Japanese Foreign Ministry showed 156,849 *nikkeijin* (members of the Japanese race) resident in Hawaii as of October 1, 1940. Of the latter number, 104,483 were listed as possessed of Japanese nationality. This figure included all *nikkeijin* of either single (Japanese) nationality or of dual (American and Japanese) nationality.

A report of the Research Bureau of the Foreign Ministry gave, however, a conflicting estimate of 91,764 residents of Japanese nationality for the same date. It is not known which of the two totals, 104,483 or 91,764, is the more accurate. Both were based on reports made by the Japanese consulate in Honolulu. The U. S. Census of 1940 listed 36,678 of Hawaii's residents of Japanese ancestry as aliens. Subtraction of 36,678 from 91,764 and from 104,483 gives the alternative totals, 55,086 or 67,805. On the basis of the data it possessed in 1940 the Japanese government could have calculated that from 45 to 55 per cent of the nisei in Hawaii were Japanese nationals. The U. S. Census of that year gave 121,312 as the total of Hawaii's residents of Japanese ancestry who were American citizens. (The Foreign Office data cited above was secured through the courtesy of Colonel M. P. Eccles, public information officer, U. S. Army, General Headquarters, Far East Command, and is contained in a letter dated October 21, 1950.)

18. *The Honolulu Star-Bulletin*, September 16, 1939. For other expressions of nisei chagrin as a result of criticism, suspicion, and discrimination, see *Statehood for Hawaii*, Hearings (1938), pp. 292, 295, 315, 322, 469, 475, 479.

CHAPTER TWO

1. Indications of the extent of Army concern can be found in U. S. Congress, Joint Committee on the Investigation of the Pearl Harbor Attack, *Pearl Harbor Attack*, Hearings, 79th Cong., 1st and 2d sess., pursuant to S. Con. Res. 27 (Washington, 1946), Part 23, pp. 863, 915; Part 27, pp. 18, 32, 143–146, 159, 208, 222, 228, 256; Part 28, pp. 1557, 1559; Part 29, p. 2081; Part 35, pp. 263, 270, 271, 452.

The functions and make-up of the Hawaiian Department's extremely limited counterintelligence apparatus are described in U. S. War Department, Army Forces, MIDPAC, "History of the United States Army Forces, Middle Pacific and Predecessor Commands during World War II," prepared by Historical Subsection, G-2, HUSAF MIDPAC, Part VIII, vol. 14, chap. 1, pp. 2988 ff.; and in *Pearl Harbor Attack*, Hearings, Part 35, pp. 87–88.

2. For information in the preceding paragraphs and for much other material in this and the following chapters on G-2's attempts to solve the internal security problem, I am indebted to Colonel George W. Bicknell's typed unpublished manuscript, compiled in 1944, "Security Measures in Hawaii during World War II." Bicknell was assistant chief of staff, G-2, in charge of counterintelligence, from October, 1940, to April, 1943. He has read chapters 1, 2, 3, and 8 of the manuscript of this book

Substantially the same kinds of reasons for suspicion as those mentioned by Bicknell are reported in *Pearl Harbor Attack*, Hearings, Part 10, p. 4912; Part 23, p. 863; Part 26,

p. 355; Part 31, pp. 3195–3198; Part 35, pp. 261–263, 271, 281–282; Part 39, p. 63.

Though American security agencies tended to suspect the kibei en masse, not all of them were more loyal to Japan than to the United States. They were regarded by the native Japanese as being too Americanized! See *The Nisei: A Study of Their Life in Japan* (Tokyo, 1939), by the Nisei Survey Committee of Keisen Girls' School, Tokyo; and the analysis of the kibei's status and problems given in U. S. War Relocation, community analysis section, "Japanese Americans Educated in Japan," Report No. 8 (Washington, 1944). A report on a survey of the attitudes of these young people, made in 1935, described many of them as feeling rejected and unhappy in the ancestral homeland. *The Honolulu Advertiser*, November 24, 1935.

3. U. S. Congress, House, Subcommittee of the Committee on the Territories, *Statehood for Hawaii*, Hearings, 74th Cong., 1st sess., pursuant to H. Res. 3034 (Washington, 1936), pp. 229, 230; U. S. Congress, Joint Committee on Hawaii, *Statehood for Hawaii*, Hearings, 75th Cong., 2d sess., pursuant to S. Con. Res. 18 (Washington, 1938), pp. 148, 151, 304, 348, 349, 370, 371, 420, 427, 464, 596, 598; *Pearl Harbor Attack*, Hearings, Part 35, pp. 263, 264, 342; Romanzo Adams, *The Education of the Boys of Hawaii and Their Economic Outlook: A Study in the Field of Race Relationship* (Honolulu, 1928), pp. 33, 34, 38, 51; Andrew W. Lind, *Hawaii's Japanese: An Experiment in Democracy* (Princeton, 1946), p. 32; William Carlson Smith, *Americans in Process: A Study of Our Citizens of Oriental Ancestry* (Ann Arbor, 1937), pp. 242–244. See also, Nisei Survey Committee report, *op. cit.*

4. Bicknell MS. General Charles D. Herron, Commander of the Hawaiian Department from October, 1937, to February, 1941, picked out "between fifty and a hundred of the top civilians in Hawaii," some of whom had been in the Islands four years, some for fifty years, and some from birth, and asked their comments on the Japanese. "I think out of the whole thing came, in general, that 10 per cent were definitely loyal to the Emperor, that 10 per cent probably were loyal to our country, that 80 per cent you could not tell about: if the going was good for us, they would be with us; if the going was good for the Japanese, they would be with the Japanese. But none of these people would tell you that they really understood the Japanese; that they had the Oriental veil that no Occidental has ever been able to get through." Testimony of Herron's chief of staff, August 9, 1944, *Pearl Harbor Attack*, Hearings, Part 27, p. 143.

Robert C. Shivers of the FBI testified January 6, 1942: "I made a tour of all the Islands in Hawaii, asking the so-called haole populace—the businessmen, the plantation managers, the plantation owners—about the Japanese conditions and the Japanese situation. I got just about as many different answers as the number of people that I talked to. So far as I could learn the haole populace in Hawaii was not in a position to give any accurate information about the Japanese populace because there had been very little intercourse between the two. They could only give you surmises, they could only tell you what they thought would happen, but for factual information it didn't exist." *Ibid.*, Part 23, p. 857.

On the matter of intercourse between the kind of person Shivers interviewed and those of Japanese ancestry, see Andrew W. Lind, *An Island Community: Ecological Succession in Hawaii* (Chicago, 1938), pp. 237, 239, 240.

5. Statement of Shivers, "Cooperation of the Various Racial Groups with Each Other and with the Constituted Authorities Before and After Dec. 7, 1941," U. S. Congress, House, Subcommittee of the Committee on the Territories, *Statehood for Hawaii*, Hearings, 79th Cong., 2d sess., H. Res. 236 (Washington, 1946), pp. 599–603; *Pearl Harbor Attack*, Hearings, Part 35, pp. 268–271; *The Honolulu Star-Bulletin*, June 14, 1941.

It should be emphasized that until the morning of December 7, 1941, prevalent opinion in military and naval circles both in Hawaii and in Washington was that if war did come, Japan would spend her effort in Asia and the Southwest Pacific, and that Hawaii would not be a prime object of attack. It was within this frame of reference as to presumed Japanese strategy that the Army in Hawaii fashioned its security policy, which envisaged sabotage on Oahu as the most imminent danger in the event of war with Japan. For illustration see *Pearl Harbor Attack*, Hearings, Part 1, pp. 2516–2519, 2636; Part 23, pp. 1081, 1238; Part 27, p. 554; Part 28, pp. 1449, 1555; Part 35, pp. 15, 16; Part 39, pp. 18, 21, 38, 73, 175, 321, 407.

6. *Pearl Harbor Attack*, Hearings, Part 23, pp. 858–862; Part 28, pp. 1556, 1557; Part 39, p. 13. In 1937 a journalist had reported two comments illustrative of the Navy attitude toward those of Japanese ancestry. He quoted a high ranking naval officer as saying, "Every Japanese, born under our flag or not, is always a Japanese. No matter how much he professes to be an American he is always thinking his Japanese thoughts, hoping secretly for Japanese victory." The writer asked a recruiting officer at Pearl Harbor why

the Navy accepted no nisei enlistments, and reported this reply: "Because a Jap is always a Jap."

Webb Waldron, "A New Star in the Union?" *American Magazine* CXXIII (April, 1937), 36, 74.

7. *Statehood for Hawaii*, Hearings (1946), Shivers statement, p. 600.

8. "History U. S. Army, MIDPAC," Part VIII, vol. 14, pp. 2991–2993.

9. Bicknell MS.

10. *Pearl Harbor Attack*, Hearings, Part 6, pp. 2692–2696.

11. These quotations are from: *14th New Americans Conference, July 15 to 21, 1940* (Honolulu, 1940); *15th New Americans Conference, July 15 to 21, 1941* (Honolulu, 1941). See also Takie and Umetaro Okamura, *Hawaii's American-Japanese Problem: A Campaign to Remove Causes of Friction Between the American People and Japanese; Report of the Campaign, January, 1921, to January, 1927* (Honolulu, n.d.); and Jisoo Sanjume, "An Analysis of the New Americans Conference from 1927–1938" (Master's thesis, University of Hawaii, 1939).

12. These letters were brought to my attention by my colleague, Dr. Charles Hunter, who had been given access to King's papers for research purposes.

Two of the men whose speeches before the "New Americans" have been quoted, had expressed sentiments similar to King's for the benefit of the Congressional Committee on Statehood of 1937. "It seems to the writer that we should think carefully before stating that these young people are not good American citizens. They are very sensitive on the subject. . . . The question of loyalty is, of course, a practical one, but it would seem wise to give fellow American citizens of whatever origins the benefit of the doubt. If we raise the issue with one group, how can we avoid implications against other groups? . . . To secure co-operation and loyalty, citizens must be treated as cooperative and their rights respected, otherwise suspicion and overt offense will engender resentment and non-cooperation. . . . And while the Defense Arm of Our Nation must be conservative, from a practical standpoint of developing reliable attitudes it would seem wise to regard these young people as loyal Americans."

"The vital thing in the event of war, as is recognized by every high-ranking Army and Navy officer with whom I have talked for the last 15 years, is the loyalty of the rank-and-file Japanese who reside in the Territory. It will be difficult enough to fight the enemy without having to fight people in our own ranks. I do believe the constant and continual questioning of the loyalty of those of Oriental ancestry—the constant bringing up for review the consideration of whether they are or will be good American citizens—is certainly not calculated to develop the object we all want, which is their ever increasing and deepening loyalty." *Statehood for Hawaii*, Hearings (1938), pp. 304, 513.

13. *The Honolulu Star-Bulletin*, November 17, 1941.

14. *Congressional Record*, 76th Cong., 3d sess.; vol. 86, part 10, pp. 10888–10895; part 11, p. 12207; *The Honolulu Star-Bulletin*, August 29, 1940; *New York Times*, August 29, September 15, 16, 1940.

15. Ralph S. Kuykendall, *Hawaii in the World War* (Honolulu, 1928), pp. 41, 42.

16. *Annual Report of the Governor of Hawaii to the Secretary of the Interior for the Fiscal Year Ending June 30, 1940*, p. 50. Frank S. Adams, in "A History of the Hawaii National Guard in Peace and War" (Master's thesis in preparation, University of Hawaii, 1954), gives Colonel Perry M. Smoot, adjutant general of the Territory from 1923 to 1946, as his authority for the statement that "there was a policy prescribed at the Washington level restricting the Japanese-Americans from enlisting freely in the National Guard."

During the statehood hearings of 1937 Senator Tom Connally of Texas commented on the disproportionately small number of nisei in that organization. A nisei witness remarked: "It would be of interest to ascertain the reaction of those who complain of the small number of such citizens in the National Guard, if the situation were reversed so that 90 per cent of the guard members were of Japanese descent." *Statehood for Hawaii*, Hearings (1938), pp. 58, 475. See pp. 288, 295, 595, on nisei reaction to this discrimination.

17. U. S. Congress, House, Committee on Public Lands, *Statehood for Hawaii*, Hearings, 80th Cong., 1st sess., pursuant to H. Res. 49, 50, 51, 52, 53, 54, 55, 56, 579, 1125, and 1758 (Washington, 1947), p. 74; Letter from General Herron to Charles R. Hemenway of Honolulu, February 26, 1947; *The Honolulu Star-Bulletin*, June 14, 1941.

18. *Pearl Harbor Attack*, Hearings, Part 6, p. 2696.

19. Information received from James W. Lovell and Farrant L. Turner, officers of the 298th Infantry at the time of the Japanese attack.

AMBASSADORS IN ARMS

CHAPTER THREE

1. Gwenfread Allen, *Hawaii's War Years, 1941–1945* (Honolulu, 1950), pp. 35, 36, 39, 141, 143.

2. Allen, *ibid.*, devotes a chapter (pp. 47 ff.) to dissection and exposure of these and numerous other falsehoods.

3. A more detailed description of these events is given in Allen, *ibid.*, pp. 44–46. An interesting analysis of the "Niihau Incident" is made by a cultural anthropologist, Edwin G. Burrows, who uses it as one of a number of illustrations of the means (e.g., aggression, withdrawal, co-operation) which he reports "Hawaiian Americans" have taken to win relief from the stress of "*haole* dominance." "Here is aggression, beyond a doubt. Though the immediate victims were Hawaiians [persons of Hawaiian ancestry] it amounted to taking arms against the United States. In evaluating this instance as a sample of nisei behavior, three points must be kept in mind. First, it is the only case of the kind. Second, the circumstances were fantastically exceptional. As to what would have happened if the Japanese had taken the islands, we can only wonder. Doubtless there would have been collaborators as in the countries occupied by Germany; but for that matter, doubtless there would have been some haoles among them; as there were, it is said, American collaborators with Germany in France. And finally, one of the aggressors—the nisei one— seems to have repented at the last moment. At any rate, he turned his aggression against himself." *Hawaiian Americans: An Account of the Mingling of Japanese, Chinese, Polynesian and American Cultures* (New Haven, 1947), p. 136. Shintani was alien, Harada nisei.

4. George W. Bicknell, "Security Measures in Hawaii during World War II," U. S. Congress, House, Subcommittee of the Committee on the Territories, *Statehood for Hawaii*, Hearings, 79th Cong., 2d sess., H. Res. 236 (Washington, 1946), pp. 855–857.

5. *Statehood for Hawaii*, Hearings (1946), Shivers' statement, p. 603.

6. Bicknell MS.

7. P. M. Smoot, "The Hawaii Home Guard in World War II" (Honolulu, 1945); "The Home Guard"; J. McE. Huey, "Record of the Activities of the Military Department (Hawaii National Guard and Hawaii Territorial Guard), December 7, 1941 to June 30, 1944"; annual report of the Adjutant General of Hawaii for year ended June, 1942; U. S. Congress, Joint Committee on the Investigation of the Pearl Harbor Attack, *Pearl Harbor Attack*, Hearings, 79th Cong., 1st and 2d sess., pursuant to S. Con. Res. 27 (Washington, 1946), Part 28, pp. 1038, 1039; Part 19, p. 3604; *The Honolulu Star-Bulletin*, January 5, August 27, 1942; *The Honolulu Advertiser*, January 12, 1942.

8. War Department, Army Forces, MIDPAC, "History of Organized Defense Volunteers in the Territory of Hawaii," prepared by the Public Relations Office, Central Pacific Base Command (Honolulu, 1945); Office of the Military Governor, Businessmen's Military Training Corps, "History of the Businessmen's Military Training Corps" (June 15, 1945); and "Brief History of Company C, 1st Battalion, BMTC" (n.d.); War Department, Army Forces, MIDPAC, "History of the United States Army Forces, Middle Pacific and Predecessor Commands during World War II," Part VIII, vol. 14, pp. 3069, 3070.

9. Bicknell MS.

10. Yutaka Nakahata, ed., *The Varsity Victory Volunteers* (Honolulu, 1943); University of Hawaii Corps of Engineers, *The Volunteer* ([Honolulu], 1943); Shigeo Yoshida, *In Memoriam: An address in honor of the University of Hawaii Varsity Victory Volunteers who died in World War II* (Honolulu, 1946); Yutaka Nakahata and Ralph Toyota, "Varsity Victory Volunteers: A Social Movement," *Social Process in Hawaii*, VIII (November, 1943); *The Honolulu Star-Bulletin*, March 2, 21, April 9, June 10, 12, July 3, 25, August 2, 1942; notes of an interview with Colonel Fielder, May 28, 1948. Colonel Fielder has read chapters 1, 2, 3, and 8 of the manuscript of this book.

11. *Pearl Harbor Attack*, Hearings, Part 23, p. 861; Part 27, p. 208; Part 35, pp. 264, 267, 287; Part 39, p. 102; "History of the U. S. Army, MIDPAC," Part VIII, vol. 14, p. 2295.

12. "History of the U. S. Army, MIDPAC," Part VIII, Appendix I, pp. 4–7, vol. 14, p. 3090.

13. Bicknell MS.

14. "History of the U. S. Army, MIDPAC," Part VIII, Appendix 2, pp. 1–2.

15. Samuel E. Morison, "Coral Sea, Midway and Submarine Actions, May 1942– August 1942," Volume IV of *History of United States Naval Operations in World War II* (Boston, 1949), pp. 69, 74–76, 79, 80; "History of the U. S. Army MIDPAC," Part VIII, Appendix 2, pp. 3, 4.

16. "History of the U. S. Army, MIDPAC," Part VIII, Appendix 2, p. 4.

Photostatic copies of General Marshall's message and of other War Department records on the activation of the 100th Infantry Battalion and the 442d Regimental Combat Team were supplied to the author through the courtesy of Dr. Kent Roberts Greenfield, Chief Historian, Office of the Chief of Military History, Department of the Army, and Dr. Stetson Conn of his staff.

17. Information based on notes of an interview with Colonel Fielder, May 28, 1948.

CHAPTER FOUR

1. See William Carlson Smith, *Americans in Process: A Study of Our Citizens of Oriental Ancestry* (Ann Arbor, 1937), pp. 81, 82.

2. The foregoing information was secured from Colonel Turner, who had a survey of personnel records made while the battalion was in training; by a questionnaire sent to AJA officers of the battalion; and by examination of records in the office of the Registrar of the University of Hawaii.

3. Gwenfread Allen, *Hawaii's War Years, 1941–1945* (Honolulu, 1950), pp. 62, 63.

4. From a first draught of the official battalion history. See note 1, chap. 5.

5. George W. Bicknell, "Security Measures in Hawaii during World War II"; *The Honolulu Star-Bulletin*, June 27, 1942.

CHAPTER FIVE

1. The foregoing, and much of the subsequent information in this and the following chapters is based on official records of the 100th Infantry Battalion and the 442d Regimental Combat Team, which are listed in detail in the bibliography.

2. Letter from Colonel Kai E. Rasmussen, December 30, 1942. Turner preserved this and similar letters, together with photographs and newspaper clippings in a personal scrapbook.

3. War Department, Army Forces, MIDPAC, Military Intelligence, reports on interpreters at Fort Snelling, "The Military Intelligence Language School," "Nisei Linguists— Eyes and Ears of Allied Pacific Forces"; *Pacific Citizen*, October 13, 1945; *Hawaii Herald*, October 23, 1945; *The Honolulu Advertiser*, December 30, 1945, January 23, 1942; John A. Rademaker, *These are Americans: The Japanese Americans in Hawaii in World War II* (Palo Alto, 1951), pp. 83–86.

CHAPTER SIX

1. *The Honolulu Advertiser*, July 9, 1942.

2. *The Honolulu Advertiser*, January 25, 1943.

3. Farrant L. Turner scrapbook.

4. For illustrations see: *New York Herald Tribune*, June 25, November 15, 1942; *Milwaukee Journal*, January 10, 1943; *Chicago Daily Times*, July 9, 13, 1942; *Chicago Sun-Parade*, October 18, 1942; *Baltimore Sunday Sun*, January 10, 1943.

I am deeply indebted to Miss Margaret Makino of Honolulu for permission to use the accurate and well-arranged volumes of newspaper and magazine clippings about Hawaii's AJA servicemen, which she compiled during the war years. From them I have secured much of the information used in this and in later chapters, as well as numerous clues to other sources of information.

5. *Hawaii Educational Review*, November, 1942, p. 75; *Chicago Sunday Times*, November 29, 1942.

CHAPTER SEVEN

1. Information based on a report prepared through the courtesy of Dr. Alvin Stauffer, Historical Section, Office of the Quartermaster General, U. S. Army.

2. *Sparta Times* (Sparta, Wisconsin), June 29, 1943.

CHAPTER EIGHT

1. Office of the Military Governor, Morale Section, "Final Report on the Emergency Service Committee" (Honolulu, 1946).

2. John A. Rademaker, *These Are Americans: The Japanese Americans in Hawaii in World War II* (Palo Alto, 1951), pp. 177–183, contains the most complete published account of the committee's activities. See also Gwenfread Allen, *Hawaii's War Years, 1941–1945* (Honolulu, 1950), pp. 91, 144, 268, 269, 277, 279, 350.

3. Testimony as to their own past and present opinions given by prominent civilians in statements before the Roberts Commission and the Army Pearl Harbor Board indicated a good deal less faith in the loyalty of those of Japanese ancestry, citizens as well as aliens, than had been expressed by civic leaders during the prewar statehood hearings. U. S. Congress, Joint Committee on the Investigation of the Pearl Harbor Attack, *Pearl Harbor Attack*, Hearings, 79th Cong., 1st and 2d sess., pursuant to S. Con. Res. 27 (Washington, 1946), Part 23, p. 908, Part 28, pp. 1413, 1440, 1441, 1443–1445, 1456, 1463–1466, 1471, 1472, 1478, 1530–1532, 1644; Part 29, pp. 1649, 2017. See also Andrew W. Lind, *Hawaii's Japanese: An Experiment in Democracy* (Princeton, 1946), p. 240; also pp. 56–61, 75, 86, 87, 115, 139.

4. George W. Bicknell, "Security Measures in Hawaii during World War II."

5. Bicknell MS.

6. *Hawaii Herald*, October 17, 1947.

7. War Department records on the activation of the 100th and 442d mentioned above, Chapter 3, n. 16. Unless otherwise specified, the remainder of this chapter is based on these materials.

8. Information based upon interview with Colonel Fielder, May 28, 1948.

9. In a letter which he sent to the Senate on September 14, the President stated that "it is established that disloyal persons among the evacuees constitute but a small minority, and that the great majority of the evacuees are loyal to the democratic institutions of the United States." He went on to comment that "In vindication of the very ideals for which we are fighting this war it is important to us to maintain a high standard of fair, considerate and equal treatment for the people of this minority as of all other minorities." *New York Times*, September 15, 1943.

10. War Department, Army Forces MIDPAC, "History of the United States Army Forces, Middle Pacific and Predecessor Commands during World War II," Part VIII, Appendix 2, pp. 5–7.

11. *The Honolulu Advertiser*, January 29, 1943. *The Honolulu Star-Bulletin*, January 28, 1943.

12. "History of the U. S. Army, MIDPAC," Part VIII, Appendix 2, pp. 7–9.

CHAPTER NINE

1. The War Department had made plans to have all male citizens of Japanese ancestry in the War Relocation Authority centers fill out "loyalty" questionnaires as a preliminary to formation of the combat team of AJA volunteers. Recruiting teams were to be sent to each center. The potential volunteers were to be assured, by a member of the recruiting team, reading from a carefully prepared document, that this Army program was not an experiment, but marked a "radical extension and broadening of a policy which has always intended that ways should be found to return you to a normal way of life," and that its fundamental purpose was "to put your situation on a plane which is consistent with the dignity of American citizenship."

The Army statement admitted the hardships of evacuation, which the evacuees had accepted with little complaint and without deviating from loyalty to the United States, and though it justified these as a temporary sacrifice of the best interests of the few for the good of the many, expressed the hope that ways would be found "to restore you as quickly as may be to your normal and rightful share in the present life and work of the people of the United States."

The "willing . . . and loyal" of military age were to be asked to volunteer. Those whose ties with the Japanese Empire were "such as to disqualify them for positions of trust in this country" (the questionnaire would help determine this) were not wanted for military service but would be treated humanely. Those who failed to volunteer would probably be taken into military service in due time, in any case, through selective service. The combat team would be composed exclusively of AJAs and its record would be "a living reproach to those who have been prejudiced against you because of your Japanese blood."

Unfortunately, the Army recruitment program became tied in with a hastily devised WRA plan for processing the whole adult population of the various centers as a preliminary to resettlement outside the camps. This included the use of another lengthy questionnaire, intended primarily for execution by female citizens and issei males and females. It was titled "War Relocation Authority Application for Leave Clearance," and like the Army questionnaire also contained certain queries devised to test "loyalty." Male citizen evacuees over 17 years of age were supposed to fill in an abbreviated form, in addition to the Army questionnaire.

WRA officials evidently expected the combined compulsory mass registration to be taken as a matter of course, and that affirmative answers would also be given the "loyalty" queries as a matter of course, despite the fact that they "had not even attempted to adapt the wording of the Army questionnaire for citizens of military age to the far different outlook and problems of the alien group."

"The questions, and their method of presentation, aroused a strong protest among Nisei, who, having had almost all their rights as citizens abrogated through evacuation and forcible confinement, questioned the justice of the restoration of just the one 'right' of serving in the armed forces. They aroused fear and resistance among Issei who, stripped of all other possessions, used every means at their disposal to hold their families intact and to avoid what they conceived to be the certainty of the loss of their sons in combat, and who, having acceded to a forced evacuation from their homes to camps, were now determined to avoid a threatened second evacuation from camps to an 'outside world' that they had every reason to believe would regard them with hostility. These protest and fear reactions were fortified by administrative procedures which inadvertently attached penalties to affirmative answers and rewards to negative answers, and by sudden and incompletely understood changes in policies."

The War Department had hoped to recruit at least 3,500 volunteers. Of the AJAs in the ten centers, only 1200 offered to join the combat team, and approximately 28 per cent refused to "swear unqualified allegiance to the United States" or to "forswear any form of allegiance or obedience to the Japanese emporer." Of the 1200 who volunteered, some 800 passed both loyalty and physical fitness tests and were accepted for service. With the addition of some other Mainland AJAs who had not been sent to relocation camps, these men formed the Mainland element of the 442d Regimental Combat Team.

"Although volunteering at the relocation centers fell considerably below the hopes of both the War Department and WRA—where there had been no mass evacuation and no confinement of nisei in government-operated centers—was more than enough to make up the complement needed for the combat team." Dorothy S. Thomas and Richard S. Nishimoto, *The Spoilage* (Berkeley, 1946), pp. 53–63; U.S. Department of the Interior, War Relocation Authority, *WRA, A Story of Human Conservation* (Washington, n.d.), pp. 54–57, 110.

For details of the varied reasons which caused so many of the evacuated AJAs to refuse to volunteer, see Thomas and Nishimoto, *op. cit.*, chaps. 3 and 4, also Robert W. O'Brien, *The College Nisei* (Palo Alto, 1949), pp. 92 ff.

2. See "Islander's Reflections on Mainland Japanese," *Social Process in Hawaii*, IX, X (1946), pp. 39–46.

A similar attitude toward the California nisei is described in the life history of a Hawaii-bred nisei published in Dorothy S. Thomas' *The Salvage* (Berkeley, 1952), pp. 297–320.

3. Quoted in *The Honolulu Star-Bulletin*, November 8, 1944. Even when confined in relocation centers the Hawaii-bred seem to have been cheerful. An irritated Mainland inmate, a parent, complained: "The Hawaiian boys have no sense of manners. They run around without shirts and bare feet, strumming their guitars and influencing the girls." O'Brien, *The College Nisei*, p. 48.

4. "Islander's Reflections," *Social Process in Hawaii*, IX, X.

CHAPTER TEN

1. For much of the information set forth in this and subsequent chapters to show the larger troop movements, dispositions, and engagements within whose orbit the 100th played its small part, I am indebted to Chester G. Starr, ed., *From Salerno to the Alps: A History of the Fifth Army, 1943–1945* (1st ed.), (Washington, 1948). For this and the following chapter, and for the same purpose, I have also used the booklets *Salerno, American Operations from the Beaches to the Volturno (6 September–6 October 1943)* (Washington, 1944) and *From the Volturno to the Winter Line (6 October–15 November 1943)* (Washington, 1944), both prepared by the Military Intelligence Division of the U. S. War Department.

2. Diary of Staff Sergeant Masaichi Goto of Honolulu.

CHAPTER ELEVEN

1. I am indebted for some details of this account to Major Gillespie's description of the action, published in *Military Journal*, December, 1944.

2. *The Daily Pinion* (McKinley High School paper), November 22, 1944.

CHAPTER TWELVE

1. U. S. War Department, Military Intelligence Division, *From the Volturno to the Winter Line (6 October–15 November 1943)* (Washington, 1944); *Fifth Army at the Winter Line (15 November 1943–15 January 1944)* (Washington, 1945).

2. This account of the attempt to take Hill 920 is very largely based on a description of the action prepared for the author by Masayoshi Kawamoto.

3. *Hawaii Times*, November 8, 1943; *The Honolulu Star-Bulletin*, November 8, 1943.

CHAPTER THIRTEEN

1. *Hawaii Herald*, October 28, 1944.

CHAPTER FOURTEEN

1. The material in this chapter on the activities of other units than those of the 133d Infantry is based on Chester G. Starr, ed., *From Salerno to the Alps: A History of the Fifth Army, 1943–1945*, (1st ed.) (Washington, 1948), chap. IV, "The Battle of Cassino."

CHAPTER FIFTEEN

1. For the foregoing information and for other background material contained in this and the next chapter, I have used Chester G. Starr, ed., *From Salerno to the Alps: A History of the Fifth Army, 1943–1945* (1st. ed.) (Washington, 1948), chaps. V–VII, pp. 122–267; also U. S. War Department, Historical Division, Department of the Army, *Anzio Beachhead (22 January–25 May 1944)*.

2. Some of the details of life on the beachhead given above are based on the series of articles, "They Were So Young," written by John C. Chinen, a veteran of the 100th, which appeared in the *Pacific Citizen*, March 29, April 5, 12, 19, 1947.

CHAPTER SEVENTEEN

1. Letter, June 26, 1944, to Leslie F. Deacon of Honolulu, from an AJA who had joined the 100th in April as a replacement from Camp Shelby. This soldier, who prefers to remain unnamed, corresponded with Mr. Deacon from April, 1944, until June, 1945. (These letters are hereafter referred to as the Deacon Letters.)

2. *The Honolulu Star-Bulletin*, October 30, 1944.

3. U. S. Congress, Senate, Subcommittee on Territories and Insular Affairs of the Committee on Public Lands, *Statehood for Hawaii*, Hearings, 80th Cong., 2d sess., on H. Res. 49 and S. 114 (Washington, 1948), p. 134.

4. *The Honolulu Star-Bulletin*, July 15, 1944.

5. "American Fighting Men Speak Out," Committee on American Principles and Fair Play (Berkeley, [1944]), p. 4.

6. *The Honolulu Star-Bulletin*, March 29, 1944.

7. *Newsweek*, November 8, 1943.

8. *The Honolulu Star-Bulletin*, August 17, 1945.

9. *The Honolulu Star-Bulletin*, October 18, 1944.

10. *The Honolulu Star-Bulletin*, November 3, 1944.

11. *The Honolulu Star-Bulletin*, October 19, 1944.

12. Gene Casey, "G. I. Jap Yank," *Collier's* (August 5, 1954); *The New Pacific* (Honolulu), September, 1944.

13. *Hawaii Times*, October 15, 1943; *Colorado Times*, October 26, 1943; *The Honolulu Star-Bulletin*, November 19, 1943, March 16, 1944.

An official report of the War Relocation Authority states that shortly after the WRA was transferred from the Department of Agriculture to the Department of the Interior in February, 1944, Secretary Harold Ickes "called upon the War Department to fullfil the commitments it had made to the evacuees at the time of the mass registration (see above, chap. 9, n. 1) and bring the full spotlight of publicity on the nisei units. The War Department readily agreed and soon found that it had excellent subject matter for such publicization." *WRA, A Story of Human Conservation* (Washington, n.d.), p. 121.

14. *The Honolulu Star-Bulletin,* January 5, 1944.

15. On September 12, 1944, Riley H. Allen, the editor of *The Honolulu Star-Bulletin,* testified before the Army Pearl Harbor Board: "I have had for many years a gerat deal of faith and confidence in the Americans of Japanese ancestry, American citizens. I have repeatedly said and written that I thought they would stand the test as American citizens, realizing that there might be exceptions to that general statement. I know that there were a great many others who were of the same mind as myself, particularly the people who deal wtith the young Japanese, not merely as servants and employees, but deal with them in a more intimate way, are better acquainted with them."

Mr. Allen gave it as his belief that the prewar preoccupation of the military and naval commands in Hawaii with the possibility of uprising and sabotage had been such that it had taken their concern away from the possibility of attack from without, and "did not sufficiently take into account what has been done in the territory over a period of a great many years to mold our young citizens of Japanese ancestry in the same beliefs and the same devotions that American citizens of other ancestries have." U. S. Congress, Joint Committee on the Investigation of the Pearl Harbor Attack, *Pearl Harbor Attack,* Hearings, 79th Cong., 1st and 2d sess., pursuant to S. Con. Res. 27 (Washington, 1946), Part 28, pp. 1619–1621.

16. *The Honolulu Star-Bulletin,* February 10, 1944.

17. *The Daily Pinion,* May 4, 1945.

18. *The Honolulu Star-Bulletin,* June 2, June 23, 1944.

19. *The Honolulu Star-Bulletin,* May 23, 1944.

20. Quoted in *Pacific Citizen,* April 22, 1944.

21. *Time,* February 15, 1944.

22. *Pacific Citizen,* February 5, 1944.

23. Reprinted in *Pacific Citizen,* September 9, 1944. Quotations from this, and other letters of similar nature are given in the War Relocation Authority pamphlet *What We're Fighting For* (Washington, 1944).

24. Quoted in *The Honolulu Star-Bulletin,* April 6, 1944.

25. *The Honolulu Advertiser,* February 26, August 18, 1944; *The Honolulu Star-Bulletin,* March 3, March 29, August 18, 1944.

CHAPTER EIGHTEEN

1. Some of the above details of the Belvedere action derive from an article by Sergeant James P. O'Neill, "The Battle of Belvedere," in *Yank* (Pacific Edition), September 1, 1944.

2. Letters from a soldier of the 100th Battalion to Leslie F. Deacon.

CHAPTER NINETEEN

1. Letters from a soldier of the 100th Battalion to Leslie F. Deacon.

2. *The Daily Pinion,* May 18, 1944. The soldier who wrote this letter later died in combat.

3. The foregoing quotations (in order given) are from letters published in *Hawaii Times,* March 11, 1944; *Maui News,* February 19, 1944; *Hawaii Times,* March 11, 1944, January 4, 1944; *Hawaii Herald,* July 12, 1944.

4. Deacon Letters, August 9, 1944.

5. *The Honolulu Star-Bulletin,* August 18, 1944; Deacon Letters, July 30, 1944.

6. *The Honolulu Star-Bulletin,* August 18, 1944.

7. Deacon Letters, July 1, July 8, 1944.

8. *The Honolulu Star-Bulletin,* July 8, 1944.

CHAPTER TWENTY

1. Letters from a soldier of the 100th Battalion to Leslie F. Deacon, October 11, 1944.

2. Deacon Letters, October 27, 1944.

CHAPTER TWENTY-TWO

1. This and the following quotations in this chapter are from letters from a soldier of the 100th Battalion to Leslie F. Deacon, December 7, 1944, February 1, 13, 22, March 7, 1945.

CHAPTER TWENTY-THREE

1. *Hawaii Herald*, July 27, 1945.

CHAPTER TWENTY-FOUR

1. Letters from a soldier of the 100th Battalion to Leslie F. Deacon.
2. Deacon Letters, May 8, 1945.
3. *Hawaii Herald*, June 8, 1945.
4. *The Honolulu Star-Bulletin*, May 23, 1945.

CHAPTER TWENTY-FIVE

1. Robert W. O'Brien, *The College Nisei* (Palo Alto, 1949), p. 99.
2. *The Honolulu Star-Bulletin*, January 21, 1944.
3. WRA, *A Story of Human Conservation* (Washington, n.d.) pp. 121–124.
4. *Chicago Sun*, September 10, 1944.
5. WRA, *A Story*, p. 126.
6. *Pacific Citizen*, August 11, 1945; July 21, 1945.
7. WRA, *A Story*, pp. 129–130.
8. *Pacific Citizen*, August 25, 1945.
9. John H. Hougen, *The Story of the Famous 34th Infantry Division* (San Angelo, Texas, 1949), chap. 10.
10. Bill Mauldin, *Back Home* (New York, 1947), pp. 165–166.
11. Letter from "Somewhere in France," December 31, 1944, to Masa Katagiri of the Emergency Service Committee. HWRD, File 45.01.
12. For description and evaluation of this phenomenon, see Andrew W. Lind, *Hawaii's Japanese: An Experiment in Democracy* (Princeton, 1946), pp. 199 ff.; Yukiko Kimura, "A Sociological Analysis of Types of Social Readjustment of Alien Japanese in Hawaii Since the War" (Master's thesis, Univeristy of Hawaii, 1947). See also Gwenfread Allen, *Hawaii's War Years, 1941–1945* (Honolulu, 1950), p. 364; and *The Honolulu Advertiser*, May 11, 1954.
13. *Hawaii Times*, November 27, 1945.
14. *The Honolulu Advertiser*, May 17, 1945.
15. *The Honolulu Advertiser*, July 16, 1945.
16. U. S. Congress, House, Subcommittee of the Committee on the Territories, *Statehood for Hawaii*, Hearings, 79th Cong., 2d sess., H. Res. 236 (Washington, 1946), pp. 243–250, 484–488, 568–573; U. S. Congress, Senate, Subcommittee on Territories and Insular Affairs of the Committee on Public Lands, *Statehood for Hawaii*, Hearings, 8th Cong., 2d sess., on H. Res. 49 and S. 114 (Washington, 1948), pp. 47–49, 91, 410–416.
17. *Hawaii Times* Jan. 17, 1946. Just how would these, and Hawaii's other nisei, have acted had the Japanese made an all-out invasion assault? One type of conjectural answer was made on May 20, 1942, by General John L. De Witt's chief of staff for civil affairs, in explanation of De Witt's orders for the mass evacuation from the West Coast of all residents of Japanese ancestry:

"Now, if you and I had settled in Japan, raised our families there and if our children and grandchildren were raised there, it is most improbable that during a period of war between Japan and the United States, if we were not interned, that we would commit any overt acts of sabotage acting individually. Doubtless, in the main, and irrespective of our inner emotions, you and I would be law abiding. But when the final test of loyalty came, if United States forces were engaged in launching an attack on Japan, I believe it is extremely doubtful whether we could withstand the ties of race and affinity for the land of our forbears, and stand with the Japanese against United States forces. To withstand such pressure seems too much to expect of any national group, almost wholly unassimilated and which has preserved in large measure to itself, its customs and traditions—a group characterized by strong filial piety." WRA, *A Story*, p. 181.

This argument seems indicative of the degree of its proponents' belief in and knowledge of the assimilative power of American institutions as compared with those of prewar Japan. It also ignores the possibility that the reaction of each individual person of American ancestry whom the officer imagined as living in Japan would have depended in very large measure on the way in which he felt that he had been treated in that country.

The person who wishes to conjecture as to what the nisei "would have done" must ask of himself how he would have acted, had he been a nisei. Loyalty is a personal matter.

18. In a paper published in March, 1943, a student at the University of Hawaii, a major in sociology, observed that the proudest families in the Japanese community were those which had sons in the U. S. Armed Forces, and quoted the remarks of several issei parents:

"I gave my sons to this country. I am very satisfied and proud. Of course, once he is in the Army, he must not think of coming back safely. I won't have him return as a coward."

"I am prepared to nurse my son if he comes back crippled. That is a small part I can share with him in his service to his country."

"My son is in Europe, fighting the enemy. I feel that I am fighting too. I make Red Cross slippers for the soldiers with my body, mind, and soul."

"My daughter-in-law and I decided not to let my son know about the death of his father. My son is in Europe and has just begun fighting. He needs courage. We must not weaken his spirit." Yukiko Kimura, "Some Effects of the War Situation Upon the Alien Japanese in Hawaii," *Social Process in Hawaii*, November, 1943, p. 27. See also, by the same author, "A Sociological Analysis of Type of Social Readjustment of Alien Japanese in Hawaii Since the War" (Master's thesis, University of Hawaii, 1947).

19. In May, 1954, seventy-four schools were in operation, and more than 13,500 students were in attendance. At first many AJA veterans had opposed reopening of the schools, but those who had served as Army interpreters saw some good in the continuance of their services, as did a large proportion of the AJA civilians. *The Honolulu Star-Bulletin*, May 26, 1954. "Japanese Language Schools, 1948," *What People in Hawaii Are Saying and Doing*, December 7, 1948, pp. 8–11.

20. As of March 25, 1954, approximately 17,000 men from Hawaii had served in the Korean War. Of these, 436 had been killed and 947 wounded. *The Honolulu Star-Bulletin*, March 10, 13, 25, 1954.

21. *The Honolulu Star-Bulletin*, July 1, 1952.

Bibliography

BOOKS

Adams, Romanzo. *Interracial Marriage in Hawaii: A Study of the Mutually Conditioned Processes of Acculturation and Amalgamation.* New York: The Macmillan Company, 1937. 353 pp.

———. "The Unorthodox Race Doctrine of Hawaii," in E. B. Reuter, ed., *Race and Culture Contacts.* New York: McGraw-Hill Book Company, 1934. Pp. 143–160.

Allen, Gwenfread. *Hawaii's War Years, 1941–1945.* Honolulu: University of Hawaii Press, 1950. 418 pp.

———. *Notes and References to Hawaii's War Years.* Honolulu: University of Hawaii Press, 1952.

Barber, Joseph, Jr. *Hawaii: Restless Rampart.* Indianapolis: The Bobbs-Merrill Company, 1941. 285 pp.

Beard, Charles A. *President Roosevelt and the Coming of the War: 1941.* New Haven: Yale University Press, 1948. 614 pp.

Benedict, Ruth. *The Chrysanthemum and the Sword.* Boston: Houghton Mifflin Company, 1946. 324 pp.

Bloom, Leonard, and Ruth Riemer. *Removal and Return: The Socio-Economic Effects of the War on Japanese Americans.* Berkeley: University of California Press, 1949. 259 pp.

Burrows, Edwin G. *Hawaiian Americans: An Account of the Mingling of Japanese, Chinese, Polynesian, and American Cultures.* New Haven: Yale University Press, 1947. 228 pp.

Clark, Mark. *Calculated Risk.* New York: Harper, 1950. 500 pp.

Clark, Sydney A. *Hawaii with Sydney A. Clark.* New York: Prentice-Hall, Inc., 1939. 304 pp.

Crawford, David. *Paradox in Hawaii: An Examination of Industry and Education and the Paradox They Present.* Boston: The Stratford Company, 1933. 262 pp.

Du Puy, William Atherton. *Hawaii and Its Race Problem.* Washington: GPO, 1932. 130 pp.

Embree, John F. *The Japanese Nation: A Social Survey*. New York: Farrar Rinehart, Inc., 1945. 308 pp.

Feis, Herbert. *The Road to Pearl Harbor*. Princeton: Princeton University Press, 1950. 356 pp.

Fergusson, Erna. *Our Hawaii*. New York: Alfred A. Knopf, 1942. 304 pp.

Gessler, Clifford. *Hawaii: Isles of Enchantment*. New York: D. Appleton-Century Company, Inc., 1937. 382 pp.

Grew, Joseph C. *Report from Tokyo: A Message to the American People*. New York: Simon and Schuster, 1942. 88 pp.

————. *Ten Years in Japan*. New York: Simon and Schuster, 1944. 554 pp.

Grodzins, Morton. *Americans Betrayed: Politics and the Japanese Evacuation*. Chicago: University of Chicago Press, 1949. 445 pp.

Gulick, Sidney L. *Mixing the Races in Hawaii: A Story of the Coming Neo-Hawaiian American Race*. Honolulu: The Hawaiian Board Book Rooms, 1937. 220 pp.

Hougen, John H. *The Story of the Famous 34th Infantry Division*. San Angelo, Texas: [privately printed], 1949. 190 pp.

Ichihashi, Yamato. *Japanese in the United States: A Critical Study of the Problems of the Japanese Immigrants and Their Children*. Stanford: Stanford University Press, 1932. 426 pp.

Inui, Kiyosue. *The Unsolved Problem of the Pacific*. Tokyo: The Japan Times, 1925. 618 pp.

Kawakami, Kiyoshi K. *The Real Japanese Question*. New York: The Macmillan Company, 1921. 269 pp.

Kuykendall, Ralph S. *Hawaii in the World War*. Honolulu: The Historical Commission, 1928. 474 pp.

————, and A. Grove Day. *Hawaii: A History; From Polynesian Kingdom to American Commonwealth*. New York: Prentice-Hall, Inc., 1948. 331 pp.

La Violette, Forrest A. *Americans of Japanese Ancestry: A Study of Assimilation in the American Community*. Toronto: Canadian Institute of International Affairs, 1945. 185 pp.

Lee, Lloyd L., ed. *In Freedom's Cause*. Honolulu: University of Hawaii Press, 1949. 176 pp.

Leighton, Alexander H. *The Governing of Men: General Principles and Recommendations Based on Experience at a Japanese Relocation Camp*. Princeton: Princeton University Press, 1945. 404 pp.

Lind, Andrew W. *Hawaii's Japanese: An Experiment in Democracy*. Princeton: Princeton University Press, 1946. 264 pp.

————. *An Island Community: Ecological Succession in Hawaii*. Chicago: University of Chicago Press, 1938. 337 pp.

MacDonald, Alexander. *Revolt in Paradise: The Social Revolution in Hawaii after Pearl Harbor*. New York: Stephen Daye, Inc., 1944. 288 pp.

McWilliams, Carey. *Prejudice; Japanese-Americans: A Symbol of Racial Intolerance*. Boston: Little, Brown & Co., 1944. 337 pp.

Mauldin, Bill. *Back Home*. New York: W. Sloane Associates, 1947. 313 pp.

Millis, Walter. *This is Pearl!* New York: William Morrow & Co., 1947. 384 pp.

Morgenstern, George Edward. *Pearl Harbor: The Story of the Secret War*. New York: The Devin-Adair Company, 1947. 425 pp.

Morison, Samuel Eliot. "Coral Sea, Midway and Submarine Actions, May 1942–August 1942." Vol. IV of *History of United States Naval Operations in World War II*. Boston: Little, Brown and Co., 1949. 307 pp.

O'Brien, Robert W. *The College Nisei*. Palo Alto, California: Pacific Books, 1949. 165 pp.

Palmer, Albert W. *The Human Side of Hawaii*. Boston: The Pilgrim Press, 1924. 144 pp.

————. *Orientals in American Life*. New York: Friendship Press, 1934. 212 pp.

Pratt, Helen G. *Hawaii, Off-Shore Territory*. New York: Charles Scribner's Sons, 1944. 392 pp.

Puleston, William D. *The Armed Forces of the Pacific*. New Haven: Yale University Press, 1941. 273 pp.

Pyle, Ernie. *Brave Men*. New York: Henry Holt & Co., 1944. 474 pp.

Rademaker, John A. *These are Americans: The Japanese Americans in Hawaii in World War II*. Palo Alto, California: Pacific Books, 1951. 259 pp.

Reischauer, E. O. *The United States and Japan*. Cambridge: Harvard University Press, 1950. 357 pp.

Sherwood, Robert E. *Roosevelt and Hopkins: An Intimate History*. New York: Harper and Brothers, 1948. 979 pp.

Shirey, Orville C. *Americans: The Story of the 442d Combat Team*. 1st ed. Washington: Infantry Journal Press, 1946. 151 pp.

Shoemaker, James H. *Labor in the Territory of Hawaii*. Washington: GPO, 1940. 244 pp.

Smith, Bradford. *Americans From Japan*. 1st ed. Philadelphia: J. B. Lippincott Co., 1948. 409 pp.

Smith, William Carlson. *Americans in Process: A Study of Our Citizens of Oriental Ancestry*. Ann Arbor: Edwards Brothers, Inc., 1937. 359 pp.

Starr, Chester G., ed. *From Salerno to the Alps: A History of the Fifth Army, 1943–1945*. 1st ed. Washington: Infantry Journal Press, 1948. 529 pp.

Stimson, Henry L., and McGeorge Bundy. *On Active Service in Peace and War*. New York: Harper and Brothers, 1948. 698 pp.

Strong, Edward K. *The Second-Generation Japanese Problem*. Stanford: Stanford University Press, 1934. 292 pp.

Thomas, Dorothy Swaine. *The Salvage*. Berkeley: University of California Press, 1952. 637 pp.

————, and Richard S. Nishimoto. *The Spoilage*. Berkeley: University of California Press, 1946. 388 pp.

Truscott, Lucian King, Jr. *Command Missions: A Personal Story*. New York: E. P. Dutton & Co., 1954. 570 pp.

Wakukawa, Ernest K. *A History of the Japanese People in Hawaii*. Honolulu: The Toyo Shoin, 1938. 439 pp.

Welles, Sumner. *Seven Decisions that Shaped History*. New York: Harper and Brothers, 1950–51. 236 pp.

Wist, Benjamin O. *A Century of Public Education in Hawaii, October 15, 1840, to October 15, 1940.* Honolulu: The Hawaii Educational Review, 1940. 221 pp.

PAMPHLETS

Adams, Romanzo. *The Education of the Boys of Hawaii and Their Economic Outlook: A Study in the Field of Race Relationship.* ("Research Publications," No. 4.) Honolulu: University of Hawaii, 1928. 59 pp.
————. *The Peoples of Hawaii.* Honolulu: American Council, Institute of Pacific Relations, 1933. 58 pp.
American Fighting Men Speak Out. Berkeley: Committee on American Principles and Fair Play, [1944]. 19 pp.
Balch, J. A. *Shall the Japanese be Allowed to Dominate Hawaii?* Honolulu: [privately printed], 1942. 38 pp.
14th New Americans Conference, July 15 to 21, 1940. Honolulu: New Americans Conference, 1940. 111 pp.
15th New Americans Conference, July 15 to 21, 1941. Honolulu: New Americans Conference, 1941. 77 pp.
Lind, Andrew W. *The Japanese in Hawaii Under War Conditions.* Honolulu: American Council, Institute of Pacific Relations, 1943. 41 pp.
Nakahata, Yutaka, ed. *The Varsity Victory Volunteers.* Honolulu: Tongg Publishing Co., 1943. 40 pp.
Nisei Survey Committee, Keisen Girls' School, Tokyo. *The Nisei: A Study of Their Life in Japan.* Tokyo: Kokusai Shuppan Insatsusha, 1939. 55 pp.
Okamura, Takie, and Umetaro Okamura. *Hawaii's American-Japanese Problem: A Campaign to Remove Causes of Friction Between the American People and Japanese; Report of the Campaign, January, 1921, to January, 1927.* Honolulu, n.d. 32 pp.
Spaulding, Ethel J., ed. *We Americans in Hawaii.* Honolulu, 1941.
University of Hawaii Corps of Engineers. *The Volunteer.* [Honolulu]: Tongg Publishing Co., 1943.
Yoshida, Shigeo. *In Memoriam: An address in honor of the University of Hawaii Varsity Victory Volunteers who died in World War II.* ("Occasional Papers," No. 44.) Honolulu: University of Hawaii, 1946. 14 pp.

ARTICLES

Akinaka, Amy. "Types of Japanese Marriages in Hawaii," *Social Process in Hawaii,* I (May, 1935), 32–33.
Casey, Gene. "G. I. Jap Yank," *Collier's,* CXIV (August 5, 1944).
Chinen, John C. "They Were So Young," *Pacific Citizen,* March 29, April 5, 12, 19, 1947.
Clark, Thomas Blake, and O. D. Russell. "Hail Our Japanese-American GIs," *Reader's Digest,* XLVII (July, 1945), 65–67.

Gillespie, James J., and Lauren E. McBride. "The 100th Battalion (Nisei) Against the Germans," *Infantry Journal*, Overseas Edition, LV (December, 1944), 8–15.

"Hawaii: Sugar-Coated Fort," *Fortune Magazine*, XXII (August, 1940).

High, Stanley. "Feudal Hawaii: Paradise, Ltd.," *Reader's Digest*, XLII (June, 1943), 19–23.

Hormann, Bernhard L. "The Caucasian Minority," *Social Process in Hawaii*, XIV (1950), 38–50.

————. "Morale in Hawaii," *ibid.*, VII (November, 1941), 41–45.

"Islander's Reflections on Mainland Japanese," *Social Process in Hawaii*, IX, X (1946), 39–49.

"Issei, Nisei, Kibei," *Fortune Magazine*, XXIX, No. 4 (April, 1944).

"Japanese in America: The Problem and the Solution," by an Intelligence Officer. *Harper's Magazine*, CLXXXV (October, 1942), 489–497.

"Japanese Language Schools, 1948," *What People in Hawaii are Saying and Doing* ("Hawaii Social Research Laboratory Reports" No. 15, December 7, 1948).

Kasibawara, James. "Japanese Etiquette in Hawaii," *Social Process in Hawaii*, I (May, 1935), 34–35.

Kawahara, Kimie, and Yuriko Hatanaka. "The Impact of War on an Immigrant Culture," *Social Process in Hawaii*, VIII (November, 1943), 36–45.

Kimura, Yukiko. "Psychological Aspects of Japanese Immigration," *Social Process in Hawaii*, VI (July, 1940), 10–22.

————. "Some Effects of the War Situation Upon the Alien Japanese in Hawaii," *ibid.*, VIII (November, 1943), 18–28.

Lind, Andrew W. "A Preliminary Study of Civilian Morale," *Social Process in Hawaii*, VIII (November, 1943), 5–17.

————. "Religious Diversity in Hawaii," *ibid.*, XVI (1952), 11–19.

Miles, Sherman. "Pearl Harbor in Retrospect," *Atlantic Monthly*, CLXXXII (July, 1948), 65–72.

Mitamura, Machiyo. "Life on a Hawaiian Plantation," *Social Process in Hawaii*, VI (July, 1940), 50–58.

Mizuta, Iwao. "Changing Attitudes Towards the Japanese Language in Hawaii," *Social Process in Hawaii*, IV (May, 1938), 28–36.

Nakahata, Yutaka, and Ralph Toyota. "Varsity Victory Volunteers: A Social Movement," *Social Process in Hawaii*, VIII (November, 1943), 29–35.

O'Neill, James P. "The Battle of Belvedere," *Yank*, Pacific Edition, III (September 1, 1944), 2–4.

Onishi, Katsumi. "Bon and Bon-Odori in Hawaii," *Social Process in Hawaii*, IV (May, 1938), 49–57.

————. "The Second Generation Japanese and the Hongwanji," *ibid.*, III (May, 1937), 43–48.

"Some Violations of Japanese Etiquette by Social Groups in Hawaii," *Social Process in Hawaii*, I (May, 1935), 36.

Theobald, Robert A. "The Final Secret of Pearl Harbor," *U. S. News and World Report*, XXXVI (April 2, 1954), 48–93.

Waldron, Webb. "A New Star in the Union?" *American Magazine*, CXXIII (April, 1937).

Welliver, Warman. "Report on the Negro Soldier," *Harper's Magazine*, CXCII (April, 1946), 333–339.

White, William Allen. "The Last of the Magic Isles," *Survey Graphic*, LVI (May 1, 1926).

Yamamoto, Bernard. "The Assimilation of the Japanese and Juvenile Delinquency," *Social Process in Hawaii*, V (June, 1939), 51–54.

Yamamoto, Misako. "Cultural Conflicts and Accommodations of the First and Second Generation Japanese," *Social Process in Hawaii*, IV (May, 1938), 40–48.

Yoshizawa, Emi. "A Japanese Family in Rural Hawaii," *Social Process in Hawaii*, III (May, 1937), 56–63.

FEDERAL DOCUMENTS

The abbreviation HWRD used below refers to the Hawaii War Records Depository at the University of Hawaii Library, Honolulu.

Congress. Senate. *Law Enforcement in the Territory of Hawaii: Letter from the Attorney General Transmitting in Response to Senate Resolution No. 134 Certain Information Relative to Law Enforcement in the Territory of Hawaii.* 72d Cong., 1st sess., S. Doc. 78. Washington, 1932. 315 pp.

———— ————. Subcommittee on Territories and Insular Affairs of the Committee on Public Lands. *Statehood for Hawaii.* Hearings, 80th Cong., 2d sess., on H. Res. 49 and S. Res. 114. Washington, 1948. 497 pp.

Congress. House. Committee on Public Lands. *Statehood for Hawaii.* Hearings, 80th Cong., 1st sess., pursuant to H. Res. 49, 50, 51, 52, 53, 54, 55, 56, 579, 1125, and 1758. Washington, 1947. 310 pp.

———— ————. Subcommittee of the Committee on the Territories. *Statehood for Hawaii.* Hearings, 74th Cong., 1st sess., pursuant to H. Res. 3034. Washington, 1936. 343 pp.

———— ———— ————. *Statehood for Hawaii.* Hearings, 79th Cong., 2d sess., H. Res. 236. Washington, 1946. 909 pp.

Congress. Joint Committee on Hawaii. *Statehood for Hawaii.* Hearings, 75th Cong., 2d sess., pursuant to S. Con. Res. 18. Washington, 1938. 735 pp.

———— ————. *Statehood for Hawaii.* Report, S. Doc. 151. Washington, 1938. 100 pp.

————. Joint Committee on the Investigation of the Pearl Harbor Attack. *Pearl Harbor Attack.* Hearings, 79th Cong., 1st and 2d sess., pursuant to S. Con. Res. 27. Washington, 1946. 39 parts.

———— ————. *Pearl Harbor Attack. Report, with additional views of Mr. Keefe together with minority views of Mr. Ferguson and Mr. Brewster.* 79th Cong., 2d sess., S. Doc. 244. Washington, 1946.

Congressional Record. 76th Cong., 3d sess., vol. 86, parts 10 and 11 (August 19, 1940—September 30, 1940).

Department of the Interior. Bureau of Education. *A Survey of Education in Hawaii.* Bulletin, No. 16. Washington, 1920. 408 pp.

———. War Relocation Authority. *The Evacuated People, A Quantitative Description.* Washington, 1946. 200 pp.

——— ———. *Myths and Facts About Japanese Americans, Answering Common Misconceptions Regarding Americans of Japanese Ancestry.* Washington, 1945. 45 pp.

——— ———. *Nisei in Uniform.* Washington, 1944. 24 pp.

——— ———. Quarterly reports.

——— ———. Semi-annual reports.

——— ———. *What We're Fighting For.* Washington, 1944. 21 pp.

——— ———. *WRA, A Story of Human Conservation.* Washington, n.d. 212 pp.

——— ———. Community Analysis Section. "Japanese Americans Educated in Japan." Report No. 8. Washington: Community Analysis Section, January 28, 1944 (mimeographed). 13 pp.

National Guard. "Memorandum Concerning 298th Infantry Regiment," by E. H. Bryan. [Honolulu], June 2, 1945 (typewritten). HWRD.

———. "Record of the Activities of the Military Department (Hawaii National Guard and Hawaii Territorial Guard), December 7, 1941 to June 30, 1944," by J. E. McE. Huey. [Honolulu], n.d. (typewritten). HWRD.

———. Adjutant General. *Annual Report of the Adjutant General, Territory of Hawaii, July 1, 1940, to June 30, 1941.* Honolulu, 1942. 24 pp.

——— ———. *Annual Report of the Adjutant General, Territory of Hawaii, July 1, 1941, to June 30, 1942.* Honolulu, 1942. 24 pp.

War Department. Army Forces, MIDPAC (and predecessor commands). "The Complete Niihau Story" (microfilm). HWRD.

——— ———. "History of the United States Army Forces, Middle Pacific and Predecessor Commands during World War II." Prepared by Historical Subsection, G-2, HUSAF MIDPAC. Part VIII, Vol. 14 (microfilm). HWRD.

——— ———. "Summary of Report of Events on the Island of Niihau, in Sequence from 7 December 1941 to 15 December 1941 (microfilm). HWRD.

——— ———. Central Pacific Base Command, Public Relations Office. "History of Organized Defense Volunteers in the Territory of Hawaii." Honolulu, 1945 (mimeographed). HWRD. 35 pp.

——— ———. Military Intelligence. Reports on interpreters at Fort Snelling (mimeographed) n.d.: "The Military Intelligence Language School"; "Nisei Linguists—Eyes and Ears of Allied Pacific Forces." HWRD.

———. Army Forces, MTO USA. Information and Education Section. *The Story of the 442d Combat Team.* MTO USA, n.d. 43 pp.

——— ———. Western Defense Command and Fourth Army. *Final Report: Japanese Evacuation from the West Coast,* by John L. De Witt. Washington, 1943. 618 pp.

———. Fifth Army Headquarters, G-3 Section. *The Advance on Rome.* N.p., [1944]. 44 pp.

————. Historical Division. *Fifth Army at the Winter Line* (*15 November 1943–15 January 1944*). Washington, 1945. 117 pp.

———— ————. *Salerno: American Operations from the Beaches to the Volturno* (*6 September–6 October 1943*). Washington, 1944. 95 pp.

——— ————. Department of the Army. *Anzio Beachhead* (*22 January–25 May 1944*). Washington, 1948. 122 pp.

————. Military Intelligence Division. *From the Volturno to the Winter Line* (*6 October–15 November 1943*). Washington, 1944. 119 pp.

————. Official records on the history of the 100th Infantry Battalion and the 442d Regimental Combat Team (in HWRD):

General Staff, Organization and Training Division, G-3, and Army Ground Forces Headquarters, Army War College, Washington. Photostatic copies of documents relative to the organization of the 100th and the 442d (28 May 1942–10 January 1943).

Office of the Adjutant General. "Historical Documents, World War II" (microfilm copies of typed originals furnished by the Office of the Adjutant General, A.G.O. Microfilming Job 500, Reels, 215, 252, Items 1402–1406):

Narrative history of the 100th Battalion, Separate, June 1942–7 September 1944: 2 September 1943–11 June 1944 (Salerno to Rome).

Unit history of the 100th Battalion, Separate (copies of organization and movement orders, rosters and awards, from 31 May 1942 to 30 April 1944).

Unit history of the 100th Battalion from 1 May 1944 to 31 October 1944.

History of the 442d Regimental Combat Team, 1 February 1943–30 April 1946, and Narrative of Events, 9 June 1944–30 April 1946.

Monthly historical reports, 442d Regimental Combat Team, 1 August 1944–31 April 1945.

————. Other official records on the history of the 100th Infantry Battalion and the 442d Regimental Combat Team (in HWRD):

Narrative history, 100th Battalion, 2 September 1943–11 June 1944 (Salerno to Rome), first and second drafts (typewritten).

Attested true copies (typewritten) of typewritten originals:

Narrative history, 100th Battalion, June-September 1944 (Rome to the Arno River).

Narrative history, 100th Battalion, September 1944–March 1945 (Bruyeres-Menton Campaign).

Narrative history, 100th Battalion, 25 March 1945–2 May 1945 (Ligurian Campaign: Leghorn to Alessandria).

Operational Report, 24 July 1945, on "The First Battle of Belvedere, 25–27 June 1944."

Presidential Citation of the 100th Battalion, General Orders No. 66, 15 August 1944.

Operational reports, 24 and 31 July 1945, on action during the periods 25–27 June 1944 (Belvedere) and 5 April–2 May 1945 (Florida Hill to Alessandria).

Headquarters, 442d Regimental Combat Team. Citation of the 100th for the Oak Leaf Cluster, for "outstanding accomplishment in combat during the periods 15 October 1944 to 30 October 1944, near Bruyeres, Biffontaine, and in the Foret Dominiale de Champ, Eastern France, and 5 and 6 April near Seravezza, Italy."

History, 133d Regiment, 34th Infantry Division, from 22 September 1943 to 31 January 1944.

In addition to the above, maps, overlays, patrol reports and rosters, and other miscellaneous documents furnished by veterans of the 100th Battalion were also consulted. HWRD.

TERRITORIAL DOCUMENTS

Governor (Civil). *Annual Report of the Governor of Hawaii to the Secretary of the Interior for the Fiscal Year Ending June 30, 1940.* Washington: GPO, 1940. 75 pp.

——. *Annual Report of the Governor of Hawaii to the Secretary of the Interior for the Fiscal Year Ending June 30, 1941.* Washington: GPO, 1941. 83 pp.

——. *Annual Report of the Governor of Hawaii to the Secretary of the Interior for the Fiscal Year Ending June 30, 1942.* Washington: GPO, 1942. 28 pp.

Office of the Military Governor (superseded July 21, 1944, by the Office of Internal Security). "Brief History of Company C, 1st Battalion, BMTC." [Honolulu], n.d. (typewritten). HWRD.

——. *Report of the Emergency Service Committee, Honolulu, T. H., March 25, 1944.* Honolulu, 1944. 10 pp.

——. *Report of the Second Territorial Conference Morale and Emergency Service Committees, Kahului, Maui, July 21–23, 1944.* Maui, T. H., 1944. 75 pp.

——. Businessmen's Military Training Corps. "History of the Businessmen's Military Training Corps." [Honolulu], June 15, 1945 (typewritten). HWRD.

——. Morale Section. *Final Report of Emergency Service Committee.* Honolulu, 1946. 52 pp.

—— ——. "Report of Second Oahu Conference of Americans of Japanese Ancestry, Honolulu, T. H., January 28, 1945." Honolulu, 1945 (mimeographed). HWRD. 41 pp.

—— ——. "Summary of Proceedings, Third Territorial Conference of Morale and Emergency Service Committees, Honolulu, T. H., March 24–26, 1945." Honolulu, 1945 (mimeographed). HWRD. 61 pp.

——. Organized Defense Volunteers. "General Staff Study, Civilian Military Defense Volunteers." [Honolulu], May, 1944 (typewritten). HWRD.

Territorial Guard. "The Hawaii Home Guard in World War II," by P. M.

Smoot. Honolulu, May 15, 1945 (mimeographed). HWRD. 43 pp.
———. "The Home Guard." [Honolulu], n.d. (typewritten). HWRD.

COUNTY DOCUMENTS

Hawaii County. Police Department. "Honolulu Police Reserves." [Honolulu], October 27, 1944 (typewritten).

NEWSPAPERS AND PERIODICALS

Daily Pinion (student newspaper of McKinley High School, Honolulu), 1942–1946.
Hawaii Hochi (formerly *Hawaii Herald*), 1938–1954.
Hawaii Times (formerly *Nippu Jiji*), 1938–1954.
The Honolulu Advertiser, 1938–1954.
The Honolulu Star-Bulletin, 1938–1954.
New York Times, 1940–1954.
Pacific Citizen (official organ of the Japanese Citizens League, published weekly), 1942–1954.

MISCELLANEOUS, UNPUBLISHED

Adams, Frank S. "A History of the Hawaii National Guard in Peace and War." Master's thesis in preparation, University of Hawaii, 1954.
Akinaka, Isaac Fukuo. "A Diary Covering from December, 1941, through May, 1942" (microfilm). HWRD.
Bicknell, George W. "Security Measures in Hawaii during World War II." 1944 (microfilm). HWRD.
Goto, Masaichi. "A Diary of the 100th Infantry Battalion, November 5, 1943–August 16, 1945." On loan to the author.
Hayashi, S. "Conflict Between First and Second Generation Japanese in Hawaii." Student research paper, Hawaii Social Research Laboratory, University of Hawaii, n.d.
Hayashida, Akiyoshi. "Japanese Moral Instruction as a Factor in the Americanization of Citizens of Japanese Ancestry." Master's thesis, University of Hawaii, 1933. 45 pp.
Kawamoto, Masayoshi. "Hill 920." Paper written for the author by a participant in this action. HWRD.
Kimura, Yukiko. "A Sociological Analysis of Type of Social Readjustment of Alien Japanese in Hawaii Since the War." Master's thesis, University of Hawaii, 1947. 248 pp.
———. "A Study of Problems and Attitudes of Second Generation Boys of Oriental Ancestry in Hawaii." Hawaii Social Research Laboratory, University of Hawaii, 1941. 74 pp.
———. "A Study of Problems and Needs of the Second Generation in Hawaii." Hawaii Social Research Laboratory, University of Hawaii, 1940. 84 pp.

Kosaki, Mildred Doi. "The Culture Conflicts and Guidance Needs of Nisei Adolescents." Master's thesis, University of Hawaii, 1949. 161 pp.

Letters from an AJA officer of the 100th Battalion to Leslie F. Deacon of Honolulu, April, 1944, to June, 1945 (microfilm). HWRD.

Makino, Margaret Y. Scrapbook of newspaper clippings and magazine articles. HWRD.

Notes on author's interviews with veterans of the 100th Infantry Battalion, written commentaries by veterans who read manuscript accounts of events in which they participated, and author's personal correspondence with other veterans of the unit. HWRD.

Onishi, Katsumi. "A Study of the Attitudes of the Japanese in Hawaii Toward the Japanese Language Schools." Master's thesis, University of Hawaii, 1943. 291 pp.

Papers written by AJA veterans for classes in English composition at the University of Hawaii, 1946–1950. HWRD.

Sanjume, Jisoo. "An Analysis of the New Americans Conference from 1927–1938." Master's thesis, University of Hawaii, 1939. 51 pp.

Territorial Conference of Social Work. "Aspects of Prejudice in the Territory of Hawaii." Honolulu, 1944 (mimeographed). HWRD. 64 pp.

Turner, Farrant L. Scrapbook of newspaper clippings, letters, photographs, awards, magazine articles, and miscellaneous. In Turner's possession.

Yamamoto, Misako. "Cultural Conflicts and Accommodations of the First and Second Generations." Hawaii Social Research Laboratory, University of Hawaii, 1938. 23 pp.

THE TABULATION below gives the most important of the unit and individual awards received by the 100th Battalion and its members:

Awards

UNIT AWARDS

Presidential Unit Citation . . .	3

INDIVIDUAL AWARDS

Congressional Medal of Honor . .	1
Distinguished Service Cross . . .	24
Silver Star	147
Legion of Merit	9
Soldier's Medal	8
Bronze Star (for valor)	238
Division Commendation	30
Purple Heart	1703
Bronze Star (for meritorious service)	2173
Croix de Guerre (France)	2
Medaglia al Valore Militare (Italy) .	5